Advances in the Treatment of Posttraumatic Stress Disorder

Cognitive-Behavioral Perspectives

Steven Taylor, Ph.D., is a clinical psychologist and professor in the department of psychiatry at the University of British Columbia. For 10 years he was associate editor of *Behaviour Research and Therapy,* and now is Associate Editor of the *Journal of Cognitive Psychotherapy.* He has published over 140 journal articles and book chapters, and seven books on anxiety disorders and related topics. He served as a consultant on the recent text revision of the *Diagnostic and Statistical Manual of Mental Disorders (DSM–IV–TR).* Dr. Taylor has received early career awards from the Canadian Psychological Association, the Association for Advancement of Behavior Therapy, and the Anxiety Disorders Association of America. He is actively involved in clinical teaching and supervision, and he maintains a private practice in Vancouver. Dr. Taylor's clinical and research interests include cognitive-behavioral treatments and mechanisms of anxiety disorders and related conditions.

Advances in the Treatment of Posttraumatic Stress Disorder

Cognitive-Behavioral Perspectives

Steven Taylor, PhD, Editor

Springer Publishing Company

Springer Publishing Company, Inc.
536 Broadway
New York, NY 10012-3955

Acquisitions Editor: Sheri W. Sussman
Production Editor: Jeanne Libby
Cover design by Joanne Honigman

01 02 03 04 05 / 5 4 3 2 1

Library of Congress Cataloging-in-Publication-Data

Advances in the treatment of posttraumatic stress disorder :
cognitive-behavioral perspectives / editor, Steven Taylor.—1st ed.
    p. cm.
  Includes bibliographical references and index.
  ISBN 0-8261-2047-4
  1. Post-traumatic stress disorder—Treatment. 2. Cognitive therapy. I. Taylor,
Steven, 1960–
RC552.P67A28 2004
616.85'21—dc22   2004012304

Printed in the United States of America by Maple-Vail Book Manufacturing Group.

For Amy Sue Janeck

CONTENTS

CONTRIBUTORS

Joyce N. Bittinger, Ph.D., Department of Psychology, University of Washington, Seattle.

Marla R. Brassard, Ph.D., Health & Behavioral Studies, Teachers College, Columbia University, New York.

Shawn P. Cahill, Ph.D., Center for the Treatment and Study of Anxiety, Department of Psychiatry, University of Pennsylvania, Philadelphia.

Amy M. Combs-Lane, Ph.D., Department of Behavioral Medicine and Psychiatry, West Virginia University School of Medicine.

Mark Creamer, Ph.D., Australian Centre for Posttraumatic Mental Health, University of Melbourne, Heidelberg, Victoria, Australia.

Carla Kmett Danielson, Ph.D., Medical University of South Carolina, Charleston.

Joanne Davis, Ph.D., Department of Behavioral Medicine and Psychiatry, West Virginia University School of Medicine, Morgantown.

Brigette A. Erwin, Ph.D., Medical University of South Carolina, National Crime Victims Research and Treatment Center, Charleston.

Sherry A. Falsetti, Ph.D., Department of Family Health and Community Medicine, University Family Health Center, College of Medicine at Rockford, University of Illinois at Chicago, Rockford.

Ingrid C. Fedoroff, Ph.D., Chronic Pain Program, St. Paul's Hospital, Vancouver, BC.

Norah C. Feeny, Ph.D., Department of Psychiatry, Case Western Reserve University, Cleveland.

Edna B. Foa, Ph.D., Center for the Treatment and Study of Anxiety, Department of Psychiatry, University of Pennsylvania, Philadelphia.

David Forbes, Ph.D., Australian Centre for Posttraumatic Mental Health, University of Melbourne, Heidelberg, Victoria, Australia.

Hyemee Han, Ph.D., Boston Department of Veterans Affairs Medical Center, Boston University School of Medicine, Boston.

Elizabeth A. Hembree, Ph.D., Center for the Treatment and Study of Anxiety, Department of Psychiatry, University of Pennsylvania, Philadelphia.

Larry Hodges, Ph.D., College of Computing, Georgia Institute of Technology, Atlanta.

Anne-Louise Humphreys, Ph.D., Department of Allied Health Professions, University of Liverpool, UK.

Brett T. Litz, Ph.D., Boston Department of Veterans Affairs Medical Center, Boston University School of Medicine, Boston.

Sally A. Moore, Ph.D., Department of Psychology, University of Washington, Seattle.

Ronald T. Murphy, Ph.D., Department of Psychology, Dillard University, New Orleans.

Marsheena Murray, Department of Psychology, Dillard University, New Orleans.

Stephen T. Peverely, Ph.D., Health & Behavioral Studies, Teachers College, Columbia University, New York.

Quaneecia Rainey, Department of Psychology, Dillard University, New Orleans.

Sheila A. Rauch, Ph.D., Center for the Treatment and Study of Anxiety, Department of Psychiatry, University of Pennsylvania, Philadelphia.

Heidi S. Resnick, Ph.D., Medical University of South Carolina, National Crime Victims Research and Treatment Center, Charleston.

Craig Rosen, Ph.D., National Center for PTSD & Stanford University School of Medicine, CA.

Barbara Olasov Rothbaum, Ph.D., Trauma and Anxiety Recovery Program, Emory University School of Medicine, Atlanta.

Anna Marie Ruef, Ph.D., Boston Department of Veterans Affairs Medical Center, Boston University School of Medicine, Boston.

Philip A. Saigh, Ph.D., Health & Behavioral Studies, Teachers College, Columbia University, New York.

Nicholas Tarrier, Ph.D., Academic Division of Clinical Psychology, Education and Research Building, Wythenshawe Hospital, Manchester, UK.

Karin Thompson, Ph.D., New Orleans Veterans Affairs Medical Center, and VISN 16 MIRECC & Department of Psychiatry and Neurology, Tulane University School of Medicine, New Orleans.

Jaye Wald, Ph.D., Department of Psychiatry, University of British Columbia, Vancouver, BC.

Lori Zoellner, Ph.D., Department of Psychology, University of Washington, Seattle.

FOREWORD

Give me your imagination for a few minutes and try to see yourself as two different creatures experiencing similar dangerous events. First, I want you to imagine yourself as a dragonfly foraging over a small swampy area. *"Wow, there are so many mosquitoes." You slip and slide in the air, foraging to your gain. Then, out of the corner of your compound eyes you see, with your motion detector retinal cells, an image of something large approaching very rapidly. You drop quickly to the right as a frog's tongue flicks past. "Whew!" you think, "That was close." You then dive on another mosquito.* The event is over.

Now let's imagine a similar situation; this time with you as a human. *A car, traveling well over the posted speed limit, roars past your position. You, a rookie police officer, slap on your siren and lights, and take off after the speeder. The offending car slows and pulls off to the side of the road. Before getting out of your police car, you radio in the speeding car's license plate. Then you step out of your car and cautiously approach. Just as you get up to the car, the driver opens the door, points a pistol, and fires twice. One bullet strikes you on your left side and knocks you to the ground, but your body armor has deflected the bullet away. The second shot misses. The felon speeds away. Afterward, you are not able to return to work because of the trauma. And, for years your waking moments, your dreams, and your imaginations are filled with horrors of that night.*

Is it a uniquely human capacity to experience psychological trauma? Is it our ability to foresee that we, or another of our species, shall ultimately die, which predisposes us to experience posttraumatic stress disorder (PTSD)? Does an organism require a sense of future to experience "fear and trembling and the sickness unto death" as the great existentialist philosopher, Kierkegaard (1954) suggested. We simply don't know. Animal behaviorists, including Jane Goodall, have described cases of animal "grief" that resemble the horrors of our own experience (de Wall, 2001). But, can animals experience PTSD? There is no question that animals, other than human beings, experience severe stress-related problems (Sapolsky, 1994). Stress responses in animals usually occur following prolonged periods of unpredictable noxious stimulation (e.g., Seligman, 1975).

There is good evidence that hormonal and brain changes in stressed animals do resemble those of people with PTSD (LeDoux, 1996). But, are those prolonged stressors equivalent to a single, horrific event in which a person believes he or she will die? Are they equal to the horror people feel when they witness (even from second-hand accounts) the death or injury of others? Or, are these uniquely human responses?

Consider a case of one of my patients. His name is Martin and he has given me permission to tell his story. (In fact, he is featured in a film by Rivard Productions on PTSD in which the editor of this book, Steve Taylor, provides expert commentary.) Martin lives in Canada and is a native Canadian. Some years ago he had an opportunity to move from his northern community to Winnipeg, a midsized Canadian city to work as a chaplain in a large metropolitan hospital. Because of her job, Martin's wife and one child continued to live in the north and he visited them as often as he could. One fall day, after a visit with his family, he was returning to Winnipeg, which is a 500– kilometer drive from his northern home. He was a passenger in a car driven by a friend. Within 100 kilometers of Winnipeg a drunk driver crossed the center lane and veered directly into Martin's car. It was estimated that the combined speed of the two cars was in excess of 200 kilometers per hour! Remarkably, both drivers escaped injury. However, Martin was trapped inside his vehicle with his left leg caught in the twisted metal. The car burst into flames, and as he lay there, Martin believed he would die. However, his primary fears were for his wife and children; what would become of them? How would they continue without his love and his income? Fortunately, Martin was rescued, but just as he was pulled to safety, the car blew up.

Several years after the accident, and after treatment, Martin still experienced symptoms of PTSD. What if Martin had been the dragonfly? Would he have experienced years of psychological and physiological agony? Not likely.

What could have been done to better understand why Martin developed PTSD, Why did his symptoms persist even after treatment? What could have been done to provide a better, more effective treatment for Martin? In the few years since Martin completed his initial treatment, we have learned so much more about the mechanisms that predispose a person to PTSD, which maintains the symptoms, and how we can more effectively treat PTSD in its various presentations. Steve Taylor, editor of *Advances in the Treatment of Posttraumatic Stress Disorder: Cognitive Behavioral Perspectives,* is one of the leaders in formulating these advancements. In this book, he has brought together an international group of experts to provide the very latest in scientifically sound information on the nature and treatment of PTSD. This book is very worthy of the attention of all who work with psychologically traumatized people.

G. Ron Norton, Ph.D.
Professor Emeritus
Department of Psychology
University of Winnipeg

REFERENCES

de Wall, F. (2001). *The ape and the suschi master.* New York, Basic Books.

Kierkegaard, S. (1954). *Fear and trembling and the sickness unto death.* New York, Doubleday.

LeDoux, J. (1996). *The emotional brain.* New York, Touchstone.

Sapolsky, R. M. (1994). *Why zebras don't get ulcers.* New York, Freeman & Company.

Seligman, M. E. P. (1975). *Helplessness.* New York, Freeman & Company.

PREFACE

Over the past two decades there have been many important advances in treating posttraumatic stress disorder (PTSD). Psychosocial treatments, particularly behavioral and cognitive-behavioral therapy, are among the most effective interventions. Although these treatments are useful, they are not universally efficacious. Some PTSD patients find these treatments to be too distressing to tolerate. Some endure treatment but fail to benefit, and some show only a partial or incomplete response. Thus, it is important to discover ways of improving treatment tolerability and outcome. Another important issue concerns the breadth of treatment effects. Are behavioral and cognitive-behavioral therapies sufficiently broad in their effects on trauma-related psychopathology and related factors? PTSD is commonly comorbid with various clinical problems, including co-occurring mental disorders and such psychosocial problems as poor quality of life. Therefore it is important to consider whether our treatments are addressing all the important trauma-related problems in people suffering from PTSD. This book strives to address these issues.

This book grew from a special issue for the *Journal of Cognitive Psychotherapy*, titled "Current Directions in the Treatment of Posttraumatic Stress Disorder." Given the clinical importance of PTSD, the journal editor, Robert L. Leahy, suggested that it would be useful to expand the special issue into an edited book by adding additional papers and by expanding existing ones. The appeal of such a book is that it would provide practitioners with a single volume that describes many of the latest advances and new directions in treating PTSD. This is what we have attempted to do. Although a single volume does not provide enough space to discuss every new development in treating PTSD, we have nevertheless sought to address many of the most promising and exciting advances in treating this common, costly, and often chronic disorder. We hope that this volume will not only be a useful resource to practicing clinicians and trainees, but also to clinical investigators actively engaged in research into the treatment of PTSD. To this end it is noteworthy that the people contributing chapters are scientist-practitioners; all are clinicians who both study and treat PTSD. As a result, the contributors to this volume seek to blend science and practice.

Steven Taylor

PART I

INTRODUCTION

CURRENT DIRECTIONS AND CHALLENGES IN THE TREATMENT OF POSTTRAUMATIC STRESS DISORDER

Steven Taylor

Posttraumatic stress disorder (PTSD) arises when a person experiences a traumatic event and then develops particular symptoms that persist for at least a month [American Psychiatric Association (APA), 2000]. Factor analyses reveal four distinct types of PTSD symptoms, each varying on a continuum of severity: reexperiencing symptoms (e.g., nightmares, flashbacks), effortful avoidance (e.g., efforts to avoid thinking about the trauma), numbing of general responsiveness (e.g., restricted range of affect), and hyperarousal symptoms (e.g., exaggerated startle response) (Asmundson et al., 2000; King, Leskin, King, & Weathers, 1998).

In North America, PTSD has a lifetime prevalence of about 8%. It persists for over a year in at least 50% of cases, and is likely to be chronic if it persists for at least 3 months (APA, 2000; Davidson et al., 1996). The disorder is associated with increased risk of other anxiety disorders, mood disorders, and substance-use disorders (APA, 2000). PTSD is associated with elevated health care costs, even after controlling for depression; chronic medical illness; and demographic variables (Walker et al., 2003). Thus, PTSD is associated with considerable personal and economic burden.

Over the past two decades there have been many important advances in understanding and treating PTSD. Contemporary cognitive-behavioral theories of this disorder emphasize expectations and appraisals about the meaning of aversive experiences (e.g., Chemtob, Roitblat, Hamada, Carlson,

& Twentyman, 1988; Ehlers & Clark, 2000; Foa, Steketee, & Rothbaum, 1989). These models propose that PTSD symptoms arise from a fear structure stored in long-term memory, which represents the stimulus, response, and meaning elements of the traumatic experience (Foa & Kozak, 1986). Traumatic events are thought to be so intense that they cause fear-conditioning to a wide range of stimuli (e.g., sights, sounds, odors, and bodily sensations associated with the trauma). Such stimuli can serve as reminders of the trauma, thus activating the fear structure and thereby producing hyperarousal and intrusive recollections of the trauma. Avoidance and numbing symptoms are thought to arise from mechanisms for deactivating the structure (Foa, Zinbarg, & Rothbaum, 1992).

Foa and Kozak (1986) proposed that effective treatment of PTSD requires exposure to corrective information. This may involve (a) imaginal exposure—i.e., imagining the trauma until emotional habituation occurs, thereby breaking the link between the traumatic event and conditioned emotional arousal; (b) in vivo exposure to distressing but harmless stimuli, which teaches the person that the stimuli are not dangerous; and (c) cognitive restructuring to help the person make sense out of the traumatic event (e.g., to realize that "I'm not a bad person for being raped, I simply was in the wrong situation at the wrong time"), and to correctly appraise their PTSD symptoms (e.g., "Repeated nightmares don't mean I'm going crazy; they're simply an indication that my mind is still processing my traumatic experience").

Following from these conceptualizations, behavioral and cognitive-behavioral therapies (CBT) have been developed, and have been found to be among the most effective methods for reducing PTSD (Chambless & Ollendick, 2001; van Etten & Taylor, 1998). This can be seen in Table 1.1, which summarizes some of the findings from our meta-analysis of PTSD treatments (van Etten & Taylor, 1998). The mean duration of the treatments was brief (8 weeks). The table shows the effect size on global, self-report measures of PTSD, as measured by the mean of d (Cohen, 1988). This statistic was defined for each treatment trial as: ($M_{pretreatment} - M_{posttreatment}$)/[Root-mean-square of pre- and posttreatment stress disorders (SDs)]. The larger the value of d, the greater the extent that symptoms declined over the course of treatment. The table shows that behavioral and cognitive-behavioral treatments performed well, compared with other treatments, in terms of treatment dropout and mean effect size. The effects of behavioral and cognitive-behavioral treatments were not significantly different from the effects of selective serotonin reuptake inhibitors

Table 1.1 Meta-analytic Comparisons of the Efficacy of PTSD Treatments (based on van Etten & Taylor, 1998)

Intervention	% Dropout	Mean pre-post effect size for (Mean d) PTSD symptoms
Waitlist control	6	0.44
Pill placebo	23	0.51
Tricyclic antidepressants	26	0.54
Carbamazepine	9	0.93
Monoamine oxidase inhibitors	36	0.61
Selective serotonin reuptake inhibitors	36	1.38
Benzodiazepines	38	0.49
Behavioral or cognitive-behavioral therapy	15	1.27
Eye movement desensitization and reprocessing	14	1.24
Hypnosis	11	0.94
Psychodynamic psychotherapy	11	0.90
Supportive psychotherapy	21	0.34

For details about the meta-analysis see van Etten and Taylor (1998).

or eye movement desensitization and reprocessing. Later research, which was a methodological improvement over many of the previous studies, provides even more encouraging support for behavioral and cognitive-behavioral therapies (see chapter 2). Follow-up studies reveal that treatment-related gains are maintained on measures of PTSD and associated depression for at least 12 to 15 months, possibly longer (Foa et al., 1999; van Etten & Taylor, 1998).

Despite these encouraging findings, these treatments are far from universally efficacious. Some PTSD patients find these treatments too stressful to tolerate. Some endure treatment but fail to benefit, and some show only a partial or incomplete response. Thus, it is important to discover ways of improving treatment tolerability and outcome. Another important issue concerns the breadth of treatment effects. Are behavioral and cognitive-behavioral therapies sufficiently broad in the problems they address? PTSD is commonly comorbid with various problems, including co-occurring disorders and symptoms, so it is important to consider whether our treatments are addressing all the important areas. Hence, the need for volume on the topic.

The book is divided into four parts. The first and second parts discuss new developments in treatment applications. From the perspective of treatment research, one of the most important recent developments was the formulation of *gold standards* for conducting studies of PTSD treatments (Foa & Meadows, 1997; see chapter 2). These are a set of rigorous criteria for conducting outcome studies. For example, making provision to ensure that treatments are delivered in the way they are supposed to be implemented (treatment fidelity). Foa and Meadows' gold standards are important for helping us judge the adequacy of outcome studies. Reliably measuring treatment fidelity and ensuring that fidelity is maintained is an arduous task. But it's necessary for the current generation of treatment-outcome studies. Gone are the days when investigators could simply compare different treatments without reporting data on whether the treatments were properly implemented. Perhaps some of the confusion in the treatment-outcome literature would have been avoided if researchers, from the outset of the treatment-outcome enterprise, had been more attentive to measuring and reporting data on treatment fidelity. Chapter 2 of this volume reports the results of a study that attempted to meet the gold standards (Taylor et al., 2003), and also reports some secondary analyses on the important question of how to predict which patient will benefit from which treatment.

Chapter 3, by Sherry Falsetti and colleagues, considers the important question of how to modify treatment when PTSD is comorbid with other clinical problems. Recent research has shown that we can treat comorbid PTSD and substance-use disorders by adding CBT for PTSD with substance-abuse programs (Ouimette, Moos, & Finney, 2003). Less is known about treating PTSD when it is comorbid with other clinical problems. Falsetti shows that a treatment that combines conventional CBT for PTSD with cognitive-behavioral interventions for panic disorder can effectively reduce PTSD and panic attacks, and has the further benefit of improving functioning and quality of life. Relatedly, Chapter 4 examines whether anxiety sensitivity—the fear of anxiety-related sensations—has important implications for understanding and treating PTSD. Elevated anxiety sensitivity is a feature of panic disorder, and interoceptive exposure (a method for reducing anxiety sensitivity) effectively reduces panic disorder (Taylor, 2000). Chapter 4 shows that anxiety sensitivity is implicated in PTSD, and that interoceptive exposure may be an effective treatment for PTSD regardless of whether the PTSD sufferer has comoribid panic attacks.

A crucial issue in treating PTSD concerns the question of how we can best engage people with PTSD in treatment. Behavioral and cognitive-behavioral PTSD treatments can be highly effective for people who complete therapy, but often patients drop out. Accordingly, methods for helping patients complete treatment are important. In chapter 5 Ronald Murphy and colleagues address the important issue of whether motivational enhancement therapy can improve treatment adherence and acceptability. This form of therapy has proved useful in motivating people to complete treatment for a variety of problems, including substance-use disorders, smoking cessation, eating disorders, and other clinical conditions. Accordingly, it may prove valuable in encouraging people to complete the anxiety-evoking interventions entailed in behavioral and cognitive-behavioral treatments for PTSD.

In chapter 6, Barbara Rothbaum and colleagues report that a recently developed form of exposure therapy—virtual reality exposure—may be useful for reducing PTSD. A strength of Rothbaum's well-designed study is the inclusion of psychophysiological data. Virtual reality interventions such as those pioneered by Rothbaum and colleagues can augment or may even replace imaginal exposure as the optimal method of therapeutic exposure to reminders of traumatic events.

Nick Tarrier and Anne-Louise Humphreys in chapter 7 provide a persuasive rationale for considering the patient's social support network in the treatment of PTSD. Interventions that improve social support may prove valuable in reducing PTSD. The importance of this chapter lies in the fact that we, as therapists, should look beyond the patient's presenting symptoms; we should consider the patient's broader social context to consider how social support is related to PTSD and its amelioration.

Chapter 8 by Sally Moore and colleagues considers the important pragmatic issues of how to combine cognitive restructuring with exposure therapy. Clinicians often combine cognitive restructuring and exposure therapy in the treatment of PTSD. Yet remarkably little is known about the optimal ways to combine these interventions. Moore and colleagues draw on the research and their extensive clinical experiences to offer some guidelines on combining these interventions.

Part III of this book considers several important issues in treating special populations and special clinical problems. Mark Creamer and David Forbes consider, in chapter 9, the special issues in treating combat veterans. These authors, based in Australia, have considerable clinical and research experience with combat-related PTSD. The problems encountered by Australian veterans are, in many ways, similar to the problems encountered by combat veterans in other countries such as the United States. Accordingly, the findings of Creamer and Forbes are likely to be broadly applicable.

Other chapters in part III consider the important clinical features that can complicate the treatment of PTSD, such as comorbid anger problems (Shawn Cahill et al., chapter 10), comorbid chronic pain (Jaye Wald et al., chapter 11), and trauma-related dissociative reactions (Norah Feeny & Carla Kmett Danielson, chapter 12). In Chapter 13 Philip Saigh discusses the treatment of PTSD in children and adolescents.

In part IV, chapter 14, the material of previous chapters is drawn together, along with other important findings, to offer a perspective on the future directions for PTSD treatment and treatment research.

The authors of this volume have strived to offer useful ideas for understanding PTSD and for improving treatment outcome. Our chapters are stepping stones toward optimal treatments of PTSD. We hope that readers find this a path worth pursuing.

REFERENCES

American Psychiatric Association. (2000). *Diagnostic and statistical manual of mental disorders* (4th ed., text revision). Washington, DC: Author.

Asmundson, G. J. G., Frombach, I., McQuaid, J., Pedrelli, P., Lenox, R., & Stein, M. B. (2000). Dimensionality of posttraumatic stress symptoms: A confirmatory factor analysis of DSM–IV symptom clusters and other models. *Behaviour Research and Therapy, 38,* 203–214.

Chambless, D. L., & Ollendick, T. H. (2001). Empirically supported psychological interventions: Controversies and evidence. *Annual Review of Psychology, 52,* 685–716.

Chemtob, C., Roitblat, H. L., Hamada, R. S., Carlson, J. G., & Twentyman, C. T. (1988). A cognitive action theory of post-traumatic stress disorder. *Journal of Anxiety Disorders, 2,* 253–275.

Cohen, J. (1988). *Statistical power analyses for the behavioral sciences* (2nd ed.). Hillsdale, NJ: Erlbaum.

Davidson, J., Foa, E. B., Blank, A. S., Brett, E. A., Fairbank, J., Green, B. L., et al. (1996). Post-traumatic stress disorder. In T. A. Widiger, A. J. Frances, H. A., Pincus, R. Ross, M. B. First, & W. W. Davis (Eds.), *DSM–IV sourcebook, Vol. 2* (pp. 577–605). Washington, DC: American Psychiatric Association.

Ehlers, A., & Clark, D. M. (2000). A cognitive model of posttraumatic stress disorder. *Behaviour Research and Therapy, 38,* 319–345.

Foa, E. B., Dancu, C. V., Hembree, E. A., Jaycox, L. H., Meadows, E. A., & Street, G. P. (1999). A comparison of exposure therapy, stress inoculation training, and their combination for reducing posttraumatic stress disorder in female assault victims. *Journal of Consulting and Clinical Psychology, 67,* 194–200.

Foa, E. B., & Kozak, M. J. (1986). Emotional processing of fear: Exposure to corrective information. *Psychological Bulletin, 99,* 20–35.

Foa, E. B., & Meadows, E. A. (1997). Psychosocial treatments for posttraumatic stress disorder: A critical review. *Annual Review of Psychology, 48,* 449–480.

Foa, E. B., Steketee, G. S., & Rothbaum, B. O. (1989). Behavioral/cognitive conceptualizations of post-traumatic stress disorder. *Behavior Therapy, 20,* 155–176.

Foa, E. B., Zinbarg, R., & Rothbaum, B. O. (1992). Uncontrollability and unpredictability in post-traumatic stress disorder: An animal model. *Psychological Bulletin, 112,* 218–238.

King, D. W., Leskin, G. A., King, L. A., & Weathers, F. W. (1998). Confirmatory factor analysis of the clinician-administered PTSD Scale: Evidence for the dimensionality of posttraumatic stress disorder. *Psychological Assessment, 10,* 90–96.

Ouimette, P., Moos, R. H., & Finney, J. W. (2003). PTSD treatment and 5–year remission among patients with substance use and posttraumatic stress disorders. *Journal of Consulting and Clinical Psychology, 71,* 410–414.

Taylor, S. (2000). *Understanding and treating panic disorder.* New York: Wiley.

Taylor, S., Thordarson, D. S., Maxfield, L., Fedoroff, I. C., Lovell, K., & Ogrodniczuk, J. (2003). Comparative efficacy, speed, and adverse effects of three treatments for PTSD: Exposure therapy, EMDR, and relaxation training. *Journal of Consulting and Clinical Psychology, 71,* 330–338.

van Etten, M., & Taylor, S. (1998). Comparative efficacy of treatments for post-traumatic stress disorder: A meta-analysis. *Clinical Psychology and Psychotherapy, 5,* 126–145.

Walker, E. A., Katon, W., Russo, J., Ciechanowski, P., Newman, E., & Wagner, A. W. (2003). Health care costs associated with posttraumatic stress disorder symptoms in women. *Archives of General Psychiatry, 60,* 369–374.

PART II

NEW DEVELOPMENTS IN TREATMENT APPLICATIONS

Chapter 2

EFFICACY AND OUTCOME PREDICTORS FOR THREE PTSD TREATMENTS: EXPOSURE THERAPY, EMDR, AND RELAXATION TRAINING

Steven Taylor

INTRODUCTION

In recent years there has been a rapidly growing amount of research on the treatment of post traumatic stress disorder (PTSD). Our recent metaanalysis suggested that exposure therapy and eye movement desensitization and reprocessing (EMDR) are among the most effective treatments for PTSD (van Etten & Taylor, 1998). Exposure therapy entails repeated, prolonged imaginal and in vivo exposure to distressing but harmless trauma-related stimuli. EMDR involves imaginal exposure (under conditions of divided attention), free association, and other techniques. The main intervention in EMDR requires the patient to recall trauma-related memories while also attending to some form of external oscillatory stimulation. Stimulation is typically induced by the therapist moving a finger from side to side across the patient's field of vision, which induces eye movements. Sets of eye movements are induced until distress is reduced (Shapiro, 1995). It has been suggested that EMDR is simply a cognitive-behavioral package, consisting of imaginal exposure plus coping skills. Shapiro (1995), however, believes that EMDR is a revolutionary treatment that works more rapidly and efficiently than c-

This research was supported by grants from the British Columbia Health Research Foundation.

onventional treatments, by activating an informational processing system in the brain responsible for processing traumatic memories. Controversial claims such as these, along with anecdotal reports of impressive treatment effects, have lead many clinical investigators (like ourselves) to become interested in examining the claims made by the proponents of EMDR.

Although the van Etten and Taylor (1998) meta-analysis suggested that EMDR and behavior therapy were equally effective, many of the studies included in the meta-analysis had important methodological limitations (Devilly, 2002; Foa & Meadows, 1997), and few studies directly compared exposure therapy to EMDR. Therefore, the meta-analytic findings are best regarded as a source of hypotheses, rather than providing definitive conclusions.

PROBLEMS WITH PREVIOUS STUDIES COMPARING EXPOSURE WITH EMDR

A handful of studies, appearing before and after our meta-analysis, have yielded conflicting findings about the relative efficacy of exposure therapy and EMDR. The four dimensions of PTSD—reexperiencing, effortful avoidance, numbing, and hyperarousal—were not separately assessed in previous studies. Instead, outcome was typically assessed by global measures of PTSD symptoms, along with separate measures of avoidance and reexperiencing.

Vaughan et al. (1994) found that imaginal exposure, relaxation training, and an early version of EMDR were equally effective at posttreatment and at 3–month follow-up, although there was some evidence that EMDR was superior in reducing reexperiencing symptoms at posttreatment. In a pilot study, Rogers et al. (1999) compared a single session of EMDR with a session of exposure therapy. The treatments were broadly equivalent in their effects, although there was some suggestion that EMDR produced greater reductions in distress and in reexperiencing symptoms. In contrast, Devilly and Spence (1999) found that a version of cognitive-behavior therapy (CBT; combining exposure therapy, relaxation training, cognitive restructuring, and other coping techniques) was more effective than EMDR on a range of measures at posttreatment. At 6–month follow-up, treatment gains were maintained for CBT but not for EMDR. Lee, Gauriel, Drummond, Richards, and Greenwald (2002) compared a similar cognitive-behavioral package with EMDR and found that the treatments generally did not differ at posttreatment, although EMDR was superior at 3–month follow-up. Ironson, Freund, Srauss, and Williams (2002) reported a pilot study comparing exposure therapy to an intervention combining EMDR and in vivo exposure therapy. The two treatments were equally effective at posttreatment and 3–month follow-up on a global measure of PTSD. However, the EMDR package resulted in a higher proportion of patients classified as treatment responders, and a midtreatment assessment suggested that the EMDR package acted more rapidly in reducing PTSD symptoms. Power et al. (2002) found that EMDR had a slight advantage over CBT on measures of depression but not on measures of PTSD symptoms. EMDR reportedly required fewer sessions than CBT.

Inconsistencies among studies could be due to methodological limitations, many of which have been highlighted in recent reviews (e.g., Devilly, 2002; Maxfield & Hyer, 2002; Spector, 2001). For example, many (22%) of Vaughan et al.'s (1994) patients did not meet diagnostic criteria for PTSD. The inclusion of such patients muddles treatment findings by (a) making it more difficult to detect symptom improvement, (b) inflating the proportion of people with mild symptoms at the end of treatment, and (c) raising concerns about whether the results can be generalized to full-blown PTSD (Foa & Meadows, 1997).

Two studies (Ironson et al., 2002; Rogers et al., 1999) failed to assess treatment outcome with structured PTSD interviews. Such interviews are widely regarded as the best way of assessing PTSD symptoms (Foa & Tolin, 2000; Tarrier, 2001). None of the other studies reported whether their interviews were reliably administered (no inter-rater reliability was reported). In three studies the therapists administered the outcome assessments instead of using blind, independent evaluators (Devilly & Spence, 1999; Ironson et al., 2002; Lee et al., 2002). Vaughan et al. (1994) did not use the current version of EMDR and their exposure therapy differed markedly from the way this treatment is usually implemented (Devilly, 2002). Rogers et al. (1999) delivered their treatments in only a single session, which also does not represent the way in which either exposure or EMDR are used in clinical practice (Foa & Meadows, 1997; Shapiro, 1999).

Only two studies reported data on whether the interventions differed in treatment integrity (Devilly & Spence, 1999; Lee et al., 2002) and even those studies reported no data on whether the integrity ratings were reliable. Within both studies it appears that treatments differed in fidelity, and commentators have argued that Devilly and Spence's EMDR was not properly implemented (Maxfield & Hyer, 2002; Spector, 2001).

Power et al. (2002) reported that EMDR was administered in significantly fewer sessions than CBT, suggesting that EMDR works more quickly.

However, those investigators had no predetermined or standardized criteria for setting the number of sessions. Treatment duration was made according to therapist judgment. It is not clear what these judgments were based on, or whether therapists were using the same criteria.

TAYLOR STUDY

More recently, we conducted a study that directly compared exposure therapy, EMDR, and relaxation training in patients with PTSD (60 trial entrants and 45 treatment completers; Taylor et al., 2003b). We included relaxation training because there has been little previous research on the efficacy of this intervention in treating PTSD. Our study attempted to meet all of Foa and Meadows's (1997) gold standards for methodologically sound outcome studies. That is, clearly defined target symptoms; reliable and valid measures; use of blind evaluators; adequately trained assessors; manualized, replicable, and specific treatments; unbiased assignment to treatment; and evaluation of treatment adherence. As per the recommendations of Foa and Meadows, we also had more than one therapist deliver the treatments in order to separate therapist effects from treatment effects. To our knowledge, ours was the first study of EMDR for PTSD that met all the gold standards.

In this chapter we take the opportunity to summarize our previously reported findings and to present some hitherto unpublished results. Our three treatments did not differ in attrition, perceived credibility of treatment, or in the incidence of symptom worsening. Dropouts and treatment completers did not differ in terms of pretreatment symptom severity or demographic variables. We found no differences in therapist efficacy across the three treatments. All three treatments were associated with symptom reduction. Treatments did not differ in their effects on numbing or hyperarousal symptoms. However, compared to EMDR and relaxation training:

- Exposure therapy tended to yield a greater proportion of participants who no longer met criteria for PTSD after treatment, as assessed by structured interview (see Figure 2.1). EMDR and relaxation did not differ from one another on any outcome variable.
- Exposure produced significantly larger reductions in avoidance and reexperiencing symptoms, as assessed before and after treatment via structured interview.

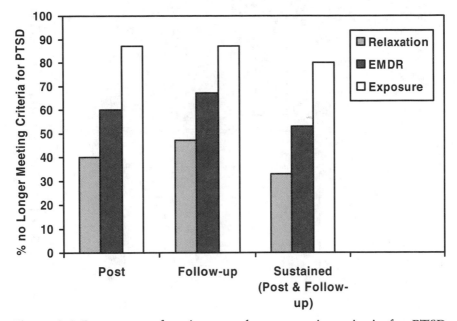

Figure 2.1 Percentage of patients no longer meeting criteria for PTSD after treatment.

• Exposure was faster at reducing avoidance, as assessed by a questionnaire administered at the beginning of each session (Figure 2.2).*

COMPARISON WITH PREVIOUS STUDIES

To compare our (Taylor et al., 2003b) study with previous trials, Table 2.1 shows the pretreatment features and treatment outcome (for treatment completers) for PTSD treatment studies of exposure, EMDR, or relaxation. Two studies (Ironson et al., 2002; Power et al., 2002) were not included because no data were reported on the variables in Table 2.1. The PTSD meta-analysis by van Etten and Taylor (1998) summarizes the early

---

*Session-by-session changes were assessed via questionnaire because it was not feasible to conduct a structured interview at the beginning of each treatment session. The limitation of this constraint is that questionnaires may be less sensitive to treatment effects than interviews (e.g., van Etten & Taylor, 1998), thereby attenuating the between-treatment differences. Greater differences between exposure and the other treatments may have been observed if session-by-session interview measures had been feasible.

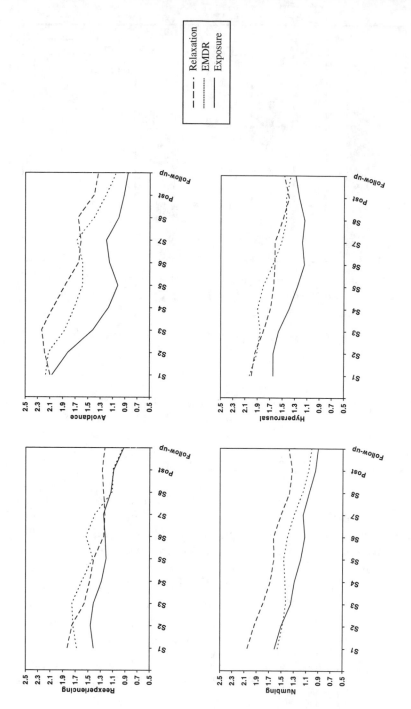

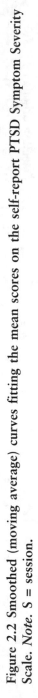

Figure 2.2 Smoothed (moving average) curves fitting the mean scores on the self-report PTSD Symptom Severity Scale. *Note. S* = session.

treatment studies (many of which have been criticized for methodological limitations: Foa & Meadows, 1997; Shapiro, 1999). The meta-analysis does not include any of the other comparison studies in the table (i.e., there is no overlap among studies). The meta-analysis summarizes the results of 13 previous trials of exposure therapy, and 11 previous trials of EMDR. Cohen's (1988) *d* was used to compare the pre-post effect sizes of our treatments with those of other studies. This statistic was defined as the difference between pre- and posttreatment means, divided by the pooled SD (i.e., root mean square of pre-and posttreatment SDs).

The table shows that treatment duration of the comparison studies was broadly similar to ours, except the EMDR trials in the meta-analysis tended to be shorter. The table also reports available data on the pretreatment severity of PTSD, as assessed by the total score on the Clinician Administered PTSD Scale (CAPS: Blake et al., 1997). The latter has been used in several studies and so provides a common metric for comparing studies. For the purpose of this table, we computed CAPS total scores for the present study, defined as the sum of the 17 items that define the four core PTSD dimensions (number of items: reexperiencing, 5; avoidance, 2; numbing, 5; hyperarousal 5). Note that avoidance symptoms are underrepresented in the total score, due to the smaller number of items assessing that dimension.

Table 2.1 indicates that the pretreatment severity of our sample tended to be as great or greater than the severity of other studies. Similarly, the duration of PTSD in our sample tended to be as great or greater than that of other studies. For exposure therapy, our effect size was as large or larger than most other studies of exposure-based therapies. (The larger the effect size, the greater the magnitude of reductions in PTSD symptoms, from pre- to posttreatment.) Our effect size for EMDR was as large or larger than the effect sizes for other EMDR studies. Our effect size for relaxation training was larger than the effect sizes of other studies of relaxation training.

A similar pattern emerges when one examines the percentage of participants who no longer met diagnostic criteria for PTSD at the end of treatment (Table 2.1). For exposure therapy, the outcome in the present study was equal to, or better than, the outcome in previous exposure studies. For EMDR, our outcome was equal to, or better than, the outcome of previous EMDR studies, with the exception of Lee et al. (2002). Note, however, that the pre-post effect size for Lee et al. was smaller than that of the present study. Lee et al.'s participants had an unusually short duration of PTSD (Table 2.1). People with a short duration of PTSD might have a better treatment response than people with long-standing

Table 2.1 Comparison of the Present Study with Other Treatment-Outcome Trials

	Treatment duration (weeks)	Pretreatment CAPS total score: M (SD)	Duration of PTSD (years): M (SD)	Pre-post effect size for PTSD total scores (interview measures)			No longer meeting criteria for PTSD at posttreatment (%)		
				Exposure	EMDR	Relaxation	Exposure	EMDR	Relaxation
Taylor et al. (2003b)	8	78.9 (15.0)	8.7 (10.8)	2.54	2.41	1.66	87	60	40
Comparison Studies									
Devilly and Spence (1999)†	8	—	9.4 (12.3)	3.63	2.37	—	83	36	—
Foa et al. (1999)	9	—	—	2.04	—	—	65	—	—
Lee et al. (2002)	7	—	1.2 (1.3)	1.55	2.07	—	75	83	—
Marks et al. (1998)	10	66.8 (18.7)	3.8 (4.8)	1.25	—	0.68	75	—	55
Tarrier et al. (1999)‡	M = 10	74.7 (17.0)	—	0.91	—	—	59	—	—
van Etten and Taylor (1998)	M = 4, 10 (EMDR, exp.)	73.2 (13.9)	8.4 (9.6)	1.89	0.69	—	59	54	—
Vaughan et al. (1994)‡	2–3	—	—	0.60	1.38	0.61	—	—	—

Note: There is no overlap among comparison studies; none of the studies included in van Etten and Taylor's (1998) meta-analysis were the other comparison studies.

†Combined exposure, cognitive restructuring, relaxation training, and breathing retraining.

‡Imaginal exposure without in vivo exposure.

PTSD (Peterson, Prout, & Schwarz, 1991). For relaxation training, the percentage of participants no longer meeting PTSD criteria in the present study was slightly lower than the percentage reported by Marks, Lovell, Noshirvani, Livanou, and Thrasher (1998). However, our pre-post effect size for relaxation was larger than that obtained by Marks and colleagues.

A recent meta-analysis of the relationship between methodological rigor and EMDR outcome (Maxfield & Hyer, 2002) found that the degree of rigor was positively correlated with the magnitude of the pre-post effect size. This is consistent with the results in Table 2.1; our study, which did not have the methodological limitations of other EMDR PTSD studies, produced effect sizes that were as large or larger than those of previous studies.

With regard to treatment attrition, the proportion of treatment dropouts for our exposure therapy (32%) was within the range of attrition reported in other studies of exposure-based therapies (0–43%: Devilly & Spence, 1999; Foa, Dancu, et al., 1999; Lee et al., 2002; Marks et al., 1998; Power et al., 2002; Tarrier et al., 1999; van Etten & Taylor, 1998). Our dropout proportion for EMDR (21%) was also within the range of attrition reported in other studies (0–35%: Devilly & Spence, 1999; Lee et al., 2002; Power et al., 2002; van Etten & Taylor, 1998). Note that the ranges of attrition for exposure therapy and for EMDR are broad. Very brief treatments tend to have very low rates of dropout compared with longer trials of therapy. For relaxation training, our proportion of dropouts (21%) was higher than the proportion of dropouts in a previous study using the same protocol (8%: Marks et al., 1998). The difference might reflect the severe, chronic nature of our sample.

PREDICTING TREATMENT OUTCOME

The remainder of this chapter reports the results of further analyses intended to identify predictors of treatment dropout and, for treatment completers, predictors whether they remitted from PTSD after therapy. We chose these broad outcome measures because they provide simple but clinically meaningful indicators of outcome. A further aim was to identify whether some predictors are more important in predicting the outcome of some treatments than others. For weaker treatments, such as relaxation training, it is possible that this therapy is most effective in producing remission in less severe PTSD. With the exception of treatment credibility (assessed at the beginning of session 2), all measures of candidate predictors were completed during a pretreatment assessment. These variables and the rationale for selecting them were as follows.

Several studies suggest that poorer treatment outcome is associated with greater pretreatment severity of various clinical variables, including global severity of PTSD and severity associated symptoms (depression, trauma-related guilt and anger) (Foa, Riggs, Massie, & Yarczower, 1995; Peterson et al., 1991; Pitman et al., 1991; Taylor et al., 2001). However, there have been a number of inconsistencies across studies in the variables that predict outcome. It may be that only the most robust predictors will consistently emerge as significant. Accordingly, more studies of these predictors need to be conducted.*

In the present study we examined the predictive importance of specific PTSD features (reexperiencing, avoidance, numbing, hyperarousal, duration of PTSD, presence vs. absence of multiple traumata), associated symptoms (trauma-related guilt and anger, depression, dissociative symptoms), and global level of functioning. Trauma-related dysfunctional thoughts and beliefs were assessed to investigate whether strongly held cognitions predict poor outcome. Strongly held ("overvalued") cognitions predict poor outcome for obsessive-compulsive disorder and panic disorder (Neziroglu, Stevens, McKay, & Yaryura-Tobias, 2001; Taylor, 2000). The same may be true of PTSD. The strength of such cognitions predicted pretreatment severity of PTSD in some studies (Foa, Ehlers, Clark, Tolin, & Orsillo, 1999) but not in others (Fedoroff, Taylor, Asmundson, & Koch, 2000). Accordingly, further research is needed. Similarly, we also examined the predictive significance of anxiety sensitivity. This is a cognitive variable defined as the fear of arousal-related sensations, arising from beliefs that these sensations have harmful consequences (e.g., the belief that palpitations lead to cardiac arrest; Taylor, 1999). Anxiety sensitivity was investigated because previous research shows that this variable predicts the pretreatment severity of PTSD (Fedoroff et al., 2000; and see Chapter 4). Intense (overvalued) anxiety sensitivity might predict poor outcome for PTSD treatments.

The predictive significance of trauma-related litigation (coded as present vs. absent) was also assessed because litigation is often a source of great distress (Mayou, Tyndel, & Bryant, 1997) and therefore might interfere with treatment outcome. Litigation might also provide disincentives for

---

*Pain severity also predicts poor outcome for PTSD arising from road traffic collisions (Taylor et al., 2001). This variable was not examined in the present study because many of our participants did not suffer from pain conditions.

overcoming PTSD; patients might fail to adhere to treatment if they believe that their compensation claims (e.g., for accident- or assault-related PTSD) would be jeopardized if their symptoms were to improve (Taylor & Koch, 1995). For similar reasons we also assessed the predictive significance of whether the patient was receiving disability benefits (from either the government or an insurance company).

Treatment credibility, as perceived by the patient, was assessed to examine the possibility that participants may be more likely to drop out of treatments that they perceive to be lacking credibility. The use of psychotropic medications was also examined (i.e., whether the patient was taking antidepressant medications such as selective serotonin reuptake inhibitors, and whether they were taking benzodiazepines). Antidepressants and benzodiazepines were examined separately because research on panic disorder suggests that behavioral and cognitive-behavioral treatments are impaired by combining them with benzodiazepines, but not by combining them with antidepressants (Taylor, 2000). The same may hold for PTSD.

METHOD

Participants

Participants were recruited from physician referrals and from advertisements in the local media. Inclusion criteria were (a) *DSM–IV* diagnosis of PTSD as the primary (most severe) presenting problem, (b) over 18 years of age and able to provide informed consent, (c) fluency in written and spoken English, and (d) willingness to suspend any concomitant psychological treatment and to keep doses of any psychotropic medication constant throughout the course of the study. Exclusion criteria were (a) mental retardation, (b) current psychotic disorder, and (c) commencement or change in dose of psychotropic medication within the past 3 months.

Sixty participants met the inclusion/exclusion criteria and entered treatment. Forty-five participants completed treatment. For the 60 people entering the study, the mean age was 37 years (SD = 10 years) and 75% were female. Most (77%) were Caucasian and most (78%) had completed some form of college education. Forty-two percent were employed full-time or part-time outside of the home, 15% were students, 5% were full-time homemakers, 13% were unemployed, and 25% were supported by some form of disability assistance. Forty-two percent were married or cohabiting, 32% were single, and 27% were separated or divorced.

The mean duration of PTSD was 8.7 years (SD = 10.8). Forty-eight percent of participants were taking some form of psychotropic medication. Sixty-five percent had experienced more than one type of traumatic event. The most common forms were sexual assault (45%), physical assault (43%), transportation accidents (43%), and being exposed to a sudden death (e.g., witnessing a homicide—22%). The most common coexisting mental disorders were major depression (42%), panic disorder with or without agoraphobia (31%), social anxiety disorder (12%), and specific phobia (10%).

Measures

Structured interviews. Intake diagnoses for Axis I disorders were assessed by the Structured Clinical Interview for DSM–IV (SCID–IV: First, Spitzer, Gibbon, & Williams, 1996). The SCID–IV was also used to rate the participant's pretreatment global level of functioning. The rating scale for global functioning, as described in DSM–IV–TR (APA, 2000, p. 34), ranges from 1 to 100, with higher scores indicating higher levels of functioning. Scores in the range of 1 to 10, for example, indicate that the person is unable to care for oneself or is in danger of seriously harming self or others. Scores in the range of 91 to 100 indicate superior functioning. We also added questions to the SCID–IV interview to assess whether the patient was in trauma-related litigation, whether they were supported by disability payments, and whether they were taking psychotropic medication.

Frequency and intensity of PTSD symptoms were assessed by the CAPS. Severity scores for each PTSD symptom were computed by adding the frequency and intensity ratings, which is the conventional scoring method (Blake et al., 1997). Recent factor analytic studies of the CAPS and similar scales (Asmundson et al., 2000; King, Leskin, King, & Weathers, 1998) indicate that the 17 core PTSD symptoms represent four dimensions: Reexperiencing (CAPS items 1–5), avoidance (items 6 and 7), numbing (items 8–12), and hyperarousal (items 13–17). We constructed CAPS scales to measure each of these dimensions. The CAPS was also used to assess PTSD duration and the number of traumata that the person had experienced.

The CAPS also included an item that assessed trauma-related guilt over acts of commission or omission, and three CAPS items were summed to measure dissociative symptoms (depersonalization, derealization, and reduction in awareness of one's surroundings). Each CAPS scale consisted of the mean of the item scores. Mean scores were computed so each scale would have the same range (0 to 8), thereby facilitating comparisons across scales. The CAPS was also used to diagnose PTSD at posttreatment and follow-up.

Self-report questionnaires. Strength of trauma-related thoughts and beliefs was assessed by the total score on the Posttraumatic Cognitions Inventory (Foa, Ehlers, et al., 1999). This scale assesses negative cognitions about oneself, negative cognitions about the world, and self-blame. Trauma-related anger was assessed by an item assessing the frequency of anger about trauma-related events over the past week. This item was rated on a 4–point scale ranging from zero (not at all) to 3 (almost always). Severity of depression was measured by the Beck Depression Inventory (Beck & Steer, 1987). Anxiety sensitivity was measured by the Anxiety Sensitivity Index (Peterson & Reiss, 1987). Treatment credibility, as perceived by the participant, was measured by the Reactions to Treatment Questionnaire (Borkovec & Nau, 1972), which was administered to participants at the beginning of session 2 (i.e., after they had received the treatment rationale and understood what treatment entailed). Other measures, not pertinent to the aims of the present study, were also administered (see Taylor et al., 2003b).

Treatments

Participants meeting study criteria were randomized to eight 90–minute individual weekly sessions of either exposure therapy, EMDR, or relaxation training. Detailed treatment manuals were used for each treatment. Exposure and relaxation were based on Marks et al. (1998), and EMDR was based on Shapiro (1995). Two female therapists administered all three treatments, under the supervision of a doctoral-level psychologist. Both therapists had completed Level I and II training from the EMDR Institute.

Exposure therapy involved four sessions of imaginal exposure to traumatic events, followed by four sessions of in vivo exposure to harmless but distressing trauma-related stimuli. Imaginal exposure was repeated several times per session, with particular focus on the most disturbing aspects of the event. Sessions were audiotaped and participants were asked to listen to the tapes for an hour each day for the first 4 weeks of treatment. In vivo exposure consisted of therapist-assisted exposure, conducted within sessions, and exposure homework assignments. The latter consisted of live exposure for an hour each day for 4 weeks.

Relaxation training involved practicing three different relaxation exercises; one per session for the first three sessions. The participant then selected an exercise to practice in subsequent sessions. This consisted of either one of the three exercises or some combination thereof. In each session the therapist read a relaxation script. The script was audiotaped and the participant was asked to listen to it for an hour each day.

EMDR commenced with the Safe Place exercise, which is a coping strategy for reducing distress. This exercise was practiced as a homework assignment and used thereafter as needed. If there was sufficient time in the first session, processing of a traumatic memory was initiated, which continued in subsequent sessions. The participant was asked to recall the memory and its associated features (e.g., negative self-statements) and then lateral sets of eye movements were induced by the therapist moving her finger across the participant's field of vision. The participant then reported any thoughts, feelings, or images that arose. This new material typically became the focus of the next set of eye movements. The process continued until the distress evoked by the memory had subsided. Other EMDR methods (e.g., cognitive interweave) were used as indicated (Shapiro, 1995).

Procedure

Potential participants contacting the clinic were given a description of the study and screened for inclusion/exclusion criteria during a telephone screening interview. Those passing the screen were invited to the clinic for an evaluation consisting of the SCID–IV, CAPS, and questionnaires. Written informed consent was obtained before commencing the clinic assessment. All interviews were conducted by clinic staff, who were trained and supervised by a doctoral-level psychologist. Clinic staff assigned diagnoses. Once the intake assessment had been conducted, the information was reviewed by a doctoral-level psychologist to confirm the diagnosis of PTSD. Interviews were audiotaped to assess inter-rater reliability.

Each therapist was randomly assigned patients from the three treatment conditions. Therapist 1 treated 27% of participants, and therapist 2 treated the remainder. Treatment sessions were videotaped for weekly supervision and to ensure treatment integrity. One month after treatment ended, participants were re-interviewed with the CAPS and completed the self-report outcome measures (posttreatment assessment). Three months later, the CAPS and self-report measures were administered again (follow-up assessment).

The CAPS interviews before and after treatment were administered by clinic staff who were not involved with treatment and were unaware of the participants' treatment assignment. Reliability of CAPS and diagnostic ratings was assessed by a doctoral-level psychologist who independently rated 12 audiotaped SCID-IV interviews and 12 audiotaped CAPS interviews. The SCID-IV interviews consisted of a random sample of participants included or excluded from the study. CAPS interviews were a random sample of pre- or posttreatment interviews (12 different participants). The agreement between raters for the diagnosis of PTSD was 92% (= .80). Reliability of ratings on the CAPS were compared by computing intraclass correlations for the four main sets of PTSD symptoms. The correlations were as follows: Reexperiencing .93, avoidance .84, numbing .85, and hyperarousal .80.

RESULTS

To identify predictors of treatment outcome, 4 step-wise discriminant function analyses were performed. The criterion variables were (a) dropout status (dropped out vs. completed treatment; $n = 60$), (b) remitted at posttreatment (i.e., whether the patient was in full or partial remission; $n = 45$), (c) remitted at follow-up ($n = 45$), and (d) remitted at posttreatment *and* follow-up (sustained remission; $n = 45$). The predictor variables were as follows: whether the patient received exposure therapy (dummy coded; 1 = yes, 0 = no), whether the patient received EMDR (1 = yes, 0 = no), perceived treatment credibility, involvement in litigation, receipt of disability assistance, use of antidepressant medications, use of benzodiazepines, global level of functioning, PTSD duration, experience of multiple traumata (1 = multiple, 0 = single trauma), and severity of reexperiencing, avoidance, numbing, hyperarousal, trauma-related guilt, trauma-related anger, dissociative symptoms, and depression. Also included as predictors were strength of trauma-related cognitions and level of anxiety sensitivity. Note that in order to control for therapy effects in predicting outcome, it was only necessary to dummy-code for exposure and EMDR. A dummy coding for relaxation would be redundant, because relaxation is indicated by a score of 0 on both the exposure and EMDR variables. Tolerance values for the discriminant analyses were all within acceptable limits (Norusis, 1988), indicating that multicollinearity was not a problem.

The only significant predictor of dropout status was treatment credibility; canonical r = .38; $\chi^2(1)$ = 8.24, p < .005, hit rate (proportion of participants correctly classified) = 87.0%. Treatment dropouts, compared to completers, had significantly lower credibility ratings. Respectively, M = 32.4 (SD = 13.7), M = 43.6 (SD = 9.5). Treatments did not differ in credibility ratings, $F(2, 48)$ = 0.16, p > .1. Similarly, the interaction between treatment type and dropout status was not significant, $F(2, 48)$ = 0.42, p > .1. (Degrees of freedom are attenuated to some extent by missing data; although, for example, all 60 participants completed the CAPS ratings, 54 participants returned to complete the credibility ratings in session 2.)

Two variables predicted remission of PTSD at posttreatment; whether the participant received exposure therapy (discriminant loading = .65) and pretreatment severity of reexperiencing symptoms (loading =-.78); canonical r = .50; $\chi^2(2)$ = 12.32, p < .005, hit rate = 75.6%. On other words, posttreatment remission from PTSD was predicted by treatment with exposure therapy and milder pretreatment reexperiencing symptoms.

One variable predicted remission of PTSD at follow-up: receipt of exposure therapy; canonical r = .30; $\chi^2(1)$ = 4.01, p < .05, hit rate = 66.7%. Sustained remission (i.e., remission at posttreatment and follow-up) was predicted by two variables: receipt of exposure therapy (loading = .72) and pretreatment severity of reexperiencing symptoms (loading =-.74); canonical r = .46; $\chi^2(2)$ = 9.99, p < .01, hit rate = 68.9%. Thus, sustained remission from PTSD was predicted by treatment with exposure therapy and milder pretreatment reexperiencing symptoms.

To investigate whether reexperiencing symptoms are more important in predicting response to one treatment than another, pretreatment severity scores for these symptoms were cluster analyzed, using Ward's method and squared Euclidean distance. This method was selected because this procedure is superior to other algorithms in identifying known clusters (Overall, Gibson, & Novy, 1993). The dendrogram indicated two clusters; cluster 1 consisted of people with more severe reexperiencing symptoms (M = 5.7, SD = 0.8, n = 27), while cluster 2 contained those with less severe symptoms (M = 3.8, SD = 0.8, n = 33). To place these numbers in context, scores on the CAPS reexperiencing range from 0 to 8.

As expected from the cluster analysis, the clusters differed significantly on reexperiencing severity, $F(1, 54)$ = 87.53, p < .001. However, the three treatments did not differ in reexperiencing, $F(2, 54) = 0.34$, $p > .1$, and the interaction between treatment and cluster was nonsignificant, $F(2, 54) = 1.41$, $p > .1$. In other words, cluster type was not confounded with treatment type.

To investigate whether the predictive importance of reexperiencing varies with treatment type, three 2–2 χ^2 tests were conducted for each treatment condition: (a) cluster type (more severe vs. less severe) by posttreatment remission (remitted vs. unremitted), (b) cluster type by follow-up remission, and (c) cluster type by sustained remission. Sample sizes for the "more severe" and "less severe" treatment completers, respectively, were as follows: relaxation ($ns = 8, 7$), EMDR ($7, 8$), and exposure ($4, 11$).

For relaxation training, the "more severe" cluster was associated with significantly poorer outcome at posttreatment, $\chi^2(1) = 11.43$, $p < .001$, and there was a trend in the same direction at follow-up, $\chi^2(1) = 3.23$, $p = .07$. For relaxation, the "more severe" cluster was also associated with significantly fewer patients achieving sustained remission, $\chi^2(1) = 8.57$, $p < .005$. Figure 2.3 illustrates these findings.

For EMDR, the "more severe" and "less severe" clusters did not differ in the proportions of patients with posttreatment, follow-up, or sustained

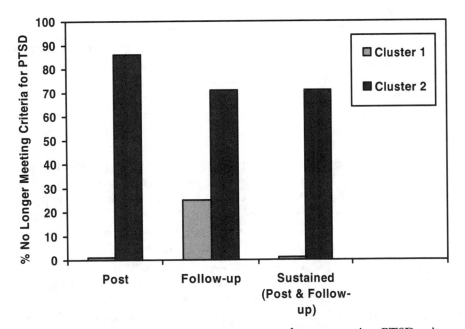

Figure 2.3 Relaxation training: Percentage no longer meeting PTSD criteria after treatment.

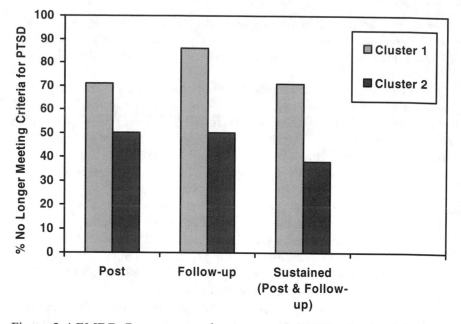

Figure 2.4 EMDR: Percentage no longer meeting PTSD criteria after treatment.

remission. Respectively, $\chi^2(1) = 0.71$, 2.14, and 1.73, $ps > .1$. Figure 2.4 shows the corresponding percentages. Although the figure suggests trends for the "more severe" cluster to have better outcome, these results do not meet the conventional criteria for trends (defined as $ps < .1$). For exposure therapy, the "more severe" and "less severe" clusters also did not differ in the proportions of patients with posttreatment, follow-up, or sustained remission. Respectively, $\chi^2(1) = 0.84$, 0.64, and 0.09, $ps > .1$ (and see Figure 2.5).

In a recent series of additional analyses, we also investigated the question of whether symptom heritability is related to treatment outcome (Taylor, Jang, & Stein, 2003a). We explored this issue because it is our impression from giving workshops and colloquia on PTSD that many clinicians, particularly those with medical backgrounds, believe that psychosocial treatments are unlikely to be useful for heritable symptoms. In other words, many practitioners seem to believe that psychosocial treatments are more efficacious for symptoms that have little or no genetic loadings, compared with symptoms with a higher heritability.

To examine this issue, Table 2.2 shows the heritability of each PTSD symptom and the effect size (d) for its treatment with exposure, EMDR,

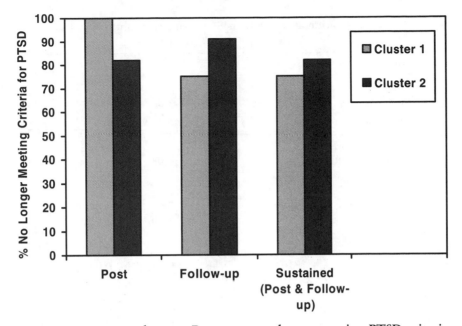

Figure 2.5 Exposure therapy: Percentage no longer meeting PTSD criteria after treatment.

or relaxation. Heritability of PTSD symptoms was measured as part of the twin study by Stein, Jang, Taylor, Vernon, and Livesley (2002), and treatment effect sizes were from Taylor et al. (2003b). (The two studies were based on different samples.) We conducted these analyses as a preliminary investigation of whether heritable symptoms are less responsive to environmental (psychosocial) interventions. Table 2.2 shows that heritability was uncorrelated with the efficacy of either exposure or relaxation. Heritability was also not significantly correlated with EMDR effect sizes, although there was a trend for EMDR to be less effective with more heritable symptoms, as suggested by the medium-sized correlation between heritability and effect size ($r = -.36$).

DISCUSSION

Despite the availability of effective treatments for PTSD, little is known about which treatment should be selected for which patient. Therapist skill and patient preference may be important considerations, although it

Table 2.2 Relationship Between Symptom Heritability (h^2) and
Treatment Effect Size (d)

PTSD symptom	h^2	d_{EMDR}	$d_{EXPOSURE}$	$d_{RELAXATION}$
Re-experiencing				
recollections	.27	1.08	1.87	2.43
dreams	.30	0.90	1.06	1.12
flashbacks	.00	1.22	0.63	0.77
psychological distress	.00	1.05	1.57	1.59
physiological reactivity	.27	0.94	1.57	0.42
Avoidance				
thoughts, feelings, conversations	.28	0.89	1.89	0.64
activities, places, people	.00	1.19	1.95	0.56
Numbing				
inability to recall	.21	0.64	0.55	0.56
diminished interest in activities	.26	0.52	1.16	1.04
detachment and estrangement	.25	0.80	0.46	1.32
restricted range of affect	.17	0.52	0.70	0.40
foreshortened future	.23	0.42	0.37	0.49
Hyperarousal				
insomnia	.20	0.72	0.27	0.39
irritability or anger	.19	0.92	0.66	0.81
difficulty concentrating	.15	0.52	0.92	1.29
hypervigilance	.22	1.15	1.07	0.57
exaggerated startle.	.20	1.21	0.56	0.83
Correlation between h^2 and ES (all $ps > .05$)		−.36	−.08	.04

Source. Taylor et al. (2003a).

is possible that regardless of patient preference, some treatments may be more effective than others. Consistent with this, a study of rape-related PTSD found that although patients found supportive counseling to be equally credible as cognitive-behavior therapy, counseling was no more effective than a wait-list control, and cognitive-behavior therapy was superior to both conditions in reducing PTSD (Foa, Rothbaum, Riggs, & Murdock, 1991).

There are several inconsistencies in the literature about the importance of outcome predictors. Some research, for example, suggests that trauma-related guilt is a predictor of poor outcome (Pitman et al., 1991), while other research failed to replicate this finding (Taylor et al., 2001). The inconsistencies might reflect the fact that many variables are not powerful predictors of outcome. Variables that are only modestly correlated with outcome may not consistently emerge as predictors. Meta-analytic studies, pooling the results of many studies, may eventually shed light on which variables are most consistently predictive of treatment outcome. Despite their limitations, meta-analyses can be useful because treatment outcome studies typically do not have large numbers of treatment completers per treatment condition (as in the present study), which means that only the most robust predictors will attain statistical significance.

Given these caveats, the findings of the present study should be interpreted with caution, and they require replication. To our knowledge, ours is the first study to attempt to identify whether different treatments are associated with different outcome predictors. If our findings are replicated, then they have a number of important clinical implications. If treatment dropout is predicted primarily with perceived treatment credibility, then steps should be taken to better improve credibility, and thereby better retain patients in treatment.

Various cognitive-behavioral strategies—known as socialization strategies—have been developed to improve credibility (Wells, 1997). These involve (a) assessing the patient's implicit model of the causes and treatment of that patient's disorder, (b) educating the patient about the disorder and introducing the therapist's model of causes and treatment, and (c) attempting to resolve any discrepancies between the models of the patient and therapist. The therapist attempts to resolve discrepancies by a variety of strategies, including the use of strategies to persuade the patient that the therapist's model is correct. For example, the therapist and patient could explore the effects of attempting to avoid (suppress) trauma-related thoughts. People with PTSD often believe that thought suppression or distraction are appropriate ways of dealing with these thoughts (Purdon, 1999). The therapist could present the rationale that avoidance perpetuates the experience of unwanted thoughts (because distracters become reminders or retrieval cues of the unwanted thoughts: Purdon, 1999). The patient could then test this model by refraining from thought suppression and monitoring the effects on the frequency of reexperiencing symptoms.

Although these socialization strategies are plausible, their benefits in limiting treatment dropout remain to be demonstrated. In particular, it remains to be seen whether they are more effective than the more limited socialization methods, such as those used in the present study. We simply provided patients with a verbal description of PTSD and its treatment, then assessed the patient's treatment goals, and discussed how the treatment was relevant to the goals.

For patients who do not drop out of treatment, our findings suggest that the most consistent predictor of good outcome is whether or not the patient receives exposure therapy. This is consistent with the conclusion of several reviews, which conclude that exposure is among the most effective treatments (Chambless & Ollendick, 2001; Foa & Meadows, 1997; van Etten & Taylor, 1998). Indeed, some studies suggest that the efficacy of treatment is not improved or even diminished when exposure is diluted by adding cognitive restructuring (Foa, Dancu, et al., 1999; Marks et al., 1998).

Our findings further suggest that the severity of reexperiencing symptoms is an important predictor of treatment outcome, largely because relaxation training has a poorer outcome when these symptoms are severe. The efficacy of exposure and EMDR does not appear to be affected by the severity of reexperiencing. These findings provide further support for the efficacy of exposure and, to a limited extent, support the use of EMDR. Our findings, however, suggest that exposure is a first-line psychosocial treatment for PTSD.

REFERENCES

American Psychiatric Association. (2000). *Diagnostic and statistical manual of mental disorders* (4th ed., text revision). Washington, DC: Author.

Asmundson, G. J. G., Frombach, I., McQuaid, J., Pedrelli, P., Lenox, R., & Stein, M. B. (2000). Dimensionality of posttraumatic stress symptoms: A confirmatory factor analysis of DSM–IV symptom clusters and other models. *Behaviour Research and Therapy, 38,* 203–214.

Beck, A. T., & Steer, R. A. (1987). *Manual for the revised Beck Depression Inventory.* San Antonio, TX: Psychological Corporation.

Blake, D., Weathers, F. W., Nagy, L. M., Kaloupek, D. G., Charney, D. S., & Keane, T. M. (1997). *Clinician administered PTSD scale* (revised). Boston, MA: Behavioral Science Division, Boston National Center for Post-Traumatic Stress Disorder.

Borkovec, T. D., & Nau, S. D. (1972). Credibility of analogue therapy rationales. *Journal of Behavior Therapy and Experimental Psychiatry, 3,* 257–260.

Chambless, D. L., & Ollendick, T. H. (2001). Empirically supported psychological interventions: Controversies and evidence. *Annual Review of Psychology, 52,* 685–716.

Cohen, J. (1988). *Statistical power analyses for the behavioral sciences* (2nd ed.). Hillsdale, NJ: Erlbaum.

Devilly, G. J. (2002). Eye movement desensitization and reprocessing: A chronology of its development and scientific standing. *Scientific Review of Mental Health Practice, 1,* 113–138.

Devilly, G. J., & Spence, S. H. (1999). The relative efficacy and treatment distress of EMDR and a cognitive-behavior trauma treatment protocol in the amelioration of posttraumatic stress disorder. *Journal of Anxiety Disorders, 13,* 131–157.

Fedoroff, I. C., Taylor, S., Asmundson, G. J. G., & Koch, W. J. (2000). Cognitive factors in traumatic stress reactions: Predicting PTSD symptoms from anxiety sensitivity and beliefs about harmful events. *Behavioural and Cognitive Psychotherapy, 28,* 5–15.

First, M. B., Spitzer, R. L., Gibbon, M., & Williams, J. B. W. (1996). *Structured Clinical Interview for Axis I DSM–IV disorders—Patient edition.* New York: Biometrics Research Department, New York State Psychiatric Institute.

Foa, E. B., Dancu, C. V., Hembree, E. A., Jaycox, L. H., Meadows, E. A., & Street, G. P. (1999). A comparison of exposure therapy, stress inoculation training, and their combination for reducing posttraumatic stress disorder in female assault victims. *Journal of Consulting and Clinical Psychology, 67,* 194–200.

Foa, E. B., Ehlers, A., Clark, D. M., Tolin, D. F., & Orsillo, S. M. (1999). The posttraumatic cognitions inventory (PTCI): Development and validation. *Psychological Assessment, 11,* 303–314.

Foa, E. B., & Meadows, E. A. (1997). Psychosocial treatments for posttraumatic stress disorder: A critical review. *Annual Review of Psychology, 48,* 449–480.

Foa, E. B., Riggs, D. S., Massie, E. D., & Yarczower, M. (1995). The impact of fear activation and anger on the efficacy of exposure treatment for posttraumatic stress disorder. *Behavior Therapy, 26,* 487–499.

Foa, E. B., Rothbaum, B. O., Riggs, D. S., & Murdock, T. B. (1991). Treatment of post-traumatic stress disorder in rape victims: A comparison between cognitive-behavioral procedures and counseling. *Journal of Consulting and Clinical Psychology, 59,* 715–723.

Foa, E. B., & Tolin, D. F. (2000). Comparison of the PTSD Symptom Scale-Interview Version and the Clinician-Administered PTSD Scale. *Journal of Traumatic Stress, 13,* 181–191.

Ironson, G., Freund, B., Strauss, J. L., & Williams, J. (2002). A comparison of two treatments for traumatic stress: A community-based study of EMDR and prolonged exposure. *Journal of Clinical Psychology, 58,* 113–128.

King, D. W., Leskin, G. A., King, L. A., & Weathers, F. W. (1998). Confirmatory factor analysis of the clinician-administered PTSD Scale: Evidence for the dimensionality of posttraumatic stress disorder. *Psychological Assessment, 10,* 90–96.

Lee, C., Gavriel, H., Drummond, P., Richards, J., & Greenwald, R. (2002). Treatment of PTSD: Stress inoculation training with prolonged exposure compared to EMDR. *Journal of Clinical Psychology, 58,* 1071–1089.

Marks, I. M., Lovell, K., Noshirvani, H., Livanou, M., & Thrasher, S. (1998). Treatment of posttraumatic stress disorder by exposure and/or cognitive restructuring. *Archives of General Psychiatry, 55,* 317–325.

Maxfield, L., & Hyer, L. (2002). The relationship between efficacy and methodology in studies investigating EMDR treatment of PTSD. *Journal of Clinical Psychology, 58,* 23–41.

Mayou, R., Tyndel, S., & Bryant, B. (1997). Long-term outcome of motor vehicle accident injury. *Psychosomatic Medicine, 59,* 578–584.

Neziroglu, F., Stevens, K. P., McKay, D., & Yaryura-Tobias, J. A. (2001). Predictive validity of the overvalued ideas scale: Outcome in obsessive-compulsive and body dysmorphic disorders. *Behaviour Research and Therapy, 39,* 745–756.

Norusis, M. J. (1988). *SPSS-X advanced statistics guide* (2nd ed.). Chicago, IL: SPSS, Inc.

Overall, J. E., Gibson, J. M., & Novy, D. M. (1993). Population recovery capabilities of 35 cluster analysis methods. *Journal of Clinical Psychology, 49,* 459–470.

Peterson, K. C., Prout, M. F., & Schwarz, R. A. (1991). *Post-traumatic stress disorder: A clinician's guide.* New York: Plenum.

Peterson, R. A., & Reiss, S. (1987). *Anxiety sensitivity index manual.* Palos Heights, IL: International Diagnostic Systems.

Pitman, R. K., Altman, B., Greenwald, E., Longpre, R. E., Macklin, M. L., Poire, R. E., & Steketee, G. S. (1991). Psychiatric complications during flooding therapy for posttraumatic stress disorder. *Journal of Clinical Psychiatry, 52,* 17–20.

Power, K., McGoldrick, T., Brown, K., Buchanan, R., Sharp, D., Swanson, V., & Karatzias, A. (2002). A controlled comparison of eye movement desensitization and reprocessing versus exposure plus cognitive restructuring versus waiting list in the treatment of post-traumatic stress disorder. *Clinical Psychology and Psychotherapy, 9,* 299–318.

Purdon, C. (1999). Thought suppression and psychopathology. *Behaviour Research and Therapy, 37,* 1029–1054.

Rogers, S., Silver, S. M., Goss, J., Obenchain, J., Willis, A., & Whitney, R. L. (1999). A single session, group study of exposure and eye movement desensitization and reprocessing in treating posttraumatic stress disorder among Vietnam war veterans: Preliminary data. *Journal of Anxiety Disorders, 13,* 119–130.

Shapiro, F. (1995). *Eye movement desensitization and reprocessing: Basic principles, protocols, and procedures.* New York: Guilford.

Shapiro, F. (1999). Eye movement desensitization and reprocessing (EMDR) and the anxiety disorders: Clinical and research implications of an integrated psychotherapy treatment. *Journal of Anxiety Disorders, 13,* 35–67.

Spector, J. (2001). EMDR: Current developments and review update. *Psicoterapia Cognitiva e Comportamentale, 7,* 25–34.

Stein, M. B., Jang, K. L., Taylor, S., Vernon, P. A., & Livesley, W. J. (2002). Genetic and environmental influences on trauma exposure and posttraumatic stress disorder symptoms: A general population twin study. *American Journal of Psychiatry, 159,* 1675–1681.

Tarrier, N. (2001). What can be learned from clinical trials? Reply to Devilly and Foa (2001). *Journal of Consulting and Clinical Psychology, 69,* 117–118.

Tarrier, N., Pilgrim, H., Sommerfield, C., Faragher, B., Reynolds, M., Graham, E., & Barrowclough, C. (1999). A randomized trial of cognitive therapy and imaginal exposure in the treatment of chronic posttraumatic stress disorder. *Journal of Consulting and Clinical Psychology, 67,* 13–18.

Taylor, S. (1999). *Anxiety sensitivity.* Mahwah, NJ: Erlbaum.

Taylor, S. (2000). *Understanding and treating panic disorder: Cognitive-behavioural approaches.* New York: Wiley.

Taylor, S., Fedoroff, I. C., Koch, W. J., Thordarson, D. S., Fecteau, G., & Nicki, R. (2001). Posttraumatic stress disorder arising after road traffic collisions: Patterns of response to cognitive-behavior therapy. *Journal of Consulting and Clinical Psychology, 69,* 541–551.

Taylor, S., & Koch, W. J. (1995). Anxiety disorders due to motor vehicle accidents: Nature and treatment. *Clinical Psychology Review, 15,* 721–738.

Taylor, S., Jang, K. L., & Stein, M. B. (2003a). *Genetic and environmental influences on PTSD: Factors influencing the risk of trauma exposure and PTSD symptoms.* Paper presented at the annual meeting of the International Society for Traumatic Stress Studies, Chicago, IL.

Taylor, S., Thordarson, D. S., Maxfield, L., Fedoroff, I. C., Lovell, K., & Ogrodniczuk, J. (2003b). Comparative efficacy, speed, and adverse effects of three treatments for PTSD: Exposure therapy, EMDR, and relaxation training. *Journal of Consulting and Clinical Psychology, 71,* 330–338.

van Etten, M., & Taylor, S. (1998). Comparative efficacy of treatments for posttraumatic stress disorder: A meta-analysis. *Clinical Psychology and Psychotherapy, 5,* 126–145.

Vaughan, K., Armstrong, M. S., Gold, R., O'Connor, N., Jenneke, W., & Tarrier, N. (1994). A trial of eye movement desensitization compared to image habituation and applied muscle relaxation in post-traumatic stress disorder. *Journal of Behavior Therapy and Experimental Psychiatry, 25,* 283–291.

Wells, A. (1997). *Cognitive therapy of anxiety disorders: A practice manual and conceptual guide.* Chichester: Wiley.

Chapter 3

MULTIPLE CHANNEL EXPOSURE THERAPY OF PTSD: IMPACT OF TREATMENT ON FUNCTIONING AND RESOURCES

Sherry A. Falsetti, Brigette A. Erwin, Heidi S. Resnick, Joanne Davis, and Amy M. Combs-Lane

INTRODUCTION

Posttraumatic stress disorder (PTSD) is a stress reaction characterized by symptoms of reexperiencing, avoidance/numbing, and hyperarousal following exposure to an extreme traumatic event. PTSD may affect 8 to10% of the general population (Kessler, Sonnega, Bromet, Hughes, & Nelson, 1995). Consistent with *DSM-IV* diagnostic criteria for PTSD (American Psychiatric Association, 1994), epidemiological and clinical studies have confirmed that PTSD is associated with significant impairment in social, occupational, and physical functioning.

As a part of the National Vietnam Veterans Readjustment Study (NV-VRS), Jordan and colleagues (1992) found that Vietnam veterans with PTSD were more likely to report marital, parental, and family adjustment difficulties than were veterans without PTSD. Zatzick and colleagues also examined data from the NVVRS in studies of male (Zatzick, Marmar, et al., 1997) and female (Zatzick, Weiss, et al., 1997) veterans. Among male veterans, the presence of PTSD was associated with greater rates of substance abuse, chronic disease, and greater functional impairment (i.e., ability to function at home, work, or school; overall life satisfaction; self-

The study reported in this chapter was supported by a grant from the National Institute of Mental Health to Sherry A. Falsetti (MH-53381–01A1).

reported physical health status; limitations in self-care, mobility, physical activities, role activities, and leisure activities; and perpetration of violent interpersonal acts in the past year). Female veterans appeared similar to males, with the exception that the presence of PTSD was additionally associated with increased numbers of days in bed due to physical illness or injury, but PTSD was not associated with increased rates of perpetration of violent interpersonal acts in the past year. Investigating health outcomes, Wagner and colleagues (2000) found that, among male and female Gulf War veterans, PTSD symptomatology assessed immediately upon return from the Gulf War was predictive of self-reported health difficulties assessed 18 to 24 months later. Among treatment-seeking Vietnam veterans, PTSD symptom severity predicted greater rates of confirmed mortality 4 to 10 years later (Erwin et al., 1996). Examining actual primary care utilization and physician-diagnosed medical conditions, Deykin and colleagues (2001) reported that PTSD among veterans is associated with greater rates of medical diagnoses, which in turn are associated with greater utilization of primary care services. Perhaps explaining these associations, Kimerling, Clum, and Wolfe (2000) found that the cluster of hyperarousal symptoms uniquely contributed to the association between traumatic exposure and subsequent self-reported health problems.

Although impairment is included as a *DSM–IV* diagnostic criterion for PTSD and there is strong empirical evidence demonstrating an association between PTSD and impairment, the systematic and comprehensive assessment of such a factor in the context of outcome studies has been neglected in clinical research. Outcome studies specifically examining functional impairment among individuals with PTSD are crucial. First, the goal of PTSD treatment is both to reduce symptoms and improve global functioning, and it is important to demonstrate empirically whether effective psychological treatments of PTSD symptoms generalize to broad- based improvement in functioning. Second, changes in symptoms and in functioning may not be highly associated. Among patients with panic disorder, symptom measures have been shown to account for only 15% (Leon, Shear, Portera, & Klerman, 1992) to 35% (Sheehan, Harnett-Sheehan, & Raj, 1996) of the variance in disability, suggesting that disability and impairment may not be assessed most validly by measures of symptom severity (Sheehan et al., 1996). Third, there is preliminary evidence suggesting that PTSD symptoms may fluctuate substantially over time (Niles et al., 1996). This suggests that measures of PTSD and related symptomatology may not be the most reliable means to determine improvement following treatment of PTSD.

Despite the importance of examining impairment in treatment out-come studies, scant clinical studies have examined changes in function-ing following treatment of PTSD. A handful of studies found evidence to suggest that short-term improvements in social adjustment are achieved following cognitive-behavioral treatment of rape-related PTSD symptoms (e.g., Resick & Schnicke, 1992). More recent studies have examined chang-es in functioning and quality of life among individuals with PTSD follow-ing double-blind, placebo-controlled pharmacotherapy trials of fluoxetine (Malik et al., 1999) and sertraline (Brady et al., 2000). Malik and col-leagues reported that, relative to 5 placebo-control participants, 11 indi-viduals who received 12 weeks of fluoxetine treatment of PTSD were found to exhibit improvement in vitality, social functioning, and mental health. In a larger study, Brady and colleagues reported that, relative to 90 placebo-control participants, 93 individuals who received 12 weeks of sertraline treatment of PTSD were found to exhibit improvement in social and occupational functioning and in life satisfaction. Currently unknown is the extent to which broad-based functioning improves following cogni-tive-behavioral treatment of PTSD.

Cognitive-behavioral techniques are commonly used for the treatment of PTSD. Improvement in PTSD symptoms following cognitive-behavior-al treatment of PTSD has been demonstrated in numerous studies (e.g., Dancu, Foa, & Smucker, 1993; Foa, Rothbaum, Riggs, & Murdock, 1991; Keane, Fairbank, Caddell, & Zimering, 1989; Marks, Lovell, Noshirvani, Livanou, & Thrasher, 1998; Resick & Schnicke, 1992). One specific set of cognitive-behavioral techniques employed in the treatment of PTSD and comorbid panic attacks is Multiple Channel Exposure Therapy (MCET; Falsetti, Resnick, Davis, & Combs-Lane, 2001). MCET is adapted from cognitive processing therapy (CPT; Resick & Schnicke, 1993) and cogni-tive-behavioral treatment of panic disorder (Mastery of Your Anxiety and Panic; Barlow & Craske, 1989). MCET is designed to maximize the effec-tiveness of exposure-based treatments of PTSD by accessing physiologi-cal, cognitive, and behavioral channels of anxiety through exposure, and by incorporating cognitive restructuring. Utilizing the same sample of participants included in the current study, patients treated with 12 weeks of MCET improved significantly compared with controls. Further, MCET patients maintained gains at 3- and 6-month follow-up (Falsetti et al., 2001). Despite the apparent efficacy of MCET at improving psychiatric symptoms of PTSD and panic, there is a strong need to determine wheth-er such gains are associated with similar improvements in overall func-tioning.

The present study examined whether female patients diagnosed with PTSD and comorbid panic attacks evidenced improvement in functioning following treatment with MCET. Based on several reviews, Sheehan and colleagues (1996) argue that, at minimum, three domains of functioning should be included when assessing disability: work impairment, social impairment, and family life/home responsibilities. Thus, participants treated with MCET and control participants were compared on measures of satisfaction with, resources for and quality of work, social life and, family at baseline and at 12 weeks (posttreatment for, the treatment condition). In addition, the treatment group was followed and assessed at 3 months and 6 months to examine further changes in functioning. It was expected that the treatment group would exhibit greater improvement in social functioning and material and emotional resources than control participants. It was also expected that the treatment group would evidence continued improvement in these areas at follow-up assessments.

METHOD

Participants

Participants were 47 women with anxiety and related symptoms subsequent to exposure to at least one traumatic event that had occurred at least 3 months prior to the time of the assessment. Before participants were accepted into the current study, they underwent a battery of self-report and interview-based instruments. All participants received a principal diagnosis of *DSM–IV* PTSD (American Psychiatric Association, 1994) and reported experiencing panic attacks. The sample reported a mean of 4.81 (SD = 2.41) traumatic events. Participants with principal diagnoses other than PTSD, with active psychosis, mental retardation, current suicidal or parasuicidal behavior, current drug or alcohol dependency, or illiteracy were excluded from the study.

The mean age of the participants was 35.72 years (SD = 9.99). Three-fourths (76.6%; n = 36) of participants were Caucasian, 21.3% (n = 10) were African-American, and 2.1% (n = 1) were Asian. More than half of the sample was single (57.4%; n = 27); 42.6% (n = 20) were married. Although 85.1% (n = 40) earned a high school education or more and 80.9% (n = 38) were employed, 51.1% (n = 24) earned an annual income of $15,000 or less and only 6.4% (n = 3) earned more than $50,000 per year. Nearly one-fifth (17.0%, n = 8) received some form of disability payments.

Treatment

All participants were assessed at baseline. Subsequently, 24 patients were randomly assigned to the treatment condition. Patients in the treatment condition met for twelve 90-minute weekly group sessions of MCET (Falsetti et al., 2001), which is a cognitive-behavioral treatment designed specifically for individuals with PTSD and comorbid panic attacks. Patients were presented with cognitive-behavioral models of PTSD and panic, and they participated in exposures directed at physiological, cognitive, and behavioral channels of anxiety. Thus, physiological reactivity was targeted with interoceptive exposure, cognitive components of anxiety were targeted through writing about the trauma, and behavioral components of anxiety were targeted through *in vivo* exposure to conditioned cues of anxiety. Further, cognitive restructuring skills (identifying maladaptive automatic thoughts, disputing cognitive errors in these automatic thoughts, and developing rational responses) were employed before, during, and after exposures; and breathing retraining (i.e., diaphragmatic breathing) was employed to manage panic symptoms. For a more detailed description of MCET, see Falsetti and colleagues (2001).

The remaining 23 patients were randomly assigned to the control condition. Participants who served as controls were contacted once every 2 weeks for 12 weeks to determine possible exacerbation of symptoms. In addition, patients in the control condition were informed that they were welcome to call if they wished to receive telephone counseling. The telephone counseling that was provided was client-centered and similar to what individuals are provided through telephone victim advocate services. All controls were informed that, at the end of 12 weeks, they would be invited to participate in the treatment condition.

Posttreatment and Follow-Up Assessments

All pretreatment assessment measures were readministered 12 weeks from baseline. For patients in the treatment condition, this assessment marked the conclusion of their treatment. For patients in the control condition, this assessment marked the conclusion of their waiting period and, if they chose to continue, the beginning of their participation in the treatment condition. Patients who had formerly served as controls were reassessed at the conclusion of their 12 weeks of treatment. Finally, all assessment measures were readministered 3 months and 6 months following treatment.

Interview Measures

Demographic measures. An interview designed by the study investigators to assess standard demographic information was administered. This interview collected information about participants' age, race, marital status, educational background, employment status, annual income, and disability status.

Clinician Administered PTSD Scale. The CAPS (Blake et al., 1990) is a structured clinical interview that is designed to assess PTSD. Current and lifetime PTSD was assessed at the pretreatment assessment with the CAPS Form 1; symptoms of PTSD experienced in the preceding week were assessed at subsequent assessments with the CAPS Form 2. The CAPS consists of standardized prompt questions; supplementary follow-up (probe) questions; and behaviorally anchored 5-point rating scales, which correspond to the frequency and intensity of each symptom assessed. The CAPS provides a means to evaluate the following: (a) self-report of exposure to potential Criterion A events (i.e., traumatic stressors); (b) frequency and intensity of each of 17 PTSD symptom and of 8 associated features; (c) the impact of the 17 PTSD symptoms on social and occupational functioning; (d) current and lifetime diagnosis of PTSD; (e) overall severity of PTSD; (f) the patient's global improvement since baseline; and (g) the validity of obtained ratings. The CAPS has been found to possess excellent psychometric properties (Weathers et al., 1992). Considering all 17 PTSD items, internal consistency was .94 and test-retest reliability measured 2 to 3 days apart ranged from .90 to .98. Using the CAPS as a continuous measure, a cutoff score of 65 was reported as having good sensitivity (.84) and specificity (.95) when measured against the SCID PTSD module. The CAPS also correlated .91 with the Mississippi Scale for Combat-Related PTSD, demonstrating excellent convergent validity.

The Anxiety Disorders Interview Schedule for DSM–IV—Lifetime (ADIS–IV–L). The ADIS–IV–L (DiNardo, Brown, & Barlow, 1994) is a semi-structured clinical interview providing *DSM–IV* diagnoses of a subset of psychiatric disorders, including panic disorder. The panic disorder section of the ADIS–IV–L was used to collect detailed information regarding panic attack symptoms. In addition to symptom ratings, this scale includes an assessment of the frequency of panic attacks, history of panic attacks, how panic attacks are managed, and distress experienced as a result of panic. Brown, DiNardo, Lehman, and Campbell (2001) reported a kappa of .72 for a principal diagnosis of panic disorder and a kappa of .56 for a principal or additional diagnosis of panic disorder in a sample of 362 anxiety disorder patients who received two independent ADIS–IV–L interviews.

Structured Clinical Interview for DSM–IV Nonpatient Version (SCID–P). The SCID–P (Spitzer, Williams, & Gibbon, 1995) is a widely used clinician-administered interview to determine *DSM–IV* psychiatric diagnoses. The PTSD module of the SCID was used to assess PTSD; the SCID II was used to assess personality disorders. The SCID has been used in many other studies of violent crime.

Self-Report Measures

Social Adjustment Scale (SAS). The SAS (Weissman & Paykel, 1974) measures social functioning in seven areas of life: m,ajor work area, social and leisure, extended family, marital, parental, family unit, and economic. In addition, the SAS provides an overall adjustment score, which combines all seven areas of life. Scores are determined by dividing the sum of each area of life by the number of items endorsed. The SAS consists of 54 items, which are rated on a 5-point or 6-point Likert-type scale. Lower scores indicate higher social functioning. The SAS has been shown to possess good discriminant validity in overall adjustment when comparing depressed patients [$M = 4.63$, $SD = 0.77$] with normal controls [$M = 2.46$, $SD = 0.72$; $t(79) = 12.86$, $p < .001$], and to be sensitive to change among patients subsequent to treatment [pretreatment: $M = 4.63$, $SD = 0.77$; posttreatment: $M = 3.63$, $SD = 0.84$; $t(39) = -6.58$, $p < .001$] (Weissman, Paykel, & Prusoff, 1974).

Family Resource Scale (FRS). The FRS (Dunst & Leet, 1987) is a 30-item instrument for assessing the adequacy of household resources ranging from basic needs to unessential resources, including food and shelter, financial resources, time for family, extrafamily support, child-care, specialized child resources, and luxuries. Items are rated on a 6-point Likert-type scale, from 0 (*does not apply*) to 5 (*almost always adequate*). The FRS provides a total score, with higher scores indicative of greater adequacy of resources. Dunst and Leet describe excellent internal consistency (.97) and moderate test-retest reliability (.52) for the FRS measured at a 2-month interval.

Van Horn, Bellis, and Snyder (2001) recently reevaluated the FRS among a sample of low-income families and derived a four-factor structure, which utilized 20 of the original 30 items. 'Basic needs' describes the presence of food, housing, clothes, heat, plumbing, furniture, and telephone access. 'Money' evaluates the presence of employment, money for self, money for entertainment, money to save, and travel or vacation. 'Time for self' assesses time to rest, time for self, time for spouse, someone to talk to, time to socialize, and time to keep in shape and looking nice. Finally, 'time for family' examines time for one's family and time for one's children. Van Horn, Bellis, and Snyder described adequate validity for these factors.

RESULTS

Social Adjustment in the Study Sample

The treatment and control groups were compared at pretreatment and posttreatment on the SAS using repeated measures analysis of variance (see Table 3.1). The combined sample evidenced improvement in overall adjustment from pretreatment to posttreatment. No group effect was found—the treatment group was not found to differ from the control group at pretreatment or at posttreatment; and no interaction between group and time was found. In order to determine whether the treatment group evidenced change on the SAS between any two time points, scores on the SAS were compared between each possible pairing of time points using paired samples t-tests. The treatment group evidenced improvement in overall adjustment from pretreatment to 3-month follow-up and from pretreatment to 6-month follow-up. No change was found among the treatment group between posttreatment and 3-month follow-up, posttreatment and 6-month follow-up, or 3-month follow-up and 6-month follow-up. The mean pretreatment overall adjustment score of the treatment group (pretreatment: $M = 2.07$; $SD = 0.44$) evidenced slightly better adjustment than that reported prior to treatment by a sample of depressed patients (2.36; Weissman, Paykel, & Prusoff, 1974). However, the mean posttreatment ($M = 1.72$; $SD = 0.34$), 3-month follow-up ($M = 1.73$; $SD = 0.50$) and 6-month follow-up ($M = 1.75$; $SD = 0.51$) overall adjustment scores of the treatment group were comparable to those reported by a sample of depressed patients after 2 months of treatment (1.99) and by a sample of controls (1.67; Weissman et al., 1974).

Table 3.1 Social Adjustment in the Study Sample

| | Treatment group n = 24 | | Control Group n = 23 | |
	M	SD	M	SD
Pretreatment	2.10	0.42	2.18	0.50
Posttreatment	1.72	0.34	1.96	0.52
3-month follow-up	1.73	0.50	—	—
6-month follow-up	1.75	0.51	—	—

Repeated measures analysis of variance

| | F | | |
	Time	Group	Interaction
Pretreatment–posttreatment	21.14***	2.04	1.56
	df = 1, 44	df = 1, 44	df = 1, 44

Paired samples t-test

	t	df
Pretreatment–3-month	2.93**	18
Pretreatment–6-month	2.71*	19
Posttreatment–3-month	−0.29	18
Posttreatment–6-month	−0.55	19
3-month–6-month	−0.31	18

Note. Lower scores on the Social Adjustment Scale indicate better adjustment.
*p < .05. **p < .01. ***p < .001.

The treatment and control groups were then compared at pretreatment and posttreatment on four of the seven individual subscales of the SAS using repeated measures multivariate analysis of variance—the sample size was insufficient to include social and leisure, extended family, and family unit in these analyses. A time effect was found [Wilks' = 0.48; F (4, 33) = 8.86; $p < .001$]. Follow-up univariate analysis of variance indicated that the combined sample evidenced improved adjustment between the pre- and posttreatment assessments in the areas of work [$F(1, 36)$ = 33.28, $p < .001$], marital [$F(1, 36)$ = 5.86, $p < .05$], and economic [$F(1, 36)$ = 4.19, $p < .05$]. No parental time effect was found. Further, no group or interaction effects were found on these subscales.

Table 3.2 Social Adjustment Subscales in the Treatment Group

	Work		Marital		Parental		Economic	
	M	SD	M	SD	M	SD	M	SD
Pretreatment	0.37	0.11	0.14	1.31	1.14	1.06	2.25	1.39
Posttreatment	0.15	0.13	0.96	1.18	1.01	0.89	1.75	1.33
3-month follow-up	0.16	0.14	0.88	1.10	0.73	0.80	1.33	1.40
6-month follow-up	0.15	0.13	0.93	1.19	0.51	0.71	1.38	1.35

Paired samples t-test

	Work		Marital		Parental		Economic	
	t	df	t	df	t	df	t	df
Pretreatment–3-month	4.79***	14	2.56*	23	2.72*	23	2.70*	23
Pretreatment–6-month	4.22***	13	2.25*	23	3.20**	23	2.48*	23
Posttreatment–3-month	−0.10	14	0.69	23	2.30*	23	1.86	23
Posttreatment–6-month	−0.88	14	0.21	23	3.03**	23	1.81	23
3-month–6-month	0.10	13	−0.85	23	2.41*	23	−0.27	23

Note. n = 24; lower scores on the Social Adjustment Scale indicate better adjustment; the sample size was insufficient to include social and leisure, extended family, and family unit in these analyses.
*p < .05. **p < .01. ***p < .001.

In order to determine whether the treatment group evidenced change on any of the four subscales of the SAS between any two time points, scores on each subscale of the SAS were compared between each possible pairing of time points using paired samples t-tests (see Table 3.2). First, the treatment group evidenced improvement on the 'work' subscale between the pretreatment and the 3-month follow-up assessments, and between the pretreatment and the 6-month follow-up assessments. Second, the treatment group evidenced improvement on the 'marital' subscale between the pretreatment and the 3-month follow-up assessments, and between the pretreatment and the 6-month follow-up assessments. Third, the treatment group evidenced improvement on the 'parental' subscale between the pretreatment and the 3-month follow-up assessments, between the pretreatment and the 6-month follow-up assessments, between the posttreatment and the 3-month follow-up assessments, between the posttreatment and the 6-month follow-up assessments, and between the 3-month follow-up and the 6-month follow-up assessments. Finally, the treatment group also evidenced improvement on the 'economic' subscale between the pretreatment and the 3-month follow-up assessments, and between the pretreatment and the 6-month follow-up assessments. The mean adjustment scores of the treatment group suggests better adjustment than those reported prior to treatment by a sample of depressed patients (work: $M = 2.65$, $SD = 0.63$; marital: $M = 2.33$, $SD = 0.51$; parental: $M = 2.52$, $SD = 0.50$; economic: $M = 1.70$, $SD = 0.00$). In fact, the mean adjustment scores of the treatment group appear superior to those reported by a sample of depressed patients after 2 months of treatment (work: $M = 1.61$, $SD = 0.35$; marital: $M = 2.06$, $SD = 0.37$; parental: $M = 1.83$, $SD = 0.35$; economic: $M = 1.70$, $SD = 0.00$) and by a sample of controls (work: $M = 1.32$, $SD = 0.25$; marital: $M = 1.71$, $SD = 0.30$; parental: $M = 1.61$, $SD = 0.31$; economic: $M = 1.15$, $SD = 0.00$; Weissman et al., 1974).

Family Resources in the Study Sample

The treatment and control groups were compared at pretreatment and posttreatment on the FRS using repeated measures analysis of variance. No group effect, time effect, or interaction effect were found (see Table 3.3). Thus, the treatment group was not found to differ from the control group at pretreatment or at posttreatment; neither the treatment nor the control group evidenced significant change in their self-rated scores on the FRS; no interaction between group and time was found. In order to determine whether the treatment group evidenced change on the FRS between any two time points, scores on the FRS were compared between each possible pairing of time points using paired samples t-tests. No change was found among the treatment group between pretreatment and 3-month follow-up, pretreatment and 6-month follow-up, posttreatment and 3-month follow-up, posttreatment and 6-month follow-up, or 3-month follow-up and 6-month follow-up. However, the mean scores of the treatment group at all time points (pretreatment: $M = 101.24$; $SD = 21.70$; posttreatment: $M = 104.17$; $SD = 21.49$; 3-month follow-up: $M = 104.16$; $SD = 21.03$; 6-month follow-up: $M = 104.20$; $SD = 23.16$) were nearly one standard deviation below the mean reported by a sample of mothers of preschool-aged children participating in an early intervention program who were mentally retarded, handicapped, and developmentally at-risk ($M = 116.54$; $SD = 17.76$; Dunst & Leet, 1987).

Table 3.3 Family Resource in the Study Sample

	Treatment group $n = 24$		Control Group $n = 23$	
	M	SD	M	SD
Pretreatment	101.20	22.26	108.84	27.44
Posttreatment	101.25	21.28	99.53	24.22
3-month follow-up	104.16	21.03	—	—
6-month follow-up	104.20	23.16	—	—

Measures analysis of variance			
		F	
	Time	Group	Interaction
Pretreatment–posttreatment	2.35	0.18	2.40
	$df = 1, 37$	$df = 1, 37$	$df = 1, 37$

Paired samples t-test		
	t	df
Pretreatment–3-month	0.21	15
Pretreatment–6-month	−0.22	16
Posttreatment–3-month	−0.21	18
Posttreatment–6-month	−0.38	19
3-month–6-month	−0.45	18

Note. Higher scores on the Family Resource Scale indicate more adequate resources. Utilizing the four-factor solution there was a trend ($p = 0.051$) for the patients to have more time for themselves at 6 months than at pretreatment.

The treatment and control groups were then compared at pretreatment and posttreatment on each of the four factors of the FRS using repeated measures analysis of variance. Again, no group, time, or interaction effects were found on basic needs, money, time for self, or time for family. In order to determine whether the treatment group evidenced change on any of the four factors of the FRS between any two time points, scores on each factor of the FRS were compared between each possible pairing of time points using paired samples t-tests. There was a trend for the treatment group to evidence improvement on the 'time for self' factor between the pretreatment ($M = 18.82$, $SD = 4.23$) and the 6-month follow-up ($M = 20.94$, $SD = 4.34$) assessments (time for self: [$t(16) = -2.11$, $p = 0.051$]). No change on 'time for self' was found among the treatment group between pretreatment and 3-month follow-up, posttreatment and 3-month follow-up, posttreatment and 6-month follow-up, or 3-month follow-up and 6-month follow-up.

DISCUSSION

This study examined changes in social adjustment and in material and emotional resources following MCET among female trauma victims diagnosed with PTSD and panic attacks. The treatment and control conditions evidenced improvement in work, marital, economic, and overall adjustment from pretreatment to posttreatment, and did not differ. In addition, the treatment group evidenced continued improvement in work, marital, economic, and overall adjustment from pretreatment to 3-month follow-up and from pretreatment to 6-month follow-up. The treatment group evidenced the most consistent amount of change on parental functioning, evidencing improvement among all assessment points. The treatment and control conditions reported having fewer overall family resources than did a normative sample; however, there was a trend for the treatment group to evidence improvement in time for self between the pretreatment and the 6-month follow-up assessment. Otherwise, neither group reported change in basic needs, money, time for self, time for family, or overall family resources at any assessment point.

Falsetti and colleagues (2001) reported that patients from this sample are less likely to be classified as having PTSD following MCET. However it is noteworthy that patients did not evidence improvement in family resources such as food and shelter, financial resources, time for self, time for family, extrafamily support, child-care, specialized child resources, and luxuries. It is possible that such resources are more resistant to change since family instability and lack of social support have been identified as risk factors associated with the development of PTSD (Byrne, Resnick, Kilpatrick, Best, & Saunders, 1999; King, King, Foy, & Gudanowski, 1996; King, King, Foy, Keane, & Fairbank, 1999; King, King, Gudanowski, & Vreven, 1995; King, King, Fairbank, Keane, & Adams, 1998). However, it is also possible that increased inadequacies in such resources develop secondary to PTSD (Byrne et al., 1999). Either way, it is likely that it is not feasible to make vast improvements in such resources during treatment because PTSD symptoms and their sequelae may make it difficult for individuals to benefit from vocational rehabilitation or educational opportunities; and it is likely that it is not feasible to make vast improvements in such resources immediately after or even 6 months after treatment since many family resources are contingent upon having adequate employment and childcare. In light of the fact that work, marital, economic and overall adjustment improved during treatment, and continued to improve along with parental adjustment 3 and 6 months following MCET, targeting vocational or educational rehabilitation, pleasurable activities scheduling, and child care during aftercare planning may facilitate the acquisition of employment, thereby improving salaries from the $15,000 or less that half of the sample reported at pretreatment.

The aftercare recommendations delineated above certainly are associated with financial cost. However, the cost of anxiety and other psychiatric disorders is immense. Thus, short-term investment in individuals who have received successful treatment of PTSD may lead to further improvement in adjustment, resources and health as well as diminish overall health care utilization. In the long term such an investment in mental health may not only diminish an economic drain on our society by reducing the number of individuals on disability, but also stimulate our economy by infusing it with active members of the workforce.

The current investigation was limited most significantly by the lack of measures available to assess functioning in samples of individuals with PTSD. Frueh and colleagues (Frueh, Turner, Beidel, & Cahill, 2001) point to the need for measures to assess the diverse array of difficulties associated with PTSD. Sheehan, Harnett-Sheehan, and Raj (1996) recommend that disability scales be short, simple, and designed so that they may be used as either patient self-report or clinician administered. However, in the absence of such a scale, Frueh and colleagues propose a multimethod approach to the assessment of end-state functioning. Such an approach would comprise self-report indices; structured interviews that include assessment of functioning such as the CAPS (Blake et al., 1990); regular patient ratings; behavioral assessments; and other objective indices of functioning such as employment status, marital status, income, and legal involvement. The assessments of functioning in the current investigation were self-report and objective indices. The sole use of self-report measures and objective indices of functioning may not provide the most accurate assessment of functioning. First, limiting the method of data collection does not account for method variance. Second, Frueh and colleagues argue that the population of individuals with PTSD is known to endorse elevations on scales of psychopathology and impairment without meaningful discrimination. Third, clinical experience suggests that patients in general may not have full insight into improvement on subjective constructs such as functioning. For instance, it is common for a patient's treatment plan to include acknowledgment of achieving treatment goals, particularly if the patient possesses a significant amount of hopelessness. Finally, objective indices of functioning may not be readily available outside of settings such as Veterans Medical Centers, where access to comprehensive patient records is more easily obtained. Thus, future studies might seek to develop a standardized measure of impairment for persons with PTSD. Until such a measure is developed, future studies should include multimethod assessment of satisfaction, resources, and health.

Another limitation to the current study is that follow-up conditions were limited to six months among the treatment group, and were ethically not appropriate for the control condition. As stated previously, greater improvements in functioning were evidenced at assessment points more distant from treatment. Future studies might include a 12- or 18-month follow-up condition to determine whether improvements in functioning are maintained over longer periods of time. Moreover, although differences between the treatment and control groups were not found at posttreatment, it is likely that had the control condition been assessed at 3- and 6-month follow-up differences would begin to emerge. Finally, future studies might compare adjustment and, resources among persons with PTSD and those of other clinical populations. Such comparisons are necessary to determine the specificity of difficulties in functioning to PTSD.

REFERENCES

American Psychiatric Association. (1994). *Diagnostic and statistical manual of mental disorders* (4th ed.). Washington, DC: Author.

Barlow, D. H., & Craske, M. G. (1989). *Mastery of your anxiety and panic.* Manual available from the Center for Anxiety and Related Disorders, 648 Beacon Street, Boston, MA 02215.

Blake, D. D., Weathers, F. W., Nagy, L. M., Kaloupek, D. G., Klauminzer, G., Charney, D. S., et al. (1990). A clinician rating scale for assessing current and lifetime PTSD: The CAPS-1. *The Behavior Therapist, 13,* 187–188.

Brady, K., Pearlstein, T., Asnis, G. M., Baker, D., Rothbaum, B., Sikes, C. R., et al. (2000). Efficacy and safety of sertraline treatment of posttraumatic stress disorder: A randomized controlled trial. *Journal of the American Medical Association, 283,* 1837–1844.

Brown, T. A., DiNardo, P. A., Lehman, C. L., & Campbell, L. A. (2001). Reliability of *DSM–IV* anxiety and mood disorders: Implications for the classification of emotional disorders. *Journal of Abnormal Psychology, 110,* 49–58.

Byrne, C. A., Resnick, H. S., Kilpatrick, D. G., Best, C. L., & Saunders, B. E. (1999). The socioeconomic impact of interpersonal violence on women. *Journal of Consulting & Clinical Psychology, 67,* 362–366.

Dancu, C. V., Foa, E. B., & Smucker, M. R. (1993, October). *Cognitive behavioral treatment of survivors of childhood sexual abuse with PTSD.* Paper presented at the International Society for Traumatic Stress Studies, San Antonio, TX.

Deykin, E. Y., Keane, T. M., Kaloupek, D. G., Fincke, G., Rothendler, J., Siegfried, M. et al. (2001). Posttraumatic stress disorder and the use of health services. *Psychosomatic Medicine, 63,* 835–841.

DiNardo, P. A., Brown, T. A., & Barlow, D. H. (1994). *Anxiety Disorders Interview Schedule for DSM–IV: Lifetime Version (ADIS–IV–L).* Albany, NY: Graywind Publications.

Dunst, C. J., & Leet, H. E. (1987). Measuring the adequacy of resources in households with young children. *Child: Care, Health and Development, 13,* 111–125.

Erwin, B. A., Niles, B. L., Newman, E., Fisher, L. M., Kaloupek, D. G., & Keane, T. M. (1996, November). *Psychopathological predictors of mortality in trauma exposed Vietnam veterans.* Paper presented at the annual convention of International Society for Traumatic Stress Studies, San Francisco.

Falsetti, S. A., Resnick, H. S., Davis, J., & Combs-Lane, A. (2001). *PTSD with panic: Multiple channel exposure therapy.* Medical University of South Carolina, National Crime Victims Research and Treatment Center, 165 Cannon Street, PO Box 250852, Charleston, SC 29425.

Foa, E. B., Rothbaum, B. O., Riggs, D. S., & Murdock, T. B. (1991). Treatment of posttraumatic stress disorder in rape victims: A comparison between cognitive-behavioral procedures and counseling. *Journal of Consulting and Clinical Psychology, 59,* 715–723.

Frueh, B. C., Turner, S. M., Beidel, D. C., & Cahill, S. P. (2001). Assessment of social functioning in combat veterans with PTSD. *Aggression and Violent Behavior, 6,* 79–90.Jordan, B. K., Marmar, C. R., Fairbank, J. A., Schlenger, W. E., Kulka, R. A., Hough, R. L., et al. (1992). Problems with families of male Vietnam veterans with posttraumatic stress disorder. *Journal of Consulting and Clinical Psychology, 60,* 916–926.

Keane, T. M., Fairbank, J. A., Caddell, J. M., & Zimering, R. T. (1989). Implosive (flooding) therapy reduces symptoms of PTSD in Vietnam combat veterans. *Behavior Therapy, 20,* 245–260.

Kessler, R. C., Sonnega, A., Bromet, E., Hughes, M., & Nelson, C. B. (1995). Posttraumatic stress disorder in the National Comorbidity Survey. *Archives of General Psychiatry, 52,* 1048–1060.

Kimerling, R., Clum, G. A., & Wolfe, J. (2000). Relationships among trauma exposure, chronic posttraumatic stress disorder symptoms, and self-reported health in women: Replication and extension. *Journal of Traumatic Stress, 13,* 115–128.

King, D. W., King, L. A., Foy, D. W., & Gudanowski, D. M. (1996). Prewar factors in combat-related posttraumatic stress disorder: Structural equation modeling with a national sample of female and male Vietnam veterans. *Journal of Consulting and Clinical Psychology, 64,* 520–531.

King, D. W., King, L. A., Foy, D. W., Keane, T. M., & Fairbank, J. A. (1999). Posttraumatic stress disorder in a national sample of female and male Vietnam Veterans: Risk factors, war-zone stressors, and resilience-recovery factors. *Journal of Abnormal Psychology, 108,* 164–170.

King, D. W., King, L. A., Gudanowski, D. M., & Vreven, D. L. (1995). Alternative representation of war zone stressors: Relationships to posttraumatic stress disorder in male and female Vietnam veterans. *Journal of Abnormal Psychology, 104,* 184–196.

King, L. A., King, D. W., Fairbank, J. A., Keane, T. M., & Adams, G. A. (1998). Resilience-recovery factors in post-traumatic stress disorder among female and male Vietnam veterans: Hardiness, postwar social support, and additional stressful life events. *Journal of Personality and Social Psychology, 74,* 420–434.

Leon, A. C., Shear, M. K., Portera, L., & Klerman, G. L. (1992). Assessing impairment in patients with panic disorder: The Sheehan Disability Scale. *Social Psychiatry and Psychiatric Epidemiology, 27,* 78–82.

Malik, M., Connor, K., Sutherland, S., Smith, R., Davidson, R., & Davidson, J. (1999). Quality of life and posttraumatic stress disorder: A pilot study assessing changes in SF-36 scores before and after treatment in a placebo-controlled trial of fluoxetine. *Journal of Traumatic Stress, 12,* 387–393.

Marks, I. M., Lovell, K., Noshirvani, H., Livanou, M., & Thrasher, S. (1998). Treatment of posttraumatic stress disorder by exposure and/or cognitive restructuring: A controlled study. *Archives of General Psychiatry, 55,* 317–325.

Niles, B. L., Newman, E., Fisher, L. M., Erwin, B. A., Kaloupek, D. G., & Keane, T. M. (1996, November). *Defining change in chronic PTSD.* Paper presented at the International Society for Traumatic Stress Studies, San Francisco.

Resick, P. A., & Schnicke, M. K. (1992). Cognitive processing therapy for sexual assault victims. *Journal of Consulting and Clinical Psychology, 60,* 748–756.

Resick, P. A., & Schnicke, M. K. (1993). *Cognitive processing therapy for rape victims: A treatment manual.* Newbury Park, CA: Sage Publications.

Sheehan, D. V., Harnett-Sheehan, K., & Raj, B. A. (1996). The measurement of disability. *International Clinical Psychopharmacology, 11* (suppl 3), 89–95.

Spitzer, R. L., Williams, J. B., & Gibbon, M. (1995). *Structured clinical interview for DSM–IV patient version.* New York: Biometrics Research Department, New York State Psychiatric Institute.

van Horn, M. L., Bellis, J. M., & Snyder, S. W. (2001). Family Resource Scale-Revised: Psychometrics and validation of a measure of family resources in a sample of low-income families. *Journal of Psychoeducational Assessment, 19,* 54–68.

Wagner, A. W., Wolfe, J., Rotnitsky, A., Proctor, S. P., & Erickson, D. J. (2000). An investigation of the impact of posttraumatic stress disorder on physical health. *Journal of Traumatic Stress, 13*, 41–55.

Weathers, F. W., Blake, D. D., Krinsley, K. E., Haddad, W., Huska, J. A., & Keane, T. M. (1992, November). *The Clinician-Administered PTSD Scale: Reliability and construct validity.* Paper presented at the Association for Advancement of Behavior Therapy, Boston.

Weissman, M. M., & Paykel, E. S. (1974). *The depressed woman: A study of social relations.* Chicago: University of Chicago Press.

Weissman, M. M., Paykel, E. S., & Prusoff, B. A. (1974). *Social Adjustment Scale handbook: Rationale, reliability, validity, scoring, and training guide.* Unpublished manuscript, Yale University School of Medicine.

Zatzick, D. F., Marmar, C. R., Weiss, D. S., Browner, W. S., Metzler, T. J., Golding, J. M., et al. (1997). Posttraumatic stress disorder and functioning and quality of life outcomes in a nationally representative sample of male Vietnam veterans. *American Journal of Psychiatry, 154,* 1690–1695.

Zatzick, D. F., Weiss, D. S., Marmar, C. R., Metzler, T. J., Wells, K. B., Golding, J. M., et al. (1997). Posttraumatic stress disorder and functioning and quality of life outcomes in female Vietnam veterans. *Military Medicine, 162,* 661–665.

Chapter 4

ANXIETY SENSITIVITY AND ITS IMPLICATIONS FOR UNDERSTANDING AND TREATING PTSD

Steven Taylor

INTRODUCTION

Empirically supported psychosocial treatments for posttraumatic stress disorder (PTSD) all entail some form of trauma-related exposure therapy (TRE). Although TRE tends to be effective, it is not effective for all PTSD sufferers. New developments in trauma treatment are needed to address this problem. This is especially important given that PTSD is a severe, prevalent, and often chronic disorder (APA, 2000). In this book there are a number of important suggestions for improving treatment outcome, such as reducing trauma-related anger, augmenting treatment with virtual reality interventions, and improving social support (Cahill, Rauch, Hembree, & Foa, 2002; Rothbaum, Ruef, Litz, Han, & Hodges, 2002: Tarrier & Humphreys, 2002).

In this chapter I would like to suggest another approach, which had some similarities to that taken by Falsetti et al. (chapter 3), but differs in its target population, conceptual basis, and treatment ingredients. Unlike the work by Falsetti and colleagues, we were interested in improving treatment outcome for PTSD sufferers in general, whereas Falsetti et al.

The work reported in this chapter was supported in part by grants from the British Columbia Health Research Foundation.

focused on PTSD with comorbid, recurrent panic attacks. Our treatment approach was derived largely from anxiety sensitivity theory (Taylor, 1999), and it emphasizes some interventions (TRE and interoceptive exposure) and deliberately omits others (cognitive restructuring and breathing retraining). In the following sections I will briefly review TRE, followed by a discussion of the theoretical and empirical reasons why anxiety sensitivity should be explicitly considered in understanding and treating PTSD.

TRAUMA-RELATED EXPOSURE THERAPY

TRE is one of the most effective treatments for PTSD (Chambless & Ollendick, 2001; van Etten & Taylor, 1998). Controlled studies, particularly the studies that do not have the methodological shortcomings of early research, indicate that TRE may be as effective or perhaps more effective than other psychosocial treatments (e.g., Foa & Meadows, 1997; Taylor et al., 2003). A recent meta-analysis further indicates that, in the short term, TRE is as effective as the most effective PTSD medications (e.g., selective serotonin reuptake inhibitors) (van Etten & Taylor, 1998). Treatment-related gains for TRE have been found to be maintained at follow-up intervals of at least 12 to15 months (Foa et al., 1999a; van Etten & Taylor, 1998). TRE may be more effective than medications at long-term follow-up, because TRE teaches patients skills that they can continue to use, as needed, once the therapy sessions have ended. In comparison, patients treated with medications are not typically trained in symptom-management skills, and they may relapse when medication is discontinued. (Little is known about the long-term effects of medication treatment for PTSD.)

TRE entails a combination of (a) imaginal exposure to traumatic memories (e.g., writing out and rereading a description of the traumatic event), and (b) in vivo exposure to distressing but harmless reminders of the trauma (e.g., returning to the scene of a traumatizing road traffic collision) (Foa & Rothbaum, 1998; Marks, Lovella, Noshirvania, Livanou, & Thrasher, 1998; Taylor et al., 2001, 2003). TRE is thought to exert its effects by exposing the person to corrective information (Foa & Rothbaum, 1998). For example, exposure exercises can modify trauma-related beliefs (e.g., the belief that the world is a dangerous place), which in turn can reduce PTSD symptoms (e.g., hypervigilance). Physiological habituation, resulting from exposure to anxiety-provoking but harmless trauma-related stimuli, also is thought to provide the person with corrective information about the harmlessness of these stimuli.

TRE is not effective for all patients; some have a partial response and others do not respond at all. Residual symptoms are often seen even in patients who no longer meet *DSM–IV* criteria for PTSD at the end of treatment (e.g., Foa et al., 1999a; Marks et al., 1998; Taylor et al., 2003). Therefore we need to search for ways of boosting its efficacy. Several investigators have examined whether outcome is improved by combining TRE with cognitive restructuring. So far the results have been disappointing, suggesting that treatment outcome is not enhanced (Foa et al., 1999a; Marks et al., 1998).

Similarly, there is no evidence that outcome is improved by teaching patients coping exercises such as breathing retraining. Foa et al. (1999a) combined TRE with breathing retraining, whereas other studies used TRE without breathing retraining (Marks et al., 1998; Taylor, et al. 2003). Foa et al.'s treatment tended to be more effective than that of Marks et al., but less effective than that of Taylor et al. Thus, it is unclear whether breathing retraining improves outcome. A concern with breathing retraining is that it can impair the efficacy of behavioral and cognitive-behavioral treatment of panic disorder, because it encourages patients to avoid feared bodily sensations (Schmidt et al., 2000; Taylor, 2000, 2001). The same may apply to PTSD. A more promising direction for improving PTSD treatment comes from recent research on anxiety sensitivity and PTSD.

ANXIETY SENSITIVITY

Several lines of evidence suggest that anxiety sensitivity plays an important role in PTSD, and that treatment outcome may be enhanced by combining TRE with interventions that reduce anxiety sensitivity. Anxiety sensitivity is the fear of arousal-related sensations, arising from beliefs that these sensations have harmful consequences. Research suggests that there are at least three basic dimensions of anxiety sensitivity: (a) fear of publicly observable anxiety reactions (e.g., fear of trembling, arising from beliefs that trembling will attract ridicule or rejection), (b) fear of cognitive dyscontrol (e.g., fear of concentration difficulties arising from beliefs that such difficulties are the harbingers of insanity), and (c) fear of somatic sensations (e.g., fear of palpitations arising from beliefs that cardiac sensations lead to heart attacks) (Taylor, 1999).

Evidence suggests that anxiety sensitivity contributes to, or amplifies, the intensity of emotional reactions (particularly anxiety), and that it also plays a role in producing panic attacks (see Taylor, 1999, 2000, for reviews).

Table 4.1 Anxiety Sensitivity in PTSD, Panic Disorder, and Normal Controls

	PTSD (without panic disorder)			Panic disorder (without PTSD)			Normal controls		
	M	SD	N	M	SD	N	M	SD	N
Taylor et al., 1992	31.6	12.8	32	36.6	12.3	151	17.8	8.8	1,013
Taylor et al., 2001	30.5	13.8	41	—	—	—	—	—	—
Taylor et al., 2003	31.0	14.6	42	—	—	—	—	—	—

To illustrate, a person who is phobic about driving would experience anxiety when required to drive. If that person had elevated anxiety sensitivity, then he or she would also become anxious about being anxious. Thus, the fear of driving would be amplified.

Although anxiety sensitivity plays a particularly important role in panic disorder, there is growing evidence of its importance in PTSD. Table 4.1 shows the mean scores (prior to treatment) for a widely used measure of anxiety sensitivity, the Anxiety Sensitivity Index (Peterson & Reiss, 1992). As suggested by the table, the severity of anxiety sensitivity in PTSD is somewhat lower than in panic disorder ($p < .06$) but people with PTSD have much greater anxiety sensitivity than normal controls ($p < .0005$) (Taylor, Koch, & McNally, 1992). Anxiety sensitivity also tends to be higher in PTSD compared with other anxiety disorders (apart from panic disorder) (Taylor et al., 1992). Research further shows that the severity of anxiety sensitivity is correlated with the severity of PTSD symptoms (Fedoroff, Taylor, Asmundson, & Koch, 2000).

There appear to be at least two ways that elevated anxiety sensitivity and PTSD may be related. Elevated anxiety sensitivity may be a predisposing factor, predating the development of PTSD. People with elevated anxiety sensitivity, compared with people with low or normal levels of anxiety sensitivity, would tend to have more intense emotional reactions to traumatic stressors because of the amplifying nature of anxiety sensitivity. That is, the person would become alarmed by the stressor, and also alarmed by their anxiety sensations, thereby amplifying their emotional response and correspondingly increasing the risk of developing PTSD.

Another possible relationship between elevated anxiety sensitivity and PTSD is that both may arise from a traumatic stressor. Such a stressor may not only trigger PTSD but also cause the person to become frightened by all stimuli associated with the stressor, including arousal-related bodily sensations. Through a process of associative learning (interoceptive conditioning) (Bouton, Mineka, & Barlow, 2001) anxiety sensitivity may be inflated by trauma exposure. Anxiety sensitivity may then amplify PTSD symptoms. For example, the person may become alarmed by reexperiencing symptoms, believing them to be harbingers of insanity. Similarly, the person may become alarmed by hyperarousal symptoms (e.g., palpitations), believing them to be signs of some physical catastrophe such as cardiac arrest (Fedoroff et al., 2000).

Regardless of the actual relations between elevated anxiety sensitivity and PTSD, the above-mentioned data and arguments suggest that the treatment of PTSD may be improved by incorporating treatments that reduce anxiety sensitivity, regardless of whether the person has comorbid panic disorder.

Additional suggestive evidence for the importance of these interventions comes from examining the effects of TRE on anxiety sensitivity. Although there are specialized interventions for reducing anxiety sensitivity (as described below), TRE can reduce anxiety sensitivity to some extent. This is because TRE encourages patients to be exposed to arousal-related sensations (as part of their exposure to trauma-related stimuli). Such exposure may help the patient learn that these sensations do not have harmful consequences (e.g., experiencing palpitations during TRE helps the patient learn that palpitations do not lead to heart attacks).

Two studies from our clinic show that TRE-related reductions in anxiety sensitivity are correlated with reductions in PTSD symptoms. In a study of the efficacy of cognitive-behavioral therapy for 28 patients with PTSD due to road traffic collisions, we computed pre- to posttreatment residual gain scores (change scores) for several measures, including a measure of anxiety sensitivity, a measure of PTSD symptoms, and measures of the strength of belief in the dangerousness of road travel (trauma-related beliefs). The latter were assessed because trauma-related beliefs are thought to play an important role in PTSD (Foa & Rothbaum, 1998; Foa, Ethers, Clark, Tolin, & Orsillo, 1999b). We found that the degree of pre- to posttreatment reduction in anxiety sensitivity was the strongest predictor of reductions in global severity of PTSD symptoms, even though anxiety sensitivity was not directly targeted during treatment (Fedoroff et al., 2000).

A similar finding emerged in another study of 15 PTSD patients treated with TRE, without targeting anxiety sensitivity (Taylor et al., 2003). The participants had PTSD arising from a number of traumata, commonly physical abuse, sexual assault, or road traffic collisions. We computed

Table 4.2 Correlations Among Change Scores (Pre- to Posttreatment Residual Gain Scores)

	Changes in PTSD symptoms			
	Reexperiencing	Avoidance	Numbing	Hyperarousal
Changes in anxiety sensitivity				
Fear of publicly observable anxiety reactions	.32	.30	.48	.34
Fear of cognitive dyscontrol	.65**	.29	.78**	.39
Fear of somatic sensations	.53*	.32	.40	.24
Changes in trauma-related beliefs				
Negative beliefs about self	.26	.09	.29	−.05
Negative beliefs about world	.18	.19	.05	−.17
Self-blame	.19	.01	.39	.00

*$p < .05$. **$p < .01$. Medium-sized or larger correlations ($\geq .30$) are in boldface.

pre- to posttreatment residual gain scores for PTSD symptoms, residual gains for the three dimensions of anxiety sensitivity, and residual gains for three dimensions of trauma-related beliefs. The latter were assessed by the recently developed Posttraumatic Cognitions Inventory (Foa et al., 1999b). All PTSD symptoms were assessed by structured interview (the Clinician Administered PTSD Scale: Blake et al., 1997).

Table 4.2 lists the variables and shows the correlations among residual gain scores. Due to the small sample size, the power to detect significant correlations was limited, and so we supplemented significance tests by classifying the correlations in terms of Cohen's (1988) criteria: Large effects are indicated by correlations of .50 and higher, medium correlations are .30 to .49, and small correlations are .10 to .29. Correlations smaller than .10 can be regarded as trivial.

Scores on all measures tended to decline from pre- to posttreatment. The table shows that changes in PTSD symptoms were significantly correlated only with changes in anxiety sensitivity. Most of the correlations with anxiety sensitivity were medium sized or larger, whereas most of the correlations among trauma-related beliefs and PTSD symptoms were small or trivial in size. These findings, like those of Fedoroff et al. (2000), are consistent with the view that reducing anxiety sensitivity may be useful in reducing PTSD. These findings are only suggestive, however, because the research was correlational, and anxiety sensitivity was not directly targeted. Nevertheless, they encourage further research to directly examine the merits of reducing anxiety sensitivity in the treatment of PTSD.

INTEROCEPTIVE EXPOSURE THERAPY (IE)

There are more powerful, direct methods than TRE for reducing anxiety sensitivity. Among the most potent is IE (Taylor, 1999, 2000). This involves deliberately inducing arousal-related bodily sensations so patients can learn that the sensations have no harmful consequences. For example, a person might be asked to hyperventilate for 2 minutes to induce palpitations and dizziness, and thereby learn that these sensations do not have catastrophic consequences such as heart attacks or insanity (see Taylor, 2000, for detailed IE protocols).

IE is widely used to reduce anxiety sensitivity in panic disorder. Little is known about whether it is useful in reducing PTSD, although the above-mentioned evidence linking PTSD and anxiety sensitivity suggests that IE may be useful. To our knowledge, only one group of investigators has considered using IE in the treatment of PTSD. Falsetti and colleagues included IE in their multicomponent treatment of patients who suffer from both PTSD and recurrent panic attacks. Their preliminary results are encouraging, although it is not known whether IE is useful in treating PTSD in general, regardless of whether the patient also suffers from recurrent panic attacks.

A potential limitation of the Falsetti protocol is its reliance on breathing retraining, which appears to undermine the efficacy of panic treatment because patients sometimes use the breathing exercises as a way of avoiding feared bodily sensations (Schmidt et al., 2000; Taylor, 2001). Another potential limitation of the Falsetti protocol is the reliance on cognitive restructuring, which does not enhance the efficacy of TRE (Foa et al., 1999a; Marks et al., 1998). A more promising protocol would be one that gives a greater emphasis to both TRE and IE.

IE may be a useful pretreatment for patients who are to undergo TRE. By first reducing the patient's anxiety sensitivity, that patient may be better able to engage in TRE, both during the treatment session and during homework assignments. That is, persons pre-treated with IE should experience less distress during TRE because their anxiety about anxiety has been reduced. As a result, the person may be more likely to complete TRE exercises, which are anxiety provoking. Clinically, it is not uncommon for people with TRE to avoid homework assignments and to limit within-session exposure exercises because the exercises are distressing. Reducing the person's anxiety sensitivity should make these exercises easier (less distressing) for the patient. Thus, TRE may be more efficacious when preceded by IE. If IE enhances the patient's adherence to, and completion of, TRE exercises, then the speed of reduction in PTSD symptoms for TRE should also be faster when this treatment is preceded by IE, because the enhanced adherence and completion of TRE will increase its "dose." The potential merits of this treatment protocol are currently under investigation in our research clinic.

REFERENCES

American Psychiatric Association. (2000). *Diagnostic and statistical manual of mental disorders* (4th ed., text revision). Washington, DC: Author.

Blake, D., Weathers, F. W., Nagy, L. M., Kaloupek, D. G., Charney, D. S., & Keane, T. M. (1997). *Clinician administered PTSD scale (revised)*. Boston, MA: Behavioral Science Division, Boston National Center for Post-Traumatic Stress Disorder.

Bouton, M. E., Mineka, S., & Barlow, D. H. (2001). A modern learning theory perspective on the etiology of panic disorder. *Psychological Review, 108,* 4–32.

Cahill, S. P., Rauch, S. A., Hembree, E. A., & Foa, E. B. (2003). Effect of cognitive-behavioral treatments for PTSD on anger. *Journal of Cognitive Psychotherapy,* in press. Vol 17, pp 113-131.

Chambless, D. L., & Ollendick, T. H. (2001). Empirically supported psychological interventions: Controversies and evidence. *Annual Review of Psychology, 52,* 685–716.

Cohen, J. (1988). *Statistical power analyses for the behavioral sciences* (2nd ed.). Hillsdale, NJ: Erlbaum.

Fedoroff, I. C., Taylor, S., Asmundson, G. J. G., & Koch, W. J. (2000). Cognitive factors in traumatic stress reactions: Predicting PTSD symptoms from anxiety sensitivity and beliefs about harmful events. *Behavioral and Cognitive Psychotherapy, 28,* 5–15.

Foa, E. B., Dancu, C. V., Hembree, E. A., Jaycox, L. H., Meadows, E. A., & Street, G. P. (1999a). A comparison of exposure therapy, stress inoculation training, and their combination for reducing posttraumatic stress disorder in female assault victims. *Journal of Consulting and Clinical Psychology, 67,* 194–200.

Foa, E. B., Ehlers, A., Clark, D. M., Tolin, D. F., & Orsillo, S. M. (1999b). The Posttraumatic Cognitions Inventory (PTCI): Development and validation. *Psychological Assessment, 11,* 303–314.

Foa, E. B., & Meadows, E. A. (1997). Psychosocial treatments for posttraumatic stress disorder: A critical review. *Annual Review of Psychology, 48,* 449–480.

Foa, E. B., & Rothbaum, B. O. (1998). *Treating the trauma of rape.* New York: Guilford.

Marks, I. M., Lovell, K., Noshirvani, H., Livanou, M., & Thrasher, S. (1998). Treatment of posttraumatic stress disorder by exposure and/or cognitive restructuring. *Archives of General Psychiatry, 55,* 317-325.

Peterson, R. A., & Reiss, S. (1992). *Anxiety Sensitivity Index Manual*. Palos Heights, IL: International Diagnostic Systems.

Rothbaum, B. O., Ruef, A. M., Litz, B.T., Han, H., & Hodges, L. (2003). Virtual reality exposure therapy of combat-related PTSD: A case study using psychophysiological indicators of outcome. *Journal of Cognitive Psychotherapy, 17*, 163-178.

Schmidt, N. B., Woolaway-Bickel, K., Trakowski, J., Santiago, H., Storey, J., Koselka, M., et al. (2000). Dismantling cognitive-behavioral treatment for panic disorder: Questioning the utility of breathing retraining. *Journal of Consulting and Clinical Psychology, 68*, 417-424.

Tarrier, N., & Humphreys, A.-L. (2002). PTSD and the social support of the interpersonal environment: The development of Social Cognitive Behaviour Therapy. *Journal of Cognitive Psychotherapy*, in press.

Taylor, S. (1999). *Anxiety sensitivity*. Mahwah, NJ: Erlbaum.

Taylor, S. (2000). *Understanding and treating panic disorder*. New York: Wiley.

Taylor, S. (2001). Invited article: Breathing retraining in the treatment of panic disorder: Efficacy, caveats, and indications. *Scandinavian Journal of Behavior Therapy, 30*, 1–8.

Taylor, S., Fedoroff, I. C., Koch, W. J., Thordarson, D. S., Fecteau, G., & Nicki, R. (2001). Posttraumatic stress disorder arising after road traffic collisions: Patterns of response to cognitive-behavior therapy. *Journal of Consulting and Clinical Psychology, 69*, 541-551.

Taylor, S., Koch, W. J., & McNally, R. J. (1992). How does anxiety sensitivity vary across the anxiety disorders? *Journal of Anxiety Disorders, 6*, 249–259.

Taylor, S., Thordarson, D. S., Maxfield, L., Fedoroff, I. C., Lovell, K., & Ogrodniciuk, J. (2003). Comparative efficacy, speed, and adverse effects of three PTSD treatments: Exposure therapy, EMDR, and relaxation training. *Journal of Consulting and Clinical Psychology, 71*, 330-338.

van Etten, M., & Taylor, S. (1998). Comparative efficacy of treatments for posttraumatic stress disorder: A meta-analysis. *Clinical Psychology and Psychotherapy, 5*, 126-145.

Chapter 5

A READINESS TO CHANGE APPROACH TO PREVENTING PTSD TREATMENT FAILURE

Ronald T. Murphy, Craig Rosen, Karin Thompson, Marsheena Murray, and Quaneecia Rainey

INTRODUCTION

The effectiveness of treatment for combat-related posttraumatic stress disorder (PTSD) has recently been called into question, at least for therapy as delivered in Veterans Administration (VA) programs (Fontana & Rosenheck, 1997; Schnurr et al., 2003). Treatment failure has long been a concern for clinicians working with individuals with PTSD, particularly Vietnam veterans who continue to seek treatment more than 30 years after their combat experiences. This chapter offers a new perspective on PTSD treatment that: (a) explains why patients may not respond to our attempts to help them eliminate their symptoms and (b) describes both general and specific approaches to improving patient response to treatment.

BASES FOR APPLYING A READINESS TO CHANGE MODEL TO PTSD TREATMENT

Why Do Treatments Fail?

There are numerous current conceptualizations of why PTSD treatment failure occurs, particularly for patients with long-standing symptoms. Generally, these theories tend not to focus on treatment methods or therapists as being at fault, but point to patient characteristics as the culprit in an unsuccessful treatment attempt. One common attribution made for treatment failure, especially when a patient has not been cooperative or compliant with treatment recommendations, is that the patient is "not ready for treatment." This implies that a trait of stubbornness or lack of insight is causing the patient to be noncompliant. Another attribution for treatment failure is that the patient's PTSD is "chronic," which seems to suggest that the disorder's resistance to treatment increases with the length of time the patient has the disorder, for reasons not clearly specified. This has become more popular as biological theories of chronic PTSD have come into vogue, and researchers in this area claim to have found permanent damage in hormonal or neuronal systems that control threat reactions and memory. These biological theories, though they have merit, cannot conclude that physiological damage causes symptoms or treatment resistance due to the correlative nature of their methods. Damage to biological systems may not be a necessary or sufficient factor for PTSD, and changes in biological systems may reflect a learned pattern of overreaction to threat arising from traumatic experiences. We posit therefore that there is still a need for examining psychological factors as important contributors to development of PTSD and symptom response to treatment.

Help Me Stop Being Angry, and Don't You Think the World is Full of Dangerous, Hostile, and Provocative People?

Our clinical experience with veterans in an inpatient VA PTSD treatment program revealed that patients often questioned the need to change their defensive approach to life, including hyperalertness to danger, social isolation, frequent anger, and mistrust of others. We witnessed therapists (including ourselves) sometimes debating with patients about the best way to handle situations involving social interactions with family, friends, and strangers. It became apparent that PTSD may mean something different for therapists and patients, or that a patient's view of what the problem is may be different from that of the therapists. We do not mean here that patients question whether or not they have PTSD, because most patients willingly accept the diagnosis. Rather, patients and therapists may have different conceptions about the presence or severity of specific PTSD symptoms or comorbid problems.

Patients may report, for example, that they have violent outbursts when in traffic or when dealing with unhelpful salespeople. Although patients may later regret angry episodes, discussion of their thoughts occurring in those situations often reveals their view that they get angry because the world is populated by people who are careless, dangerous, hostile, and provocative. The connection between their responses and their personal trauma history is that their experiences have taught them that it is necessary to take a protective and defensive approach to daily life. In other words, these patients do not share the therapist's belief that PTSD-related coping responses are overreactions based on earlier life events.

Why Are You Ruining My Beautiful Treatment Plan?
The Readiness to Change Model

If patients are not convinced of the need to change certain PTSD symptoms and trauma-based coping responses, what happens in treatment when patients don't do what therapists want them to? Certainly some therapists react with surprise and frustration when patients don't follow carefully crafted treatment plans or question their validity. These patients often are labeled as "resistant" or "not ready for treatment" and confrontation of the patients by treatment staff often results. If patients do not acquiesce or comply with demands for change, they may be discharged or referred elsewhere.

New approaches to treatment-resistant patients have been implemented in other areas, such as alcoholism treatment, where similar patient problems are common. The best developed theoretical work on readiness to change is the Transtheoretical Model (Prochaska & DiClemente, 1983). The model has most often been applied to smoking and substance abuse (Prochaska, DiClemente, & Norcross, 1992) but has been extended to a variety of other patient populations (Rosen, 2000). The Transtheoretical Model assumes that behavioral change and response to treatment are a function of modifiable beliefs about the need to change and not personality traits of denial or negative attitude. The Stages of Change component of the model describes five stages associated with different beliefs about the need to change and actions toward change. These stages include a lack of awareness that a problem exists (Precontemplation), ambivalence about the need to change (Contemplation), initial steps toward change (Preparation), engagement in efforts to change (Action), and maintaining change (Maintenance). A key assumption in the Stages of Change is that different psychoeducational or therapeutic techniques are needed at each stage to help individuals resolve questions about the need or ability to change that behavior and move to the next stage. Readiness to change variables have been found to predict psychotherapy dropout (Brogan, Prochaska, & Prochaska, 1999; Smith, Subich, & Kalodner, 1995) and substance use (Belding, Iguchi, & Lamb, 1997; Heather, Rollnick, & Bell, 1993). Among trauma victims, researchers have applied the Transtheoretical Model to readiness for change in adult survivors of child abuse (Koraleski & Larson, 1997) and battered women (Feuer, Meade, Milstead, & Resick, 1999; Wells, 1998).

Concurrent with this theoretical work has been Miller's development of clinical interventions that enhance individuals' readiness to change and facilitate movement through the Stages of Change (Miller & Rollnick, 2002). Developed in response to confrontation-based approaches to alcohol problems, Motivational Interviewing encompasses both general style and specific methods for addressing patients who are apparently unaware or ambivalent about the need to change problematic behaviors. The general therapeutic approach is nonconfrontational and objective, relying heavily on reflective listening. Specific techniques for facilitating problem acknowledgment include norm comparison, decision balance, the development of discrepancy between values and behavior, and ambivalence amplification. Motivation enhancement interventions based on Miller's Motivational Interviewing approach have been found to be effective in modifying beliefs about the need to change and facilitating change for a variety of behaviors (Bien, Miller, & Tonigan, 1993). For example, such approaches have been effective in reducing HIV risk behaviors (Carey et al., 1997) and alcohol use by college students (Borsani & Carey, 2000), problem drinkers (Miller, Benefield, & Tonigan, 1993), and alcoholics high in anger (Project Match Research Group, 1998).

Finally, Newman (1994) has provided an insightful approach to conducting a functional analysis of patient resistance in cognitive therapy. He emphasizes that client behavior labeled as resistance is understandable in the context of an individual's developmental history and current environment, and often serves a protective or fear avoidance function.

Evidence for Ambivalence or Lack of Awareness About the Need to Change PTSD Symptoms Among Veterans

What evidence is there that veterans with PTSD are unaware of or ambivalent about the need to change particular symptoms and modes of responding? Only two studies have directly addressed this issue. Murphy et al. (in press) collected data on beliefs about the need to change PTSD symptoms and other problems from 243 male veterans in an inpatient VA

PTSD treatment program over an 18-month period. Patients were asked to list on a form any problems they classified as "Might Haves," defined as "Problems I'm not sure I have" or "Problems others have told me I have, but I disagree." Patients were asked to list separately any problems they were sure that they had. These open-ended responses were coded into various PTSD symptoms and other problem categories. For example, patient reports of "flying off the handle," "rage," and "aggression" were all categorized as Anger; "distrust" and "suspicious" were classified under the Trust category. Participants classified a wide range of PTSD symptoms and related behaviors as "Might Have" problems, with the highest percentage of patients (48%) classifying Anger as a "Might Have." Approximately one third of the patients labeled Isolation, Depressive Symptoms, Trust, and Health as a "Might Have," and about one fourth reported Conflict Resolution, Alcohol, Communication, Relationship/Intimacy, Restricted Range of Affect, and Drugs as "Might Have" problems. Other types of PTSD-Related problems, for example, Hypervigilance, were reported as "Might Haves" by 15 to 21% of the patients. Reexperiencing problems were rarely identified as "Might Haves."

A study by Rosen et al. (2001) sought to determine if there were distinct subgroups of combat PTSD patients that differed in their readiness to change alcohol or anger problems. Male combat veterans ($N =$ 102) entering a PTSD rehabilitation program completed the University of Rhode Island Change Assessment (URICA) and process of change questionnaires based on the Transtheoretical Model (Prochaska et al., 1992). Separate assessments were made for alcohol abuse and anger control. Patients varied in their readiness to address these two problems, and could be categorized into four motivational subtypes consistent with the Transtheoretical Model. Strikingly, 35% of the PTSD inpatients with severe anger were in Precontemplation or Contemplation stage for anger as a problem. Motivation to change alcohol problems was independent of that for anger. For both alcohol abuse and anger management, patients in the Action/Maintenance stage for that problem reported more frequent use of change strategies than did patients in the Precontemplation stage.

Problem Endorsement Versus Belief About the Need to Change: Two Different Things Entirely

Patients may not always appear to lack awareness of the need to change PTSD-related behaviors and beliefs. On symptom checklists and in structured interviews, patients will frequently endorse a wide variety of PTSD symptoms. Clinicians can be misled into thinking that patients are sure that they need to change these symptoms or PTSD-based beliefs, yet patients' true beliefs about the need to change these problems can contradict their symptom report. How can this occur? Generally, patients may see certain problematic behaviors or beliefs as being different from a symptom as typically labeled. Some patients, for example, will endorse hypervigilance as a symptom because they always feel "on guard" or hyperalert to danger, but will not see related behaviors or beliefs as problematic. They may see problems such as mistrust of others, isolation, needing to be in control, or owning multiple weapons as reasonable ways of responding to potential threat, and not as a psychiatric symptom.

Patients may also believe that they have a problem but not believe that it is truly their problem. To illustrate, patients will usually endorse anger as a PTSD symptom, and frequently regret times when they lost control of their temper. Yet some of the same patients will state that if other people or certain situations did not provoke them, they would not have an anger problem. When describing instances of anger outbursts, they will justify their response (e.g., "The other driver was careless and was going to get someone killed" in cases of road rage). In general, the issue is one of responsibility for the problem that usually involves externalizing the symptomatic reaction or cause of the symptom. Thus, patients may report that they have an anger problem, yet be unconvinced of the need to change. Some patients will even use their combat experience as a justification of their response. Patients may report, for example, that they are highly mistrustful of others, yet defend this PTSD symptom by stating, "I've seen what happens when you depend on other people," or "Combat showed me reality—life is dangerous, you've got to protect yourself from other people." Similarly, we have seen patients endorse anger as a problem, yet later report that they disagree with others' complaints that they are short-tempered or irritable, again often justifying the behavior with statements like "You've got to be hard on people because they just won't do things right."

Finally, the reality of the compensation system often causes patients to report PTSD symptoms that they really do not think are problematic or wish to change. Because most patients are concerned that service-connected disability payments may be put at risk if their symptom report does not continue to confirm their diagnosis, there is a natural bias toward overendorsement of symptoms on checklists and structured interviews. Open-ended assessment of what problems trouble patients, and their understanding of PTSD symptoms they have endorsed, may be a better method for revealing what they believe they need to change in order to improve their lives.

WHY WOULD SOMEONE NOT BE READY TO CHANGE?

One of the less well-developed areas in the readiness to change literature has been explanation of how individuals with serious problems can be unaware of the need to change. Miller's work certainly examines some of these factors, because they are related to the targets of particular techniques. What is needed, and what we present here, is a fuller discussion of what we see as the reasons why individuals may not be convinced of the need to change behaviors, beliefs, and coping styles that are maladaptive. Consistent with the work of Miller, Prochaska, DiClemente, Newman, and others, we posit that most of these reasons or causative factors are products of normal cognitive processes and background familial, social, and cultural events and influences, and are not particularly pathological, in that they may apply to anyone regardless of the presence of a mental disorder.

Cognitive Roadblocks to Admitting a Problem to Myself

There are numerous reasons why an individual might not be willing to consider the need to change that are not specific to PTSD or psychopathology in general. One set of these reasons relates to why someone might be unwilling to admit a problem to oneself.

What's normal for our patients (and for us)? The role of perceived norms. What determines our sense that our behavior or beliefs need change? One factor may be our consideration of where our responses to stress, social interactions (e.g., intimacy), or daily life challenges fit in a normal or average range of behavior. From an early age, we begin to view as "normal" that which happens in our family, regardless of the dysfunctional nature of our family's behaviors or beliefs about people and methods for coping with life's challenges. This can apply to family norms for behavior itself, like expressing feelings and needs, asking for help, drinking alcohol, or using aggression in intimate relationships and child rearing. In addition, we can learn early on in our families what is "normal" for the severity and types of behavioral consequences, such as doing time in jail or family disruption due to alcohol. Constant exposure to these experiences in the family does not leave a child with a clear understanding of societal norms for problem behaviors or their consequences. The main point here is that when experiencing difficulties later in life, an individual lacks a sense that "something is wrong," that is, something is occurring that is out of the range of what happens to the average person.

For veterans, an additional factor hindering consideration of the need to change problematic behaviors is that an additional set of norms can be learned in the military and in the combat zone. We have frequently heard veterans say that they were trained that it was shameful and "unmanly" to ask others for help or show certain emotions such as fear. Norms for survival in combat can include suppression of grief or fear (especially by the use of anger), avoidance of close attachment to others, a life-or-death sense of control, and refusal to allow the decisions of others to impact one's life. For many soldiers, these behaviors and beliefs can be a normal and understandable part of military life, especially in the war zone. As with childhood experiences, adult exposure to civilian norms for at least some individuals does not always erase the sense of what are personally acceptable behaviors. And for many veterans seeking treatment, their post–military life involved dangerous jobs (e.g., police work) or outlaw lifestyles (such as being in gangs or dealing drugs) that reinforced their notions of normative behavior.

Internal stereotypes. Consideration of the presence of a problem can elicit "internal stereotypes," or incorrect perceptions of what it means to have a particular disorder. Alcoholics may not want to admit to a drinking problem or seek treatment because their stereotypes of people so labeled involve images of the town drunk, a homeless person, or some other extreme and inaccurate depiction (Cunningham, Sobell, & Chow, 1993; Cunningham, Sobell, Sobell, & Gaskin, 1994). This can be particularly true for a problem drinker who maintains a job and family life, and whose mental picture of an alcoholic includes social isolation and unemployment. These persons may not see themselves as similar to those stereotypes, and thus they cannot have the same problem, or they find thought of having the same problem as those individuals to be so aversive that they will avoid taking on the same label. Sometimes these stereotypes come from more personal experiences, such as having a parent with a particular problem. In these cases in particular, if the parent elicited shame, anger, or disgust due to their behavior, the person can be particularly averse to admitting to a similar problem. Similarly, veterans may have internal stereotypes of psychiatric patients that involve inaccurate images of a "raving lunatic" or the "crazy Vietnam vet" who needs a straitjacket and cannot function in society. Therefore, their negative reaction to suggestions that they seek psychiatric care for PTSD-related behaviors is understandable. Early exposure to media depiction of people with mental disorders can contribute to these stereotypes. For many veterans who came home from Vietnam in the late '60s and were experiencing difficulties adjusting to civilian life, their only exposure to what psychiatric care involved came from the movie *One Flew Over the Cuckoo's Nest*, which portrayed not only very disturbed individuals but horrific conditions of confinement and care.

Avoidance of negative emotions elicited by problem recognition. Often people do not acknowledge a problem because they are avoiding some type of fear (Newman, 1994). This includes including fear of incapacity or death elicited by recognition of a mental or physical disorder. For example, medical patients with cardiac problems or diabetes may not follow treatment regimens or make lifestyle changes because compliance means acceptance of the presence of disease or condition, which can elicit fears of dying, becoming disabled, or being reliant on others. Also, problem recognition can be hindered by a feeling of being overwhelmed by problems already acknowledged, which may be particularly true for persons with multiple ongoing difficulties. For many individuals, adding another problem to their list of things to deal with is simply seen as another opportunity for failure, and so they avoid consideration of additional problems to recognize. Other negative emotions that can be elicited by problem recognition include feeling weak or stupid due to an inability to handle or solve problems on one's own, and feeling ashamed or "crazy" if there is a potential mental health problem.

The pros and cons of change. Another nonpathological cognitive process that guides decision-making about the need for change is the relative balance of the advantages or "payoffs" of behavior and the disadvantages or negative consequences. An individual's engagement in a behavior despite negative consequences is often more understandable to both patient and therapist when there is clear understanding of the balance of subjective advantages and disadvantages of that behavior. Since immediate consequences of behavior have more reinforcement value than long-term consequences, it is also critical to understand that patients will persist in behaviors that have short-term rewards despite long-term negative consequences (e.g., alcohol consumption or isolation to avoid conflict). This may be particularly important to motivation enhancement approaches since patients may be unaware of how this weighing of pros and cons controls behavior.

Cognitive Roadblocks to Admitting a Problem to Others

Problem acknowledgment can be limited by factors related to the social context of admitting a problem. Individuals may fear various consequences of publicly acknowledging a problem, including rejection or other negative reactions by family members, partners, or friends. They may be reluctant to admit the need to change to others to avoid shame or being judged as "damaged," weak, sick, or crazy.

External Roadblocks to Considering the Need to Change

There are sometimes realistic environmental or social factors that make it difficult for an individual to consider the need to change or could get in the way of change (Miller & Rollnick, 2002). Patients who rely on disability compensation, for example, may fear that any responsibility-taking implied by problem acknowledgment could cause agencies to attribute responsibility for ongoing difficulties to the patient and not to life circumstances or continued illness. They therefore may be concerned that problem acknowledgment may put their compensation at risk of termination. Further, problem acknowledgment and its consequences, including the need for treatment, may cause family disruption or other unwanted life changes. Other realistic concerns that patients may have related to publicly admitting a problem involve issues of confidentiality, job security, and employer reactions, as well as a host of other environmental disincentives to change (Newman, 1994).

Why PTSD Patients May Be Ambivalent About Changing

"The average guy is stupid": Beliefs about trauma-based coping. In addition to perceived norms and the other roadblocks previously discussed, other factors that limit consideration of the need to change problematic behaviors can include the apparent functionality of maladaptive behavior, which

can be maintained by short-term positive consequences and a perceived lack of options for responding due to a lack of models for adaptive coping. This may be particularly true for trauma victims, for whom Criterion C and D trauma symptoms "feel right" (i.e., appropriate responses regarding safety and minimization of fear, for example, hypervigilance and avoidance of trauma reminders). We have heard many PTSD veterans who acknowledge that their own behavior is not typical of most people defend their coping style by saying "The average guy is stupid" with respect to levels of danger inherent in daily life.

Another factor that may hinder PTSD patients' recognition of problems is guilt. For those veterans who feel guilty that they survived combat when many of their friends did not, any problem solving related to their difficulties in life brings up guilty feelings of not deserving to feel good or live a satisfying life. This may be further compounded by guilt over postwar substance use and relationship problems. They therefore may hesitate to actively pursue therapeutic tasks such as consideration of previously unacknowledged problems that may be causing them difficulties. This can be particularly true for Vietnam veterans, for whom problem acknowledgment can mean facing an enormous sense of loss and guilt over almost 40 years of personal difficulties and mistreatment of loved ones that they have staved off by the belief that their behavior was justified.

Low Self-Efficacy as a Roadblock to Acknowledging the Need to Change

Taking action to address a problem after acknowledging the need to change may at least partly depend on an individual's self-efficacy (Bandura, 1989), or belief that change is possible and will have a positive outcome. Low self-efficacy about the ability to change can result from a number of factors, including lack of understanding about how therapy works (Newman, 1994; Zweben & Li, 1981). The public is rarely exposed to appropriate examples of good therapists, and popular media presentations of therapy often depict inept or unethical therapists (e.g., *The Sopranos* TV series or the film *Analyze This*). Good therapy involves time spent on goal setting, development of a therapeutic relationship using reflective listening, and skills training, which do not lend themselves to creation of dramatic scenes or talk-show segments where self-change gurus emphasize charismatic persuasion and confrontational interpretations of guests' misbehaviors and problems.

Two other factors related to low self-efficacy about change are the need for social support in facilitating change and resource availability. Social support is a critical predictor of therapeutic success (e.g., alcohol treatment; Sobell, Sobell, Toneatto, & Leo, 1993). The importance of this factor may be underestimated by therapists and patients. Some patients believe they must "go it alone." They understandably have anxiety about their ability to change. In addition, patients may have real roadblocks to implementing change, which are not acknowledged by therapists and are sometimes mistaken for resistance or denial. As Miller and Rollnick (2002) have emphasized, patients must have the resources needed for change available to them. Any single working parent, for example, would understand the importance of finances, time, energy, and day care in attempting to engage fully in treatment for a disorder.

A STAGES OF CHANGE MODEL FOR PREVENTING PTSD TREATMENT FAILURE

Treatment Outcome Implications of a Stages of Change Approach to PTSD

A readiness to change conceptualization of PTSD treatment failure posits that treatment outcome depends primarily on matching interventions to the patient's Stage of Change regarding particular symptoms. Treatment failure can then be explained as being due to therapist or treatment program mismatching interventions to a patient's Stage of Change, which can be caused by misreading or ignoring the patient's Stage of Change for specific problems. Mismatch can result in patients exiting treatment unconvinced that their particular ways of coping and thinking are maladaptive (e.g., hypervigilance, isolation, anger). When this occurs, patients don't see a need to use new coping skills, thus continuing or returning to trauma-based coping. The end result is poor posttreatment adjustment and a return of symptoms.

Assessing Stage of Change

Although there are psychometrically validated instruments for assessing Stage of Change for specific problems (e.g., alcohol, smoking, spouse abuse), methods for assessing Stage of Change for PTSD symptoms and related problems are still being developed. One general approach to assessing readiness to change is the University of Rhode Island Change Assessment scale (URICA; McConnaughy, et al., 1983). The URICA contains 32 items assessing beliefs about the need to change and action toward change, each rated on a 5-point scale, from 1, strongly disagree, to 5, strongly agree. Items include "I guess I have faults, but there is nothing I need to change" (Precontemplation), "It might be worthwhile to work on my problem" (Contemplation), "I am really working hard to change" (Action), and "I'm here to prevent myself from having a relapse of my problem" (Maintenance). The instructions ask the patients to respond to the items in terms of whatever problem is listed in a space on the top of the form by the clinician or researcher. The URICA generates continuous scores on four scales related to the Stages of Change: Precontemplation (don't see a problem), Contemplation (thinking about changing), Action (making changes), and Maintenance (concerned about avoiding relapse).

Support for the reliability and validity of the URICA questionnaire in assessing readiness to change a wide variety of problems has been obtained (Carney & Kivlahan, 1995; DiClemente & Hughes, 1990; Greenstein, Franklin, & McGuffin, 1999; McConnaughy, DiClemente, Prochaska, & Velicer, 1989; McConnaughy, et al., 1983). With respect to PTSD-related problems, the URICA has been used to assess Stages of Change for posttraumatic stress in general from sexual abuse (Koraleski & Larson, 1997), and for specific problems of anger and alcohol use among combat veterans in PTSD treatment (Rosen et al., 2001).

Another approach has been used by Murphy and colleagues (Murphy, Rosen, Cameron, & Thompson, 2002) to identify problems for which patients may be in Precontemplation or Contemplation stage as a way to identify targets for a motivation enhancement intervention, the PTSD Motivation Enhancement (PTSD ME) Group described toward the end of this chapter. A key part of the group is having patients generate a list of behaviors or beliefs that might be a problem for them. Patients fill out a worksheet (PTSD ME Group Form No. 1), which is divided into three columns: "Definitely Have," "Might Have," or "Definitely Don't Have." The "Might Have" column is further divided into two categories: "A Problem You Have Wondered If You Have" and "A Problem Others Say You Have (But You Disagree)." We have defined "Might Have" problems in these two ways to elicit not only problem areas that they have considered as possibly needing change, that is, on which they are in Contemplation Stage, but also problems that they might be unaware of or unwilling to change, that is, Precontemplation Stage. The goal is for patients to eventually sort items listed under "Might Have" into "Definitely Have" or "Definitely Don't Have." Also in development is a checklist version of the PTSD ME Group Form No. 1, called the PTSD Readiness to Change Problem Checklist, in which specific PTSD symptoms and related problems are listed for which patients are asked to check which of the following categories the problem falls under for them: (a) A Problem You Definitely Have, (b) A Problem You "Might Have:" A Problem You Have Wondered If You Have, (c) A Problem You "Might Have": A Problem Others Say You Have (But You Disagree), and (d) A Problem You Definitely Don't Have. Psychometric validation of these instruments, which have been used extensively in clinical trials of the PTSD ME Group, is ongoing.

PREVENTING PTSD TREATMENT FAILURE: A PRACTICAL MODEL BASED ON THE STAGES OF CHANGE

In this section we present a model for preventing PTSD treatment failure that describes specific assessment and intervention techniques appropriate for patients at various Stages of Change regarding PTSD-related symptoms and problems. Before describing this model, we would like to briefly note the importance of general therapeutic style in facilitating patient movement through the Stages of Change. The reader is referred to Miller and Rollnick (2002), who describe in detail the response style and tactics that motivate patient change most effectively. An objective, nonconfrontational stance is critical, and Miller and Rollnick describe key skills and techniques that are part of this stance, including reflective listening, avoiding argumentation, rolling with resistance, highlighting discrepancies between patient behavior and goals and values, and supporting self-efficacy. These and other techniques presented by Miller and Rollnick are essential ingredients to successful implementation of the model for preventing PTSD treatment failure outlined here.

The key assumption in this approach to preventing PTSD treatment failure is that ignoring or mismatching interventions to a patient's Stage of Change for important symptoms causes problems in patient engagement in treatment and poor posttreatment outcome. This mishandling of patients in terms of their Stage of Change can impact their beliefs about the relevance of treatment components as well as their posttreatment functioning. For each Stage of Change, the following model describes signs that a mismatch is occurring between the stage and therapy inter-ventions, assessment strategies, and intervention recommendations. The model uses an understanding of the reasons why patients do not recog-nize the need to change as a basis for recommendations for assessment and intervention. For each stage, use of the structured measures for as-sessing Stage of Change described above will be useful, although we also suggest additional open-ended questions that are stage-specific.

Precontemplation Stage

In Precontemplation stage, a patient does not believe they have a partic-ular PTSD-related problem (e.g., anger, alcohol, or isolation) when in reality they do. We have found it helpful to conceptualize a patient's cognitive state at each of the Stages of Change in terms of a question in the patient's mind that needs to be answered before the patient can move to the next stage. For Precontemplation, the goal of the therapist is to help the patient answer the question, "What problem?" The cause of poor treatment engagement or outcome at this stage is that therapists assume that the patient is convinced of the need to change regarding a problem (or problems) that seems obvious to everyone else, including the thera-pist. Acting on this incorrect assumption, therapists often begin interven-tions for the problem (e.g., skills training), or use argumentation, reason, and listing of negative consequences the patient has experienced in an attempt to persuade the patient of the need to change. These approaches are unlikely to be effective and will have the effect of distancing and discouraging the patient.

Precontemplation stage: Signs of stage-by-intervention mismatch. These signs include the patient missing appointments, not doing therapy tasks, attempt-ing to reduce but not eliminate behavior, minimizing or externalizing re-sponsibility for changing, and blaming others for causing consequences to their behavior (e.g., "The police didn't need to arrest me for the anger-related incident"). Also, the patient doesn't see similarity between themselves and others with the same problems (e.g., "I'm not like those vets who go off"). Additional signs include the therapist feeling frustrated, and using the term "not ready for treatment" with respect to the patient.

Precontemplation stage: Assessment. Based on the analysis of why someone might not acknowledge the need to change, assessing a patient's readiness to change at this stage should include an empathic discussion of the patient's opinion about why others see need for change. Also, it would help clarify what might be getting in the way of the patient acknowledging a problem by asking what it would mean to the patient to have that problem.

Precontemplation stage: Intervention. Helping patients answer the question "What problem?" primarily involves education about PTSD in general or the nature of a particular symptom. For example, what exactly hyperarousal is and how it can manifest itself in daily life and social interactions. As part of this education, it is important to translate clinical symptom labels into concrete descriptions of behavior. Again using hyperarousal as an example, it may be useful to talk about irritability, short-temperedness, or as the patients often state, "intolerance" of other people's shortcomings in social, family, and work settings (e.g., blowing up in response to slow or inefficient salespeople). It may also be helpful to talk to the patient about how internal stereotypes, cognitive distortions (e.g., "If I have one more problem, it will be a disaster"), and other internal roadblocks prevent people from recognizing or acknowledging problems. The goal of this approach at this stage is only to support the patient in acknowledging that there may be a problem, at which point the patient would be in Contemplation stage.

Contemplation Stage

In Contemplation stage, the patient is unsure or ambivalent about the need to change, with their question being "Do I need to change?" Difficulties in treatment engagement result if a therapist wrongly assumes that such a patient is convinced, as the therapist is, that: (a) the patient's coping responses are maladaptive and rooted in past conflicts, (b) their perceptions are cognitive distortions, and (c) that they are overreacting (or underreacting) with respect to present-day situations and likelihood of potential negative consequences (e.g., danger in trusting others).

Contemplation stage: Signs of stage-by-intervention mismatch. These include patients still resorting to old coping patterns (e.g., drinking, hypervigilance, isolation, anger outbursts) and inconsistent compliance with treatment plans despite a generally cooperative attitude. In addition, therapists may question patients' motivation or ability to change.*Contemplation stage:*

Assessment. Assessing a patient's readiness to change at this stage should include empathic discussion of the patient's view of where the problem comes from, and their view of their level of responsibility for changing the problem. Also, the patient should be asked what it would mean to admit the problem to other people.

Contemplation stage: Intervention. To help patients answer the question "Do I need to change?", therapists should focus on processes that facilitate making a decision that change is necessary. First, decision-balance techniques, in which patients weigh the pros and cons of changing a behavior or belief, help to clarify the advantages and disadvantages of maintaining or changing a behavior or attitude. For example, a patient who is unsure about the need to change the feeling of always wanting to be in control may list the pros or benefits to this behavior as "get things done quickly," "get things done my way," and "don't need to depend on others for input to make decisions." Cons or disadvantages may be "often make mistakes," "hurt others' feelings," "feel isolated," and "don't know how to ask for help."

Another useful technique is norm comparison, in which patients see where their behavior fits on a continuum from "average" to "extreme problem." Although this can be done informally, there are structured approaches. As practiced by Miller and colleagues (Miller & Rollnick, 2002), this can include using the results of medical or psychological tests, with the intervention being an objective, non-confrontational review of the how the patient's "numbers" compare with similar-age population norms and cutoff scores. Another technique is the "Comparison to the Average Guy" group module that is part of the PTSD ME Group (see following). In addition, therapist use of clear, understandable metaphors for problem origin and function can help clarify how the patient learned a particular behavior as a coping device, why it worked in past environments, and what makes the behavior maladaptive today (Newman, 1994). For example, we have often used the "getting in the house" metaphor, which describes a person who long ago could not get into a house that he needed to be in, and had to learn to get in by sneaking in the back door. Later in life, the person continues to use this method, never realizing that the front door is now unlocked. The goal of such interventions at this stage is for a patient to be convinced that they need to change maladaptive coping behaviors, that their response is an overreaction to current situations based on past negative situations or childhood environment, that their perceptions are distorted because of past events, and that advantages to change outweigh the disadvantages.

Preparation Stage

Once convinced of the need to change, individuals in Preparation stage frequently make initial steps toward addressing a particular problem. We feel that a key component of this stage is a person's uncertainty about the outcome of these change efforts (DiClemente, 1991), and so we propose that an important question in the mind of someone in Preparation stage is "I know I should change, but can I change?" In this stage, patient response to treatment can be negatively affected when treatment providers underestimate patients' confidence or self-efficacy about the ability to change. In addition, problems arise when a therapist mistakenly assumes that a patient understands how change occurs in therapy, feels capable of change, and feels participation will yield positive results. This can be a critical point for patients in that realizing the need to change but feeling one is incapable of change is a very discouraging or even depressing experience. In such a state, patients may question the need to change and thus regress to earlier stages of change (DiClemente, 1991).

Preparation stage: Signs of stage-by-intervention mismatch. These include relapse (to PTSD-based coping) and missed sessions after apparent therapy advances, reappearance of doubts about the need to change, depression, and anxiety about future progress.

Preparation stage: Assessment. To determine a patient's confidence in the ability to change it may be useful to allow that patient to rate self-efficacy in coping with situations related to the problem, behavior, or belief that the person has acknowledged the need to change. More informal discussion can focus on patient's beliefs that they can cope successfully, their understanding of how therapy works and what it involves, and the belief that using therapy tools will have beneficial effect, or be "worth it."

Preparation stage: Intervention. Therapists can best help patients answer the question "Can I change?" by spending some time in educating patients about how therapy works (Newman, 1994) and facilitating their participation in support groups. Allowing the patient to experience success in brief role-play or behavioral rehearsal tasks or periods of exposure to problem-related cues or situations also increases self-confidence in the ability to change. Related to the earlier discussion of practical roadblocks to initiating change, therapists should first recognize that these might exist and not immediately blame problems in carrying out change on low motivation or resistance. Then, clinicians must coach patients in problem solving these external roadblocks (e.g., lack of finances, time, or energy, such as experienced by working single or even married, parents). Peer modeling is also most useful at this stage, as patients recognize the similarities between themselves and others with the same problems, and can gain encouragement, increased self-efficacy, and specific skills from observing these individuals. Therefore, maximizing patient involvement with more advanced or senior patients is critical at this stage. The goal of these efforts is to maximize self-confidence so that the patient can cope successfully and promote realistic but positive expectations of posttreatment recovery.

OTHER FACTORS THAT CAN RUIN PERFECTLY GOOD THERAPY FOR PTSD

Breakdown in the Therapeutic Relationship

As Miller and colleagues have emphasized, facilitating patient recognition of the need to change depends heavily on therapist behavior, specifically the use of an empathic, objective approach. Although somewhat beyond the scope of this chapter, we wish to at least briefly note the critical role that a strong therapeutic relationship plays in the success of any psychotherapeutic treatment, including PTSD treatment of combat vets. A strong therapeutic relationship or "working alliance" is best fostered by therapists using reflective techniques, resulting in patients feeling understood, listened to, and more willing to trust (Horvath & Luborsky, 1993; Miller, 1985). Numerous studies of psychotherapy suggest that therapist empathy and client report of the working alliance are the best predictors of patient outcome (Horvath & Symonds, 1991; Miller, et al., 1993). This approach may be critical for enhancing treatment adherence for combat veterans in treatment in PTSD.

What can disrupt or prevent the development of a good therapeutic relationship? Although PTSD patients can be mistrustful, argumentative, and uncooperative, this is often a direct manifestation of the problems for which they are in treatment (whether they realize it themselves or not). These instances should be seen as unique opportunities for forging a strong therapeutic alliance and not as signs of a patient resisting help or the treatment not working (Newman, 1994). Meeting argumentativeness with reflective listening is often a surprising but powerful experience for patients, increasing their trust in the process of therapy and enhancing their willingness to explore unacknowledged problems or undertake therapeutic tasks. Therapists who argue with patients hoping to convince them of the right way to see the world or to see the negative consequences of their behavior lose this opportunity to gain patient trust and build the therapeutic relationship. Patients then become reluctant to engage in treatment, and treatment failure can result.

Race, Gender, and Social Class

Therapists must also be aware of issues related to race, gender, and social class that can hinder the development of a strong therapeutic relationship. Regarding race, racial differences between participants and leaders can elicit mistrust and bias that goes unaddressed. In addition, therapists must be sensitive to ethnic minority group members who have experienced lifelong exposure to racism, both obvious and subtle, and may be hesitant to engage in treatment in settings run by nonminority staff or populated by largely nonminority patients. It is the job of the therapist to not mistake this "cultural suspiciousness" for treatment resistance or even paranoia. Further, therapists must take into account cultural and ethnic differences in the expression or even the experience of strong emotion, which in some cultures feels like "going crazy."

A number of factors related to gender can influence patient response to treatment which therapists must consider. Although too numerous to enumerate here, these include male taboos about expressing feelings or appearing "weak," expectations for women to be passive and not express anger, and gender-specific attachment of shame for certain types of problems (e.g., alcoholism for women). In general, male-female power dynamics can arise in the therapeutic process and may need to be addressed during treatment.

With respect to social class, therapists must recognize differences in everyday language and vocabulary when working with patients from underprivileged or working-class backgrounds. We are often unaware of the extent of our use of psychology jargon in our work with patients, thus overestimating the degree of "psychological mindedness" among our patients. That is, the notion that emotions and perceptions are shaped by past events and affect current behavior. In addition, therapists may be insensitive to class-related norms for anger, safety, emotional expressivity, and relationship/intimacy behaviors of patients from poor or working class environments.

AN EXAMPLE OF A STRUCTURED APPROACH TO MOTIVATING CHANGE IN PTSD PATIENTS

Applying a readiness to change model to PTSD symptomatology is still a new and developing area of treatment and research. This chapter offers a rationale for the potential clinical value of this approach in PTSD treatment and ideally will foster research on the role of problem awareness in PTSD treatment failure and the effectiveness of PTSD interventions based on the readiness to change model. We would like to end this chapter by describing a specific group intervention that has been designed to enhance motivation to change among combat veterans in PTSD treatment. The PTSD Motivation Enhancement Group is described in detail elsewhere (Murphy et al., in press) and will be briefly summarized here as an example of a structured treatment component aimed at preventing treatment failure from a readiness to change perspective.

The PTSD Motivation Enhancement Group

The PTSD ME Group, a manualized brief intervention, is conceptually based on the Stages of Change and utilizes Motivational Interviewing principles and techniques (Miller & Rollnick, 2002) that have been modified for group treatment of PTSD-related problems. The rationale for the PTSD ME Group is that increased recognition of the need to change specific PTSD symptoms and other problems will lead to better PTSD treatment adherence and outcome because patients will perceive coping skills learned in treatment as more personally relevant to their problems. As explained to the patients, the purpose of the group is to help them avoid being "blindsided" by unrecognized problems. For example, a patient who believes that social isolation is an acceptable coping strategy will likely withdraw from family or other social support under stress or after interpersonal conflict, which can lead to a downward spiral or sequence of other problems such as depression, hypervigilance, substance use, and reexperiencing symptoms. A patient who recognizes that social isolation is definitely a problem will be more likely to use adaptive coping skills to address problems directly or use social support instead of withdrawing from others.

The PTSD ME Group protocol consists of four 90-minute sessions that focus on the use of decision-making skills to help patients recognize the need to change any unacknowledged PTSD-related problems. A key part of the group is having patients generate a list of behaviors or beliefs that might be a problem for them, called "Might Have" problems. These possible unrecognized problems are defined as problems they have wondered if they have, or problems that others have told them they have, but they disagree. Participants then use decision-making tools employed in the PTSD ME Group to help them decide if these "Might Have" problems are actually problems they definitely have. In the first PTSD ME Group session, "Rationale and Review," group leaders review the purpose, procedures, and potential value of the group. In the second session, "Pros & Cons," patients use decision balance techniques to determine the need to change specific behaviors or coping styles that they are unsure are problematic. The third session is called "Comparison to the Average Guy," in which patients compare their behavior to estimated age-appropriate norms to help them judge how problematic their behavior might be. For example, patients who are constantly hyperalert to danger but feel that this approach to daily life is appropriate are asked to compare their own behavior with safety-related behaviors that might be considered normative in terms of frequency (e.g., number of times checking locks at night), severity of consequences (e.g., impact on family), or purpose (e.g., caution vs. a sense of "life or death"). The fourth session, "Roadblocks," focuses on identification of individual cognitive and emotional factors (as described earlier) that may be preventing the patient from considering changing problematic behaviors. For example, veterans have often reported that fears of being perceived as weak, or shame about the distress they have brought to loved ones, will inhibit their willingness to admit or even think about a possible problem they have. Cognitive distortions that may be roadblocks include "all or nothing thinking" such as "If I admit to having one more problem, I will have to acknowledge being a complete failure."

Initial findings from an uncontrolled study of the effectiveness of the PTSD ME Group for 243 combat veteran participants have been encouraging (Murphy et al., in press). With respect to changes in problem awareness and ambivalence during the course of the group, veterans on average reclassified approximately 40% of all items they initially listed as "Might Have" to either "Definitely Have" or "Definitely Don't Have." For patients who classified various problems as "Might Have," by the end of their participation in the group significantly more veterans reclassified the following problems as "Definitely Have" than "Definitely Don't Have": Anger, Isolation, Anxiety, Authority, Guilt, Emotional Masking, Relationship/Intimacy, Smoking, and Trust. Group participants reported high levels of satisfaction with all aspects of group content and process, and gave high ratings on perceived helpfulness (Franklin et al., 1999). Although conclusive statements about the effectiveness of the group await controlled trials, these initial findings indicate that patients are responding to the group as predicted. A randomized control study of the effectiveness of inclusion of the PTSD ME Group in a yearlong PTSD outpatient program is ongoing. The predictions are that participation in the intervention will result in increased recognition of PTSD-related problems, greater perceived relevance of treatment, increased engagement in the PTSD program treatment components (e.g., attendance rates and lower dropout over the year of treatment), and greater life satisfaction. Such findings would support the need for integrating a readiness to change approach into PTSD treatment programs in order to maximize patient benefit from treatment and prevent PTSD treatment failure.

REFERENCES

Bandura, A. (1989). Human agency in social cognitive theory. *American Psychologist, 44*, 1175–1184.

Belding, M., Iguchi, M., & Lamb, R. (1997). Stages and processes of change as predictors of drug use among methadone maintenance patients. *Experimental and Clinical Psychopharmacology, 5*, 65–73.

Bien, T. H., Miller, W. R., & Tonigan, J. S. (1993). Brief interventions for alcohol problems: A review. *Addiction, 88*, 315–336.

Borsani, B., & Carey, K. B. (2000). Effects of a brief motivational intervention with college student drinkers. *Journal of Consulting and Clinical Psychology, 68*, 728–733.

Brogan, M. M., Prochaska, J. O., & Prochaska, J. M. (1999). Predicting termination and continuation status in psychotherapy using the transtheoretical model. *Psychotherapy, 36*, 50–60.

Carey, M. P., Maisto, S. A., Kalichman, S. C., Forsyth, A. D., Wright, E. M., & Johnson, B. T. (1997). Enhancing motivation to reduce the risk of HIV infection for economically disadvantaged urban women. *Journal of Consulting and Clinical Psychology, 65*, 531–541.

Carney, M. M., & Kivlahan, D. R. (1995). Motivational subtypes among veterans seeking substance abuse treatment: Profiles based on stages of change. *Psychology of Addictive Behaviors, 9*, 135–142.

Cunningham, J. A., Sobell, L. C. , & Chow, V. M. (1993). What's in a label? The effects of substance types and labels on treatment considerations and stigma. *Journal of Studies on Alcohol, 54,* 693–699.

Cunningham, J. A., Sobell, L. C., Sobell, M. B., & Gaskin, J. (1994). Alcohol and drug abusers' reasons for seeking treatment. *Addictive Behavior,19,* 691–696.

DiClemente, C. C. (1991). Motivational Interviewing and the Stages of Change. In W. R. Miller & S. Rollnick (Eds.), *Motivational Interviewing.* New York: Guilford.

DiClemente, C. C., & Hughes, S. O. (1990). Stages of change profiles in outpatient alcoholism treatment. *Journal of Substance Abuse Treatment, 2,* 217–235.

Feuer, C., Meade, L., Milstead, M., & Resick, P. (1999, November). *The transtheoretical model applied to domestic violence survivors.* Paper presented at the annual meeting of the International Society for Traumatic Stress Studies, Miami, FL.

Fontana, A., & Rosenheck, R. (1997). Effectiveness and cost of the inpatient treatment of posttraumatic stress disorder: Comparison of three models of treatment. *American Journal of Psychiatry, 154,* 758–765.

Franklin, C. L., Murphy, R. T., Cameron, R. P., Ramirez, G., Sharp, L. D., & Drescher, K. D. (1999, November). *Perceived helpfulness of a group targeting motivation to change PTSD symptoms.* Poster presented at the annual meeting of the International Society for Traumatic Stress Studies, Miami, FL.

Greenstein, D. K., Franklin, M. E., & McGuffin, P. (1999). Measuring motivation to change: An examination of the University of Rhode Island Change Assessment Questionnaire (URICA) in an adolescent sample. *Psychotherapy, 36,* 47–55.

Heather, N., Rollnick, S., & Bell, A. (1993). Predictive validity of the Readiness to Change questionnaire. *Addiction, 88,* 1667–1677.

Horvath, A. O., & Luborsky, L. (1993). The role of the therapeutic alliance in psychotherapy. *Journal of Consulting and Clinical Psychology, 61,* 561–573.

Horvath, A. O., & Symonds, B. D. (1991). Relation between working alliance and outcome in psychotherapy: A meta-analysis. *Journal of Counseling Psychology, 38,* 138–149.

Koraleski, S. F., & Larson, L. M. (1997). A partial test of the Transtheoretical Model in therapy with adult survivors of childhood sexual abuse. *Journal of Counseling Psychology, 44,* 302–306.

McConnaughy, E. A., DiClemente, C. C., Prochaska, J. O., & Velicer, W. F. (1989). Stages of change in psychotherapy: A follow-up report. *Psychotherapy, 26,* 494–503.

McConnaughy, E. A., Prochaska, J. O., & Velicer, W. F. (1983). Stages of change in psychotherapy: Measurement and sample profiles. *Psychotherapy: Theory, Research & Practice, 20,* 368–375.

Miller, W. R. (1985). Motivation for treatment: A review with a special emphasis on alcoholism. *Psychological Bulletin, 99,* 84–107.

Miller, W. R., Benefield, R. G., & Tonigan, J. S. (1993). Enhancing motivation for change in problem drinking: A controlled comparison of two therapist styles. *Journal of Consulting and Clinical Psychology, 61,* 455–461.

Miller, W. R., & Rollnick, S. (2002). *Motivational interviewing* (2nd ed.). New York: Guilford.

Murphy, R. T., Cameron, R. P., Sharp, L., Ramirez, G., Rosen, C., Drescher, K., et al. (in press). Readiness to change PTSD symptoms and related behaviors among veterans participating in a Motivation Enhancement Group. *The Behavior Therapist.*

Murphy, R. T., Rosen, C. S., Cameron, R. P., & Thompson, K. E. (2002). Development of a group treatment for enhancing motivation to change PTSD symptoms. *Cognitive & Behavioral Practice, 9,* 308–316.

Newman, C. F. (1994). Understanding client resistance: Methods for enhancing motivation to change. *Cognitive and Behavioral Practice, 1,* 47–69.

Prochaska, J. O., & DiClemente, C.C. (1983). Stages and processes of self-change in smoking: Toward an integrative model of change. *Journal of Consulting & Clinical Psychology, 40,* 432–440.

Prochaska, J. O., DiClemente, C. C., & Norcross, J. C. (1992). In search of how people change: Applications to addictive behaviors. *American Psychologist, 47,* 1102–1114.

Project Match Research Group. (1998). Matching alcoholism treatments to client heterogeneity: Project MATCH three-year drinking outcomes. *Alcoholism: Clinical and Experimental Research, 22,* 1300–1311.

Rosen, C. S. (2000). Is the sequencing of change processes by stage consistent across health problems? A meta-analysis. *Health Psychology, 19,* 593–604.

Rosen, C. S., Murphy, R. T., Chow, H. C., Drescher, K. D., Ramirez, G., Ruddy, R., et al. (2001). Posttraumatic stress disorder patients' readiness to change alcohol and anger problems. *Psychotherapy, 38,* 233–244.

Schnurr, P. P., Friedman, M. J., Foy, D. W., Shea, M. T., Hsieh, F. Y., Lavori, P. W., et al. (2003). Randomized trial of trauma-focused group therapy for posttraumatic stress disorder. *Archives of General Psychiatry, 60,* 481–489.

Smith, K. J., Subich, L. M., & Kalodner, C. (1995). The transtheoretical model's stages and processes of change and their relation to premature termination. *Journal of Counseling Psychology, 42,* 34–39.

Sobell, L. C., Sobell, M. B., Toneatto, T., & Leo, G.I. (1993). What triggers the resolution of alcohol problems without treatment? *Alcoholism: Clinical and Experimental Research, 17,* 217–224.

Wells, M. T. (1998, November). *Assessing battered women's readiness to change: An instrument development study.* Paper presented at the annual meeting of the International Society for Traumatic Stress Studies, Washington, DC.

Zweben, A., & Li, S. (1981). Efficacy of role induction in preventing early dropout from outpatient treatment of drug dependency. *American Journal of Drug and Alcohol Abuse, 8,* 171–183.

Chapter 6

VIRTUAL REALITY EXPOSURE THERAPY OF COMBAT-RELATED PTSD: A CASE STUDY USING PSYCHOPHYSIOLOGICAL INDICATORS OF OUTCOME

Barbara Olasov Rothbaum, Anna Marie Ruef, Brett T. Litz, Hyemee Han, and Larry Hodges

INTRODUCTION

Posttraumatic stress disorder (PTSD) is a pervasive and chronic disorder in veterans of the Vietnam War (Kulka, et al., 1990; Weiss et al., 1992). Although research has demonstrated the effectiveness of cognitive-behavioral treatments in reducing symptoms of PTSD in veterans (e.g., Keane, Fairbanks, Caddell, & Zimmering, 1989a), many veterans remain untreated or are unresponsive to treatment (Kulka et al., 1990). Treatment is generally time intensive and demanding, especially exposure therapy, which requires considerable therapist expertise and resources. Participants are generally not thought to be good candidates for exposure ther-

This research was supported by NIMH Grant R41 MH60015-01 awarded to the first author. We wish to thank Dr. Mark Miller, who programmed and prepared the psychophysiological procedures for the study. We also thank Jason Hall and Mathew Jakupcak for their assistance.

Disclosure Statement: Drs. Rothbaum and Hodges receive research funding and are entitled to sales royalty from Virtually Better, Inc., which is developing products related to the research described in this article. In addition, they serve as consultants to and own equity in Virtually Better, Inc. The terms of this arrangement have been reviewed and approved by Emory University and Georgia Institute of Technology in accordance with their conflict of interest policies.

apy if they fail to imagine vividly their painful memories of combat or if they avoid processing their feelings to a sufficient degree.

Virtual reality is a relatively new medium for exposure therapy. It integrates real-time computer graphics, body-tracking devices, visual displays, and other sensory input devices to immerse a participant in a computer-generated virtual environment. Virtual reality exposure (VRE) therapy may be more advantageous than other exposure treatments (e.g., imaginal exposure) since it may require fewer therapist resources and may be a more efficient vehicle to meet the necessary conditions of therapeutic emotional processing of traumatic memories (Rothbaum et al., 1999). Preliminary studies using VRE in the treatment of phobias have shown promising effects for this mode of treatment (Carlin, Hoffman, & Weghorst, 1997; Rothbaum et al., 1995; Rothbaum, Hodges, Smith, Lee, & Price, 2000) as well as lasting effects of treatment (Rothbaum, Hodges, Anderson, Price, & Smith, 2002).

Rothbaum and colleagues (1999) recently demonstrated the efficacy of VRE in the treatment of a Vietnam veteran suffering from PTSD. Their findings indicated that the participant showed clinically significant reductions in PTSD, anxiety, and depressive symptomatology following virtual reality exposure treatment. These results were replicated in an open clinical trial with Vietnam veterans, finding significant symptoms reductions with treatment that lasted following treatment termination (Rothbaum, Hodges, Ready, Graap, & Alarcon, 2001).

The purpose of this single case study was to replicate Rothbaum et al.'s (1999) findings, namely, to examine the efficacy of VRE therapy in the treatment of a Vietnam veteran with chronic PTSD symptomatology. As in Rothbaum et al.'s (1999, 2001) studies, standardized interview and self-report measures of psychiatric symptomatology and functioning were used. However, this study is unique in that psychophysiological responses were measured throughout the treatment. While all prior studies of VRE therapy relied on patients' report of outcome and process, which are subject to bias and demand, psychophysiological assessment provides an objective indicator of outcome and an online index of emotional processing *during* the VRE sessions. In addition, the psychophysiological procedure provides a vehicle to evaluate whether negative affect and arousal are attenuated within session which would indicate extinction of the conditioned emotional response. Although it is assumed that the principal change agent in exposure therapy is extinction, within-session extinction is rarely achieved (e.g., Boudewyns & Hyer, 1990) and measurement of psychophysiological process across sessions may inform the mechanisms of change.

The participant of this case report is a veteran who experienced severe guilt and shame about acts of unnecessary violence in the warzone. Although we may never know the extent to which veterans with chronic PTSD suffer from guilt about acts of omission or commission of violence in the warzone, clinicians who treat veterans tend to agree that these experiences are difficult to address in treatment, and may be one of the causes of chronicity (e.g., Kubany, 1997). Furthermore, exposure therapy is typically seen as contraindicated for sufferers of PTSD who also perpetrated acts of unnecessary violence in the warzone and present with severe guilt and shame. The argument is that if patients feel guilt, these feelings will only be intensified from their narrative accounts of acts of perpetration, and guilt and shame are assumed to be emotions that fail to attenuate upon repeated exposure (Pitman et al., 1991). However, this loose heuristic is based on a commonly held view of exposure therapy as a fear extinction–based procedure exclusively. More recently, it has been suggested that an additional mechanism of change in exposure therapy is the re-appraisal and reconstruction of the meaning of a traumatic event, especially in important dimensions of the self-schema (Cason, Resick, & Weaver, 2002). In this framework, a veteran who describes, in vivid detail, the causes of an act of perpetration, the act itself, his emotional responses at the time, and the meaning he attributes to the events, lays the groundwork for belief change. This case study examines the efficacy of this process in treating PTSD-related guilt and shame.

METHOD

Participant

The participant was a 52-year-old, married Caucasian male Vietnam veteran who had served as a mortarman for 13 months in Vietnam during 1967–68 and was seeking clinical services at the National Center for PTSD in Boston. Unlike the modal Vietnam veteran seeking services at the center, the participant was not seeking financial compensation for war trauma and PTSD. His presenting complaints were extreme anxiety, depression, intrusive thoughts, and nightmares. Although he received some psychiatric services in the early 1970s, he had never been in therapy or received treatment specifically for PTSD. The participant reported experiencing a recent exacerbation of a long history of PTSD symptoms as a result of reuniting with some of his comrades from the war.

At the time of the study, the participant was in a stable marriage of 23 years, residing with his wife and one of four children. The participant was a practicing Catholic, and his religion was an important source of coping and comfort to him. He had a severe alcohol and drug dependence history, which impaired his relationships and his capacity to work. Nevertheless, he managed to retain a steady job for 30 years, and had been sober of alcohol for the last 20 years. He had a lengthy history of marijuana abuse, which he reported helped him calm down and "relive Vietnam experiences," in order to imagine he could control them and change the outcome. He reported an intensification of his PTSD symptoms, anxiety, and anger since he stopped his marijuana use in 1999.

The participant's experiences in Vietnam left him with very chronic and severe guilt about acts of commission and shame about transgression. He reported a chronic history of bouts of anger interspersed with severe anxiety and other negative affect. When upset, he reported being "jittery" and "shaking with rage." Typically, the participant would cope with his guilt and shame by externalizing, blaming, and expressing rage at the Vietcong. As would be expected, the veteran struggled with depression chronically and was hospitalized in the early 1970s for depression and suicidality.

While in the warzone, the participant reported the following events as the most distressing.

Traumatic event 1: One of the most distressing events for the participant occurred on the day he learned his close friend had been killed in action. Feeling helpless, angry, and overwhelmed by the news, the participant deliberately fired one mortar blindly into a nearby village. The following day, he learned that someone had been seriously injured as a result of the attack. The participant reported that he felt no remorse at the time of the event, but that he now feels deep guilt about what he did.

Traumatic event 2. Another very distressing event occurred when the participant and his comrades entered a village and came upon the mutilated body of a young girl. They soon realized that this was a trap, and they were ambushed. Soon after, he was horrified to witness a sergeant ordering the demolition of a village hut that held ammunition, despite knowing that civilians had taken shelter there.

Traumatic event 3. The participant described witnessing one of his own men being hit by friendly fire. He stated that the man "disintegrated before my eyes."

Traumatic event 4. Another particularly distressing event, which the participant described, was an entire day of battle, which began by a surprise attack by the North Vietnamese. He reported that his company had incurred many casualties, and one of his close friends had been wounded. During this battle, the veteran stated that he was filled with anger and anxiety, and he had "lost it," taking revenge on the North Vietnamese.

Traumatic event 5. After being ambushed by the North Vietnamese, the participant described the "shocking" experience of having to walk through bodies of wounded fellow soldiers.

Procedure

The participant described in this report was part of a larger research study. In that study, an independent assessor administered a standardized pretreatment evaluation consisting of clinical interviews and self-report measures to potential subjects. Participants had to currently meet PTSD diagnostic criteria to be included in the study, and participants were allowed to continue any concurrent psychosocial treatments during the course of the study. Exclusion criteria were as follows: A documented history or current clinical evidence of mania, schizophrenia, psychosis, or organic mental disorders; unstable medication conditions; prominent suicidal ideation; current alcohol or drug abuse/dependence; and panic disorder or any other physical or emotional problem that would interfere with wearing the virtual reality helmet. If the potential participant met the eligibility criteria, he was provided information about the study and asked to sign an informed consent.

The participant in this study failed to meet the formal diagnostic criteria for PTSD, using the "1–2" DSM–IV decision rule* on the Clinician-Administered PTSD Scale (CAPS; Blake et al., 1995) by only one criterion C symptom (avoidance and numbing symptoms). Rather than avoiding Vietnam-related cues, the participant reported a history of approaching these cues in attempts to gain mastery, to make sense out of what happened to him, and to change the outcome. Despite his subthreshold PTSD symptomatology according to the CAPS, a consensus judgment was made to include this participant in the study based on the following information: (a) The veteran met or exceeded the diagnostic threshold on the

---

*A frequency of "1" or higher and an intensity of "2" or higher for a given item indicates symptom endorsement.

two paper-and-pencil measures of PTSD: PTSD Checklist (PCL; Weathers, Lit, Hermann, Huska, & Keane, 1993) and the Mississippi Scale (Keane, Caddell, & Taylor, 1988). (b) The participant's wife completed a collateral version of the Mississippi Scale (Niles, Herman, Segura-Schultz, Joaquim, & Litz, 1993; Taft, King, King, Leskin, & Riggs, 1999), and reported that the participant experienced severe symptoms (total score of 123 out of 195). (c) The independent evaluator described the participant as having a very exacting and concrete reporting style, rather than the global overendorsing style, which often characterizes veterans seeking compensation. In addition, he had avoided seeking treatment for many years, because he thought, "I should be able to handle it myself," and he experienced significant shame about seeking treatment. As a result, he may have minimized his presentation to the evaluator. (d) In the interview, the veteran endorsed severe and specific re-experiencing symptoms and was emotive and reactive in moments of sharing his trauma, which suggested that he would be a good candidate for exposure therapy.

Instruments

Standardized psychometric measures of PTSD and comorbid psychopathology were used to assess change across time. Assessments were administered pre- and posttreatment, and at follow-ups of 3 and 6 months posttreatment to explore treatment effects. The assessments consisted of the following measures: CAPS (Blake et al., 1995); PCL (Weathers et al., 1993); psychotic screen module from the Structured Clinical Interview for DSM–IV (SCID; First, Spitzer, Gibbon, & Williams, 1995); Beck Depression Inventory (BDI; Beck, Ward, Mendelsohn, Mock, & Erbaugh, 1961); Brief Symptom Inventory (BSI; Derogatis, 1993); Combat Exposure Scale (CES; Keane et al., 1989b); Mississippi Scale (Keane et al., 1988); Boston Life Satisfaction Inventory (Smith, Niles, King, & King, 2001).

In addition, the participant also participated in an assessment of psychophysiological reactivity at pre- and posttreatment, using a script-driven imagery procedure (see Keane et al., 1998). More specifically, psychophysiological responses were measured while the participant listened to 30-second taped descriptions of two of his combat traumas (events 1 and 2 described above), interspersed with two neutral scripts (e.g., sitting on the beach); he was instructed to imagine each of these scenes as vividly as possible while listening to each script.

Psychophysiological reactivity during the virtual Vietnam environments was also measured to examine the process of change within and between sessions. Psychophysiological data was collected for heart rate (HR) and skin conductance (SC). HR activity was recorded from 9-mm-diameter SensorMedics Ag-AgCl electrodes (SensorMedics, Yorba Linda, CA) filled with Beckman electrolyte and attached by adhesive collars at standard lead I (arm) sites. Electrodes were connected to a Coulbourn Instruments high gain bioamplifier (S75-01, Coulbourn Instruments, Allentown, PA), and output from the amplifier was directed to a Coulbourn Instruments tachometer (S77-26) to yield a beats-per-minute (BPM) equivalent of each interbeat interval. SC was recorded from adjacent sites on the hypothenar eminence of the nondominant hand using 1-cm Beckman Ag/AgCl electrodes filled with Unibase-saline paste (Lykken & Venables, 1971) and connected to a Coulbourn-isolated SC coupler (S71-23). Digital sampling (20 Hz) of data occurred twice a second in 60-second blocks (i.e., trials); trials were initiated by a button press by experimenter. Prior to each recording session, the SC coupler was calibrated to register activity from 0 to 40 Siemens. Digitized measurements (A-D units) were converted to conductance values (uSiemens) using the appropriate calibration parameters.

For each VRE session, psychophysiological data was collected at minute 5 of the 5-minute pre-baseline period (i.e., neutral virtual environment), minutes 1 and 25 of the virtual Vietnam environment, and minute 5 of the post-baseline period (i.e., neutral virtual environment). In addition, data were collected during moments selected by the experimenter, which seemed particularly evocative in the virtual Vietnam environment. Thus, on average, each VRE session consisted of approximately 25 one-minute trials of psychophysiological data.

Treatment

In the therapy phase, the participant was treated twice per week over a 5-week period. During the VRE sessions the participant wore a head-mounted display with stereo earphones that provided visual and audio cues consistent with being near, outside, and inside a Huey helicopter (refer to Rothbaum et al., 1999, for a more extensive description of the VRE apparatus). The therapist asked the participant to give a Subjective Units of Distress (SUDS) rating approximately every 5 minutes during all exposures as an indication of his level of anxiety. The therapist made comments and encouraged the patient to sustain his focus on critical elements of a traumatic memory and negative affect in the service of maximizing exposure and facilitating extinction. The participant was allowed to progress at his own pace. The therapist simultaneously viewed on a video monitor the virtual environment in which the participant was interacting, and therefore was able to comment appropriately.

Two different virtual Vietnam scenarios were used. In the virtual landing zone (jungle clearing), the participant stood on a platform, which had a woofer underneath to provide vibrations. He used a joystick to give the illusion of walking forward and backward in the virtual environment. Audio effects included recordings of jungle sounds (e.g., crickets), gunfire, helicopters, mine explosions, and men yelling, "Move out! Move out!" which could be increased in intensity. Visual effects included muzzle flashes from the jungle, helicopters flying overhead, landing and taking off, and fog.

In the virtual helicopter, audio effects included the sound of the rotors, gunfire, bombs, B52s, engine sounds, radio chatter, and men yelling various commands. Visual effects included the interior of a Huey helicopter in which the backs of the pilot's and copilot's heads with patches were visible, instruments, controls, as well as the view out of the helicopter side door. This view included aerial shots of other helicopters flying by, clouds, and the terrain below, which consisted of rice paddies, jungle, and a river. To increase the effectiveness of the illusion of actually being in a helicopter, the participant sat in a chair that had a woofer under the seat that provided vibrations.

Treatment proceeded in an additive manner. During session 1, the participant was made familiar with the treatment procedures. He was able to try on the virtual reality helmet and explore a neutral virtual environment, namely a room with a few pieces of furniture. The therapist reviewed his five most traumatic combat memories, obtained in the diagnostic session, and determined a hierarchy of traumatic events based on the participant's level of distress (i.e., SUDS rating) evoked by the particular memory. Finally, he was instructed in breathing retraining, a relaxation technique frequently used in exposure therapy (Rothbaum et al., 1999).

During session 2, the participant was exposed to the virtual landing zone, and he was encouraged to explore it. Virtual effects were added gradually, as he was able to tolerate them. The participant spent 30 to 45 minutes of this and all remaining therapy sessions with the helmet on: 5 minutes in the neutral environment, then 20 to 35 minutes in the "virtual

Vietnam," then the last 5 minutes back in the neutral environment. The remainder of each 90-minute session was spent on an initial check-in, attachment and detachment of physiological sensors, postexposure breathing retraining, and debriefing. Session 3 was similar to session 2, but in this session the participant was exposed to the Huey helicopter virtual environment.

In sessions 4 and 5, VRE therapy continued, but the participant was asked to share any memories that were triggered by the virtual environment. He described each memory in the present tense with his eyes open to view the virtual environment. The therapist attempted to match the virtual stimuli to the participant's description of his traumatic experiences.

From sessions 6 to 10, the participant was asked to recount his most traumatic memories, which were discussed in session 1. The therapist had the participant focus on one memory at a time, beginning with the least traumatic in the hierarchy and gradually proceeding to more difficult memories. The participant was encouraged to focus his attention on the memory and any negative affect elicited. These sessions were audiotaped, and the tapes were given to the participant to practice imaginal exposure as daily homework. At the end of each VRE session, the therapist debriefed the participant for at least 15 minutes. These conversations were deemed to be a critical aspect to the VRE therapy. The therapist asked the participant to share what it was like to disclose the trauma and to share his feelings and the meaning of the experience. These conversations were poignant for both the therapist and the participant and resulted in an examination of beliefs and constructions, which over time were less maladaptive. All sessions were videotaped to ensure adherence to treatment protocol.

RESULTS AND DISCUSSION

Psychometric Measures

The participant reported considerable change in PTSD symptoms at post-treatment and the two follow-up intervals as seen in Table 6.1. Most noteworthy is the change in the two categories of PTSD symptoms referenced to the targets of the VRE treatment, namely reexperiencing symptoms (all Category B symptoms) and the two strategic avoidance symptoms (Categories C-1 & C-2). Immediately posttreatment, the participant's

Table 6.1 Self-Report Measures

Measure	Pre	Mid	Post	3-month	6-month
CAPS—Total Score	40	—	49	49	30
reexperiencing (B symptoms)	21	—	18	13	2
avoidance (C1 & C2)	0	10	0	5	
arousal (D symptoms)	12	—	11	18	16
PCL	48	42	38	34	41
BSI—Global Severity Index	1.12	—	—	0.83	0.81
BDI	16	14	10	13	10
BAI	16	—	16	13	13
Mississippi Scale	107	—	99	96	100
Boston Life Satisfaction Inventory	103	—	135	131	134
Combat Exposure Scale	28	—	—	—	—

Note. CAPS = Clinician Administered PTSD Scale; PCL = PTSD Checklist; BSI = Brief Symptom Inventory; BDI = Beck Depression Inventory; BAI = Beck Anxiety Inventory.

reexperiencing symptoms showed only a slight decrease compared to their pretreatment baseline values. This is consistent with the therapist's observation that at the end of the 5 weeks of treatment, the participant was still grappling with new ways of construing the traumatic events processed during the VRE procedure.

During and immediately after the VRE treatment, the veteran was attempting to reconcile being a young victim of the horrors of the Vietnam War who tried his best to survive the experience, and being a perpetrator of violence. However, at the end of treatment the veteran was no longer vacillating severely between cognitive assimilation of his acts of brutality in the war, by indignantly expressing rage and dehumanizing the enemy, and excessive overaccommodation of the meaning or implication of the acts of perpetration. The latter entailed absorbing too much blame and experiencing despair from guilt about responsibility for others' suffering. The veteran was nevertheless still raw and quite sensitive and continued to have some reexperiencing symptoms immediately posttreatment as he continued to process his trauma memories. Over the course of the 3-month and 6-month follow-ups, however, he reported a dramatic decrease in reexperiencing symptoms.

In terms of the participant's posttreatment increases in strategic avoidance symptoms, this was the result of a noteworthy shift in coping strategy. Prior to treatment, the participant reported no avoidance of thoughts and feelings related to his trauma and no avoidance of situations that trigger recall of the trauma, which is highly unusual given the extent of his exposure to combat trauma. The veteran would seek out reminders of Vietnam combat (e.g., regularly viewing his medals) and feel as much as he could, particularly anger and rage, and sadness and guilt, which was in the service of contrition and shame. At the end of the 5 weeks of therapy, the participant ostensibly learned to be more strategic in avoiding reminders and feelings related to the trauma. This was seen as a step in the trajectory of change of these behaviors, which, as can been seen in Table 6.1, were reduced considerably over time.

Overall, the participant reported very significant gains, which were maintained at the 6-month assessment interval. At this last assessment, his CAPS total score as well as his reexperiencing and strategic avoidance symptoms were reportedly low. Furthermore, his life satisfaction had increased. However, there were a variety of life stressors and demands (e.g., an increase in job stress, family conflicts) that may have served to maintain a degree of stress symptoms (as indexed by Criterion D PTSD symptoms and BSI Global Severity Index) as well as mild anxiety (indexed by the BAI) and depression (as indexed by the BDI), at all assessment intervals. This is not unusual, particularly given that the exposure therapies such as VRE are primarily designed to target reexperiencing symptoms and strategic avoidance behaviors as opposed to stress management and problem-solving approaches to PTSD treatment that attempt to address stress symptoms more broadly.

In terms of the participant's guilt and shame about acts of perpetration of unnecessary violence in the war zone, the patient made considerable gains. At the outset of treatment, the participant expressed that he periodically saw himself as a War criminal who should go to prison for his actions in the warzone, and at other times he would completely blame the enemy. He could see himself as a young man who experienced loss, but he did not know how to cope with the loss or he refused to take responsibility for his actions and forgive himself. At the outset of the VRE procedure the participant was unable to think about the victim of his retaliatory rage without becoming enraged at the Vietnamese or being consumed by self-blame. At the end of treatment, the participant expressed concern about his victim and could appreciate her humanity and would brainstorm spontaneously about ways to help victims of war. At the end of treatment, the participant could also focus on the sadness he felt about his lost comrade (the event that provoked the retaliatory rage) and could acknowledge that he too was victimized generally as a young soldier.

Physiological responsivity across sessions

Figures 6.1 and 6.2 show the participant's heart rate and skin conductance reactivity, respectively, across each VRE session. For each treatment session, values are provided for the pre- and post-baseline periods in which the participant was in the neutral virtual reality environment. The graphs also include mean values for the first, highest, and last 1-minute trials of data collection during the virtual Vietnam environment for each session. Figure 6.3 provides a graph of the participant's SUDS ratings across each treatment session, and Figure 6.4 shows mean heart rate.

In general, the participant appeared to be physiologically reactive in the first VRE session, when he was exposed to the virtual landing zone. However, his response levels dropped for session 3, when he rode in the helicopter. As it turned out, the participant did ride in helicopters in Vietnam, but they were not a particular source of trauma for him, so this virtual scenario was not used again. As seen in Figure 6.1, his peak responses were relatively high for sessions 4 and 5, when he began to explore actual memories of combat that were triggered by the virtual environment. Notably, in session 5, the virtual Vietnam environment had triggered memories about an enemy attack and the battle that followed,

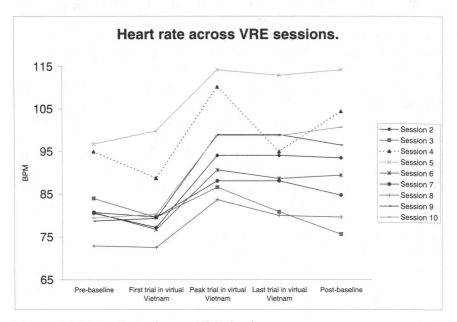

Figure 6.1 Heart Rate Across VRE Sessions

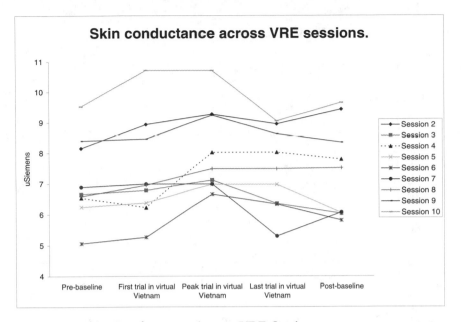

Figure 6.2 Skin Conductance Across VRE Sessions

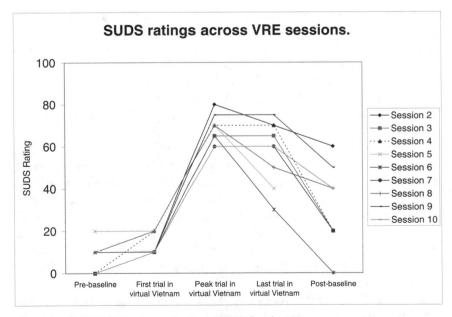

Figure 6.3 SUDS Ratings Across VRE Sessions

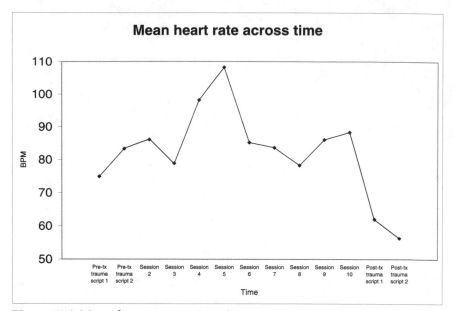

Figure 6.4 Mean heart rate across time.

which the participant reported he had forgotten until then. The participant was very emotionally engaged in reliving these experiences. As expected, the other highest values in Figures 6.1 and 6.2 occurred in sessions 9 and 10 when the participant explored his most traumatic memories, which were of his most severe battle (see event 4 on pg 7).

The psychophysiological data and SUDS ratings collected within the VRE sessions are suggestive of three main findings. First, the participant's physiological reactivity to the virtual Vietnam stimuli indicated significant emotional processing, which is a necessary ingredient to exposure therapy. Compared with his baseline values in the neutral environment, the participant showed a substantial increase in responsivity when exposed to the virtual Vietnam environment. For example, as seen in Figure 6.1, during the participant's most intense session (i.e., session 5), his HR reached a peak of 114 BPM, which was a significant increase from his pre-baseline HR of 97 BPM. Moreover, as Figure 6.2 indicates, the participant's SC also showed substantial increases within the VRE sessions compared with his baseline values.

Second, although there were signs of within-session extinction of conditioned responses to trauma cues in some sessions, more often than not, the participant maintained a high level of physiological activity at the end of the session. In contrast, in nearly all the sessions, as can be seen in Figure 6.3, the participant reported reduced SUDS ratings at the end of the session, which suggests extinction of conditioned response to trauma memories. It is unclear why there was a disconnect between the SUDS ratings and the physiological indicators of emotional behavior despite that these are always only moderately correlated (e.g., Keane et al., 1998). It may be that the SUDS ratings were in part influenced by a demand effect, or it may be that this participant was not sufficiently in-tune with his bodily response to trauma cues. In any case, the data suggests that a diminution of reaction to trauma memory processing during the VRE was not the sole change agent.

It should be noted that at the end of every session, the therapist would spend at least 15 minutes carefully discussing the participant's experience, which in every instance appeared to lead to a reduction in tension and negative affect. Thus, it may be that in exposure therapy, residual hyperarousal can be redressed by systematically allowing patients time at the end of a session to decompress and process their experiences. This should not be underestimated as a possible change agent in exposure therapy with Vietnam veterans and follows the recommendations for exposure therapy (Foa & Rothbaum, 1998).

Third, it appears that there was some decrease in physiological responsivity over the course of treatment. During the first VRE session (session 2), the participant was exposed to very few trauma cues, but nonetheless, his reaction was quite strong. For instance, his heart rate reached 94 BPM, up from 77 BPM when he first entered the virtual landing zone, and his SUDS ratings reached a peak value of 80. Comparing this with the participant's last two sessions, when he was repeatedly going over his worst combat trauma, an ambush and brutal firefight with many casualties, his heart rate reached a maximum of 99 BPM which is not much higher than when he was simply exploring the virtual Vietnam environment in session 2, despite the fact that in the last two treatment sessions, he was experiencing a virtual battle. Furthermore, his SUDS ratings peaked at 75 in session 9, which is lower than his SUDS ratings during the first, relatively benign VRE session.

Physiological Assessment Pre- and Posttreatment

As can be seen in Table 6.2, the participant's resting pretreatment heart rate was discrepant with his post-assessment baseline as well as his pre-

Table 6.2 Psychophysiological Data at Pre- and Post-Treatment While Listening to Idiographic Trauma Scripts

Parameter	Pre-treatment				Post-treatment			
	Baseline	Trauma	Trauma Script 1	Post-Script 2	Baseline baseline	Trauma Script 1	Trauma Script 2	Post-baseline
Heart rate (beats/min)	74.09	74.90	83.30	58.65	58.30	62.02	56.33	58.88
Skin conductance (μSiemens)	6.53	7.29	8.17	6.99	7.92	8.64	7.25	8.73
Systolic blood pressure (μm)	137	142	153	—	133	134	129	129
Diastolic blood pressure (mm)	84	88	92	—	82	90	89	90

and post-baseline during the posttreatment assessment, suggesting that the participant initially experienced anticipatory anxiety about the laboratory procedure, which is quite common (e.g., Keane et al., 1998). Thus, it appears that the participant's "true" baseline heart rate was approximately 58 BPM, which is consistent with his degree of aerobic fitness. Using 58 BPM as the baseline index, the participant exhibited severe increases in cardiac activity in response to both trauma-scripts (event 1 and event 2, respectively; see previous). In contrast, the participant's posttreatment cardiac reactivity was equivocal relative to his baseline. Table 6.2 also shows that there was an 8-point drop in systolic blood pressure from pre- to posttreatment for the first trauma script, and a 24-point drop for the second trauma script. However, diastolic blood pressure did not change substantially, which is not unexpected, since systolic blood pressure is known to be more sensitive to phasic stress responses compared to diastolic blood pressure (Llabre, Spitzer, Saab, & Scheiderman, 2001).

The participant's skin conductance responses did not match up well with his cardiovascular response at the pre- and posttreatment assessments (see Table 6.2). The skin conductance values were uniformly very high suggesting a ceiling effect [the mean skin conductance values in a large study of veterans was 3.8 (SD=3.6); Keane et al., 1998]. In any event, it appears that this particular participant was a cardiovascular reactor more than any other channel of response. Nevertheless, the participant did show modest reactivity to trauma scripts at the pretreatment assessment, and a slight decrease in reactivity at posttreatment relative to his baseline. These results, taken as a whole, strongly suggest that at the end of VRE, the participant was substantially less physiologically reactive to two key trauma memories compared with his pretreatment assessment.

CONCLUSION

We have described the treatment of a Vietnam veteran for PTSD related to his war experiences by virtual reality exposure therapy. Psychophysiological monitoring occurred throughout the treatment as well as at pre- and posttreatment. Although the treatment was considered successful, that would not be clearly evident by the usual standards. His scores on standardized measures of PTSD and related symptoms decreased, but in many cases not until 6 months after the termination of therapy. Much of his distress was triggered by acts committed by him or with his participation in Vietnam and he responded with guilt and anger. In many ways, the most important aspects of his therapy occurred in each session *after* the exposure therapy when the material was discussed in a more cognitive therapy type of discussion. We have found this processing of the traumatic material that comes up in exposure therapy not just useful, but mandatory, for effective emotional processing.

Regarding his physiological responding to the virtual Vietnam stimuli, there were clear signs of significant emotional engagement, although, more often than not, the participant maintained a high level of physiological activity at the end of the session. Consistent with this finding, we have found in conducting exposure therapy with sexual assault survivors with PTSD that the between-session habituation is more important than the within-session habituation (Jaycox, Foa, & Morral, 1998). It is also interesting that his physiological reactivity did not always match his self-report of distress. Despite these difficulties and inconsistencies, the patient did well in therapy. We chose this case to highlight some of the interesting aspects of exposure therapy, virtual reality exposure therapy, and psychophysiological monitoring.

REFERENCES

American Psychiatric Association. (1994). *Diagnostic and statistical manual of mental disorders* (4th ed.). Washington, DC: Author.

Beck, AT, Word, CH, Mendelson, M, Mock, J. & Erbaugh (1961). An inventory for measuring Depression. *Archives of General Psychiatry, 4.* 561–571.-

Blake, D. D., Weathers, F. W., Nagy, L. M., Kaloupek, D. G., Gusman, F. D., Charney, D. S., et al. (1995). The development of a clinician-administered PTSD scale. *Journal of Traumatic Stress, 8,* 75–90.

Boudewyns, P. A., & Hyer, L. (1990). Physiological response to combat memories and preliminary treatment outcome in Vietnam veteran PTSD patients treated with therapeutic exposure. *Behavior Therapy, 21,* 63–87.

Carlin, A. S., Hoffman, H. G., & Weghorst, S. (1997). Virtual reality and tactile augmentation in the treatment of spider phobia: A case report. *Behaviour Research and Therapy, 35,* 153–158.

Cason, D. R., Resick, P. A., & Weaver, T. L. (2002). Schematic integration of traumatic events. *Clinical Psychology Review, 22,* 131–153.

Derogatis, L.R. (1993). *Brief Symptom Inventory: Administration, scoring and procedures manual.* Minneapolis, MN: National Computer Systems, Inc.

First, M.D., Spitzer, R.L., Gibbon, M., & Williams, J.B.W. (1995). *Structured clinical interview for DSM–IV Axis I disorders, Patient edition.* New York: Biometrics Research, New York State Psychiatric Institute.

Foa, E. B., & Rothbaum, B. O. (1998). *Treating the trauma of rape: A cognitive-behavioral therapy for PTSD.* Guilford: New York.

Jaycox, L. H., Foa, E. B., & Morral, A. R. (1998). Influence of emotional engagement and habituation on exposure therapy for PTSD. *Journal of Consulting and Clinical Psychology, 66,* 185–192.

Keane, T. M., Caddell, J. M., & Taylor, K. L. (1988). Mississippi Scale for Combat-Related Posttraumatic Stress Disorder: Three studies in reliability and validity. *Journal of Consulting and Clinical Psychology, 56,* 85–90.

Keane, T. M., Fairbank, J. A., Caddell, J. M., & Zimering, R. T. (1989a). Implosive (flooding) therapy reduces symptoms of PTSD in Vietnam combat-veterans. *Behavior Therapy, 20,* 245–260.

Keane, T. M., Fairbank, J. A., Caddell, J. M., Zimering, R. T., Taylor, K. L., & Mora, C. A. (1989b). Clinical evaluation of a measure to assess combat exposure. *Psychological Assessment, 1,* 53–55.

Keane, T. M., Kolb, L. C., Kaloupek, D. G., Orr, S. P., Blanchard, E. B., Thomas, R. G., et al., (1998). Utility of psychophysiology measurement in the diagnosis of posttraumatic stress disorder: Results from a department of Veterans Affairs cooperative study. *Journal of Consulting and Clinical Psychology, 66,* 914–923.

Kubany, E. S. (1997). Application of cognitive therapy for trauma-related guilt (CT-TRG) with a Vietnam veteran troubled by multiple sources of guilt. *Cognitive and Behavioral Practice, 4,* 213–244.

Kulka, R. A., Schlenger, W. E., Fairbank, J. A., Hough, R. L., Jordan, B. K., Marmar, C. R., et al., (1990). *Trauma and the Vietnam War generation: Report of findings from the National Vietnam Veterans Readjustment Study.* New York: Brunner/Mazel.

Llabre, M.M., Spitzer, S.B., Saab, P.G., & Scheiderman, N. (2001). Piecewise latent growth curve modeling of systolic blood pressure reactivity and recovery from the cold pressor test. *Psychophysiology, 38,* 951–960.

Lykken, D. T., & Venables, P. H. (1971). Direct measurement of skin conductance: A proposal for standardization. *Psychophysiology, 8,* 656–672.

Niles, B. L., Herman, D. S., Segura-Schultz, S., Joaquim, S. J., & Litz, B. T. (1993). *The Spouse/Partner Mississippi Scale: How does it compare?* Paper presented at the annual meeting of the International Society for Traumatic Stress Studies, San Antonio, TX.

Pitman, R. K., Altman, B., Greenwald, E., Longpre, R. E., Macklin, M. L., Poire, R. E., et al., (1991). Psychiatric complications during flooding therapy for posttraumatic stress disorder. *Journal of Clinical Psychiatry, 52,* 17–20.

Rothbaum, B. O., Hodges, L., Alarcon, R., Ready, D., Shahar, F., Graap, K., et al., (1999). Virtual reality exposure therapy for PTSD Vietnam veterans: A case study. *Journal of Traumatic Stress, 12,* 263–271.

Rothbaum, B.O., Hodges, L., Anderson, P.L., Price, L., & Smith, S. (2002). 12-month follow-up of virtual reality exposure therapy for the fear of flying. *Journal of Consulting and Clinical Psychology, 70,* 428–432.

Rothbaum, B. O., Hodges, L., Kooper, R., Opdyke, D., Williford, J., & North, M.

M. (1995). Effectiveness of virtual reality graded exposure in the treatment of acrophobia. *American Journal of Psychiatry, 152,* 626–628.

Rothbaum, B.O., Hodges, L., Ready, D., Graap, K., & Alarcon, R. (2001). Virtual reality exposure therapy for Vietnam veterans with posttraumatic stress disorder. *Journal of Clinical Psychiatry, 62,* 617–622.

Rothbaum, B.O., Hodges, L., Smith, S., Lee, J.H., & Price, L. (2000). A controlled study of virtual reality exposure therapy for the fear of flying. *Journal of Consulting and Clinical Psychology, 68,* 1020–1026.

Smith, A. A., Niles, B. L., King, L., & King, D. (2001). *Psychometric properties of the Boston Life Satisfaction Inventory among veterans with PTSD.* Poster presented at the annual conference of the International Society for Traumatic Stress Studies, New Orleans, LA.

Taft, C. T., King, L. A., King, D. W., Leskin, G. A., & Riggs, D. S. (1999). Partners' ratings of combat veterans' PTSD symptomatology. *Journal of Traumatic Stress, 12,* 327–334.

Weathers, F.W., Litz, B.T., Herman, D.S., Huska, J.A., & Keane, T.M. (1993). *The PTSD Checklist (PCL): Reliability, validity, and diagnostic utility.* Paper presented at the annual meeting of the International Society for Traumatic Stress Studies, San Antonio,TX.

Weiss, D. S., Marmar, C. R., Schlenger, W. E., Fairbank, J. A., Jordan, B. K., Hough, et al., (1992). The prevalence of lifetime and partial posttraumatic stress disorder in Vietnam theater veterans. *Journal of Traumatic Stress, 5,* 365–376.

Chapter 7

PTSD AND THE SOCIAL SUPPORT OF THE INTERPERSONAL ENVIRONMENT: THE DEVELOPMENT OF SOCIAL COGNITIVE BEHAVIOR THERAPY

Nicholas Tarrier and Anne-Louise Humphreys

INTRODUCTION

Although case studies and uncontrolled trials can provide evidence for treatment efficacy, this evidence is generally regarded as weak and potentially suffers from bias. The randomized controlled trial (RCT) remains the "gold standard" for evaluating treatment efficacy (Doll, 1998). A number of RCTs have demonstrated that cognitive-behavioral treatments are efficacious in the prevention and treatment of posttraumatic stress disorder (PTSD) (see Foa, Davidson, & Frances, 1999). Treatments have been applied to prevent the development of PTSD and to alleviate PTSD once it has developed.

Without treatment, approximately 70% of people who reach criteria for acute stress disorder (ASD) will go on to meet criteria for PTSD (Harvey & Bryant, 1998; Holeva, Tarrier, & Wells, 2001). Cognitive-behavioral therapy (CBT) delivered within the first month after the trauma in subjects suffering from ASD can significantly reduce the number who subsequently develop PTSD (Bryant, Harvey, Dang, Sackville, & Basten, 1998; Foa, Hearst-Ikeda, & Perry, 1995). In chronic PTSD, clinical trials have demonstrated that exposure therapy (Foa, et al.,1999; Foa, Rothbaum, Riggs, & Murdoch,1991; Keane, Fairbanks, Caddell, & Zimmering, 1989; Marks, Lovell, Nashirvani, Livanour, & Thrasher, 1998; Paunovic & Ost, 2001; Tarrier, Pilgrim, et al., 1999), cognitive therapy

(Marks et al., 1998; Paunovic & Ost, 2001; Resick & Schnicke, 1992; Tarrier, Pilgrim, et al.,1999) and stress inoculation (Foa et al., 1999; Foa et al., 1991) all result in clinical benefit and significant symptom reduction. Evidence has also been published in favor of eye movement desensitization (EMDR), but this technique remains controversial and opinion on its utility varies (Davidson & Parker, 2001). Applied relaxation (Marks et al., 1998) and supportive counseling (Foa et al., 1991) appear less effective.

Where the comparative efficacy of these interventions has been assessed there appears to be no superiority between cognitive therapy and exposure (Marks et al., 1998; Paunovic & Ost, 2001; Tarrier, Pilgrim et al., 1999) or between exposure and stress inoculation (Foa et al., 1999). There also appears to be little advantage in combining treatments, so that exposure plus cognitive therapy (Marks et al., 1998) and exposure plus stress inoculation (Foa et al., 1999) were not superior to each intervention alone. Benefits from such therapies appear to be maintained in the short term (Foa et al., 1991; Marks et al., 1998; Tarrier, Sommerfield, Pilgrim, & Humphreys, 1999), with some evidence that exposure is more effective than stress inoculation (Foa et al., 1999).

With most follow-ups being no more than 12 months, little is known about longerterm maintenance. Patient groups have included Vietnam veterans (Keane et al., 1989), rape victims (Foa et al., 1999; Foa et al.,1991; Resick & Schnicke, 1992), refugees (Paunovic & Ost, 2001), and mixed civilian traumas (Marks et al., 1998; Tarrier, Pilgrim, et al., 1999). Little is known about differences in treatment outcomes between these groups except that victims of accidents appear to respond better to CBT than victims of criminal assault (Tarrier, Sommerfield, et al., 1999).

Despite significant improvements in PTSD reported in these trials, a significant number of patients remain disordered. Foa et al. (1999) reported that at 12 month follow-up 40% of those treated with exposure, 58% of those treated with stress inoculation, and 60% of those treated with the combined treatment remained PTSD cases. Similarly, Tarrier, Sommerfield, et al., (1999) found 39% of their mixed trauma sample treated with exposure or cognitive therapy were PTSD cases at 12-month follow-up.

INFLUENCE OF THE INTERPERSONAL ENVIRONMENT AND SOCIAL SUPPORT

A small but significant number of patients suffering from PTSD appear not to respond, or only partially respond, to cognitive-behavioral treatments. It is important to attempt to understand what factors may be maintaining high levels of psychopathology, both to aid understanding of the development of psychological disorders after trauma and to inform the innovation and development of more effective treatments.

It is well established that the quality of social support is associated with mental health outcomes (Rhodes & Lakey, 1999). The lack of social support has been found by Brewin, Andrews and Valentine (2000) in a meta-analysis to be a risk factor for PTSD. However, it has yet to be resolved clearly which aspects of support are necessary to promote health (Cwikel & Israel, 1987). Social support is a multifarious concept, which may be conceptualiszed as the resources provided by other people (Cohen & Symes, 1985). It consists of a number of factors including the nature of the interpersonal and emotional environment created by the quality of the relationship with the person's key relative, significant other, or support network. House (1981) defines four broad classes of resources: (a) behavioral resources, (b) emotional resources, (c) instrumental resources, and (d) informational and appraisal support. Both emotional support, when coupled with either informational or instrumental support (Cwikel & Israel, 1987), and having a close confiding reciprocal relationship (Israel, 1982) are associated with more positive outcomes. However it is important to be aware that there are both positive and negative aspects to social support and some people may be more vulnerable to the negative effects (Lefrancois, Leclerc, Hamel, & Gaulin, 2000; Swickert, Rosentreter, Hittner, & Mushrush, 2002).

The complexity of the concept of social support inevitably leads to difficulties when attempting to study or measure it, particularly because the individual's perspective of support is related to mental health, not the actual support provided (Solomon, Mikulincer, & Hobfoll, 1987). One productive approach to assessing the quality of the interpersonal environment has been to measure expressed emotion (EE). This is derived from a semi-structured interview with the key relative or significant other. From the audiotape of this interview respondents can be classified as either high or low on EE depending on ratings of criticism, hostility, and emotional over-involvement (Leff & Vaughn, 1985). Most research on EE and its effects has been carried out in schizophrenia, in which there is a consistent finding that living with a high EE relative is associated with increased rates of relapse (Butzlaff & Hooley, 1998; Kavanagh, 1992). Similar findings have also been found in depression and other psychological and behavioral disorders (Wearden, Tarrier, Barrowclough, Zastowny, & Rahill, 2000). Tarrier, Sommerfield, and Pilgrim (1999) demonstrated in a prospective study that the EE of the key relative was strongly associated with clinical outcome in PTSD patients receiving treatment by cognitive therapy or exposure. The EE of the key relative was measured and rated prior to randomization and entry into a treatment trial, patients living with a high EE relative showed no differences in clinical measures when compared with those living with low EE relatives prior to treatment. However, at post-treatment those patients living with a high EE relative showed significantly less improvement across all outcome measures. It was concluded that the quality of the patient's social environment, as reflected in their relatives' EE measure, had a significant effect on their response to treatment.

EE is directly obtained from the relative as respondent. In addition, proxy measures of EE have been developed, which measure the patient's perception of the quality of the interpersonal support that patient has obtained from significant others. These measures have the advantage of economy although the disadvantage is that they are derived from the same source as the measurement of psychopathology. Perception of social support has found to be predictive of relapse in unipolar depression (Hooley & Teasdale, 1989), onset of seasonal affective disorder (McCarthy, Tarrier, & Gregg, in press), exacerbation of anxiety in ovarian cancer patients (Hipkins, Whitworth, Tarrier, & Jayson, 2002) and in the development of ASD and PTSD in victims of road traffic accidents (Holeva et al., 2001). In the latter study it was found that seeking social support generally reduced subsequent levels of PTSD, except when the perception of available social support was of poor quality. In these cases, when seeking social support was a coping strategy but the quality of available support was perceived as poor, the chances of developing later PTSD was eight times greater than in other patients (Holeva et al., 2001).

A Model of the Action of the Interpersonal Environment

Investigation into the beliefs of key relatives of patients with a range of disorders, through the measurement of causal attributions, has suggested that the cognitions of the key relative may influence their behaviour toward the patient (Barrowclough, Johnston, & Tarrier, 1994). These studies have found that if the relative believes that the patient's behaviour is, to some extent, under volitional control, then this is associated with the relative being more critical and in some extremes, hostile and rejecting (Barrowclough et al., 1994; Hooley, 1987; Tarrier, Barrowclough, Ward, Donaldson, & Burns, 2002). Emotionally over-involved relatives on the other hand tend to view the patient's problem behaviour as due to factors beyond the control of the patient (Barrowclough et al., 1994; Brewin, MacCarthy, Duda, & Vaughn, 1991; Tarrier et al., 2002). Relatives who are low EE tend to identify fewer problems and attribute these to benign causes (Barrowclough et al., 1994; Tarrier et al., 2002). It has been suggested that these underlying beliefs, held by relatives about the patient's behaviour, may determine how they themselves behave toward the patient and that this may have consequences for the patient and the development and maintenance of his or her psychopathology. Relatives who attribute the patient's problems to factors internal and controllable by them will be more likely to be critical or hostile to the patient and attempt to bring about restitution to normality through coercive coping strategies. It is assumed that these coping strategies will be stressful and detrimental to the patient. Whereas, relatives who attribute problems to factors external and outside the patient's control are more likely to be emotionally over-involved and be over-protective and intrusive (Barrowclough et al., 1994). Relatives who are warm and show low EE are more likely to foster a supportive interpersonal environment (Tarrier et al., 2002).

Evidence from a range of psychological disorders indicates that the quality of the interpersonal environment created by the interaction between the patient and key relative or significant other can affect both the development of a disorder after trauma or the course of the disorder once it has been established. It is proposed that the beliefs held by the relatives about the nature of the patient's problems can determine their emotional and behavioral reaction to the patient. This set of emotional and behavioral reactions creates a psychosocial or emotional climate to which the patient is exposed. It is concluded that because the research on EE, perceived social support, and causal attributions has produced similar results across a range of disorders, the association between a negative interpersonal environment and poor clinical outcome is a general one, although there may well be disorder-specific factors or elements. Furthermore, we suggest that the findings from different disorders will be generally relevant to PTSD and will be able to guide further treatment development.

TREATMENT IMPLICATIONS AND FAMILY INTERVENTIONS

The consistent finding that high EE is associated with elevated relapse in schizophrenia and depression stimulated attempts to design family interventions to improve clinical outcome in these disorders. There is very good evidence that family interventions result in clinical benefits in schizophrenia (Pharoah, Mari, & Streiner, 2000; Pitschel-Waltz, Leucht, Bauml, Kissling, & Engel, 2001) and preliminary evidence for depression (Leff et al., 2000). By the same reasoning, if the interpersonal environment created by the significant other is important in the maintenance of PTSD, then an intervention with the family or including the significant other should result in clinical benefits with PTSD patients. Support for this comes from content analysis of the critical comments made by relatives of PTSD patients, which indicates that the criticisms made by the relatives are very similar to those of schizophrenic patients. Of the six most cited complaints, five are similar to the complaints of relatives of patients with other disorders: (a) Patient irritability and moodiness, (b) laziness and lack of interest, (c) lack of affection, (d) heavy drinking, and (e) being withdrawn (Tarrier, 1996). Only a preoccupation with the trauma is specific to PTSD.

One study has examined the effect of family intervention in the treatment of PTSD, but with negative results. Glynn et al. (1999) allocated 42 Vietnam veterans and a family member to either (a) a waiting list control, (b) exposure therapy; or (c) exposure therapy followed by behavioral family intervention. Patients receiving exposure therapy showed significant improvements in positive PTSD symptoms (e.g., reexperiencing) but not negative symptoms (e.g., numbing). Positive and negative symptoms were classified on the basis of a principle-component analysis. Family intervention did not add anything to exposure.

There are three possible reasons for the rather disappointing result. First, the sample was small and the study statistically underpowered to demonstrate a significant difference between two active treatments (a Type II error). Second, the family intervention was based on communication training (Mueser & Glynn, 1995), which may not be appropriate because there is no evidence that the relatives have specific communication skill deficits. This intervention would not, therefore, specifically target important maladaptive beliefs and behaviours of the relative. Third, Vietnam veterans are a special population with a 25-plus year history of intractable PTSD with significant comorbid and social problems. It may well have been that the chronicity and severity of their problems have resulted in so well-established emotional and behavioral patterns that they would require more than 18 sessions to exert an additional effect over exposure. Despite Glynn et al.'s (1999) failure to demonstrate the efficacy of family interventions, the investigation of this type of intervention is potentially productive with a noncombat population with less chronicity.

RECIPROCITY AND SOCIAL EXCHANGE

Salkovskis (2002) suggested that the further development of CBT could be addressed through attention to empirically grounded clinical interventions. Such an approach would enable further understanding of the association between social support and PTSD and facilitate the development of relevant interventions. As poor social support is a risk factor for chronic PTSD, the development of interventions designed to enhance such support are inherently appealing as an adjunct to cognitive-behavioral therapy. However the social support literature is theoretically diverse and interventions need to be implemented with caution, as some studies have demonstrated deleterious effects between support and health (Helgeson, Cohen, Schultz, & Yasko, 2000; Krause 1997). A range of social support-based interventions have been investigated but the results are frequently difficult to interpret since they are often neither theoretically based nor include pre- and post-intervention measures of social support (Hogan, Linden, & Najariana, 2002). The range of measurement tools utilized is also an area of concern because these often lack reliability or validity.

Despite these difficulties, the social support literature may offer further understanding of PTSD and inform interventions to improve the efficacy of current treatments. Such approaches may be particularly useful for those patients with significant levels of comorbid depression, substance abuse, or complex bereavement problems wherein social support interventions have already been demonstrated to exert an effect (Harris, Borwn, & Robinson, 1999; Humphreys, Mankowski, Moos, & Finney, 1999; Vachon, Lyall, Rogers, Freedman, Letowsky, & Freeman, 1980).

An emergent concept from social support studies, with potential relevance to PTSD patients, is reciprocity. Accidental injury or assault accounts for a large proportion of PTSD prevalence. Such events may result in both physical and psychological injury with the patient requiring considerable long-term support. The need for extensive support with physical and psychological problems can place a significant and sustained burden on the support network, with the focus often centering upon the family rather than the wider network (Pearlin, 1985). In addition, patients may lack opportunities to offer assistance and support to others and hence the reciprocal relationship between patients and their network is affected. Reciprocity, the ability to give and receive support, while not specifically studied in relation to PTSD, has been identified as important to the mental health for people with a range of chronic problems (Anson, Stanwyck, & Krauser, 1993).

Social support may be conceptualized by individuals as an insurance policy against adversity whereby the paying in of supportive actions to others may provide access to support in the event of a future crisis (Bruhn, 1991). Reciprocity can be considered as the cognitive process by which persons balance their support account. For people with chronic problems they may perceive that they continually have to rely on past payments with limited opportunity to deposit new income. Overdrawing on this account could then be equated with a perceived risk of losing support. Fear of losing vital support may exacerbate the perception of future threat and enhance their sense of vulnerability. This may manifest itself as patients fearing their partners will leave them or an avoidance of talking about their problems for fear of burdening friends and relatives. Identifying such cognitions may elucidate the value of some frequent behavioral responses of PTSD such as avoidance of talking about the event or emotional withdrawal from significant others.

Gender differences observed between the social support patterns of men and women may be significant (Fuhrer & Stansfeld, 2002) and the type of support that is protective following a crisis may differ between the sexes (Craig & Pathare, 2000). Women have been reported to gain emotional support from wide groups of confidants with partners being less heavily relied on for this role. They also appear to place greater importance on providing emotional support to others (Fuhrer & Stansfeld, 2002). In contrast a man relies more heavily on his partner as his sole confidant and places greater value on practical support (Fuhrer & Stansfeld, 2002). Men who receive support from friends are at greater risk for stress related problems (Husaini, Heff, Newborough, & Moore, 1982). The stress-enhancing aspect of such support may arise from reduced reciprocity within the friendship.

How Can Reciprocity Be Utilized Therapeutically?

Assessment of perceived social support would appear important. In those people who identify a deficiency within their supportive network it may be beneficial to consider interventions to redress this balance. A range of intervention options are available here from structured family interventions to modification of beliefs about the intention and actions of others (see Figure 7.1). If no specific problems are identified, it may only be necessary to continue to monitor the person's support needs during the process of therapy.

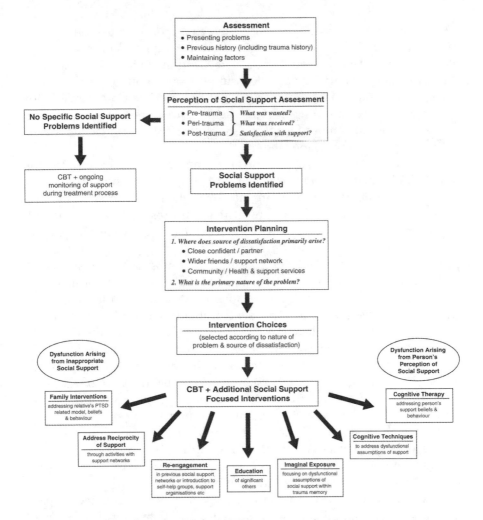

Figure 7.1 Clinical pathway for PTSD interventions.

Such interventions have yet to be investigated for PTSD. However, interventions may be incorporated into cognitive-behavioral therapy to specifically address areas of dysfunction in social support. Education of both patients and their significant others about PTSD symptoms is central and can be used by the therapist to encourage the reengagement into previous support networks and confiding relationships. Addressing reciprocity with an existing network such as a spouse or partner may be most beneficial. This may be brought about through an agreed exchange of support between the couple negotiated within therapy. For example, the agreement to contribute practical support (e.g., household chores) in exchange for emotional support (e.g., talking about their problems), with their partner. The aim being to both ease the burden on the caregiver and increase the opportunities for the person with PTSD to contribute meaningful support to the relationship.

Self-help groups and support organizations may also be utilized for those with limited support or problems utilizing previous support. Groups or "buddy" support may be more effective when structured to provide opportunities to enter into reciprocal relationships with similar others. However, such support may prove more valuable to women given the greater value placed on providing emotional support to a wider circle of people (Fuhrer & Stansfeld, 2002). Self-help groups have been suggested to be most valued by those with stigmatizing problems (Hogan et al., 2002) so they may be most relevant for those traumatized in potentially stigmatizing events such as rape, sexual abuse, and domestic violence. This may be due to a fear of burdening their relatives with the horror of their experience while also being able to use the experience reciprocally to benefit others who have suffered in a similar way. However, further investigation is required to understand the therapeutic value of this support group-seeking phenomenon. Reengagement in previous social activities and family life may provide natural opportunities for reciprocal support to occur, but as discussed previously, supportive relationships can also have a negative impact. Where this is identified it may be necessary to address the understanding of PTSD, beliefs and behaviours of close supportive others through family interventions.

A key impact of social support is its subjective nature. Individuals' perceptions may be influenced by their pretrauma history, disruption in their recall of the trauma or in their interpretation of actions of others after the trauma, and during recovery. Dysfunction arising from distorted perceptions may indicate the need to utilize specific cognitive restructuring techniques to address these problems. Following assessment of the nature and sources of support the therapist needs to consider whether identified problems arise primarily from inappropriate support or from a distorted perception of their support or somewhere on the continuum between these. It is then possible to consider which adjunctive interventions may be the most appropriate to address the social support needs of their individual patients.

CONCLUSION

Cognitive-behavioral therapists routinely use some of the strategies discussed in this chapter, while other treatment options are more speculative. However, the value of such interventions have rarely been considered within the context of reciprocity and social support theories. If therapists are to seek to enhance the efficacy of currently available therapies through the milieu of social support, it is imperative that this is conducted through well-designed empirical studies and the application of theory to the intervention design and measurement (Cwikel & Israel, 1987; Hogan et al., 2002). Without such an approach it will be difficult to increase understanding of the role of social support as a risk factor for PTSD or to design interventions to buffer individuals from the consequences of traumatic events. The recent call for a closer integration between the psychotherapy and social support literature by Barker and Pistrang (2002) and within the context of individual case formulation by Tarrier and Calam (2002), may well afford opportunities to enhance the efficacy of current therapies. A failure to pay attention to social support studies as well as failure to build interventions on apparent common sense may result at best in ineffective interventions and at worst harmful ones.

REFERENCES

Anson, C. A., Stanwyck, D. J., & Krause, J. S. (1993). Social support and health status in spinal cord injury. *Paraplegia, 31,* 632–638.

Barker, C., & Pistrang, N. (2002). Psychotherapy and social support: Integrating research on psychological helping. *Clinical Psychology Review, 22,* 361–379.

Barrowclough, C., Johnston, M., & Tarrier, N. (1994). Attributions, expressed emotion and patient relapse. An attributional model of relatives' response to schizophrenic illness. *Behavior Therapy, 25,* 67–88.

Brewin, C.R., Andrews, B., & Valentine, J. D. (2000). Meta-analysis of risk factors for posttraumatic stress disorder in trauma-exposed adults. *Journal of Consulting and Clinical Psychology, 68,* 748–766.

Brewin, C. R., MacCarthy, B., Duda, K., & Vaughn, C. E. (1991). Attribution and expressed emotion in the relatives of patients with schizophrenia. *Journal of Abnormal Psychology, 100,* 546–554.

Bruhn, J. G. (1991). People need people. *Integrating Physiological & Behavioral Science, 26,* 325–329.

Bryant, R.A., Harvey, A., Dang, S.T., Sackville, T., & Basten C. (1998). Treatment of acute stress disorder: A comparison of cognitive-behavioral therapy and supportive counseling. *Journal of Consulting and Clinical Psychology, 66,* 802–806.

Butzlaff, R. L., & Hooley, J. M. (1998). Expressed emotion and psychiatric relapse: A meta-analysis. *Archives of General Psychiatry, 35,* 547–552.

Cohen, S., & Symes, S. L. (1985). Issues in the study and application of social support. In S. Cohen & S. L. Symes (Eds.), *Social support and health.* Orlando, FL: Academic Press.

Craig, T. & Pathare, S. (2000). Gender differences in the experience and response to adversity. In T. Harris (Ed.), *Where inner and outer worlds meet* (pp. 211–225). London: Routledge.

Cwikel, J. M., & Israel, B.A. (1987). Examining the mechanisms of social support and social networks: A review of health-related intervention studies. *Public Health Review, 15,* 159–193.

Davidson, P.R., & Parker, K.C.H. (2001). Eye movement desensitization and reprocessing (EMDR): A meta-analysis. *Journal of Consulting and Clinical Psychology, 69,* 305–316.

Doll, R. (1998). Controlled trials: The 1948 watershed. *British Medical Journal, 317,* 1217–1220.

Foa, E.B., Davidson, J.R.T., & Frances, A. (1999). Treatment of posttraumatic stress disorder: The expert consensus guideline series. *Journal of Clinical Psychiatry, 60* (Suppl. 16), 1–76.

Foa, E.B., Hearst-Ikeda, D., & Perry, K.J. (1995). Evaluation of a brief cognitive-behavioral program for the prevention of chronic PTSD in recent assault victims. *Journal of Consulting and Clinical Psychology, 63,* 948–955.

Foa, E.B., Rothbaum, B.O., Riggs, D.S., & Murdock, T.B. (1991). Treatment of posttraumatic stress disorder in rape victims: A comparison between cognitive-behavioral procedures and counseling. *Journal of Consulting and Clinical Psychology, 59,* 715–723.

Fuhrer, R., & Stansfeld, S. A. (2002). How gender affects patterns of social relations and their impact on health: A comparison of one or multiple sources of support from close persons. *Social Science & Medicine, 54,* 811–825.

Glynn, S.M., Eth, S., Foy, D.W., Randolph, E.T., Urbaitis, M., Boxer, L., et al., (1999). A test of behavioral family therapy to augment exposure for combat-related posttraumatic stress disorder. *Journal of Consulting and Clinical Psychology, 67,* 243–251.

Harris, T., Brown, G. W., & Robinson, R. (1999). Befriending as an intervention for chronic depression among inner city women. *British Journal of Psychiatry, 174,* 219–232.

Harvey, A., & Bryant, R.A. (1998). The relationship between acute stress disorder and posttraumatic stress disorder: A prospective evaluation of motor vehicle accident survivors. *Journal of Consulting and Clinical Psychology, 66,* 507–512.

Helgeson, V. S., Cohen, S., Schultz, R., & Yasko, J. (2000). Group support interventions for women with breast cancer: Who benefits from what? *Health Psychology, 19,* 107–114.

Hipkins, J., Whitworth, M., Tarrier, N., & Jayson, G. (2002). *Psychological morbidity after chemotherapy in ovarian cancer.* Submitted for publication.

Hogan, B., Linden, W., & Najarian, B. (2002). Social support interventions: Do they work? *Clinical Psychology Review, 22*, 381–440.

Holeva, V., Tarrier, N. & Wells, A. (2001). Prevalence and predictors of acute stress disorder and PTSD following road traffic accidents: Thought control strategies and social support. *Behavior Therapy, 32*, 65–83.

Hooley, J. (1987). The nature and origins of expressed emotion. In M. J. Goldstein & K. Hahlweg (Eds.), *Understanding major mental disorder. The contribution of family interaction research* (pp. 176–194). New York: Family Process Press.

Hooley, J.M., & Teasdale, J.D. (1989). Predictors of relapse in unipolar depressives: Expressed emotion, marital distress and perceived criticism. *Journal of Abnormal Psychology, 98*, 229–235.

House, J. (1981). *Work stress and social support.* Reading, MA: Addison-Wesley.

Humphreys, K., Mankowski, E. S., Moos, R. H., & Finney, J. W. (1999). Do enhanced friendship networks and active coping mechanisms mediate the effect of self-help groups on substance abuse? *Annals of Behavioral Medicine, 21*, 54–60.

Husaini, B. A., Neff, J. A., Newborough, J. R., & Moore, M. C. (1982). The stress buffering role of social support and personal competence among the rural married. *Journal of Community Psychology, 10*, 409–26.

Israel, B. A. (1982). Social networks and health status: Linking theory, research and practice. *Patient Counselling and Health Education, 4*, 65–79.

Kavanagh, D. J. (1992). Recent developments in expressed emotion and schizophrenia. *British Journal of Psychiatry, 160*, 601–620.

Keane, T.M., Fairbank, J.A., Caddell, J.M., & Zimering, R.T. (1989). Implosive (flooding) therapy reduces symptoms of PTSD in Vietnam combat veterans. *Behavior Therapy, 20*, 245–260.

Krause, N. (1997). Received support, anticipated support, social class and mortality. *Research in Ageing, 19*, 387–422.

Leff, J., & Vaughn, C. (1985). *Expressed emotion in families: Its significance for mental illness.* New York: Guilford.

Leff, J.P., Vearnals, S., Brewin, C.R., Wolff, G., Alexander, B., et al., (2000). The London Depression Intervention Trial: A randomized controlled trial of antidepressants v. couple therapy of people with depression living with a partner: Clinical outcomes and costs. *British Journal of Psychiatry, 177*, 95–100.

Lefrancois, R., Leclerc, G., Hamel, S., & Gaulin, P. (2000). Stressful life events and psychological distress of the very old: Does social support have a moderating effect? *Archives of Gerontology, 31*, 243–255.

Marks, I., Lovell, K., Noshirvani, H., Livanou, M., & Thrasher, S. (1998). Exposure and cognitive restructuring alone and combined in PTSD: A controlled study. *Archives of General Psychiatry, 55*, 317–325.

McCarthy, E., Tarrier, N., & Gregg, L. (in press). The nature and timing of seasonal affective symptoms and the influence of self-esteem and social support: A longitudinal prospective study. *Psychological Medicine.*Mueser, K.T., &

Glynn, S.M. (1995). *Behavioral family therapy for psychiatric disorders.* New York: Simon & Schuster.Paunovic, N., & Ost, L-G (2001). Cognitive-behaviour therapy vs exposure therapy in the treatment of PTSD in refugees. *Behaviour Research & Therapy, 39,* 1183–1198.

Pearlin, L. (1985). Social structure and processes of social support. In S. Cohen & L. Syme (Eds.), *Social support and health* (pp. 43–60). Orlando, FL: Academic Press.

Pharoah, F. M., Mari, J. J., & Streiner, D. (2000). Family interventions for schizophrenia (Cochrane review). *The Cochrane Library, 1.* Oxford: Update software.

Pitschel-Waltz, G., Leucht, S., Bauml, J., Kissling, W., & Engel, R.R. (2001). The effect of family interventions on relapse and rehospitalisation in schizophrenia: A meta-analysis. *Schizophrenia Bulletin, 27,* 73–92.

Resick, P.A., & Schnicke, M.K. (1992). Cognitive processing therapy for sexual assault victims. *Journal of Consulting and Clinical Psychology, 60,* 748–756.

Rhodes, G. L., & Lakey, B. (1999). Social support and psychological disorder: Insights from social psychology. In R. M. Kowalski & M. R. Leary (Eds.), *The social psychology of emotional and behavioral problems: Interfaces of social and clinical psychology* (pp. 281–309). Washington, DC: American Psychological Association.

Salkovskis, P., M. (2002). Empirically grounded clinical interventions: Cognitive-behavioral therapy progresses through a multi-dimensional approach to clinical science. *Behavioral and Cognitive Psychotherapy, 30,* 3–10.

Solomon, Z., Mikulincer, M., & Hobfoll, S.E. (1987). Objective versus subjective measurement of stress and social support: Combat related reactions. *Journal of Consulting and Clinical Psychology, 55,* 577–583.

Swickert, R., Rosentreter C. J., Hittner, J. B., & Mushrush, J. E. (2002). Extraversion, social support processes and stress. *Personality and Individual Differences, 32,* 877–891.

Tarrier, N. (1996). An application of expressed emotion to the study of PTSD: Preliminary findings. *Clinical Psychology and Psychotherapy, 3,* 220–229.

Tarrier, N., Pilgrim, H.. Sommerfield, C., Farragher, E.B., Reynolds, M., Graham, E., et al., (1999). A randomized controlled trial of cognitive therapy and imaginal exposure in the treatment of chronic posttraumatic stress disorder. *Journal of Consulting and Clinical Psychology, 67,* 13–18.

Tarrier, N., Sommerfield, C., Pilgrim, H., & Humphreys, L. (1999). Twelve month follow-up of a trial of cognitive therapy or imaginal exposure in the treatment of PTSD. *British Journal of Psychiatry, 175,* 571–575.

Tarrier, N., Sommerfield, C. , & Pilgrim, H. (1999). The effect of the relatives' level of expressed emotion (EE) on the outcome of psychological treatment of PTSD patients. *Psychological Medicine, 29,* 801–812.

Tarrier, N., & Calam, R. (2002). New developments in cognitive-behavioral case formulation. Epidemiological, systemic and social context: An integrative approach. *Behavioral & Cognitive Psychotherapy, 30,* 335–352.

Tarrier, N., Barrowclough, C., Ward, J., Donaldson, C., & Burns, A. (2002). Expressed emotion and attributions in the carers of patients with Alzheimer's disease: The effect on carer burden. *Journal of Abnormal Psychology, 111,* 340–349.

Vachon, M., Lyall, W., Rogers, J., Freedman-Letofsky, K., & Freeman, S. (1980). A controlled study of a self-help intervention for widows. *American Journal of Psychiatry 137,* 1380–1384.

Wearden, A. J., Tarrier, N., Barrowclough, C., Zastowny, T. R., & Rahill, A. A. (2000). A review of expressed emotion research in health care. *Clinical Psychology Review, 20,* 633–666.

Chapter 8

COMBINING COGNITIVE RESTRUCTURING AND EXPOSURE THERAPY: TOWARD AN OPTIMAL INTEGRATION

Sally A. Moore, Lori A. Zoellner, and Joyce N. Bittinger

INTRODUCTION

Both cognitive and exposure therapies are highly effective for the treatment of chronic posttraumatic stress disorder (PTSD). In clinical practice, the integration of these therapies for treatment of this disorder is often quite common. However, in light of recent treatment outcome research indicating that their combination may not increase the efficacy of comprehensive exposure or cognitive monotherapies, clinicians are left wondering how to proceed. First, this chapter reviews theory and research on cognitive features common to PTSD. Second, this chapter reviews treatment outcome research that explores our ability to enhance patient response by combining cognitive and exposure approaches. Third, this chapter discusses advantages and disadvantages of combining these approaches. Finally, this chapter suggests some practical methods aimed at obtaining an "optimal integration" of exposure and cognitive interventions. While no simple answers are forthcoming regarding such optimal integration, clinicians are urged to use the information and recommendations that follow to guide their decision making about appropriate PTSD treatment.

This chapter was supported in part by the "Moving PTSD Treatment into the Real World" Grant awarded by the Anxiety Disorders Association of America to Lori A. Zoellner, PI, and by a National Research Scientist Award 1F31MH068050 from the National Institutes of Health, awarded to Sally A. Moore.

COGNITIVE THEORIES: CORE BELIEFS AND NEGATIVE INTERPRETATIONS

A variety of cognitive theorists posit that individuals core beliefs about themselves, others, and the world around them both prior to experiencing a traumatic event and the alterations of these core beliefs posttrauma impact whether individuals will develop long-term psychological difficulties such as PTSD and depression. Cason, Resick, and Weaver (2002) suggested that one of the ways to conceptualize current theories in this area is to differentiate between content-focused and process-focused theories.

Seminal content-focused theorists highlight the content of core schemas, or belief systems, in the development of posttrauma psychopathology. Although all content-focused theorists emphasize trauma-related cognitions, theorists vary on the precise substance of these core beliefs. Specifically, Janoff-Bulman (1989a,b, 1992) identified common themes of world benevolence, meaningfulness, and self-worth and proposed that traumatic experiences shatter fundamental assumptions about a safe and meaningful world. Similarly, Epstein (1991) emphasized four key beliefs that can change as a result of trauma exposure: (1a) the self is worthy, (b) people are trustworthy, (c) the world is benign, and (d) the world is meaningful. In contrast to these views of shattering positive beliefs, McCann and colleagues (McCann & Pearlman, 1990; McCann, Sakheim, & Abrahamson, 1988) identified five specific cognitive themes of safety, trust, power, esteem, and intimacy and posited that preexisting beliefs could be either positive or negative based on prior life experience. Trauma exposure then either further confirms preexisting negative beliefs or shatters positive ones. Overall, content-focused theorists postulate that certain core beliefs are susceptible to disruption via traumatic experiences and that the identification and reconciliation of these schemas are necessary for resolving posttrauma psychopathology.

In contrast, process-focused theorists emphasize the formation, activation, and modification of fear-related schemas (Cason et al., 2002). For example, emotional processing theory (e.g., Foa & Jaycox, 1999, Foa & Riggs, 1993) proposes that special efforts are required to process the traumatic event, and that the completion of processing is necessary for recovery. Thus, chronic psychological disturbances are viewed as signs that this processing has not occurred (Foa & Kozak, 1986; Rachman, 1980) and that the representation of the traumatic experience in memory contains pathological elements (Foa & Rothbaum, 1998). According to this theory, two dysfunctional cognitions underlie the development and maintenance of chronic PTSD: the conception of the world as completely dangerous and of oneself as totally incompetent. Individuals who have rigid pretrauma conceptions of the world and oneself (both positive and negative) are vulnerable to PTSD, whereas individuals who have a finer discrimination regarding safety and competence are more able to interpret the trauma as unique and without broader implications influencing their views of the world and their ability to cope.

In a similar vein, Ehlers and Clark's cognitive model (2000) emphasizes the role of current threat in the development of chronic PTSD. PTSD becomes persistent when individuals process the trauma in a way that leads to a sense of serious current threat. This model focuses on dysfunctional meanings attributed to PTSD symptoms themselves (i.e., intrusive thoughts) and suggests that these interpretations play an important role in the maintenance of the disorder. Ehlers and Clark (2000) hypothesize that these negative meanings (e.g., "These thoughts mean I'm insane/incompetent") increase the level of distress associated with the intrusions and determine the extent of cognitive and behavioral avoidance. As with emotional processing theory, this conceptualization suggests that cognitive interventions for PTSD should focus on trauma-related negative or distorted perceptions of across domains, such as symptoms, self, others, and the world.

Evidence regarding negative interpretations and PTSD

Along with the theoretical emphasis on the role of negative interpretations, research is emerging suggesting a pivotal role of these cognitive factors in the development and maintenance of chronic PTSD. Specifically, the way an individual interprets initial PTSD symptoms (e.g., "I am going crazy," "I will never recover") predicts the development of chronic PTSD, beyond what can be accounted for by initial symptom severity (e.g., Dunmore, Clark, & Ehlers, 2001; Ehlers, Mayou, & Bryant, 1998). In a similar vein, Andrews, Brewin, Rose, and Kirk (2000) found that shame predicted the course of PTSD symptoms, also beyond what can be accounted for by initial severity. Indeed, other cognitive variables have also been empirically implicated in the development of chronic PTSD such as guilt, alienation, and perception of permanent change (e.g., Ehlers, Maercker, & Boos, 2000).

Individual differences in the interpretation of the traumatic experience and its sequelae have also been shown to discriminate between trauma victims with PTSD and those without (Foa, Ehlers, et al., 1999). Cognitions that discriminate between these groups include cognitions about the self, negative cognitions about the world, and self-blame on the Posttraumatic Cognitions Inventory (PTCI; Foa et al., 1999); beliefs about the self, others, safety, undoing, trust, power, esteem, intimacy and self-blame on the Personal Beliefs and Reactions Scale (PBRS; Resick, Schnicke, & Markway, 1991); and assumptions about justice, benevolence of the world, self-worth, luck, and self-controllability on the World Assumptions Scale (Janoff-Bulman, 1989a, 1992). Thus, a number of cognitive variables discriminate between individuals with and without PTSD. Furthermore, both the PBRS and the PTCI subscales are sensitive to PTSD treatment effects, changing with successful PTSD treatment (Foa, 1997; Resick, Nishith, Weaver, Astin, & Feuer, 2002; Resick & Schnicke, 1992).

EFFICACY OF COMBINING COGNITIVE AND EXPOSURE THERAPY

Given both the growing theoretical and research emphasis on the role of cognition, treatment approaches have often sought to directly or indirectly target core dysfunctional cognitions in the treatment of chronic PTSD. In the following section, we will briefly review the efficacy of various cognitive behavioral treatments, highlighting combined cognitive and exposure therapy approaches.

Cognitive therapies typically directly focus on the identification, evaluation, and modification of trauma-related cognitive distortions; whereas exposure therapies directly focus on engagement and habituation with feared trauma reminders, incorporating imaginal exposure (i.e., repeated recounting of the traumatic experience) and in vivo exposure (i.e., systematic approaching of nondangerous, previously avoided trauma reminders). Both cognitive and exposure therapies are effective in significantly reducing chronic PTSD and related symptoms such as anxiety and depression, with treatment gains lasting over time (see Harvey, Bryant, & Tarrier, 2003). Furthermore, these treatments are effective across a variety of precipitating trauma experiences (Devilly & Spence, 1999; Foa, Dancu, et al., 1999; Marks, Lovell, Norshirvani, Livanou, & Thrasher, 1998; Taylor et al., 2001). When cognitive and exposure therapies are directly compared, the treatments usually show comparable symptom reduction (Marks et al., 1998; Resick et al., 2002; Tarrier et al., 1999). Yet, while each monotherapy is generally highly effective and well tolerated, not all patients experience significant symptom reduction. Indeed, theorists have postulated that some individuals may have idiosyncratic symptom patterns that are better addressed through the use of treatments more specifically targeting maladaptive cognitions or learning patterns (e.g., Tarrier et al., 1999).

As such, in an effort to increase the efficacy of our current therapies, studies have begun to examine the impact of augmenting exposure-based treatment with cognitive techniques, such as cognitive restructuring (CR), with the idea that adding such components may increase treatment effectiveness (Bryant, Moulds, Guthrie, Dang, & Nixon, 2003; Foa et al., 1999; Foa, Rothbaum, & Furr, 2003; Marks et al., 1998; Paunovic & Ost, 2001). This "augmentation hypothesis" was first tested in a randomized controlled study by Marks et al. (1998). Specifically, for men and women with chronic PTSD, prolonged exposure (PE, including imaginal and in vivo exposure), CR, and their combination (PE/CR) were compared to a relaxation only control condition. Contrary to the augmentation hypothesis, all three active treatments showed similar reductions in PTSD symptoms and each produced greater symptom reduction than relaxation. Furthermore, no differences appeared through 6-month follow-up.

In a second augmentation study, Foa and colleagues (1999) compared PE, stress inoculation training (SIT; including a cognitive restructuring component), a combined PE/SIT treatment, and a waitlist control condition in female assault survivors with chronic PTSD. Rather than supporting their main hypothesis that the combined treatment would produce an additive benefit, results were very similar to those seen in Marks et al. (1998): all active treatments produced comparable outcome. Observed differences between active treatments were minor, with modest evidence for the superiority of PE alone in terms of overall effect sizes. Furthermore, no differences on PTSD severity, depression, or end-state functioning appeared through 12-month follow-up.

Importantly, in Foa et al. (1999), SIT only included a small component of cognitive restructuring. In order to more specifically address the augmentation of exposure with cognitive therapy, in a subsequent study, Foa and colleagues (Foa et al., 2003) directly compared PE alone, the combination of PE and CR (PE/CR), and a wait-list control in female assault victims with chronic PTSD. Again, contrary to the augmentation hypothesis, preliminary analyses indicated that PE and PE/CR produced comparable treatment gains across a variety of outcome measures and that both treatments were more effective than the wait-list control. In addition, no differences appeared through the 1-year follow-up.

In a smaller augmentation study, Paunovic and Ost (2001) compared exposure-only (imaginal and in vivo exposure) therapy to cognitive-behavioral therapy (CBT, including both exposure and cognitive therapy) in Swedish refugees with chronic PTSD. Again, both intervention groups showed comparable decreases in PTSD symptoms, generalized anxiety, and depression at posttreatment and through the 6-month follow-up period.

In summary, across four well-controlled studies (Foa et al., 1999; Foa et al., 2003; Marks et al., 1998; Paunovic & Ost, 2001), no additional benefits of including cognitive components were seen above the impact of exposure therapy alone (imaginal and in vivo exposure). Furthermore, in one study (Marks et al., 1998) no additive benefits of including exposure could be seen above cognitive therapy alone.

However, the picture changes slightly when studies examine dismantling exposure therapy into either its imaginal or in vivo components. In one such dismantling study, Bryant and colleagues (2003) compared imaginal exposure alone (IE), IE combined with CR (IE/CR), and a supportive counseling control condition in male and female nonsexual assault and motor vehicle accident victims with chronic PTSD. Participants in both IE and IE/CR showed a marked reduction in PTSD related symptoms beyond those seen in supportive counseling. Consistent with the augmentation hypothesis, however, combined therapy (IE/CR) showed a greater reduction in PTSD symptom intensity and maladaptive coping style than IE alone. Thus, when imaginal exposure was used in isolation, the inclusion of cognitive restructuring increased therapeutic efficacy. Bryant recently reported results from another dismantling study comparing imaginal exposure alone, in vivo exposure alone, their combination, and supportive counseling (Bryant, 2003). Interestingly, patients receiving in vivo exposure alone and supportive counseling therapies had smaller reductions in symptoms than those in the imaginal exposure alone therapy, who in turn had smaller reductions than those in the combined imaginal and in vivo exposure therapy. Thus, in comparison to imaginal exposure alone, the delivery of in vivo exposure plus imaginal exposure increased therapeutic efficacy.

Overall, as we reviewed previously, studies that have attempted to examine the efficacy of augmenting exposure therapy with cognitive therapy for PTSD consistently are unable to detect advantages of such augmentation. In contrast, when exposure therapy is broken into separate imaginal and in vivo components, augmenting imaginal exposure with either in vivo exposure or cognitive restructuring does appear to enhance its efficacy. Accordingly, the "optimal integration" of cognitive restructuring and exposure therapy may not be necessary, as the combination of cognitive restructuring and exposure therapy (using both in vivo and imaginal exposure components) typically does not fair better than either monotherapy alone. Furthermore, pretreatment predictors of who would benefit from one type of therapy or the combination are also elusive (e.g., Tarrier, Sommerfield, Pilgrim, & Faragher, 2000). However, our ability to explore the question of what works for whom is limited by a couple of factors. First, thankfully, the *majority* of patients in CBT trials are making good clinical gains. Second, the treatment trials to date are not powered to detect individual differences in responses to particular treatments. Thus, in most cases, even if real differences exist, they may not be detectable or clinically meaningful.

Combining Cognitive and Exposure Therapies: Advantages and Disadvantages

It also should be noted though that the combination of cognitive and exposure therapies does not generally appear to hurt outcome: patients are improving within the same number of sessions and making comparable treatment gains. In addition, as we noted in the introduction, in clinical practice, the combination of these therapies for the treatment of PTSD is quite common. Therefore, it is worthwhile to consider the therapeutic advantages and disadvantages of their combination. On the one hand, combining cognitive restructuring and exposure therapy in the treatment of PTSD has intuitive appeal, including specifically addressing the cognitive components of PTSD and providing an additional avenue through which change can occur. Moreover, some postulate that their combination may increase the tolerability of the treatment and increase therapy effectiveness and efficiency. On the other hand, others have urged caution when considering their combination, citing evidence that CR may not add to the effectiveness of the therapy and that the transportability and intellectual requirements of these therapies are areas of concern. The evidence and discourse surrounding these claims will be reviewed in the following.

One of the potential advantages of combining exposure and cognitive restructuring is that cognitive restructuring may increase the tolerability of exposure. Indeed, some have expressed concern about the tolerability of exposure, particularly imaginal exposure; and research suggests that for a minority of patients, symptom exacerbation at the onset of imaginal exposure occurs (Foa, Zoellner, Feeny, Hembree, & Alvarez-Conrad, 2002). Additionally, therapists themselves may experience distress at the onset of imaginal exposure (e.g., et al., 2003), possibly resulting in "vicarious traumatization." However, several lines of research do not support the hypothesis that the addition of CR increases the tolerability of imaginal exposure. First, if exposure therapy alone is indeed more difficult to tolerate for patients, treatment dropout should be higher in exposure-based–therapies than in therapies that do not include exposure components. Hembree and colleagues (Hembree, et al., in press) recently completed a comprehensive analysis of PTSD treatment research addressing the issue of differential dropout. While active treatments had higher rates of dropout compared to the control conditions, no differences in drop out rates were found between exposure and non-exposure–based treatments. Furthermore, in studies that directly compare therapies with and without exposure components, there is typically no reliable difference in dropout rates (Foa et al., 1999; Marks et al., 1998; Nishith, Resick, & Griffin, 2002; Resick et al., 2002). Second, if cognitive components help reduce distress during exposure, patterns of symptom exacerbation may be different between therapies that do and do not include cognitive components. However, Nishith et al. (2002) found similar patterns of initial exacerbation preceding symptom reduction in prolonged exposure and cognitive processing therapy, a primarily cognitive therapy with modest exposure elements. Thus, treatment dropout rates and patterns of recovery over time appear generally comparable, arguing against the notion that combined treatments increase tolerability. For patients with significantly impaired affect tolerance, however, in particular there is still the potential that cognitive therapy, alone or in combination with exposure, would be less emotionally distressing than exposure alone.

As previously discussed, another hypothesized advantage of adding cognitive components to exposure therapy is that the combination may result in greater symptom reduction. Specifically, the addition of cognitive components may further reduce overall symptoms such as PTSD, depression, and anxiety beyond what is seen in exposure therapies alone, or it may specifically reduce particular cognitive symptoms identified in PTSD. As we have already reviewed, however, enhancement of overall symptom reduction with the addition of CR to exposure therapy has not received strong empirical support. Interestingly, the possibility of greater reductions on *specific cognitive symptoms* with combined treatment has also been examined. For example, Lovell, Marks, Norshirvani, Thrasher,

& Livanou (2001) reported on data from the augmentation study conducted by Marks et al. (1998) but focused explicitly on potential differences in specific cognitive symptom reduction (including cognitive symptoms such as guilt, hopelessness, and disillusionment with authority) across the three treatment groups. No differences across treatments emerged, with the exception of one detachment item. The authors concluded that there was no evidence to support selection of cognitive or exposure-based therapies based on particular symptoms and features of PTSD (Lovell et al., 2001). Similarly, in a study comparing cognitive processing therapy to prolonged exposure therapy (Resick et al., 2002), both therapies evidenced comparable reduction across cognitive variables, with the exception of two subscales assessing guilt, where there was an advantage in favor of cognitive therapy. As with the Lovell et al. (2001) study, the importance of this finding is not inherently apparent and further information is needed in order to assess whether these reported differences are replicable or clinically meaningful. Finally, Foa et al. (2003) reported that both PE and PE/CR decrease negative cognitions concerning the self, others, and the world, with neither therapy emerging as superior. Cleary, further investigation is needed to elucidate the effects of cognitive and exposure components on both psychopathology symptoms and erroneous cognitions, specifically examining whether any differences have clinically meaningful implications such as decreasing the likelihood of relapse over time. However, there is currently little evidence demonstrating that treatment selection, namely including (or not including) cognitive components based on specific symptom or cognitive profiles, is possible. Despite the fact that our intervention studies up until this point have not been powered to detect individual differences, it is still possible that for specific patients (e.g., those with extremely negative, pervasive trauma-related cognitions) the combination of exposure and cognitive therapies would be more beneficial than either therapy alone.

One possible disadvantage of combining treatments is the difficulty that learning multiple treatment methods may pose to therapists. Combined exposure and cognitive restructuring may be less transportable to practitioners in the community compared with exposure or cognitive therapy alone, given the need to master both techniques as well as the integration of the two. Indeed, therapists in the Marks et al. (1998) study indicated that the combination of exposure and cognitive restructuring was more difficult to conduct than either alone. They also reported that exposure alone was easier for therapists than cognitive restructuring. It may be that exposure is a more clearly delineated, teachable process in that the procedures are comparable across types of trauma exposure and modalities (in vivo/imaginal) and may therefore be easier to learn, whereas cognitive restructuring can vary widely in content depending on the particular client's beliefs and experiences. However, dissemination studies of treatments for PTSD are in their infancy and little information exists at this time regarding the ease or difficulty with which therapists learn various treatment modalities.

Another possible disadvantage for the combination of exposure and cognitive restructuring components is the abstract intellectual capabilities and insight that cognitive restructuring requires from patients. Given that patients with PTSD often display attention difficulties, memory impairments, and generally lower cognitive abilities, it may be difficult for some to identify, evaluate, and generate rational alternatives to cognitive distortions. When cognitive therapies and exposure therapies are directly compared, however, differences do not emerge, arguing against this hypothesis. Still, PTSD patients with extreme attention, memory, and overall cognitive difficulties may not be good candidates for cognitive restructuring. More research is needed to investigate the interaction between these obstacles and cognitive therapy procedures.

In conclusion, therapists need to think carefully about the potential advantages and disadvantages of combining treatment approaches. Utilizing more treatment techniques is not necessarily better. For most patients with PTSD, as discussed previously, the combination of exposure and cognitive therapies does *not* appear necessary. Current monotherapies are effective across a variety of patients, even among those with severe trauma histories, multiple comorbidities, and severe symptom presentations. To be cautious though, given the relative infancy of our current knowledge about predictors of treatment efficacy for *individuals,* the combination of both or the differential preference for one treatment or the other *may* be warranted for patients with very extreme symptom presentations, such as severely impaired distress tolerance, excessive dysfunctional cognitions, and severe cognitive impairment.

WHAT IS THE "OPTIMAL INTEGRATION" OF COGNITIVE RESTRUCTURING AND EXPOSURE THERAPY?

To reiterate, available data report that "optimal integration" of cognitive restructuring and exposure therapy is, at best, an elusive, and at worst, an unnecessary pursuit. From a practical perspective, lack of differences across cognitive, exposure, or combination therapies is very good news to the clinician with expertise in one modality or the other: A clinician with expertise in imaginal and in vivo exposure for PTSD should use this therapy as a first line intervention, and a clinician with expertise in cognitive therapy for PTSD should use it as a first-line intervention. Thus, in many respects, the optimal integration may not include integration at all. That said, in reality, the differentiation between cognitive and exposure therapies may set up a false dichotomy, incorrectly assuming that cognitive components are ignored in exposure therapy and that behavioral components are ignored in cognitive therapy. We would argue, instead, that often the distinction between cognitive and exposure therapists is one of emphasis, and that many therapists, even within each modality, seek "optimal integration" of cognitive and exposure components. Accordingly, in the following section, we will review several clinical methods aimed at obtaining this integration, including assessment and psychoeducation regarding core cognitive distortions, formal cognitive restructuring techniques, and the integration of these techniques in both imaginal and in vivo exposure. Finally, we will conclude with a discussion of general principles from the cognitive literature that can be incorporated to enhance treatment efficacy.

Identification of Core Cognitive Distortions and Psychoeducation

One of the best ways for a therapist to initially understand a patient's erroneous cognitions is via formal assessment. Fortunately, a variety of psychometrically validated measures exist that allow clinicians to have a sense for key cognitive distortions. These include the Posttraumatic Cognitions Inventory (PTCI; Foa, Ehlers et al., 1999), the World Assumptions Scale (WAS; Janoff-Bulman, 1989a, 1992), the Personal Beliefs and Reactions Scale (PBRS; Resick et al., 1991), and the Trauma-Related Guilt Inventory (TRGI; Kubany et al., 1996). All of these measures are relatively brief, and thus clinically it is possible to give all of them to patients. However, this is probably overly time consuming and redundant, given the convergent validity among measures and subscales. With these measures, it is helpful to be aware of both normative and relative scores. Normative scores help place a particular patient within a larger context (e.g., on "self-blame," this patient is substantially elevated compared with other individuals with chronic PTSD). Relative scores allow for the identification and exploration of the more salient cognitive themes for a particular patient (e.g., although this patient is substantially elevated on all subscales, "negative cognitions about world" shows greater elevation than the other subscales). For convergent validity and normative information on the PTCI, WAS, and PBRS, see Foa, Ehlers, et al., (1999).

A common component of treatment regimens for PTSD is education about the nature of trauma response and trauma-related symptoms. This psychoeducation normally occurs within the first two treatment sessions and, as such, is an opportunity to both assess and address patients' cognitive distortions. Typically, psychoeducation is primarily didactic and highlights common reactions following trauma exposure, including the definition of PTSD, the role of fear and anxiety, the description of other common symptoms (e.g., depression, guilt, shame), and common maladaptive shifts in beliefs about oneself, the world, and other people. Psychoeducation often directly addresses several common cognitive distortions, as trauma victims are often confused and upset by the persistence of symptoms, and they often view this persistence as a sign that they are no longer in control, or that they are inadequate or weak in some way. By allowing psychoeducation about common reactions to trauma to be interactive, the therapist may further gain insight into persistent cognitive themes.

Teaching Patients Formal Cognitive Restructuring

Depending on the expertise or preference of the therapist, *formal* cognitive restructuring may or may not be introduced during the initial stages of treatment. The main focus of formal cognitive restructuring is to help the patient to identify, evaluate, and modify negative thoughts such as the ones outlined previously. As suggested by cognitive theorists and just discussed in more detail, common themes include negative views about oneself, the world, and the future. Examples of dysfunctional thoughts include: "I can't trust anyone," "I should have been able to prevent the trauma," "I need to be in control at all times," and "I must be a bad person or this wouldn't have happened to me." Additionally, therapists should look for dramatic shifts in thinking (e.g., "I thought I was invulnerable, but now I know that I can be hurt at any time") or for confirmation of previously held beliefs (e.g., "Bad things always happen to me").

One of the easiest ways of teaching cognitive restructuring is using the A-B-C model for automatic thoughts, where A = antecedent, B = belief, and C = consequences (Beck, Rush, Shaw, & Emery, 1979). When teaching the A-B-C model, it is important to illustrate to the patient how a particular event (e.g., a loud noise in the other room) can be interpreted in different ways (e.g., "Someone is breaking into my home!" or "What did the dog break this time?") can lead to utterly distinct emotional responses (e.g., fear or anger). Often an example such as the one just given is useful in illustrating this relationship. After a general example, it is helpful to have the patient provide a personal example of a recent emotion-evoking situation. The therapist then often uses a worksheet to help identify the situation, the feelings and their intensity, and the negative thoughts or images that occurred. The rationality/helpfulness of the beliefs is then assessed by challenging them using a series of questions (e.g., "What evidence do you have for this thought?", "How would someone else look at the situation?"), and then replacing them with more realistic thoughts. More specifically for PTSD, for example, Resick and Schnicke (1993) seek to identify incongruities between prior beliefs and the traumatic event, terming these incongruities as "stuck points" and teaching their patients cognitive therapy techniques (e.g., Beck & Emery, 1985) to address the incongruities without blaming themselves or over-generalizing. The goal over the course of therapy is for the patient to learn how to identify negative thoughts, to challenge these negative thoughts, and to be able to generate more rational responses throughout their lives. Detailed descriptions of how to conduct cognitive restructuring may be found in Beck and Emory (1985), Resick and Schnicke (1993), and Foa and Rothbaum (1998), with the latter two references more specifically oriented to cognitive restructuring and PTSD.

Incorporating Cognitive Restructuring During Imaginal and In Vivo Exposure

One of the clear advantages of teaching formal cognitive restructuring skills is that the patient then can draw upon these skills, when necessary, during imaginal exposure (i.e., repeated recounting of the traumatic experience) and in vivo exposure (i.e., systematic approaching of nondangerous, previously avoided trauma reminders). As discussed previously, however, formal cognitive restructuring does not appear to be a necessary component when using both imaginal and in vivo exposure. However, if a therapist is planning on using *only* imaginal exposure or *only* in vivo exposure, the addition of formal cognitive restructuring may provide additive treatment gains. Regardless of whether a therapist incorporates formal cognitive restructuring or not, it is helpful to be aware of and address persistent cognitive themes that emerge over the course of exposure therapy. Foa and Rothbaum (1998) provide detailed descriptions of how to conduct both imaginal and in vivo exposure. Although they focus on treating the psychological consequences following rape, the information they provide can easily be generalized to other types of trauma events. Basic principles seen in their work and others to remember when conducting either form of exposure include the collaborative relationship between therapist and patient in deciding when, where, and how to approach feared stimuli (i.e., a strong therapeutic alliance); the necessity of the patient choosing to approach the feared situation (i.e., never forced or coerced); the therapist's responsibility to help modulate patient distress (i.e., designing and modifying exposures so that the patient is neither over- or underengaged); and the necessity for both extended and repeated exposure to the fear provoking stimuli for fear reduction (i.e., allowing enough time and practice). Additional clinical resources in this area are Feeny, Hembree, and Zoellner (2003), Hembree, Marshall, Fitzgibbons, and Foa (2001), and Jaycox, Zoellner, and Foa (2002).

With both imaginal and in vivo exposure, the therapist needs to pay particular attention to persistent cognitive themes that emerge over the course of therapy. During imaginal exposure, the therapist should be aware of both the *content* and the *emotions* aroused during recounting of the trauma memory. Often it is helpful to write brief notes during imaginal exposure so that important aspects of the trauma memory or the recounting experience can be discussed following its completion. For example, a patient may rush through an important section of the trauma narrative and his or her mood may shift from fear to sadness. Further discussion of this experience may bring up themes of guilt or shame and stimulate more informal cognitive restructuring. Furthermore, awareness of salient dysfunctional themes often helps the therapist shift the emphasis of the imaginal exposure over the course of sessions to particular "hot spots," where imaginal exposure narrows to particular aspects of the trauma memory. In the example just given, during imaginal exposure, the therapist would encourage the patient to considerably slow down the recounting during this section of the narrative, increasing focus on thoughts and feelings; over the course of the therapy, the therapist would encourage the patient to repeat this section over and over rather than recounting the whole narrative; and at the end of each imaginal exposure, the therapist and patient would spend time discussing feelings of guilt or shame. Thus, often the awareness of dysfunctional beliefs helps guide important therapeutic choices and points of emphasis during imaginal exposure.

Similarly, during in vivo exposure, the therapist also should pay careful attention to persistent cognitive themes that emerge over the course of therapy; these themes may also guide decision making regarding choice of in vivo exposure assignments. Often, exposure assignments can be structured around cognitive themes (e.g., increasing sense of competence) rather than content themes (e.g., going to shopping malls). In many respects, exposure assignments aimed at shifting cognitive distortions across a variety of content areas (a shopping mall, a bank, a bar) may be as important to recovery as the functional benefit of regaining the ability to do these tasks without extreme distress. Another method to integrate formal or informal cognitive restructuring skills into in vivo exposure is its use as a form of "self talk" during in vivo exposure assignments. This self talk can be used to help patients approach a situation ("Before the assault, I went to the mall all the time."), stay in the exposure situation ("I know it's bad now, but my fear usually decreases over time"), and reevaluate the situation or oneself after the exposure ("I did it. I really am not as incompetent as I thought I was"). Thus, by including cognitive restructuring skills, either formally or more informally, the therapist either may help increase the relevance of the in vivo exposure assignments or may help the patient more successfully accomplish these assignments.

General Therapeutic Principles Based on Cognitive Information Processing Abnormalities in PTSD

Finally, individuals with PTSD evidence several information-processing difficulties that have clear implications for how we conduct our current therapies. Understanding these deficits has direct clinical implications, leading to practical suggestions that may be incorporated to optimize overall treatment efficacy. In the following section, we will review general memory deficits, automatic/strategic processing deficits, and autobiographical memory deficits often seen in individuals with PTSD and discuss general therapeutic strategies to address these deficits.

Individuals with PTSD evidence *memory deficits* in a variety of domains. For example, these deficits have been found in areas of attention, short-term memory, verbal memory, and retroactive interference (see Buckley, Blanchard, Neill, 2000, for a review). Recognizing these possible deficits, therapeutic work often should be adjusted to maximize retention of relevant information. For example, the therapist can give the patient written educational materials (e.g., handouts describing typical posttrauma reactions) to highlight issues covered during therapy, and the therapist should ensure that homework assignments are written down before ending a session. In addition, therapists can review each session's most important themes, repeating and summarizing key information. These therapeutic techniques and others aimed at maximizing cognitive retention can help prevent patients from becoming overwhelmed and discouraged by the demands of CBT treatment.

Individuals with PTSD also tend to display *deficits in the automatic and strategic processing of information* (Beck, Freeman, Shipherd, Hamblen, & Lackner, 2001; Bryant & Harvey, 1995; Buckley, Blanchard, & Hickling, 2002; Foa, Feske, Murdock, Kozak, & McCarthy, 1991; Harvey et al., 2003). Automatic processing refers to processing of information that is involuntary, fast, and occurs without conscious awareness (Buckley et al., 2000; McNally, 1998). For example, intrusive memories in PTSD may often involve automatic processes in which external or internal cues trigger the traumatic memory regardless of one's efforts to inhibit the intrusion. Strategic processing refers to processing of information that has greater conscious control, is slower, and is sequential in nature. For example, avoidance symptoms seen in PTSD may often involve strategic processes, whereby the individual with PTSD consciously avoids situations or distracts themselves from thoughts or feelings associated with trauma reminders. Therapeutically, helping the patient understand the varying nature of PTSD symptoms, some being more automatic and others being more strategic, is often helpful in the psychoeducation phase of treatment. Indeed, understanding the distinction between automatic and strategic processing of information often facilitates the explanation of the "out of the blue" nature of some symptoms. Furthermore, this understanding also helps normalize the patient's experience of feeling out of control, often further helping reduce self-blame and guilt about PTSD symptoms.

Finally, individuals with PTSD also often display *deficits in autobiographical memory retrieval* (i.e., memories for personal life events). Specifically, impaired voluntary retrieval of specific, positive autobiographical memories (McNally, Lasko, Macklin, & Pitman, 1995; McNally, Litz, Prassas, Shin, & Weathers, 1994) is evident in both PTSD and depression (for a review, see Williams, 1995). Thus, it is often difficult for individuals with PTSD to remember details about positive life experiences, whereas details about negative life experiences are more easily retrieved. During therapy, patients with PTSD may tend to focus on their personal failures rather than their successes. When patients make significant advances in therapy, it may be necessary for the therapist to remind them of these successes and of other positive experiences. Furthermore, in clinical populations, this type of overgeneral retrieval is associated with problem-solving difficulties (Evans, Williams, O'Loughlin, & Howells, 1992; Sidley, Whitaker, Calam, & Wells, 1997). Problem-solving impairments present a variety of obstacles for patients, which can be addressed therapeutically. For example, the therapist can specify when and how homework will be conducted, examine complications that may interfere with homework completion or session attendance, and develop plans for carrying out other difficult or new tasks.

Ultimately, by understanding some of the cognitive information processing deficits seen in individuals with PTSD, the therapist can modify procedures to enhance retention of information, better explain various symptom presentations, highlight gains made during treatment, and address problem solving difficulties ahead of time. In summary, the awareness of the possible limitations of these patients and the modification of therapeutic procedures to address these limitations can lead to more effective, validating, and appropriate PTSD treatment.

CONCLUSION

Through some may be discouraged by the apparent lack of evidence for the additive efficacy of combining treatments, the news is actually quite good. As stated previously, comprehensive cognitive and exposure monotherapies generally appear equivalent in terms of efficacy, meaning that it does not seem necessary to combine therapies to benefit our patients. As stated earlier, if one is a successful cognitive therapist, or a successful exposure therapist, each of these approaches to the treatment of PTSD is empirically supported and therefore represents the highest standards of care. Therefore, as a therapeutic community, we have the freedom to focus on issues such as ease of training, treatment transportability, therapist preference, and patient preference in making choices between exposure and cognitive therapies. In addition, in routine clinical practice, it is now possible to monitor and compare individual patient patterns of outcome to those seen in controlled trials (e.g., Nishith et al., 2002). Thus, clients identified as "delayed" or "partial responders" may benefit additionally from the introduction of formal augmentation procedures. It may be through case reports of treatment tailoring that we gain vital insight into the most beneficial shifts of techniques with individual PTSD and personality presentations.

REFERENCES

Andrews, B, Beck, A. T., & Emery, G. (1985). *Anxiety disorders and phobias: A cognitive perspective.* New York: Basic Books.

Beck, A. T., Rush, A. J., Shaw, B. F., & Emery, G. (1979). *Cognitive therapy of depression.* New York: Guilford Press.

Beck, J. G., Freeman, J. B., Shipherd, J. C., Hamblen, J. L., & Lackner, J. M. (2001). Specificity of Stroop interference in patients with pain and PTSD. *Journal of Abnormal Psychology, 110,* 536–543.

Bryant, R. A., Moulds, M. L., Guthrie, R. M., Dang, S. T., & Nixon, R. D. V. (2003). Imaginal exposure alone and imaginal exposure with cognitive restructuring in treatment of posttraumatic stress disorder. *Journal of Consulting and Clinical Psychology, 71,* 706–712.

Bryant, R. (2003, October). *Imaginal exposure vs. in vivo exposure in treating PTSD.* Paper presented at the International Society for Traumatic Stress Studies. Chicago, IL.

Bryant, R.A,, & Harvey, A.G. (1995). Processing threatening information in posttraumatic stress disorders: *Journal of Abnormal Psychology. 104.* 537–541.

Buckley, T. C., Blanchard, E. B., & Hickling, E. J. (2002). Automatic and strategic processing of threat stimuli: A comparison between PTSD, panic disorder, and nonanxiety controls. *Cognitive Therapy & Research, 26,* 97–115.

Buckley, T. C., Blanchard, E. B., & Neill, W. T. (2000). Information processing and PTSD: A review of the empirical literature. *Clinical Psychology Review, 28,* 1041–1065.

Cason, D., Resick, P., & Weaver, T. (2002). Schematic integration of traumatic events. *Clinical Psychology Review, 22,* 131–153.

Devilly, G. J., & Spence, S. H. (1999). The relative efficacy and treatment distress of EMDR and a cognitive-behavior trauma treatment protocol in the amelioration of posttraumatic stress disorder. *Journal of Anxiety Disorders, 13,* 131–157.

Dunmore, E., Clark, D. M., & Ehlers, A. (2001). A prospective investigation of the role of cognitive factors in persistent posttraumatic stress disorder (PTSD) after physical or sexual assault. *Behaviour Research & Therapy, 39,* 1063–1084.

Ehlers, A. & Clark, D. M. (2000). A cognitive model of posttraumatic stress disorder. *Behaviour Research & Therapy, 38,* 319–345.

Ehlers, A., Maercker, A., & Boos, A. (2000). Posttraumatic stress disorder following political imprisonment: The role of mental defeat, alienation, and perceived permanent change. *Journal of Abnormal Psychology, 109,* 45–55.

Ehlers, A., Mayou, R. A., & Bryant, B. (1998). Psychological predictors of chronic posttraumatic stress disorder after motor vehicle accidents. *Journal of Abnormal Psychology, 107*, 508–519.

Epstein, S. (1991). Impulse control and self destructive behavior. In L. P. Lipsitt & L. L. Mitick (Eds.), *Self regulatory behavior and risk taking: Causes and consequences* (pp. 273–249). Norwood, NJ: Ablex.

Evans, J., Williams, J. M. G., O'Loughlin, S., & Howells, K. (1992). Autobiographical memory and problem-solving strategies of parasuicide patients. *Psychological Medicine, 22*, 399–405.

Feeny, N. C., Hembree, E. A., & Zoellner, L. A. (2003). Myths regarding exposure therapy for PTSD. *Cognitive and Behavioral Practice, 10*, 85–90.

Foa, E. B. (1997). Psychological processes related to recovery from a trauma and an effective treatment for PTSD. In R. Yehuda & A. McFarlane (Eds.), *Psychobiology of posttraumatic stress disorder. Annals of the New York Academy of Sciences, 821* (pp. 410–424). New York: New York Academy of Sciences.

Foa, E. B., Dancu, C. V., Hembree, E. A., Jaycox, L. H., Meadows, E. A., & Street, G. P. (1999). A comparison of exposure therapy, stress inoculation training, and their combination for reducing posttraumatic stress disorder in female assault victims. *Journal of Consulting and Clinical Psychology, 67*, 194–200.

Foa, E. B., Ehlers, A., Clark, D., & Tolin, D. F, & Orsillo, S. (1999). Posttraumatic cognitions inventory (PTCI): Development and comparison with other measures. *Psychological Assessment, 11*, 303–314.

Foa, E. B., Feske, U., Murdock, T. B., Kozak, M. J., & McCarthy, P. R. (1991). Processing of threat-related information in rape victims. *Journal of Abnormal Psychology, 100*, 156–162.

Foa, E. B., & Jaycox, L. (1999). Cognitive-behavioral theory and treatment of posttraumatic stress disorder. In D. Spiegel (Ed), *Efficacy and cost-effectiveness of psychotherapy. Clinical practice;* Vol. 45 (23–61). Washington, DC: American Psychiatric Press.

Foa, E. B., & Kozak, M. J. (1986). Emotional processing of fear: Exposure to corrective information. *Psychological Bulletin, 99*, 20–35.

Foa, E.B., & Riggs, D. S. (1993). Posttraumatic stress disorder in rape victims. In J. Oldham, M. B. Riba, & A. Tasman (Eds.) *American psychiatric press review of psychiatry,* Vol. 12 (pp. 273–303). Washington, D. C.: American Psychiatric Press.

Foa, E. B., & Rothbaum, B. O. (1998). *Treating the trauma of rape: Cognitive behavioral therapy for PTSD.* New York: Guilford Press.

Foa, E. B., Rothbaum, B. O., & Furr, J. M. (2003). Is the efficacy of exposure therapy for posttraumatic stress disorder augmented with the addition of other cognitive behavior therapy procedures? *Psychiatric Annals, 33*, 1–7.

Foa, E. B., Zoellner, L. A., Feeny, N. C., Hembree, E. A., & Alvarez-Conrad, J. (2002). Does imaginal exposure exacerbate PTSD symptoms? *Journal of Consulting and Clinical Psychology, 70*, 1022–1028.

Harvey, A. G., Bryant, R. A., & Rapee, R. M. (1996). Preconscious processing of threat in posttraumatic stress disorder. *Cognitive Therapy and Research, 20*, 613–623.

Harvey, A. G., Bryant, R. A., & Tarrier, N. (2003). Cognitive behaviour therapy for posttraumatic stress disorder, *Clinical Psychology Review, 23,* 501–522.

Hembree, E. A., Foa, E. B., Dorfan, N. M., Street, G. P., Kowalski, J., & Tu, X. (in press). Do patients drop out prematurely from exposure therapy for PTSD? *Journal of Traumatic Stress.*

Hembree, E. A., Marshall, R., Fitzgibbons, L., & Foa, E. B. (2001). The difficult to treat PTSD patient. In M. Dewan & R. Pies (Eds.), *The difficult to treat psychiatric patient (pp.149–178).* Washington, DC: American Psychiatric Press.

Hembree, E. A., Rauch, S. A.M., & Foa, E. B. (2003). Beyond the manual: The insider's guide to prolonged exposure therapy for PTSD. *Cognitive & Behavioral Practice, 10* (1), 22–30.

Janoff-Bulman, R. (1989a). Assumptive worlds and the stress of traumatic events: applications of the schema construct. *Social Cognition, 7,* 113–136.

Janoff-Bulman, R. (1989b). The benefits of illusions, the threat of disillusionment, and the limitations of inaccuracy. *Journal of Social and Clinical Psychology, 8,* 158–175.

Janoff-Bulman, R. (1992). *Shattered assumptions: Towards a new psychology of trauma.* New York: The Free Press.

Jaycox, L., Zoellner, L., & Foa, E. (2002). Current Perspectives: Cognitive behavior therapy for PTSD in rape survivors. *Journal of Clinical Psychology, 58,* 891–906.

Kubany, E., Haynes, S., Abueg, F., Manke, F., Brennan, J., & Stahura, C. (1996). Development and validation of trauma related guilt inventory. *Psychological Assessment, 8,* 428–444.

Lovell, K., Marks, I. M., Norshirvani, H., Thrasher, S., & Livanou, M. (2001). Do cognitive and exposure treatments improve various PTSD symptoms differently? A randomized controlled trial. *Behavioural & Cognitive Psychotherapy, 29,* 107–112.

Marks, I., Lovell, K., Norshirvani, H., Livanou, M., & Thrasher, S. (1998). Treatment of posttraumatic stress disorder by exposure and/or cognitive restructuring: A controlled study. *Archives of General Psychiatry, 55,* 317–325.

McCann, I. L., & Pearlman, L. A. (1990). *Psychological trauma and the adult survivor: theory, therapy, and transformation.* New York: Brunner/Mazel.

McCann, I. L., Sakheim, D. K., & Abrahamson, D. J. (1988). Trauma and victimization: a model of psychological adaptation. *The Counseling Psychologist, 16,* 531–594.

McNally, R. J. (1998). Experimental approaches to cognitive abnormality in posttraumatic stress disorder. *Clinical Psychology Review, 18,* 971–982.

McNally, R. J., Lasko, N. B., Macklin, M. L., & Pitman, R. K. (1995). Autobiographical memory disturbance in combat-related posttraumatic stress disorder. *Behavior Research & Therapy, 33,* 619–630.

McNally, R. J., Litz, B. T., Prassas, A., Shin, L. M., & Weathers, F. W. (1994). Emotional priming of autobiographical memory in posttraumatic stress disorder. *Cognition & Emotion, 8,* 351–367.

Nishith, P., Resick, P. A., & Griffin, M. G. (2002). Pattern of change in prolonged exposure and cognitive-processing therapy for female rape victims with post-traumatic stress disorder. *Journal of Consulting & Clinical Psychology, 70,* 880–886.

Paunovic, N. & Ost, L. G. (2001). Cognitive behavioral therapy vs. exposure therapy in treatment of PTSD in refugees. *Behaviour Research and Therapy, 39,* 1183–1197.

Rachman, S. (1980). Emotional processing. *Behaviour Research and Therapy, 18,* 51–60.

Resick, P. A., Nishith, P., Weaver, T. L., Astin, M. C., & Feuer, C. A. (2002). A comparison of cognitive-processing therapy with prolonged exposure and a waiting condition for the treatment of chronic posttraumatic stress disorder in female rape victims. *Journal of Consulting & Clinical Psychology, 70,* 867–879.

Resick, P. A., & Schnicke, M. D. (1992). Cognitive processing therapy for sexual assault victims. *Journal of Consulting and Clinical Psychology, 60,* 748–756.

Resick, P. A., & Schnicke, M. (1993). *Cognitive processing therapy for rape victims: A treatment manual.* Newbury Park, CA: Sage.

Resick, P., Schnicke, M., & Markway, B. (1991, November). *The relationship between cognitive content and posttraumatic stress disorder.* Paper presented at the annual meeting of the Association for the Advancement of Behavior Therapy, New York.

Sidley, G. L, Whitaker, K., Calam, R. M., & Wells, A. (1997). The relationship between problem-solving and autobiographical memory in parasuicide patients. *Behavioural and Cognitive Psychotherapy, 25,* 125–202.

Tarrier, N., Pilgrim, G., Sommerfield, C., Faragher, B., Reynolds, M., Graham, E., et al. (1999). A randomized trial of cognitive therapy and imaginal exposure in the treatment of chronic posttraumatic stress disorder. *Journal of Consulting and Clinical Psychology, 67,* 13–18.

Tarrier, N., Sommerfield, C., Pilgrim, H., & Faragher, B. (2000). Factors associated with outcome of cognitive-behavioural treatment of chronic posttraumatic stress disorder. *Behaviour Research & Therapy, 38,* 191–202.

Taylor, S., Koch, W. J., Fecteau, G., Fedoroff, I. C., Thordarson, D. S., & Nicki, R. M. (2001). Posttraumatic stress disorder arising after road traffic collisions: Patterns of response to cognitive-behavioral therapy. *Journal of Consulting and Clinical Psychology, 63,* 541–551.

Williams, J. M. G. (1995). Depression and the specificity of autobiographical memory. In D.C. Rubin (Ed.), *Remembering our past: Studies in autobiographical memory* (pp. 218–243). New York: Cambridge University Press.

PART III

TREATING SPECIAL POPULATIONS AND PROBLEMS

Chapter 9

MILITARY POPULATIONS

Mark Creamer and David Forbes

INTRODUCTION

The development of mental health problems, particularly posttraumatic stress disorder (PTSD) and related conditions, is a major issue for defense forces around the world, with serious implications for operational performance, readiness to deploy, retention rates, and compensation. Although little adequately controlled treatment research exists with the military population, there is evidence to suggest that cognitive-behavioral treatments for military-related PTSD may be beneficial, albeit perhaps less so than for some other populations. This chapter commences with some contextual information designed to assist clinicians in formulating such cases and in understanding some of the complexities relevant to the treatment of PTSD in this population. The chapter goes on to provide a brief review of literature on cognitive-behavioral therapy (CBT) outcome research with military populations, before discussing specific aspects of treatment and foreshadowing future directions.

PREVALENCE

Although the focus is usually on post-deployment mental health, it is important to emphasize that much PTSD in military populations may result not from deployments but from other non-operational traumatic events. These may include motor vehicles and training accidents, as well as physical and sexual assaults. The prevalence of psychiatric problems following such events has been well documented in civilian populations (see, for example, Creamer, Burgess, & McFarlane, 2001; Kessler, Sonnega,

Hughes, & Nelson, 1995) and there is little reason to suppose that rates among military personnel would be markedly different. Bolton, Litz, Britt, Adler, & Roemer, (2001), for example, found that 74% of soldiers about to deploy to Bosnia had been previously exposed to potentially traumatizing events, the majority of which were not related to their military careers, and that 6% of these soldiers met the cut-off for PTSD caseness prior to deployment. Thus, it would be a mistake to assume that the recognition and management of posttrauma reactions in the military should be an initiative confined solely to deployed troops or to post-deployment psychopathology.

Comprehensive reviews of the epidemiological literature pertaining to military-related PTSD are available elsewhere (Creamer & Forbes, 2003; Schlenger, Fairbank, Jordan, & Caddell, 1999). In summary, the history of posttraumatic mental health problems in soldiers is probably as old as war itself, and literature throughout the ages is replete with descriptions of traumatic stress reactions following combat. It is only since the Vietnam war, however, that well-designed epidemiological studies have produced reliable figures on the scope of the problem. The National Vietnam Veterans Readjustment Study (NVVRS: Kulka et al., 1990) investigated the prevalence of postwar problems in 1,632 Vietnam veterans. They found a lifetime PTSD prevalence of 31% for men and 27% for women, with current rates of 15% for men and 9% for women. These figures are important for understanding the chronicity of the disorder—half of those Vietnam veterans who had ever had PTSD still had it 20 or so years later. Comparable rates have been reported among other Vietnam veteran populations (O'Toole et al., 1996). Importantly, both those studies highlighted the prevalence of comorbid psychopathology with PTSD, an important consideration in treatment design.

More recently, estimates of the prevalence of PTSD among troops deployed to the Persian Gulf in 1991 have ranged from a low of 4% (Wolfe, Brown, & Kelley, 1993) to a high of 19% (Sutker, Uddo, Brailey, & Allain, 1993) depending on the specific population of interest. Importantly, the prevalence of PTSD in this population seems to have increased over time (Southwick et al., 1995), raising questions about the possibility of delayed onset (or, at least, delayed reporting) of combat-related PTSD. Finally, studies of peacekeeping and peacemaking deployments, which have become common over recent years, indicate comparable levels of PTSD in those troops. Litz and his colleagues (Litz, Orsillo, Friedman, Ehlich, & Batres, 1997), for example, investigating 3,461 troops who served as part of a U.S. force in Somalia, found a PTSD prevalence of around 8% shortly after their return.

UNIQUE CHARACTERISTICS: THE POPULATION AND THE STRESSORS

In considering the nature, development, and treatment of mental health problems among military personnel, it is important to consider several factors that may make this population unusual, if not unique. While not claiming to be all-inclusive, this section raises some issues that may be important for the clinician to consider when formulating the case and designing cognitive-behavioral interventions for PTSD among past or present members of the defense forces.

Recruitment and Selection

An initial consideration is whether certain types of individuals, especially those with characteristic histories, are more likely to join the military. Some evidence suggests increased rates of childhood physical and sexual abuse, as well as neglect, among military recruits compared to community averages (Merrill et al., 1998; Rosen & Martin, 1996). Rosen and Martin speculate that a history of neglect may negatively impact upon the individual's ability to access and use social support, a factor consistently found to predict adjustment following trauma (Brewin, Andrews, & Valentine, 2000; Ozer, Best, Lipsey, & Weiss, 2003). Research has also revealed high rates of family dysfunction among new recruits (Goyne, 2001). Such findings may have implications for the person's ability to engage in a strong therapeutic relationship, suggesting that more time may need to be devoted to this in the initial stages of treatment. Since prior trauma has been established as a risk factor in the subsequent development of PTSD (Brewin et al., 2000; Ozer et al., 2003), these findings further suggest that this preexsisting vulnerability may be a factor in the development of PTSD in at least a portion of military cases. Thus, treatment may need to address preexsisting issues of unresolved trauma or other premilitary factors rather than focussing exclusively on the precipitating event.

Military Training

Military personnel have undergone a specific type of training, characterized in many cases by expectations of obedience without question to the commands of their superiors. A high level of emotional "toughness" and resilience is expected by the miliary organization, as well as by their colleagues and commanders, in order to optimise operational effectiveness. Such training and expectations, which were ingrained over many years and which may have stood the soldier well during their deployment, may serve as an impediment when it comes to seeking and engaging in treatment. Such training may promote a "shutting down" of affective states in order to successfully function in the high stress operational environment. The pairing of stress and anger is rehearsed through training to increase the likelihood of responding to threat with anger or aggression rather than with fear and vulnerability. Interestingly, in subsequent clinical contexts, the task of distinguishing these learned characteristics from the symptomatic anger and numbing associated with PTSD can be difficult. Certainly, clinical experience suggests that engagement in therapy, and formation of a strong therapeutic relationship, can take considerable time with veteran and currently serving military personnel. This is likely to be an important issue for therapists to consider when embarking upon CBT interventions with this population.

Operational Deployment

The operational deployment—the context in which the individual traumatic events are likely to occur—is itself characterized by several features that may be assumed to increase vulnerability. It is likely to involve travel to distant lands, with different language and culture, which may require considerable adjustments. It takes people away from nonmilitary support networks such as family and friends, leaving the unit as the main, if not only, source of support. It is likely that the environment will be, at best, unpleasant in terms of climate and conditions; indeed, experience of a "malevolent environment" has been shown to be a powerful predictor of subsequent adjustment among Vietnam veterans (King, King, Gudanowski, & Vreven, 1995). The constant presence of threat to oneself and others that characterizes many military deployments may result in prolonged periods of autonomic arousal (often for many months at a time), a sustained stress response that may contribute to the persistent hyperarousal characteristic of chronic, combat-related PTSD. This state of hypervigilance was appropriate while on deployment; it is the failure to "recalibrate" the threat arousal system on return that causes problems. Thus, considerable time should be devoted in the early stages of treatment to teaching strategies for effective reduction of arousal. Certainly, clinical experience suggests that more intensive exposure-based or cognitive interventions with this population are extremely difficult until improved arousal management has been achieved.

Military deployments often include biochemical exposure of various kinds. There may be prophylactic medical interventions, such as predeployment vaccinations or daily administration of drugs to counteract chemical weapons. There may be actual or threatened exposure to noxious agents in the form of biological, chemical, or nuclear weapons; "smoil" (smoke from oil well fires during the Gulf conflicts); or defoliants (in Vietnam). These factors complicate the clinical picture, since they provide an alternative etiology, an opportunity for the veteran to avoid psychological formulations of the problem and to focus on purely physical explanations. It is probably not helpful for the therapist to engage in a debate about etiology; rather, it is important to acknowledge these alternative explanations but to focus on the more important issue that, regardless of the cause, CBT approaches have demonstrated efficacy in ameliorating both physical and psychological symptoms.

The nature of military deployments is such that fundamental beliefs about the self, the world, and humanity may be shattered. Military personnel are likely to be confronted with death and destruction, particularly relating to civilians, on a scale that is often unimaginable and for which the person has had little preparation. Personnel themselves, or their colleagues, may have committed atrocities—or acts of violence that, with the benefit of hindsight, may be deemed to be atrocities—that shatter previously held beliefs about themselves and that may have considerable impact on self-image and self-esteem. The changing nature of war, and the increase in peacekeeping and peacemaking missions, has brought with it a new type of stress. The "rules of engagement" that severely limit the extent to which troops can intervene in violent situations and protect innocent civilians may lead to feelings of frustration, powerlessness, and lack of control that, in turn, may serve to increase subsequent adjustment problems. Personnel may be left with powerful perceptions that the deployment was a failure or was, from the outset, immoral and unjustified. Increasing questioning of deployment decisions by the media and the general public, and increasing scrutiny of the behavior of deployed troops by the media, may serve to decrease a sense of "being on the side of good and right" that has tended to provide an element of psychological protection for combatants in the past. These issues are very likely to emerge and will need to be addressed actively in treatment.

Finally, given the nature and often lengthy duration of military deployments, it is not uncommon for personnel to experience a number of traumatic events. Multiple traumatization may influence the range and severity of subsequent symptoms, as well as treatment response (Shalev, 1997). Thus, it is important to take a thorough trauma history, both in order to formulate the case effectively and in order to plan treatment (e.g., exposure hierarchies).

CBT OUTCOME LITERATURE

Surprisingly little empirical treatment outcome research has been published in the area of CBT with military-related PTSD. This is despite the fact that the Department of Veterans Affairs and its equivalent in several countries spend millions of dollars on treating veterans with a diagnosis of PTSD resulting from military service. Of the controlled studies that do exist with this population, most have focused upon exposure therapy. Several uncontrolled studies of broader, group-based intervention models with a generally CBT focus, however, have also appeared in the literature.

It should be noted at the outset that most clinical treatment trials with veteran populations, both pharmacological and psychological, have shown less efficacy than trials with nonveterans whose PTSD was related to other traumatic experiences such as sexual assaults, accidents, and natural disasters (Foa, Keane, & Friedman, 2000; Shalev, Bonne, & Eth, 1996). There are several possible explanations, however, making this observation difficult to interpret. First, as discussed previously, poorer treatment outcome may be explained by characteristics of military personnel themselves. Second, the duration (potentially many months of hypervigilance and hyperarousal) and nature of military deployments may result in a specific form of "treatment resistant PTSD." Detailed phenomenological data to inform this question are not yet available. Third, veteran treatment trials are routinely composed exclusively of males, while nonveteran trials tend to have predominantly female participants (often sexual assault survivors). There is some evidence to suggest that females may be more responsive to pharmacological and psychological treatment for PTSD than males (Foa et al., 2000) and, therefore, the poorer outcomes may be explained more by gender than veteran status. Fourth, most veteran trials have been conducted with Vietnam-era veterans, several decades posttrauma, who have high levels of comorbidity. While some of the nonveteran trials include a wide range of participants, the same consistent pattern of chronicity and high comorbidity is rarely seen. Fifth, implementation of best-practice CBT treatments has been less rigorous with veteran than with non-veteran samples. Many of the exposure studies discussed next, for example, suffer from problems such as inadequate session length and inconsistent application of best practice principles for imaginal exposure. There are, as yet, no studies examining the efficacy of cognitive processing therapy (CPT; Resick & Schnicke, 1993) with veterans, despite the fact that this intervention would seem to hold considerable promise. Finally, compensation, pensions, and other entitlements may have the potential for greater impact on treatment outcome among military than civilian populations. At this stage, given the meager amount of adequately controlled research with veteran populations, the reasons for poorer treatment outcome must remain largely speculative.

Individual Treatment

In a review of exposure therapy in combat-related PTSD, Frueh, Turner, and Beidel (1995) were able to find only four controlled studies to that date (Boudewyns & Hyer, 1990; Boudewyns, Hyer, Woods, Harrison, & McCranie, 1990; Cooper & Clum, 1989; Keane, Fairbank, Caddell, & Zimering, 1989). All four reported positive results, suggesting that exposure therapy does have a therapeutic effect in combat-related PTSD. Treatment effects, however, were clinically small, perhaps due in part to the fact that exposure was not always implemented in an optimum fashion. Nevertheless, those studies suggest that the technique has promise and further investigation is warranted.

More recently, a few studies have investigated the efficacy of eye movement desensitization and reprocessing (EMDR) in the treatment of PTSD in veterans (Carlson, Chemtob, Rusnak, Hedlund, & Muraoka, 1998; Rogers et al., 1999). Considerable attention has been devoted to this approach in PTSD and much has been written about its efficacy with other PTSD populations (Davidson & Parker, 2001). Certainly, the technique has appeal in its brevity and relative ease of administration. Though some research has produced encouraging results, with EMDR producing greater symptom improvement than control conditions, those studies have been criticized on methodological grounds (McNally, 1999). Other studies with veteran populations have found less positive results (Devilly, Spence, & Rapee, 1998). With our current state of knowledge, it is hard to be definitive about the benefits of EMDR with veteran populations but, like exposure, it clearly warrants further investigation.

Group Treatment

Government-funded veterans affairs mental health services in most countries are likely to offer group treatments for veterans presenting with a diagnosis of PTSD. Although randomized controlled trials are lacking, several naturalistic studies reported in the literature contribute to our understanding of the potential benefits of these approaches. Early program evaluations of these programs were disappointing, with long-term outcomes showing no symptom improvement, or even deterioration, in the group as a whole (Johnson et al., 1996). This was the case even when a more CBT-oriented approach was adopted (Solomon et al., 1992). Slightly more positive findings, however, were reported from CBT-oriented cohort-based group programs for Vietnam veterans with PTSD in Australia (Creamer, Morris, Biddle, & Elliott, 1999). That study found significant improvements in group means, maintained through to 9-month follow-up, although the overall size of treatment response was only moderate and large variations among veterans were evident.

Several questions are raised regarding the optimum way of conducting this kind of group treatment. Early models, for example, were conducted on an inpatient basis on the grounds that it would not be possible to adequately contain the effect if veterans were returning home each evening. A comparison of inpatient and day-hospital models offering comparable treatment to Vietnam veterans with PTSD, however, revealed no difference in treatment effects at either 3- or 9-month follow-up (Creamer, Forbes, Biddle, & Elliott, 2002). Also contrary to popular clinical opinion, the outcome data do not support the notion that veterans will do better if treatment takes place in homogeneous groups comprising only veteran participants than in mixed trauma groups (Johnson et al., 1999). Although participants in a veteran-only group reported higher satisfaction on several indices than those who undertook the same program in a mixed group of veterans and nonveterans, there was no difference in outcome.

The group program data must be interpreted cautiously, since those reports represent program monitoring rather than controlled trials. Indeed, a recently published study represents the only randomized controlled trial of group CBT treatment for PTSD in veterans to have appeared in the literature (Schnurr et al., 2003). In the U.S. Department of Veterans Affairs Cooperative Study 420, 360 male Vietnam veterans were randomly assigned to receive either trauma-focused group psychotherapy or a present-centered comparison treatment that avoided any trauma focus work. Cohorts of 6 veterans per group received weekly treatment for 30 weeks, followed by 5 monthly booster sessions. Both groups improved significantly from intake to post-treatment, with gains maintained at follow-up. Though average improvement was modest, approximately 40% of participants showed clinically significant change. Contrary to expectations, no overall differences were found between treatment conditions. Importantly, however, analyses suggested that those who received an "adequate" dose of trauma focus treatment (attending at least 80% of sessions) did respond slightly better than those in the control condition. Again, the results are encouraging but steps are clearly needed to reduce dropout (perhaps using motivational interviewing—see chapter 5) and to enhance the delivery of CBT treatments in routine clinical practice.

ISSUES IN THE TREATMENT OF PTSD IN VETERANS

A review of controlled CBT treatment outcome studies with veterans provides little cause for optimism. Not only are there few studies in the published literature, but those that do exist suggest that the prognosis is poor and that treatment effects are, at best, modest. Despite this gloomy picture, however, important work is being published in a range of associated areas that has the potential to shed light on the key issues in treatment for this complex disorder and to improve the application of CBT with veteran and military populations. Although not all these factors are unique to military populations, they are important considerations when working with this population.

Perhaps the most significant advances in the treatment of military-related PTSD have occurred in the area of interventions targeting specific symptoms (such as nightmares and anger) or associated features (such as trauma-related guilt and alcohol abuse or dependence). Attempts to establish effective treatments for these symptoms and associated features are important not only because of the distress associated with these phenomena themselves, but also because of emerging evidence of the negative impact of these phenomena on treatment outcome for PTSD more broadly. While some of these interventions apply across a range of traumatized populations, others have more specific implications for combat or military veterans.

Posttraumatic Nightmares

Until recently, little attention has been paid to direct cognitive behavioral treatment of posttraumatic nightmares. Such treatments are of particular relevance for individuals with residual nightmares following completion of exposure or other CBT approaches.

Recent treatment efforts targeted at posttraumatic nightmares have focused on a procedure known as imagery rehearsal therapy (IRT), a cognitive-behavioral intervention in which the patient consciously alters, or rescripts, the content of the nightmare. The rescripted content promotes mastery or control over the threat contained in the nightmare. The altered script is then repeatedly rehearsed.

Investigations into the use of IRT in the treatment of posttraumatic nightmares have been promising. Krakow et al. (2001) conducted a randomized controlled trial using IRT to treat nightmares in female sexual assault survivors, reporting that three sessions of IRT reduced chronic nightmares, as well as improving sleep quality and overall PTSD symptomatology as assessed at 6 month follow-up. With regard to military populations, Forbes, Phelps, and McHugh (2001) conducted a pilot study examining the efficacy of IRT on posttraumatic nightmares in male Vietnam veterans with chronic PTSD. That study demonstrated significant reductions in the frequency and intensity of nightmares, with the targeted nightmare having ceased completely at 3-month follow-up in 60% of cases. These changes were associated with improvements in overall PTSD severity, mood, and more general symptomatology, with gains maintained to 12 months posttreatment (Forbes et al., 2003). The reductions in nightmare frequency and intensity reported in these studies are encouraging, particularly given clinical reports that nightmares frequently remain as a residual symptom following treatment.

Guilt

Another interesting innovation in recent years is the emergence of a systematic approach to the treatment of trauma-related guilt using cognitive therapy. This is a particularly important development, since guilt has been found to negatively influence outcome for PTSD more broadly (Davidson et al., 1993). The most prominent work in the area of combat-related guilt is to be found in Kubany's Cognitive Therapy for Trauma Related Guilt (CT-TRG: Kubany, 1994, 1997; Kubany & Watson, 2003), although his treatment has also been used with other posttraumatic populations (Kubany, Hill, & Owens, 2003).

<txt>This treatment involves a series of semistructured procedures that identify and challenge key thinking errors characteristic of combat-relat-

ed guilt. The strength of this treatment is its systematic approach and rational rigor, addressing the guilt-related issues one by one and further dismantling and addressing guilt-related cognitions within each issue.

Anger

As discussed in chapter 10, anger may adversely affect the outcome of CBT in PTSD. This is an issue of considerable concern for military populations in view of the finding that anger is a particularly prominent feature of combat-related PTSD (Novaco & Chemtob, 2002). Evidence supporting the negative influence of anger on outcome has been reported for sexual assault survivors (Foa, Riggs, Massie, & Yarczower, 1995) and combat veterans (Forbes et al., 2002). Several possible explanations have been proposed for the manner in which anger may influence treatment outcome in PTSD. Foa et al. (1995), for example, hypothesized that anger interfered with the client's engagement with the trauma-related fear during exposure treatment, thereby preventing habituation. Forbes et al. (2002) drew on existing work that identified the therapeutic alliance as a significant predictor of outcome for Axis 1 disorders more generally (Hatcher & Barends, 1996). They speculated that anger has the potential to interfere with the engagement of the client in the therapeutic alliance, resulting in a reasonably global negative impact on symptom change or, indeed, in premature termination of treatment (Stevenson & Chemtob, 2000). Similarly, anger may also interfere by impeding the client's capacity to engage with social and familial supports during and following treatment, which may otherwise assist them in reinforcing and consolidating any treatment gains. Finally, it may be speculated that severe anger reflects a general tendency toward externalization of responsibility and blame, inhibiting the self-reflection required for meaningful longer term change (Deffenbacher, 1999). Whatever the explanation, anger has the potential to adversely affect treatment response in combat veterans with PTSD and may, in part, account for the modest recovery rates quoted elsewhere in the literature for military populations (Shalev, 1997).

Such findings, of course, raise the potential to improve outcomes of CBT treatment for combat-related PTSD by directly addressing severe anger prior to the use of exposure or other CBT interventions. Although a 12-session CBT intervention reduced anger reactions and improved anger control in veterans with PTSD and severe anger (Chemtob, Novaco, Hamada, & Gross, 1997), empirical studies examining the benefits of applying such interventions prior to addressing the core symptoms of PTSD have not yet been published. Nevertheless, this does appear to be an appropriate avenue for further investigation and development.

Somatic Presentations

Early descriptions of traumatic stress, characterized by terms such as "shell shock" and "neurasthenia", placed heavy emphasis on physical symptoms and somatoform clinical presentations. With the advent of DSM–III and the introduction of PTSD as a diagnosis, the emphasis shifted to psychological and behavioral aspects of the disorder. There has been a renewed interest n recent times in somatic aspects of postdeployment conditions driven to a large extent by widespread reports of physical symptoms and ill-health among veterans of the 1991 Gulf War. The fact that exposure to various noxious agents may have occurred during the deployment may serve to reinforce expectations of physical pathology. Although attempts to define a "Gulf War Syndrome" have been unsuccessful, the research is consistent in reporting increased rates of multiple physical symptoms among Gulf veterans, greater functional impairment, lower general health perception, and greater health care utilization (see, for example, Goss Gilroy Inc., 1998; Iowa Persian Gulf Study Group, 1997; Unwin et al., 1999). While associations between these physical symptom constellations and PTSD remain unclear, CBT treatments for these somatic presentations are proving very promising (Donta et al., 2003) and may serve as useful adjuncts to PTSD treatment in some cases.

Comorbidity Management

Comorbidity is, of course, common in all chronic PTSD presentations (Creamer et al., 2001; Kessler et al., 1995) and clinical decisions are routinely required about how best to manage these aspects of the presentation. It is, perhaps, a particularly difficult problem among veteran populations, especially with regard to the high level of substance use disorders (Kulka et al., 1990; O'Toole et al., 1996). The debate about order of treatment is complex: Is the substance Use best conceptualized as being secondary to the PTSD (as a way of managing the painful symptoms). Is the PTSD secondary to preexisting substance abuse, or are the two comorbid but independent conditions? Although early approaches argued for the importance of treating the substance use first, this runs the risk that the untreated PTSD symptoms will precipitate a relapse. Clinicians may also argue that engaging veterans in treatment is so difficult that to treat the substance abuse and send them away for a period of sobriety before allowing them to commence treatment for PTSD would be to run the risk not only of relapse but also of losing the veteran to treatment for a considerable time. More recent approaches have argued for concurrent treatment models that address both substance Use and PTSD symptoms as part of an integrated approach to treatment (Najavits, 2003; Najavits, Weiss, Shaw, & Muenz, 1998; Ouimette & Brown, 2003). In such models, integrated treatment focuses on education, symptom management, and coping skills development, with exposure- based interventions introduced only when there has been a cessation of alcohol use or abuse is stable at low risk levels for a sustained period.

Treatment Goals

Quite reasonably, the efficacy of CBT treatment for PTSD is routinely judged against symptom reduction as the primary outcome measure. Though empirical data in this area are lacking, it is reasonable to assume that the treatment of certain clinical populations, including past and present members of the defense forces, requires the clinician to consider the most appropriate goals for treatment in each case. If the person is still a serving member, and intends to return to active duty, the goals of treatment may be different from those for a veteran with a chronic condition who completed military service several decades ago. In the latter example, there is likely to be considerable impairment across a broad range of social and occupational areas of functioning. It may be that psychosocial rehabilitation, with an emphasis on improved relationships, social reintegration, and vocational functioning (for example, voluntary work), may be an equally appropriate focus for intervention as a reduction in core PTSD symptoms.

For the serving member, however, the goals are different. While symptom reduction is clearly important, this in itself may not be sufficient. A key goal will be that of increasing resilience and reducing the risk of relapse upon future traumatic exposure (for example, during another deployment). This represents a major challenge for the field. It is reasonable to assume that a prior diagnosis of PTSD (or of any psychiatric condition) is a risk factor for the development of PTSD following subsequent exposure. At this stage, there is little or no information regarding the extent to which successful CBT treatment for PTSD impacts upon the risks following subsequent exposure. Clearly, this has major implications for advice that clinicians may provide regarding return to active duty.

FUTURE DIRECTIONS

Although progress has been made in some areas, it is hard to escape the conclusion that the cognitive-behavioral treatment of PTSD in past and current military personnel has advanced little in the past decade. With the number of military deployments showing no sign of reducing, the human and financial cost of mental health problems to defense forces around the world must remain an issue of considerable concern. There is an urgent need for further work in this area to improve our understanding of the development and treatment of mental health conditions in the military. The final section of this chapter will propose some of the key areas that require attention.

Research Directions

From the scant review of solid empirical research, it is clear that we have yet to see adequate trials of accepted best practice CBT treatment for PTSD in military and veteran populations. Exposure, for example, the core of demonstrably effective CBT treatment, has not really been tested effectively in this population to date. This is not to detract from the very important studies that examined exposure in the late 1980s and early 1990s. It is, however, reasonable to say that treatment was generally not administered with the same level of rigor as has characterized the most successful treatment outcome studies in nonveteran populations (e.g., Foa et al., 1999). Similarly, cognitive processing therapy (CPT) has demonstrated a level of efficacy in rape victims with PTSD comparable to that of exposure (Resick, Nishith, Weaver, Astin, & Feuer, 2002). It is reasonable to assume that CPT may prove an effective treatment for veterans, particularly those from recent peacekeeping deployments. For such veterans, the trauma is not restricted solely to personal threat but, rather, is often characterized by exposure to the widespread death and suffering of others, combined with severe restrictions on their ability to intervene. Thus, cognitive appraisals are an important aspect of the clinical presentation for these veterans and a properly conducted trial of CPT for this PTSD population is long overdue.

Finally, there are many innovative approaches discussed in other chapters of this volume that may improve treatment outcome with this population and that warrant examination. These include the application of virtual reality approaches to exposure (see chapter 6), the potential benefits of combining pharmacological approaches with CBT and the most appropriate ways to manage comorbidity.

Treatment Goals

Careful consideration of the most appropriate goals for treatment in military populations, particularly with regard to chronic PTSD in middle-aged or elderly veterans, is an important future direction. It may be that a shift in focus toward a greater emphasis on psychosocial rehabilitation would be an appropriate way to proceed with more chronic combat-related PTSD. Often these veterans display considerable comorbidity, along with widespread occupational and social dysfunction. It may be that some relatively simple lifestyle changes would help to improve their quality of life and perhaps ameliorate some of the PTSD symptoms. Again, though there is a paucity of adequately controlled research in this area, CBT has a great deal to offer and good reviews appear elsewhere (Penk & Flannery, 2000). An important factor in the success of these approaches will be the willingness of veterans to commit themselves to this alternative treatment approach. In that context, it is vital to see psychosocial rehabilitation as having a much broader focus than simply a return to paid employment. Indeed, in many cases, that would be a highly unrealistic goal. Rather, interventions need to cover areas such as relationships, family functioning, conflict resolution, socialization and social reintegration, and vocational rehabilitation in the broadest sense of the construct (i.e., including the development of hobbies and pastimes, new skills, leisure activities, and voluntary work). If, as is reasonable to expect, such changes result in improved quality of life for veterans, then they are a very valid focus for the powerful interventions available under the rubric of CBT. Of course, there is an urgent need also for adequate research in this area in order to demonstrate outcomes and to refine such interventions for this population.

EARLY INTERVENTION AND PREVENTION

Early intervention and prevention is perhaps the most significant and important challenge facing the field of traumatic stress. Although it is beyond the scope of this chapter, it is important to recognize that military populations are ideally placed to inform our understanding of these crucial issues. The potential for interventions at the point of recruit selection and training, subsequent training, pre-deployment, during deployment, post-deployment, and at discharge from the military are enormous. All have the potential to reduce the long-term mental health sequelae of military service, with resultant savings in terms of human suffering and financial costs.

CONCLUSION

Veteran and military populations constitute a high-risk group in terms of the development of posttraumatic mental health problems in general and PTSD in particular. Despite the human and financial costs of these problems to defense forces and governments around the world, surprisingly little attention has been paid to the systematic application of evidence-based CBT interventions for this population. It may be that this will change as governments accept greater responsibility for the long-term health outcomes of deployed personnel. Certainly, the opportunities for research and world's best clinical practice in military-related PTSD, from selection and prevention through to the management of chronic and severe psychiatric illness, are considerable. Though advances in the CBT treatment of PTSD with military populations over recent years have been modest, it is hoped that the next decade will see a more systematic approach to clinical research that will lead to improvements in outcome for this deserving population.

REFERENCES

Bolton, E. E., Litz, B. T., Britt, T. W., Adler, A., & Roemer, L. (2001). Reports of prior exposure to potentially traumatic events and PTSD in troops poised for deployment. *Journal of Traumatic Stress, 14,* 249–256.

Boudewyns, P. A., & Hyer, L. (1990). Physiological response to combat memories and preliminary treatment outcome in Vietnam veteran PTSD patients treated with direct therapeutic exposure. *Behavior Therapy, 21,* 63–87.

Boudewyns, P. A., Hyer, L., Woods, M. G., Harrison, W. R., & McCranie, E. (1990). PTSD among Vietnam veterans: An early look at treatment outcome using direct therapeutic exposure. *Journal of Traumatic Stress, 3,* 359–369.

Brewin, C. R., Andrews, B., & Valentine, J. D. (2000). Meta-analysis of risk factors for posttraumatic stress disorder in trauma-exposed adults. *Journal of Consulting and Clinical Psychology, 68,* 748–766.

Carlson, J. G., Chemtob, C. M., Rusnak, K., Hedlund, N. L., & Muraoka, M. Y. (1998). Eye Movement Desensitization and Reprocessing (EMDR) treatment for combat-related posttraumatic stress disorder. *Journal of Traumatic Stress, 11,* 3–24.

Chemtob, C. M., Novaco, R. W., Hamada, R. S., & Gross, D. M. (1997). Cognitive-behavioral treatment for severe anger in posttraumatic stress disorder. *Journal of Consulting and Clinical Psychology, 65,* 184–189.

Cooper, N. A., & Clum, G. A. (1989). Imaginal flooding as a supplementary treatment for PTSD in combat veterans: A controlled study. *Behavior Therapy, 20,* 381–391.

Creamer, M., Burgess, P., & McFarlane, A. C. (2001). Posttraumatic stress disorder: findings from the Australian National Survey of Mental Health and Well-being. *Psychological Medicine, 31,* 1237–1247.

Creamer, M., & Forbes, D. (2003). The long term effects of traumatic stress. In G. E. Kearney, M. Creamer, R. Marshall, & A. Goyne (Eds.), *Military Stress and Performance: The Australian Defense Force Experience* (pp. 175–186). Melbourne: Melbourne University Press.

Creamer, M., Forbes, D., Biddle, D., & Elliott, P. (2002). Inpatient versus day hospital treatment for chronic, combat-related posttraumatic stress disorder: A naturalistic comparison. *Journal of Nervous & Mental Disease, 190,* 183–189.

Creamer, M., Morris, P., Biddle, D., & Elliott, P. (1999). Treatment outcome in Australian veterans with combat-related posttraumatic stress disorder: A cause for cautious optimism? *Journal of Traumatic Stress, 12,* 545–558.

Davidson, J. R., Kudler, H. S., Saunders, W. B., Erickson, L., Smith, R.D., Stein, R.M., et al. (1993). Predicting response to amitriptyline in posttraumatic stress disorder. *American Journal of Psychiatry, 150,* 1024–1029.

Davidson, P. R., & Parker, K. C. (2001). Eye movement desensitization and reprocessing (EMDR): A meta-analysis. *Journal of Consulting & Clinical Psychology, 69,* 305–316.

Deffenbacher, J. L. (1999). Cognitive-behavioral conceptualization and treatment of anger. *Journal of Clinical Psychology. Special Issue: Treating Anger in Psychotherapy, 55,* 295–309.

Devilly, G. J., Spence, S. H., & Rapee, R. M. (1998). Statistical and reliable change with eye movement desensitization and reprocessing: Treating trauma within a veteran population. *Behavior Therapy, 29,* 435–455.

Donta, S. T., Clauw, D. J., Engel, C. C., Jr., Guarino, P., Peduzzi, P., Williams, D. A., et al. (2003). Cognitive behavioral therapy and aerobic exercise for Gulf war veterans illnesses: A randomized controlled trial. *Journal of the American Medical Association, 289,* 1396–1404.

Foa, E. B., Dancu, C. V., Hembree, E. A., Jaycox, L. H., Meadows, E. A., & Street, G. P. (1999). A comparison of exposure therapy, stress inoculation training, and their combination for reducing posttraumatic stress disorder in female assault victims. *Journal of Consulting and Clinical Psychology, 67,* 194–200.

Foa, E. B., Keane, T. M., & Friedman, M. J. (2000). *Effective Treatments for PTSD.* New York: Guilford Press.

Foa, E. B., Riggs, D. S., Massie, E. D., & Yarczower, M. (1995). The impact of fear activation and anger on the efficacy of exposure treatment for posttraumatic stress disorder. *Behavior Therapy, 26,* 487–499.

Forbes, D., Creamer, M., Allen, N., Elliott, P., McHugh, T., Debenham, P., et al. (2002). The MMPI–2 as a predictor of symptom change following treatment for posttraumatic stress disorder. *Journal of Personality Assessment, 79,* 321–336.

Forbes, D., Phelps, A., & McHugh, T. (2001). Treatment of combat-related nightmares using imagery rehearsal: A pilot study. *Journal of Traumatic Stress, 14,* 433–442.

Forbes, D., Phelps, A. J., McHugh, A. F., Debenham, P., Hopwood, M., & Creamer, M. (2003). Imagery rehearsal in the treatment of posttraumatic nightmares in Australian veterans with chronic combat-related PTSD: 12–month follow-up data. *Journal of Traumatic Stress, 16,* 509–513.

Frueh, B. C., Turner, S. M., & Beidel, D. C. (1995). Exposure therapy for combat-related PTSD: A critical review. *Clinical Psychology Review, 15,* 799–817.

Goss Gilroy Inc. (1998). *Health study of Canadian Forces personnel involved in the 1991 conflict in the Persian Gulf* (Vol. 1). Ontario: Goss Gilroy Inc., Management Consultants.

Goyne, A. (2001). Family breakdown, child-parent conflict, and adjustment amongst male applicants for the Australian Army. In G. Kearney, M. Creamer, R. Marshall, & A. Goyne (Eds.), *The Management of Stress in the Australian defense force: Human factors, families, and the welfare of military personnel away from the combat-zone* (pp. 93–106). Canberra: Defense Publishing Service.

Hatcher, R. L., & Barends, A. W. (1996). Patients' view of the alliance in psychotherapy: Exploratory factor analysis of three alliance measures. *Journal of Consulting & Clinical Psychology, 64,* 1326–1336.

Iowa Persian Gulf Study Group. (1997). Self-reported illness and health status among Gulf War Veterans: A population based study. *Journal of the American Medical Association, 277,* 238–245.

Johnson, D. R., Lubin, H., Rosenheck, R., Fontana, A., Charney, D., & Southwick, S. (1999). Comparison of outcome between homogeneous and heterogeneous treatment environments in combat-related posttraumatic stress disorder. *Journal of Nervous and Mental Disease, 187,* 88–95.

Johnson, D. R., Rosenheck, R., Fontana, A., Lubin, H., Charney, D., & Southwick, S. (1996). Outcome of intensive inpatient treatment for combat-related posttraumatic stress disorder. *American Journal of Psychiatry, 153,* 771–777.

Keane, T. M., Fairbank, J. A., Caddell, J. M., & Zimering, R. T. (1989). Implosive (flooding) therapy reduces symptoms of PTSD in Vietnam combat veterans. *Behavior Therapy, 20,* 245–260.

Kessler, R. C., Sonnega, A., Hughes, M., & Nelson, C. B. (1995). Posttraumatic stress disorder in the national comorbidity survey. *Archives of General Psychiatry, 52,* 1048–1060.

King, D. W., King, L. A., Gudanowski, D. M., & Vreven, D. L. (1995). Alternative representations of war zone stressors: Relationships to posttraumatic stress disorder in male and female Vietnam veterans. *Journal of Abnormal Psychology, 104*, 184–196.

Krakow, B., Hollifield, M., Johnston, L., Koss, M., Schrader, R., Warner, T. D., et al. (2001). Imagery rehearsal therapy for chronic nightmares in sexual assault survivors with posttraumatic stress disorder—A randomized controlled trial. *Journal of American Medical Association, 286*, 537–545.

Kubany, E. S. (1994). A cognitive model of guilt typology in combat-related PTSD. *Journal of Traumatic Stress, 7*, 3–19.

Kubany, E. S. (1997). Application of cognitive therapy for trauma-related guilt (CT-TRG) with a Vietnam veteran troubled by multiple sources of guilt. *Cognitive and Behavioral Practice, 4*, 213–244.

Kubany, E. S., Hill, E. E., & Owens, J. A. (2003). Cognitive trauma therapy for battered women with PTSD: Preliminary findings. *Journal of Traumatic Stress,16*, 81–91.

Kubany, E. S., & Watson, S. B. (2003). Guilt: Elaboration of a multidimensional model. *Psychological Record, 53*, 51–90.

Kulka, R. A., Schlenger, W. E., Fairbank, J. A., Jordan, B. K., Marmar, C. R., Weiss, D. S., et al. (1990). *Trauma and the Vietnam war generation: Report of findings from the Vietnam veterans readjustment study.* New York: Brunner/Mazel.

Litz, B. T., Orsillo, S. M., Friedman, M., Ehlich, P., & Batres, A. (1997). Posttraumatic stress disorder associated with peacekeeping duty in Somalia for U.S. military personnel. *American Journal of Psychiatry, 154*, 178–184.

McNally, R. J. (1999). Research on eye movement desensitization and reprocessing (EMDR) as a treatment for PTSD. *PTSD Research Quarterly of the National Center for PTSD, 10* (1), 1–7.

Merrill, L. L., Newell, C. E., Milner, J. S., Koss, M. P., Hervig, L. K., Gold, S. R., et al. (1998). Prevalence of premilitary adult sexual victimization and aggression in a navy recruit sample. *Military Medicine, 163*, 209–212.

Najavits, L. M. (2003). Seeking safety: A treatment manual for PTSD and substance abuse. *Psychotherapy Research, 13*, 125–126.

Najavits, L. M., Weiss, R. D., Shaw, S. R., & Muenz, L. R. (1998). "Seeking safety": Outcome of a new cognitive-behavioral psychotherapy for women with posttraumatic stress disorder and substance dependence. *Journal of Traumatic Stress, 11*, 437–456.

Novaco, R. W., & Chemtob, C. M. (2002). Anger and combat-related posttraumatic stress disorder. *Journal of Traumatic Stress, 15*, 123–132.

O'Toole, B. I., Marshall, R. P., Grayson, D. A., Schureck, R. J., Dobson, M., French, M., et al. (1996). The Australian Vietnam veterans health study: III. Psychological health of Australian Vietnam veterans and its relationship to combat. *International Journal of Epidemiology, 25*, 331–339.

Ouimette, P., & Brown, P. J. (2003). *Trauma and substance abuse: Causes, consequences, and treatment of comorbid disorders*. Washington, DC: American Psychological Association.

Ozer, E. J., Best, S. R., Lipsey, T. L., & Weiss, D. S. (2003). Predictors of posttraumatic stress disorder and symptoms in adults: A meta-analysis. *Psychological Bulletin, 129,* 52–73.

Penk, W., & Flannery, R.-B., Jr. (2000). Psychosocial rehabilitation. In E. B. Foa, T. M. Keane, & M. J. Friedman (Eds.), *Effective treatments for PTSD: Practice guidelines from the International Society for Traumatic Stress Studies* (pp. 347–350). New York: The Guilford Press.

Resick, P. A., Nishith, P., Weaver, T. L., Astin, M. C., & Feuer, C. A. (2002). A comparison of cognitive-processing therapy with prolonged exposure and a waiting condition for the treatment of chronic posttraumatic stress disorder in female rape victims. *Journal of Consulting & Clinical Psychology, 70,* 867–879.

Resick, P. A., & Schnicke, M. K. (1993). *Cognitive processing therapy for sexual assault victims: A treatment manual*. Newbury Park CA: Sage Publications.

Rogers, S., Silver, S. M., Goss, J., Obenchain, J., Willis, A., & Whitney, R. L. (1999). A single session, group study of exposure and Eye Movement Desensitization and Reprocessing in treating posttraumatic stress disorder among Vietnam War veterans: Preliminary data. *Journal of Anxiety Disorders, 13,* 119–130.

Rosen, L. N., & Martin, L. (1996). Childhood antecedents of psychological adaptation to military life. *Military Medicine, 161,* 665–668.

Schlenger, W. E., Fairbank, J. A., Jordan, B. K., & Caddell, J. M. (1999). Combat-related posttraumatic stress disorder: Prevalence, risk factors, and comorbidity. In P. A. Saigh & J. D. Bremner (Eds.), *Posttraumatic stress disorder: A comprehensive text* (pp. 69–91). Needham Heights, MA: Allyn & Bacon.

Schnurr, P. P., Friedman, M. J., Foy, D. W., Shea, M. T., Hsieh, F. Y., Lavori, P. W., et al. (2003). Randomized trial of trauma-focused group therapy for posttraumatic stress disorder—Results from a Department of Veterans Affairs Cooperative Study. *Archives of General Psychiatry, 60,* 481–489.

Shalev, A. Y. (1997). Treatment of prolonged posttraumatic stress disorder: Learning from experience. *Journal of Traumatic Stress, 10,* 415–423.

Shalev, A. Y., Bonne, O., & Eth, S. (1996). Treatment of posttraumatic stress disorderd: A review. *Psychosomatic-Medicine, 58,* 165–182.

Solomon, Z., Shalev, A., Spiro, S. E., Dolev, A., Bleich, A., Waysman, M., et al. (1992). Negative psychometric outcomes: Self-report measures and a follow-up telephone survey. *Journal of Traumatic Stress, 5,* 225–246.

Southwick, S. M., Morgan, C. A., Darnell, A., Bremner, D., Nicolaou, A. L., Nagy, L., et al. (1995). Trauma-related symptoms in veterans of Operation Desert Storm: A 2–year follow-up. *American Journal of Psychiatry, 152,* 1150–1155.

Stevenson, V.-E., & Chemtob, C.-M. (2000). Premature treatment termination by angry patients with combat-related posttraumatic stress disorder. *Military Medicine, 165,* 422–424.

Sutker, P. B., Uddo, M., Brailey, K., & Allain, A. N. (1993). War-zone trauma and stress-related symptoms in Operation Desert Shield/Storm (ODS) returnees. *Journal of Social Issues, 49,* 33–50.

Unwin, C., Blatchley, N., Coker, W., Ferry, S., Hotopf, M., Hull, L., et al. (1999). Health of UK.. servicemen who served in Persian Gulf War. *Lancet, 353,* 169–178.

Wolfe, J., Brown, P. J., & Kelley, J. M. (1993). Reassessing war stress: Exposure and the Persian Gulf War. *Journal of Social Issues, 49,* 15–31.

Chapter 10

EFFECT OF COGNITIVE-BEHAVIORAL TREATMENTS FOR PTSD ON ANGER

Shawn P. Cahill, Sheila A. Rauch,
Elizabeth A. Hembree, and Edna B. Foa

INTRODUCTION

Several studies have documented a relationship between anger and posttraumatic stress disorder in veterans (e.g., Chemtob, Hamada, Roitblat, & Muraoka, 1994; Frueh, Henning, Pellegrin, & Chobot, 1997; Kubany, Gino, Denny, & Torigoe, 1994) and civilian populations (Riggs, Dancu, Gershuny, Greenberg, & Foa, 1992). Yet the nature of this relationship is not completely understood. Increased anger following the experience of a traumatic event is one of the possible symptoms of posttraumatic stress disorder (PTSD) (APA, 1987). Therefore, it is not entirely surprising that some individuals with PTSD also obtain elevated scores on separate measures of anger. Furthermore, paper and pencil measures of negatively valenced emotions, such as anger, anxiety, and depression, are frequently correlated with one another, suggesting such measures may share a common core of negative affect (Watson & Clark, 1984). It therefore is possible that the relationship between anger and PTSD may reflect a common core of negative affect.

This study was supported in part by Grant MH42178 from the National Institute of Mental Health awarded to Edna B. Foa.

The authors would like to thank David S. Riggs for his comments on an earlier draft of this manuscript.

Results from longitudinal studies of natural recovery following trauma, however, suggest a more complex relationship between anger and PTSD. Riggs et al. (1992) found that state-anger assessed approximately 1 week after a sexual or nonsexual assault predicted PTSD severity 1 month following the assault even after first entering life threat and guilt into the regression equation. Andrews, Brewing, Rose, & Kirk (2000) replicated and extended these findings among a group of victims of violent crime who were assessed 1 and 6 months following the index crime. Anger at others, but not at the self, was predictive of PTSD severity 6 months after the assault even after first entering other predictors of PTSD into the regression, including PTSD severity at 1 month, degree of injury, and gender.

One possible explanation for such results is that anger impedes the emotional processing (Foa & Kozak, 1986) of the trauma memory that would normally take place as the survivor talks about the experience with supportive others and encounters trauma reminders in their daily life in the absence of harmful consequences (Riggs et al., 1992; cf. Foa & Cahill, in press). Specifically, Riggs et al. (1992) proposed that, similar to fear, non-fear emotions following trauma such as anger are represented in memory as cognitive structures that include stimulus, response, and meaning elements. Such "anger structures" may share several stimulus elements with fear structures so that the same stimuli that activate the fear structure may also activate the anger structure. To the extent that anger inhibits fear responses, as suggested by several authors (e.g., Butler, 1975; Goldstein, Serber, & Piaget, 1970), and that activation of the fear structure is a necessary condition for modifying the fear structure (Foa & Kozak, 1986), then activation of the anger structure would prevent the modification of the fear structure and thereby impede natural recovery. Indeed, individuals may even learn cognitive strategies to activate anger in response to trauma-related thoughts in order to avoid feelings of anxiety.

A number of different cognitive-behavioral treatments (CBTs) have been found effective in reducing PTSD severity and associated anxiety and depression. Such treatments include prolonged exposure (PE; e.g., Fecteau & Nikki, 1999; Foa, Rothbaum, Riggs, & Murdock, 1991; Foa et al., 1999; Keane, Fairbank, Caddell, & Zimmering, 1989; Marks, Lovell, Noshirvani, & Thrasher, 1998; Tarrier et al., 1999), stress inoculation training (SIT; Foa et al., 1991; Foa et al., 1999), and variations of cognitive therapy (Marks et al., 1998; Resick & Schnicke, 1992; Tarrier et al., 1999). The effects of CBT for PTSD on anger and the impact of anger on treatments for PTSD have not yet been well studied. Pitman et al. (1991) reported a series of case studies that illustrated psychiatric complications that developed during a larger study of exposure therapy for a group of veterans with chronic PTSD (Pitman et al., 1996). Pitman et al. (1991) proposed that:

> Going over the situation again and again as called for in the flooding proce-dure appeared to have the effect not of alleviating but rather exacerbating the anger, shame, guilt, self-accusations, feelings of failure, and "What if" rumina-tion associated with performance in the traumatic situation. (p. 19)

Pitman et al. further recommend that therapists instead utilize cogni-tive or insight oriented therapy to address these problems. Similarly, Resick and Schnicke (1992) suggested that:

> Although activation of the [trauma] network, or schema, may sufficiently alter perceptions of danger, and hence, fear, there may be no change in emotional reactions other than fear without direct confrontation of con-flicts, misattributions, or expectations. Victims may still blame themselves, feel they have not recovered or handled the event quickly enough, feel shame or disgust, or experience anger, all of which appear sufficiently intense to facilitate intrusive memories and avoidance reactions.(p. 749; cf. Cason, Resick, & Weaver, 2002, p. 148)

While clinical lore and some cognitive theories of PTSD predict that exposure therapy for PTSD should not be effective in reducing non-fear emotions, the research literature on this question is limited and contra-dictory. Brom, Kleber, and Defares (1989) investigated the efficacy of trauma desensitization, hypnotherapy, and psychodynamic therapy com-pared with a waitlist control utilizing a group of male and female survi-vors of a variety of civilian traumas. All three treatments produced significant improvement on PTSD symptom severity, while there was no significant change for those in the waitlist condition, and the active treat-ments were comparable to one another. By contrast, no significant im-provement was observed for state-anger in any condition. However, this null finding may be the result of a floor effect, as the mean pretreatment state-anger scores were close to the minimum possible score (less than 14 on a scale ranging from 10 to 40). Foa, Riggs, Massie, and Yarczower (1995) similarly reported no significant reduction in state-anger from pre- to posttreatment among a group of 12 female sexual and nonsexual assault victims who were treated with exposure therapy. Again, however, the mean pretreatment score was close to the minimum possible score, thus raising the possibility that the null finding was the result of a floor effect. The previously noted Pitman et al. (1996) study incorporated a psychophysiological assessment during exposure therapy sessions and also collected self-reported levels of fear, sadness, guilt, and anger. The results revealed a pattern of within-session activation, within-session habituation, and across-session habituation not only for the psychophysiological indicators (heart rate, skin conductance, facial EMG) and levels of fear, but also for the self-report levels of non-fear emotions. Interestingly, Chemtob, Novaco, Hamada, and Gross (1997) targeted the treatment of anger among a group of veterans with PTSD and elevated levels of anger by adding stress inoculation training (SIT) to routine VA clinical care. Results revealed that, compared to a control group receiving routine care only, adding SIT was effective in significantly reducing state-anger, increasing anger control, decreasing general anxiety, and decreasing PTSD reexperiencing symptoms.

The effect of anger on non-anger outcome measures following targeted treatment for PTSD has also been evaluated. The previously mentioned study by Foa, Riggs, Masse, and Yarczower (1995) investigated the relationships among PTSD severity and anger at pretreatment; activation of fear during the first exposure therapy session, as measured by facial expressions of fear and self-reported fear (SUDs); and a composite outcome measure combining PTSD symptom severity and general anxiety. Correlation analyses revealed that fear activation measured by facial expressions during exposure therapy was positively associated with improvement. Fear activation during exposure was also positively associated with PTSD severity prior to treatment. Thus greater initial PTSD severity was positively correlated with fear activation during exposure therapy, which in turn was positively correlated with symptom improvement. Pretreatment anger, by contrast, was negatively correlated with fear activation during exposure therapy. Foa, Riggs, et al. (1995) proposed that anger hampers the efficacy of exposure therapy for PTSD by reducing activation of the fear structure. Taylor et al. (2001) utilized dynamic cluster analysis to investigate patterns of response to a treatment that combined cognitive restructuring, applied relaxation, and imaginal and in vivo exposure among survivors of road traffic collisions. Their analysis yielded two reliable patterns: responders (60% of their sample) and partial responders (40% of their sample). Among several pretreatment variables that differed between clusters, anger about the road traffic accident measured by a five-item scale devised for this study was significantly greater in the partial responder group than in the responder group. However, the magnitude of this difference was relatively small, less than two points on a scale ranging from 0 to 15. The previously mentioned study by Pitman et al. (1996) investigated the relationship between theoretical predictors of emotional processing (activation of fear, within- and between-session fear reduction; cf. Foa & Kozak, 1986) and treatment outcome. As expected, heartrate activation, within-session habituation and between-session habituation were correlated with reductions in reexperiencing symptoms. By contrast, measures of non-fear emotions elicited during exposure therapy were not related to outcome. Thus, anger during exposure did not appear to interfere with treatment outcome for measures of PTSD and general distress.

Given the paucity of data and conflicting results of studies investigating the effects of treatment for PTSD on anger and the effects of anger on treatment for PTSD, the present investigation addressed three related issues regarding the relationship between CBT for PTSD and anger, utilizing data from a study by Foa et al. (1999) that compared outcomes for two different CBT interventions [prolonged exposure (PE and SIT)] individually and their combination (PE/SIT) with a waitlist (WL) control group. First, we investigated the efficacy of each of the three active treatments targeted at PTSD on concomitant anger. Second, we compared the relative efficacy of PE, SIT, and PE/SIT on anger reduction. Third, we investigated whether high levels of pretreatment anger were associated with poorer outcome on measures of PTSD and related psychopathology.

METHOD

Participants

Participants in the current study were 67 women who completed treatment in the Foa et al. (1999) study and for whom pre- and posttreatment state-anger scores on the State-Trait Anger Expression Inventory (STAXI; Spielberger, 1988) were available. Entry into the parent study was determined during a pretreatment evaluation, which included the Structured Clinical Interview for *DSM–III–R* Disorders with Psychotic Screen (SCID; Spitzer, Williams, & Gibbon, 1987) and the PTSD Symptom Scale Interview (PSS-I; Foa, Riggs, Dancu & Rothbaum, 1993). All participants met *DSM–III–R* (APA, 1987) criteria for chronic PTSD resulting from an assault that occurred after age 16. Exclusion criteria included current diagnosis of organic mental disorder, schizophrenia, bipolar disorder, current alcohol or drug abuse or dependence, and having an ongoing intimate relationship with the perpetrator.

Participants in the current sample averaged 34.6 years in age (SD = 10.5). Sixty-seven percent were Caucasian and 33% were African American. Forty-eight percent were single, 22% married or co-habitating, and the remainder divorced, separated, or widowed. Forty-eight percent were employed full-time, 19% were employed part-time, and 33% were unemployed. Twelve percent did not complete high school, 15% had high school diplomas, 42% had some college education, and 32% had earned bachelor's degrees or higher. Household income was $10,000 or less for 38% of participants and above $30,000 for 41%.

Measures

The SCID was administered only at the pretreatment evaluation. All other measures were administered at pre- and posttreatment assessment points.

Structured Clinical Interview for DSM–III–R Disorders (SCID). Developed by Spitzer et al. (1987), the SCID is a semistructured interview designed to assess major Axis I disorders according to DSM–III–R (APA, 1987) criteria. In the present study, it was used to assess study eligibility and comorbid disorders.

PTSD Symptoms Scale—Interview (PSS-I). The PSS-I consists of 17 questions that correspond to the DSM–III–R PTSD symptoms each rated on a 0 to 3 point scale for frequency and severity. Inter-rater reliability for both the diagnosis of PTSD (Kappa = .91) and overall severity ratings (r = .97) are excellent (Foa et al., 1993).

State-Trait Anger Expression Inventory (STAXI). The STAXI (Spielberger, 1988) is a 44-item scale that evaluates feelings of anger and anger expression styles. It has three subscales: a 10-item State-Anger scale that evaluates the intensity of anger at the time the instrument is completed, a 10-item Trait-Anger scale that evaluates general feelings of anger, and a 24-item Anger-Expression scale. The internal consistency for the State-Anger scale, which is the focus of the current investigation, is .93.

Beck Depression Inventory (BDI; Beck, Ward, Mendelson, Mock, & Erbaugh, 1961). This is a 21-item measure of cognitive and vegetative symptoms that is widely used to assess depression in a variety of populations, including rape victims (Atkeson, Calhoun, Resick, & Ellis, 1982; Foa et al., 1991; Rothbaum, Foa, Riggs, Murdock, & Walsh, 1992; Resick & Schnicke, 1992). The inventory has a split half reliability of .93. Correlations with clinician ratings of depression range from .62 to .65.

State-Trait Anxiety Inventory (STAI). The STAI (Spielberger, Gorsuch, & Lushene, 1970) contains 20 items for state anxiety and 20 items for trait anxiety. Test-retest reliability for the state-anxiety scale is .40 and for the trait-anxiety scale is .81. Internal consistency ranges from .83 to .92. Only data from the state-anxiety scale (STAI-S) were used in the present study.

Procedures

Participants were first screened by phone and then invited to the clinic for an evaluation. Evaluators were female clinicians with at least a master's degree who were blind to treatment assignment. Eligible women who provided consent were randomized into four conditions: PE ($n = 19$), SIT ($n = 18$), PE/SIT ($n = 17$), and WL ($n = 13$). Seven female Ph.D. level clinical psychologists provided the individually administered treatments over a series of nine twice-weekly sessions, each lasting between 90 and 120 minutes. A brief description of the PE, SIT, and PE/SIT treatments is given below; see Foa et al. (1999) for a more detailed description of the treatment conditions and information about treatment fidelity.

PE treatment consisted of psycho-education about common reactions to trauma, breathing retraining, invivo exposure, imaginal exposure, and homework (for more details see Foa & Rothbaum, 1998). Imaginal exposure consisted of reliving the traumatic event in imagination and recounting the memory in the present tense. Imaginal exposure was tape-recorded and participants were instructed to listen to the tapes daily at home. Additional homework included invivo exposure to objectively safe situations that provoke trauma-related anxiety and avoidance. SIT treatment (adapted from Veronen & Kilpatrick, 1982) consisted of the acquisition and practice of coping skills aimed at management of assault-related anxiety and other post-assault problems. Skills included deep muscle relaxation, cue-controlled and differential relaxation, thought stopping, cognitive restructuring, guided self-dialogue, covert modeling, and roleplaying. Homework assignments consisted of practicing the various coping skills. The combined PE/SIT treatment followed the nine-session format and included education, invivo exposure, imaginal exposure, and training in all the SIT skills. Participants randomized to WL were informed that they would receive treatment in five weeks and were encouraged to call at anytime if they were having problems. During this period, WL participants were contacted one time by a therapist to check on them. At the completion of the WL phase, these participants were offered active treatment. Only WL data from these participants were used in the present study. Follow-up assessments were conducted on participants who received immediate treatment, but not those who received WL, at 3 months, 6 months, and 12 months posttreatment.

RESULTS

Preliminary Analyses: Effect of Treatments on PTSD, Anxiety, and Depression

We conducted preliminary analyses to determine whether outcomes for the current subsample were similar to those of the full study reported by Foa et al. (1999) for measures of PTSD, depression, and state-anxiety. The upper section of Table 10.1 presents means and standard deviations for the PSS-I, BDI, and STAI-S obtained at pretreatment, posttreatment, follow-up assessment points. Inspection of the means suggests that all three active treatments resulted in substantial decreases on all three measures, compared with little or no change in the WL condition, and that these treatment gains were maintained at follow-up. To assess the acute response to treatment, scores on each measure were submitted to separate one-way analyses of covariance (ANCOVAs), with treatment condition (PE, SIT, PE/SIT, WL) as the sole between-group factor, posttreatment scores as the dependent variable, and the corresponding pretreatment score as the covariate. Consistent with findings from the parent study (Foa et al., 1999), significant main effects for treatment condition were obtained for each measure: for the PSS-I, $F (3,62) = 9.95$; the BDI, $F (3, 62) = 8.03$; and the STAI-S, $F (3, 61) = 7.06$ ($ps < .001$). (One WL participant did not have a pretreatment score on the STAI-S, accounting for one less df compared to the PSS-I and BDI.)

Follow-up pair-wise comparisons were conducted using the least significant difference (LSD) method. For the PSS-I, PE ($M_{adj} = 10.5$, $SE = 1.82$), SIT ($M_{adj} = 13.3$, $SE = 1.87$), and PE/SIT ($M_{adj} = 13.2$, $SE = 1.93$) were each significantly ($p < .001$) different from WL ($M_{adj} = 25.6$, $SE = 2.23$)

Table 10.1 Summary of Treatment Group Means and Standard Deviations for Measures of PTSD, Depression, Anxiety, and Anger

Measure		PE			SIT			PE/SIT			WL	
		Pre	Post	FU	Pre	Post	FU	Pre	Post	FU	Pre	Post
PSS-I	M	29.4	10.2	9.0	29.9	13.2	13.6	28.6	12.6	12.6	33.2	26.9
	SD	10.3	6.5	8.2	8.6	9.1	13.9	7.3	9.9	12.3	6.1	8.9
	n	19	19	16	18	18	18	17	17	16	13	13
BDI	M	17.4	5.1	5.9	22.5	10.3	13.9	20.7	10.3	10.4	25.9	22.2
	SD	11.8	4.8	6.3	10.8	8.2	15.5	11.6	10.0	9.2	11.5	15.2
	n	19	19	16	18	18	18	17	17	16	13	13
STAI-S	M	47.7	29.6	33.7	51.5	39.3	41.0	49.3	39.5	40.1	50.8	50.7
	SD	13.1	9.1	9.6	13.8	11.8	17.0	15.8	15.0	13.1	12.9	14.5
	n	19	19	16	18	18	18	17	17	16	12	13
STAXI-S	M	14.2	10.7	10.7	19.8	10.8	12.9	16.1	13.5	13.5	18.7	18.4
	SD	6.4	1.9	1.4	9.2	1.6	6.2	8.6	5.8	6.4	9.2	10.0
	n	19	19	16	18	18	18	17	17	15	13	13

Note. PSS-I = PTSD Symptom Scale–Interview, BDI = Beck Depression Inventory, STAI-S = State-Trait Anxiety Inventory (State-Anxiety Index), and STAXI-S = State-Trait Anger Expression Inventory (State-Anger Index).

($ps < .001$), but no differences were obtained among the active treatments. Similarly for the BDI, PE ($M_{adj} = 7.34$, $SE = 1.62$), SIT ($M_{adj} = 9.59$, $SE = 1.64$), and PE/SIT ($M_{adj} = 10.64$, $SE = 1.69$) were each significantly different from WL ($M_{adj} = 19.51$, $SE = 1.96$) ($ps < .001$), with no differences among the active treatments. On the STAI-S, PE ($M_{adj} = 30.41$, $SE = 2.65$), SIT ($M_{adj} = 38.59$, $SE = 2.72$), and PE/SIT ($M_{adj} = 39.68$, $SE = 2.79$) were each significantly different from WL ($M_{adj} = 49.90$, $SE = 3.33$) ($ps < .05$). In addition, PE was significantly lower on the STAI-S than either SIT or PE/SIT ($ps < .05$). SIT and PE/SIT were not significantly different from one anther.

Data for the PSS-I, BDI, and STAI-S data were available from at least one follow-up time point on all but four of the participants initially assigned to active treatment. Three of the participants for whom no follow-up data are available received PE and one participant received PE/SIT. Follow-up data were not available on WL participants. To assess long-term effects of the active treatments, we conducted mixed-factorial ANCOVAs on each of the three outcome measures in which treatment condition (PE, SIT, or PE/SIT) served as the sole between-group factor, time of assessment (posttreatment or follow-up) served as the repeated measure, and pretreatment scores served as the covariate. These analyses were limited to those participants with a least one follow-up score ($n = 50$) and utilized the last available observation. The results revealed a significant main effect of treatment condition on the STAI-S, $F(2, 46) = 3.99$, $p < .05$. Follow-up pair-wise comparisons using the LSD method revealed that STAI-S scores in the PE condition ($M_{adj} = 32.4$, $SE = 2.18$) were significantly lower than in either the SIT ($M_{adj} = 39.1$, $SE = 2.06$) or PE/SIT ($M_{adj} = 40.5$, $SE = 2.18$) conditions ($ps < .05$), while the latter two conditions did not differ from one another. No main effect for treatment condition was obtained on the PSS-I or BDI. No main effect for time of assessment was detected on any measure, nor were there any significant treatment condition X time of assessment interactions.

Effect of Treatments on State-Anger

We next examined the effects of treatment for PTSD on state-anger. The lower section of Table 10.1 presents means and standard deviations for the STAXI-S obtained at pretreatment, posttreatment, and follow-up assessment points for each active treatment condition and WL. Inspection of the STAXI-S means suggests that all three active treatments resulted in a modest pre- to posttreatment decrease, while no change was observed in the WL condition, and that treatment gains were maintained at follow-up. To assess the acute response to treatment, STAXI-S scores were submitted to an ANCOVA, with treatment condition (PE, SIT, SIT/PE, and WL) as the between-group variable, posttreatment scores as the dependent variable, and pretreatment scores as the covariate. The results revealed a significant effect of treatment condition, F (3, 62) = 7.46, $p < .001$. Follow-up pair-wise comparisons utilizing the LSD method revealed that PE (M_{adj} = 11.6, SE = 1.13), SIT (M_{adj} = 9.9, SE = 1.16), and PE/SIT (M_{adj} = 13.8, SE = 1.18) were each significantly different from WL (M_{adj} = 17.9, SE = 1.35) ($ps < .05$). In addition, the SIT group reported significantly less state-anger than PE/SIT ($p < .05$), while PE was not different from either SIT or SIT/PE.

STAXI-S data were available from at least one follow-up time point on all but five of the participants initially assigned to active treatment. Three of the participants for whom no STAXI-S follow-up data are available received PE and two participants received PE/SIT. To assess long-term effects of the active treatments, we conducted a mixed-factorial ANCOVA on the STAXI-S scores in which treatment condition (PE, SIT, or PE/SIT) served as the sole between-group factor, time of assessment (posttreatment or follow-up) served as the repeated measure, and pretreatment scores served as the covariate. This analysis was limited to those participants with at least one posttreatment follow-up score for the STAXI-S (n = 49) and utilized the last available observation. The main effect for treatment condition approached significance ($F(2, 45)$ = 3.11, p = .054). Follow-up pair-wise comparisons utilizing the LSD method revealed the PE (M_{adj} = 11.2, SE = 0.86) and SIT (M_{adj} = 11.1, SE = 0.89) groups reported significantly ($p < .05$) less anger than PE/SIT (M_{adj} = 13.9, SE = 0.91). PE and SIT did not differ from one another. Neither the main effect for time of assessment nor the treatment condition X time of assessment interaction was significant.

Effects of Treatment on Participants with High and Low State-Anger

Although there was a statistically significant effect of treatment for PTSD on state-anger, inspection of the means in Table 10.1 reveals that, on average, our sample reported low pretreatment state-anger scores. It may be that the effects of treatment for PTSD on anger are limited to those who are generally low in anger. Therefore, it is of interest to determine whether individuals who are high in levels of anger also benefited from treatment. To investigate this question, we performed a subgroup analysis by comparing treatment outcome for high and low anger participants among the treatment sample. High anger participants were defined as those individuals having a pretreatment state-anger score two or more standard deviations above the mean for women in a normative sample (Spielberger et al., 1979).

Nine participants in the treatment samples (5 in the SIT group and 2 each in the PE and PE/SIT groups) had clinically elevated pretreatment STAXI-S scores. Of these high state-anger participants, eight also had STAXI-S data from at least one follow-up assessment. Of the 45 low state-anger anger participants, 41 also had STAXI-S data from at least one follow-up assessment. The STAXI-S data for the 49 treatment participants with at least one follow-up were submitted to a state-anger condition (low vs. high) X time of assessment (pretreatment, posttreatment, follow-up) mixed factor analysis of variance (ANOVA). This analysis revealed significant main effects for state-anger condition [$F(1, 47) = 63.66$, $p < .001$] and time of assessment [$F(2, 94) = 50.06$, $p < .001$], which were qualified by a significant interaction [$F(2, 94) = 28.91$, $p < .001$]. The means for this interaction are depicted in Figure 10.1. Follow-up one-

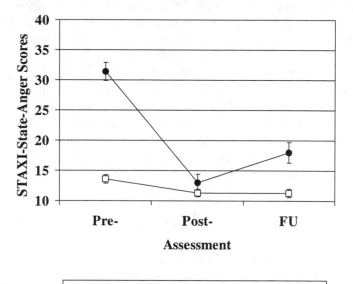

Figure 10.1 Mean state-anger over the course of treatment and at follow-up for groups of low and high state-anger women who received treatment for PTSD. Bars indicate standard errors.

way ANOVAs revealed that, as would be expected, state-anger groups differed significantly at pretreatment [$F(1, 47) = 112.60, p < .001$]. STAXI-S scores declined significantly over the course of treatment for both the low [$F(1, 40) = 7.89, p < .01$] and high [$F(1, 7) = 52.54, p < .001$] anger groups, with no difference detected between groups at posttreatment ($F(1, 47) = 1.29$, ns). No significant changes from posttreatment to follow-up were detected for either the low anger [$F(1, 40) < 1.0$, ns] or high anger group [$F(1, 7) = 2.85$, ns], although a significant difference between the groups emerged at follow-up [$F(1, 47) = 13.89, p < .001$]. Levels of anger at follow-up remained significantly lower than they had been at pretreatment for both the low [$F(1, 40) = 9.79, p < .01$] and high anger groups [$F(1, 7) = 10.44, p < .05$].

Within-group effect sizes comparing pre- to posttreatment means were calculated according to the formula ES = $(M_{Pre} - M_{Post})/SD_{Pooled}$, where SD_{Pooled} = (SQRT)[$(SD^2_{Pre} + SD^2_{Post})/2$], modified from Cohen's d statistic. Similar effect sizes comparing pre- to follow-up means were also computed by replacing the posttreatment mean and standard deviation with the corresponding follow-up statistics. Results are interpreted as recommended by Cohen (1988): small $\geq$ .20, medium $\geq$ .50, large $\geq$ .80. The high state-anger group showed large effect sizes of 3.43 and 1.88 for pre- to posttreatment and pre- to follow-up comparisons, while the low state-anger group showed a medium effect sizes of .59 for both post- and follow-up assessments.

In order to examine the hypothesis that the results of the high state-anger group reflected mere regression towards the mean, we computed reliable change index scores (RCI: Jacobson & Truax, 1991) at posttreatment and follow-up for each participant in this group. RCI scores are based upon both the magnitude of change over treatment and test-retest reliability of the instrument, with any values over 1.96 indicating that the change seen in treatment is likely to reflect reliable improvement ($p < .05$). Immediately after treatment, eight of the nine participants in the high state-anger treatment group obtained RCI scores above the cutoff, with all five of the participants in the SIT condition meeting the cutoff score, as did both participants in the PE condition, and one of the two participants in the SIT/PE condition. At follow-up, five of eight participants achieved RCI scores above the cutoff, with three of the five participants in the SIT condition meeting the cutoff score, as did both of the participants in the PE condition, but not the participant in the PE/SIT condition. These results suggest that regression to the mean alone is an unlikely explanation for the observed improvement among the high state-anger participants.

Further evidence consistent with the conclusion that the reduction in anger for the high state-anger participants is not due simply to regression to the mean is the pre- ($M = 32.7$, $SD = 6.0$) and posttreatment ($M = 32.3$, $SD = 2.1$) means from three high state-anger participants who did not receive treatments. The participants who did not receive treatment showed essentially no change across the two assessments despite having similar pretreatment scores as those who received treatment.

PTSD symptom severity, depression and anxiety. Eight of the 9 high state-anger participants (5 in the SIT group, 2 in the PE group, and 1 in the PE/SIT group) and 42 of the low state-anger participants had PSS-I, BDI, and STAI-S data from at least one follow-up assessment. To examine whether participants with high pretreatment state-anger scores benefit as much from treatment on measures of PTSD symptom severity, depression, and anxiety as those participants with low pretreatment state-anger scores, we calculated pretreatment, posttreatment, and follow-up means and standard deviations for the PSS-I, BDI, and STAI-S for each state-anger group, which are presented in Table 10.2. Scores from each measure were sub-

Table 10.2 Summary of State-Anger Group Means and Standard Deviations for PTSD, Depression, and Anxiety Among Participants Receiving Treatment

Measure		State-Anger group					
		Low			High		
		Pre	Post	FU	Pre	Post	FU
PSS-I	M	28.4	11.5	10.3	33.8	14.6	19.5
	SD	8.8	8.4	10.7	7.4	8.9	14.5
	n	45	45	42	9	9	8
BDI	M	18.0	7.4	8.7	30.8	13.8	18.4
	SD	10.4	6.4	10.1	10.6	13.0	15.4
	n	45	45	42	9	9	8
STAI-S	M	47.9	34.8	36.6	57.3	41.7	47.5
	SD	13.7	12.4	12.0	14.0	13.7	19.7
	n	45	45	42	9	9	8

Note. PSS-I = PTSD Symptom Scale—Interview, BDI = Beck Depression Inventory, STAI-S = State-Trait Anxiety Inventory (State-Anxiety Index).

mitted to separate state-anger group (low vs. high) X time of assessment (pretreatment vs. posttreatment vs. follow-up) mixed ANOVAs. These analyses were limited to data from the 50 participants with at least one follow-up data point.

Results for the PSS-I revealed a significant main effect for time of assessment [$F(2, 96) = 54.78$, $p < .001$]. Follow-up analyses revealed a significant decrease from pre- [$M = 29.5$, $SD = 8.9$] to posttreament [$M = 11.6$, $SD = 8.3$; $F(1, 49) = 176.9$. $p < .0$], with no change from posttreatment to follow-up [$M = 11.8$, $SD = 11.7$; $F(1, 49) < 1$, ns]. Scores at follow-up remained significantly lower than at pretreatment [$F(1, 49) = 121.9$, $p < .001$]. Large effects sizes were obtained pre- to posttreatment (2.08) and pre-to-follow-up (1.70). The was no significant main effect for state-anger condition nor state-anger X time of assessment interaction.

Results for the BDI revealed a significant main effect for state-anger group [$F(1, 48) = 10.24$, $p < .01$], with participants in the high state-anger group reporting greater depression [$M = 21.3$, $SD = 13.6$] than those in the low state-anger group [$M = 11.4$, $SD = 9.1$]. There was also a main effect for the time of assessment [$F(2, 96) = 30.07$, $p < .001$]. Follow-up ANOVAs indicated that BDI scores declined significantly from pretreatment [$M = 20.0$, $SD = 11.4$] to posttreatment [$M = 8.6$, $SD = 8.2$; $F(1, 49) = 94.56$, $p < .001$], but no difference from posttreatment to follow-up [$M = 10.2$, $SD = 11.5$; $F(1, 49) = 1.5$, ns]. Scores at follow-up remained significantly lower than they were at pretreatment [$F(1, 49) = 35.13$, $p < .001$]. Large effect sizes were obtained pre- to posttreatment (1.14) and pre- to follow-up (0.86). The interaction between state-anger condition and time of assessment was not significant.

Results for the STAI revealed a significant main effect for state-anger group [$F(1, 48) = 4.73$, $p < .05$], with participants in the high state-anger group reporting greater anxiety [$M = 48.6$, $SD = 16.3$] than those in the low state-anger group [$M = 39.9$, $SD = 12.5$]. There was also a main effect for the time of assessment [$F(2, 96) = 12.4$, $p < .001$]. Follow-up ANOVAs indicated that STAI scores declined significantly from pre-treatment [$M = 49.2$, $SD = 13.6$] to posttreatment [$M = 36.4$, $SD = 12.8$; $F(1, 49) = 38.63$, $p < .001$], but no difference from posttreatment to follow-up [$M = 38.3$, $SD = 13.8$; $F(1, 49) < 1.0$, ns]. Scores at follow-up remained significantly lower than they were at pretreatment [$F(1, 49) = 35.46$, $p < .001$]. Large effect sizes were obtained pre- to posttreatment (.97) and pre- to follow-up (.80). The interaction between state-anger condition and time of assessment was not significant.

Effect of Anger on Treatment Outcome of PTSD, Anxiety, and Depression: Regression Analyses

Dividing participants into high and low state-anger groups is a relatively insensitive method to investigate the effects of state-anger on non-anger outcome measures. Therefore, we also conducted a series of regression analyses on the 54 participants in the three active treatments to determine if pretreatment state-anger predicted posttreatment scores on measures of PTSD symptoms severity, depression, and general anxiety. Similar analyses were conducted on data from the 50 participants in the three active treatments with at least one follow-up assessment to determine if pretreatment state-anger predicted follow-up scores on the non-anger outcome measures.

PSS-I. Pearson correlations revealed that pretreatment PSS-I scores and STAXI-S scores were each significantly related to posttreatment PSS-I scores ($r = .37$, $p < .01$ and $r = .27$, $p < .05$, respectively) but were not significantly related to one another ($r = .21$, ns). In order to determine the unique contribution of pretreatment STAXI-S scores to posttreatment PSS-I scores, we conducted a hierarchical multiple regression analysis, entering pretreatment PSS-I scores first followed by pretreatment STAXI-S scores. Pretreatment STAXI-S scores did not contribute significantly to the regression equation beyond the contribution of the pretreatment PSS-I scores. Pretreatment PSS-I scores were significantly correlated with follow-up PSS-I scores ($r = .42$, $p < .01$) but pretreatment STAXI-S scores were not ($r = .23$, ns).

BDI. Pearson correlations revealed that pretreatment BDI scores and STAXI-S scores were significantly related to posttreatment BDI scores ($r = .68$, $p < .001$ and $r = .35$, $p < .01$, respectively). These pretreatment measures were also significantly related to each other ($r = .42$, $p < .01$). In order to determine the unique contribution of pretreatment STAXI-S scores to posttreatment BDI scores, we conducted a hierarchical multiple regression analysis, entering pretreatment BDI scores first followed by pretreatment STAXI-S scores. Pretreatment STAXI-S scores did not contribute significantly to the regression equation beyond the contribution of the pretreatment BDI. Pretreatment BDI scores were significantly correlated with follow-up BDI scores ($r = .48$, $p < .001$), but pretreatment STAXI-S scores were not ($r = .27$, ns).

STAI-S. Pearson correlations revealed that pretreatment STAI-S scores were significantly related to posttreatment STAI-S scores ($r = .40$, $p < .01$) but pretreatment STAXI-S scores were not significantly related to posttreatment STAI-S scores ($r = .25$, ns). These pretreatment measures were, however, significantly related to each other ($r = .37$, $p < .05$). Pretreatment STAI-S scores and STAXI-S scores were each significantly correlated with follow-up STAI-S scores ($r = .56$, $p < .001$ and $r = .30$, $p < .05$, respectively). In order to determine the unique contribution of pretreatment STAXI-S scores to follow-up STAI-S scores, we conducted a hierarchical multiple regression analysis, entering pretreatment STAI-S scores first followed by pretreatment STAXI-S scores. Pretreatment STAXI-S scores did not contribute significantly to the regression equation beyond the contribution of the pretreatment STAI-S scores.

DISCUSSION

The current study demonstrated that PE, SIT, and their combination (PE/SIT), which had been administered to ameliorate PTSD symptoms, also decreased anger. This was especially apparent for participants with high pretreatment levels of anger. Indeed, the subgroup analyses indicated that, on average, participants with high pretreatment levels of anger displayed normal levels of anger at posttreatment. Indeed, high and low state-anger groups did not differ from one another at the posttreatment assessment. Although participants with high levels of pretreatment anger were subsequently found to have higher levels of anger at the follow-up assessment than their low anger counterparts, the level of anger among the high angry participants at the follow-up assessment was still significantly lower than it had been prior to treatment and was not significantly greater than it had been immediately following treatment.

These findings, together with prior results showing that CBT interventions (e.g., PE, SIT, cognitive therapy) for PTSD also reduce depression and anxiety (e.g., Foa et al., 1991, 1999; Marks et al., 1998; Tarrier et al., 1999), suggest that CBT has broad effects on negative emotions beyond those targeted by the treatment. Consistent with this view is the complementary finding by Chemtob et al. (1997) that, among veterans with PTSD, treatment for anger resulted not only in decreased anger but also in decreased PTSD reexperiencing symptoms.

In the current study PE and SIT produced comparable reductions in anger, whereas the PE/SIT program was less effective than SIT alone. The finding that PE and SIT produced similar reductions in anger is inconsistent with previous findings that exposure therapy does not reduce anger and suggestions that anger therefore requires the use of additional or alternative interventions (Pitman et al., 1991; Resick & Schnicke, 1992). However, the finding that SIT, but not PE, produced a greater decrease in anger than PE/SIT may lend support to the view that interventions included in SIT may be particularly suitable for anger management. The finding is also consistent with studies showing that combining treatments (e.g., PE/SIT, PE plus cognitive restructuring) does not result in better outcome, and sometime results in slightly worse outcome, than obtained by the individual treatments (Foa et al., 1999; Marks et al., 1998; Paunovic & Ost, 2001). An alternative explanation for the superiority of SIT over PE/SIT lies in possible sample differences. Of the nine participants with high levels of state-anger, the individuals who showed the greatest reduction in anger after treatment, five were in the SIT condition versus two in each of the other conditions.

In the current study high levels of pretreatment state-anger did not impede the efficacy of CBT in reducing symptoms of PTSD, depression, and anxiety. These findings are inconsistent with Foa et al.'s (1995) results that pretreatment anger predicted low fear activation during PE sessions, which in turn predicted less improvement in trauma-related psychopathology. One possible explanation for the inconsistency is sample differences: while the pre- and posttreatment anger means were similar in the Foa et al. 1995 and the current study, the standard deviation of the former was lower than in the current study. This suggests that Foa et al.'s (1995) sample did not include high-anger participants, the very participants who showed the greatest reduction in anger in the present study. The present results are also at odds with Taylor et al.'s (2001) finding that partial responders to cognitive behavior therapy for PTSD following road collisions were angrier about the accident than were responders. Here we note that studies differed in their assessment of anger, with Taylor et al. (2001) focusing on anger related to the traumatic event while we measured state-anger regardless of the object of the anger. Finally, the current finding that pretreatment anger levels did not impede outcome are discrepant with studies indicating that high levels of anger impede natural recovery (e.g., Feeny, Zoellner, & Foa, 2000; Riggs et al., 1992), and question Foa's (1997) proposition that common mechanisms underlie natural recovery from PTSD and the benefits of CBT with regard to anger.

Three questions regarding the clinical significance of the current results can be raised. First, did state-anger scores in the high-anger condition reflect clinically significant levels of anger? Probably, given that the cutoff used to categorize participants as highly angry was two standard deviations above the mean of a normative sample. Additionally, the pretreatment mean score of our high-anger female participants (M = 32.3) was similar to the corresponding mean of Chemtob et al.'s (1997) sample of angry male veterans with PTSD (M = 32.4). Second, did the reduction in anger seen in the high-anger participants represent clinically significant change? Again, probably. As noted earlier, although anger scores in the low- and high-anger groups differed significantly at pretreatment, this difference disappeared after treatment. Furthermore, the mean posttreatment anger scores for both groups fell within the "normal" range, based on the normative sample. Indeed, the mean posttreatment anger score for our highly angry group (M = 13.3) was less than four points above the minimum score for this instrument, and numerically lower than that reported by Chemtob et al. (1997) following their targeted treatment of anger among veterans with PTSD (M = 19.5).

Third, can the reduction in anger found in the high-anger participants be explained by regression to the mean, rather than actual improvement in anger? This question was addressed in two ways. In the current sample, three waitlist participants had clinically significant elevations in anger. Due to low sample size, formal analyses were not conducted comparing treated versus non-treated high-anger participants. However, the average change from pre- to posttreatment among the three untreated participants was less than a single point on the STAXI-S, thus failing to lend any support to the regression to the mean hypothesis. Furthermore, computation of RCI scores, which factors in both test-retest reliability of the measurement instrument and symptom change, indicated that, immediately after treatment, eight of the nine high anger participants who received treatment displayed change that was greater than would be expected if treatment had no effect on anger.

In summary, the results of the current study suggest that (a) the effects of PE, SIT, and their combination implemented for PTSD on anger are genuine; (b) the effects hold for both clinically angry and non-clinically angry participants; (c) anger reduction for is both statistically and clinically meaningful; and (d) high levels of anger did not impede the effectiveness of treatments for PTSD and associated psychopathology. These results challenge clinical lore that exposure therapy, the best–validated treatment for PTSD, should not be implemented with highly angry individuals (Jaycox & Foa, 1996; Hembree, Marshall, Fitzgibbons & Foa, 2001; Pitman et al., 1991).

REFERENCES

American Psychiatric Association. (1987). *Diagnostic and statistical manual of mental disorders* (3rd ed., rev.). Washington, DC: Author.

Andrews, B., Brewin, C. R., Rose, S., & Kirk, M. (2000). Predicting PTSD symptoms in victims of violent crime: The role of shame, anger, and childhood abuse. *Journal of Abnormal Psychology, 109*, 69–73.

Atkeson, B. M., Calhoun, K. S., Resick, P. A., & Ellis, E. M. (1982). Victims of rape: Repeated assessment of depressive symptoms. *Journal of Consulting and Clinical Psychology, 50*, 96–102.

Beck, A. T., Ward, C. H., Mendelson, M., Mock, J., & Erbaugh, J. (1961). An inventory for measuring depression. *Archives of General Psychiatry, 4*, 561–571.

Brom, D., Kleber, R. J., & Defares, P. B. (1989). Brief psychotherapy for posttraumatic stress disorders. *Journal of Consulting and Clinical Psychology, 57*, 607–612.

Butler, P. (1975). The treatment of severe agoraphobia employing induced anger as an anxiety inhibitor: A case study. *Journal of Behavior Therapy and Experimental Psychiatry, 6*, 327–329.

Cason, D. R., Resick, P. A., & Weaver, T. L. (2002). Schematic integration of traumatic events. *Clinical Psychology Review, 22*, 131–153.

Chemtob, C. M., Hamada, R. S., Roitblat, H. L., & Muraoka, M. Y. (1994). Anger, impulsivity and anger control in combat-related posttraumatic stress disorder. *Journal of Consulting and Clinical Psychology, 62*, 827–832.

Chemtob, C. M., Novaco, R. W., Hamada, R. S., & Gross, D. M. (1997). Cognitive-behavioral treatment for severe anger in posttraumatic stress disorder. *Journal of Consulting and Clinical Psychology, 65*, 184–189.

Cohen, J. (1998). *Statistical power analysis for the behavioral sciences* (2nd ed.) Hillsdale, NJ: Erlbaum.

Fecteau, G., & Nikki, R. (1999). Cognitive behavioural treatment of posttraumatic stress disorder after motor vehicle accident. *Behavioural and Cognitive Psychotherapy, 27*, 201–214.

Feeny, N., Zoellner, L., & Foa, E. B. (2000). Anger, dissociation, and posttraumatic stress disorder among female assault victims. *Journal of Traumatic Stress, 13*, 89–100.

Foa, E. B. (1997). Psychological processes related to recovery from a trauma and an effective treatment for PTSD. In R. Yehuda & A. McFarlane (Eds.), Psychobiology of PTSD. *Annals of the New York Academy of Sciences, 410–424.*

Foa, E. B., & Cahill, S. P. (in press). Emotional processing in psychological therapies. In N. J. Smelser & P. B. Bates (Eds.), *International Encyclopedia of the Social and Behavioral Sciences.* Oxford: Elsevier.

Foa, E. B., Dancu, C. V., Hembree, E. A., Jaycox, L. H., Meadows, E. A., & Street, G. P. (1999). A comparison of exposure therapy, stress inoculation training, and their combination for reducing posttraumatic stress disorder in female assault victims. *Journal of Consulting and Clinical Psychology, 67*, 194–200.

Foa, E. B., & Kozak, M. J. (1986). Emotional processing of fear: Exposure to corrective information. *Psychological Bulletin, 99*, 20–35.

Foa, E. B., Riggs, D. S., Dancu, C. V., & Rothbaum, B. O. (1993). Reliability and validity of a brief instrument for assessing posttraumatic stress disorder. *Journal of Traumatic Stress, 6,* 459–473.

Foa, E. B., Riggs, D. S., Massie, E. D., & Yarczower, M. (1995). The impact of fear activation and anger on the efficacy of exposure treatment for posttraumatic stress disorder. *Behavior Therapy, 26,* 487–499.

Foa, E. B., & Rothbaum, B. O. (1998). *Treating the trauma of rape: Cognitive-behavioral therapy for PTSD.* New York: Guilford.

Foa, E. B., Rothbaum, B. O., Riggs, D. S., & Murdock, T. B. (1991). Treatment of posttraumatic stress disorder in rape victims: A comparison between cognitive-behavioral procedures and counseling. *Journal of Consulting and Clinical Psychology, 59,* 715–723.

Frueh, B. C., Henning, K. R., Pellegrin, K. L., & Chobot, K. (1997). Relationship between anger measures and PTSD symptomatology, employment, and compensation-seeking status in combat veterans. *Journal of Clinical Psychology, 53, 8,* 871–878.

Goldstein, A. J., Serber, M., & Piaget, G. (1970). Induced anger as a reciprocal inhibitor of fear. *Journal of Behavior Therapy and Experimental Psychiatry, 1,* 67–70.

Hembree, E.A., Marshall, R., Fitzgibbons, L., & Foa, E.B. (2001). The difficult-to-treat patient with posttraumatic stress disorder. In M. J. Dewan & R. W. Pies (Eds.), *The Difficult to Treat Psychiatric Patient* (pp. 149–178). Washington, DC: American Psychiatric Press.

Jacobson, N. S., & Truax, P. (1991). Clinical significance: A statistical approach to defining meaningful change in psychotherapy research. *Journal of Clinical and Consulting Psychology, 59,* 12–19.

Jaycox, L. H., & Foa, E. B. (1996). Obstacles in implementing exposure therapy for PTSD: Case discussions and practical solutions. *Clinical Psychology and Psychotherapy, 3,* 176–184.

Keane, T. M., Fairbank, J. A., Caddell, J. M., & Zimmering, R. T. (1989). Implosive (flooding) therapy reduces symptoms of PTSD in Vietnam combat veterans. *Behavior Therapy, 20,* 245–260.

Kubany, E. S., Gino, A., Denny, N. R., & Torigoe, R. Y. (1994). Relationship of cynical hostility and PTSD among Vietnam veterans. *Journal of Traumatic Stress, 7,* 21–31.

Marks, I., Lovell, K., Noshirvani, H., Livanou, M., & Thrasher, S. (1998). Treatment of posttraumatic stress disorder by exposure and/or cognitive restructuring: A controlled study. *Archives of General Psychiatry, 55,* 317–325.

Paunovic, N., & Ost, L. G. (2001). Cognitive-behavior therapy vs exposure therapy in the treatment of PTSD in refugees. *Behaviour Research and Therapy, 39,* 1183–1197.

Pitman, R. K., Altman, B., Greenwald, E., Longpre, R. E., Macklin, M. L., Poire, R. E., et al. (1991). Psychiatric complications during flooding therapy for posttraumatic stress disorder. *Journal of Clinical Psychiatry, 52,* 17–20.

Pitman, R. K., Orr, S. P., Altman, B., Longpre, R. E., Poire, R. E., Macklin, M. L., et al. (1996). Emotional processing and outcome of imaginal flooding therapy in Vietnam veterans with chronic posttraumatic stress disorder. *Comprehensive Psychiatry, 37,* 409–418.

Resick, P. A., & Schnicke, M. K. (1992). Cognitive processing therapy for sexual assault victims. *Journal of Consulting and Clinical Psychology, 60,* 748–756.

Riggs, D. S., Dancu, C. V., Gershuny, B. S., Greenberg, D., & Foa, E. B. (1992). Anger and posttraumatic stress disorder in female crime victims. *Journal of Traumatic Stress, 5,* 613–625.

Rothbaum, B. O., Foa, E. B., Riggs, D. S., Murdock, T., & Walsh, W. (1992). A prospective examination of posttraumatic stress disorder in rape victims. *Journal of Traumatic Stress, 5,* 455–475.

Spielberger, C.D. (1988). Anger expression scale. In M. Hersen & A.S. Bellack (Eds.), *Dictionary of behavioral assessment techniques* (pp. 446–448). New York: Pergamon Press.

Spielberger, C. D., Gorsuch, R. L., & Lushene, R. E. (1970). *Manual for the State-Trait Anxiety Inventory (self-evaluation questionnaire).* Palo Alto, CA: Consulting Psychologists Press.

Spielberger, C.D., Jacobs, G., Crane, R. Russell, S., Westberry, L., Johnson, E., et al. (1979). *Preliminary manual for the State-Trait Personality Inventory (STPI).* Tampa, FL: University of South Florida Human Resources Institute.

Spitzer, R. L., Williams, J. B. W., & Gibbon, M. (1987). *Structured clinical interview for DSM–III-R-nonpatient version.* New York: Biometric Research Department, New York State Psychiatric Institute.

Tarrier, N., Pilgrim, H., Sommerfield, C., Faragher, B., Reynolds, M., Graham, E., et al. (1999). A randomized trial of cognitive therapy and imaginal exposure in the treatment of chronic posttraumatic stress disorder. *Journal of Consulting and Clinical Psychology, 67,* 13–18.

Taylor, S., Fedoroff, I. C., Koch, W. J., Thoradarson, D. S., Fecteau, G., & Nicki, R. M. (2001). Posttraumatic stress disorder arising after road traffic collisions: Patterns of response to cognitive-behavior therapy. *Journal of Consulting and Clinical Psychology, 69,* 541–551.

Veronen, L. J., & Kilpatrick, D. G. (1982, November). Stress inoculation training for victims of rape: Efficacy and differential findings. In *Sexual Violence and Harassment,* symposium conducted at the 16th Annual Convention of the Association for Advancement of Behavior Therapy, Los Angeles, CA.

Watson, D., & Clark, L. A. (1984). Negative affectivity: The disposition to experience aversive emotional states. *Psychological Bulletin, 96,* 465–490.

Chapter 11

THE CHALLENGE OF TREATING PTSD IN THE CONTEXT OF CHRONIC PAIN

Jaye Wald, Steven Taylor, and Ingrid C. Fedoroff

INTRODUCTION

Acute pain is an adaptive, protective response, typically coinciding with actual or potential tissue damage. This type of pain produces a withdrawal response from the noxious stimuli to allow the injured area to heal and to prevent further injury. Acute pain typically abates with physical recovery. In comparison, chronic pain is defined by the persistence of pain beyond the usual healing time, usually beyond 3 months (Merskey & Bogduk, 1994). There are many different kinds of chronic pain (e.g., chronic low-back pain, fibromyalgia, myofascial pain syndrome). Unlike acute pain, chronic pain typically has no adaptive purpose and the onset and cause may be unclear. Chronic pain can be recurrent, intermittent, or continuous. It can evolve into an entrenched, self-perpetuating cycle of psychological distress and suffering, physical deconditioning (i.e., muscle wasting and loss of physical fitness due to inactivity), functional interference, withdrawal from activities, as well as dependence on medication and health care services (Eimer & Freeman, 1998).

Chronic pain and posttraumatic stress disorder (PTSD) commonly co-occur, resulting in substantial disability, health care utilization, and public health costs. Often, a traumatic injury is the source of both PTSD and chronic pain. Common examples include injuries arising from motor vehicle accidents (MVAs), industrial accidents involving burns or amputation, and assault- or combat-related injuries. Research suggests that 20 to 75% of patients with chronic pain have comorbid PTSD (Asmundson, Norton, & Allerdings, 1998; Chibnall & Duckro, 1994; Geisser, Rth, Bachman, & Eckert, 1996; Hickling & Blanchard, 1992; Hickling, Blanchard, Scwartz, & Silverman, 1992). The wide range of estimates probably reflects differences in patient characteristics across studies, such as differences in the type of tissue damage.

Comorbid pain and PTSD present a number of treatment challenges. This chapter will review what is currently known about the relationship between pain and PTSD, as well as review the small but growing literature on the treatment of comorbid PTSD and chronic pain. Assessment issues and treatment strategies are discussed and illustrated with case examples.

DEVELOPMENT AND MAINTENANCE OF COEXISTING PAIN AND PTSD

Predisposing Factors

The risk for developing coexisting PTSD and chronic pain may depend on pretrauma factors common to both disorders. Pretrauma risk factors implicated in PTSD include the experience of previous trauma and previous psychopathology (Breslau, Davis, Andreski, & Peterson, 1991). Premorbid psychopathology and prior traumatic events have similarly been associated with the development of chronic pain (Dersh, Dolatin, & Gatchel, 2002; Eimer & Freeman, 1998; Gasma, 1994). There might also be a shared genetic vulnerability for PTSD and chronic pain (Asmundson, Coons, Taylor, & Katz, 2002).

One promising area of research is to clarify the role of anxiety sensitivity in both development and maintenance of pain and PTSD. Anxiety sensitivity is the fear of arousal-related bodily sensations, arising from beliefs that the sensations have harmful physical, social, or psychological consequences (e.g., the belief that palpitations lead to heart attacks, or the belief that stress-related depersonalization leads to insanity: see chapter 4). PTSD and chronic pain are both associated with elevated anxiety sensitivity, and people with elevated anxiety sensitivity tend to fear the arousal sensations associated with pain and with PTSD (Asmundson et al., 2002). In turn, this fear leads to further arousal, thereby amplifying the person's distress. Thus, anxiety sensitivity appears to contribute to pain-related fear and avoidance, and to the fear and avoidance of PTSD reexperiencing and hyperarousal symptoms.

Although there is suggestive evidence that elevated anxiety sensitivity may be a predisposing factor for PTSD and chronic pain, further research is needed to establish whether elevated anxiety sensitivity actually precedes these disorders. It is possible that anxiety sensitivity could become elevated as a result of PTSD or chronic pain, and then in turn exacerbate PTSD and pain. If this is the case then anxiety sensitivity might be a perpetuating factor rather than a predisposing factor. Either way, interventions that reduce anxiety sensitivity may be useful for treating comorbid pain and PTSD. Such interventions include interoceptive exposure and cognitive restructuring of catastrophic beliefs about arousal-related sensations (Taylor, 2000; and see chapter 4).

PRECIPITATING FACTORS

Severe pain conditions (e.g., complex regional pain syndrome) can be traumatizing, and may lead to full-blown PTSD (Amir et al., 1997; Lebovitz, Yarmush, & Lefkowitz, 1990). Thus, the underlying medical condition producing the pain disorder may sometimes indirectly precipitate PTSD. Similarly, a severe, life-threatening injury may be sufficient to precipitate both chronic pain and PTSD.

PERPETUATING FACTORS

Reinforcement contingencies. Reinforcement contingencies, such as sympathy or attention from significant others in response to expressions of pain, can perpetuate chronic pain (Holzman & Turk, 1986). However, it is unclear whether reinforcement contingencies can perpetuate PTSD. Accordingly, it is unclear whether reinforcement contingencies can play a role in the persistence of comorbid pain and PTSD.

With regard to the relationship between protracted litigation and PTSD, some studies suggest that PTSD and litigation are related, while other studies find no relationship (Blanchard et al., 1996; Bryant & Harvey, 1995; Mayou, Tyndel, & Bryant, 1997). Case settlements do not typically result in symptom resolution in either PTSD or chronic pain (Bryant & Harvey, 2003; Gasma, 1994). Thus, it appears that litigation may not be a strong incentive (reinforcer) for either pain behavior or PTSD symptoms. Financial difficulties and litigation involvement might contribute to the chronicity of these conditions owing to their stressful nature and to the fact that they also provide ongoing reminders of the traumatic event (Ehlers, Mayou, & Bryant, 1998; Taylor & Koch, 1995). Further research is required to examine this possibility.

Mutual maintenance. People with PTSD and chronic pain, compared with people with only one of these disorders, tend to have more severe symptoms, greater distress, and more functional impairment (Amir et al., 1997; Bryant, Marasszeky, Crook, Baguley, & Gurka, 1999; Geisser et al., 1996). This observation led investigators to consider whether pain and PTSD symptoms mutually maintain or exacerbate one another (Sharp & Harvey, 2001). There are several ways in which chronic pain and PTSD could mutually perpetuate one another.

It is common for people with pain and PTSD to describe inescapable reminders of the traumatic event, such as the permanent functional limitations, disfigurement, and other secondary stressors associated with the trauma (e.g., loss of major life roles, litigation). Similarly, recurrent episodes of pain can serve as potent interoceptive cues that trigger recollections of the traumatic event (Schreiber & Galai-Gat, 1993). Thus, recurrent pain can perpetuate PTSD-reexperiencing symptoms. In turn, these distressing PTSD symptoms can heighten muscle tension, thereby leading to further pain (e.g., headache, muscle spasms).

The mechanisms underlying PTSD may also contribute to the recurrence of pain. It appears that trauma reminders can trigger pain as a form of somatosensory flashback (Salomons, Osterman, Gagliese, & Katz, in press). These flashbacks consist of pain that resembles, in quality and location, the pain experienced during the trauma. To illustrate, PTSD in one patient was triggered by awareness under anesthesia, in which she experienced the pain associated with intubation and surgical incisions, but was unable to move or signal for help. She later experienced pain flashbacks, consisting of "painful pressure pushing against my sternum," which coincided with the location of pain during intubation. Pain flashbacks were triggered by surgery-related stimuli, such as the sight of a nurse in a blue surgical scrub suit (Salomons et al., in press).

Avoidance of pain and PTSD also is involved in the mutual maintenance of these conditions. People with comorbid pain and PTSD typically strive to avoid things that worsen pain or provoke PTSD symptoms. A person with MVA-related PTSD and chronic pain, for example, might avoid driving because it triggers pain (e.g., lower-back pain due to muscle spasms), and because driving triggers PTSD symptoms (e.g., intrusive recollections of the MVA). This strategy is maladaptive and disabling over the long term because (a) it perpetuates PTSD, and (b) leads to physical deconditioning and, consequently, the perpetuation of pain (Foa & Rothbaum, 1998; Vlaeyen & Linton, 2000). Pain avoidance is linked to fear of re-injury and to beliefs that pain is unendurable (Asmundson, 1999; Vlaeyen & Linton, 2000). Similarly, the avoidance of PTSD symptoms is associated with beliefs that the symptoms themselves are harmful (Fedoroff, Taylor, Asmundson, & Koch, 2000). Thus, the tendency to hold catastrophic beliefs about one's pain and PTSD symptoms appears to motivate avoidance, which in turn perpetuates comorbid pain and PTSD.

Other types of thinking styles also have been implicated in pain and PTSD. The tendency to engage in angry rumination about the traumatic event (e.g., angry thoughts about the person responsible for a severe MVA) is correlated with the persistence of PTSD and with pain severity and pain-related functional interference (Ehlers et al., 1998; Fernandez & Turk, 1995; Riggs, Dancun, & Gershuny, 1992). This ruminative tendency therefore could perpetuate both pain and PTSD.

ASSESSMENT OF PAIN AND PTSD

In clinical settings where patients present with PTSD as the primary complaint, pain symptoms may go undetected. Similarly, people who present for pain treatment may not be assessed for PTSD. Brief screening for comorbidity in individuals who present with either pain or PTSD can facilitate early detection and appropriate treatment planning. For example, asking the patient with PTSD a few direct questions about the presence and severity of pain can be helpful in identifying pain problems. Similarly, asking questions about the patient's trauma history and current PTSD symptoms (e.g., unwanted memories of the trauma, recurrent nightmares) can be a quick and effective screening method for PTSD symptoms. When patients are suspected of having this type of comorbidity, a comprehensive assessment of pain and PTSD should then be undertaken. Relevant diagnostic information can be obtained through a structured diagnostic interview such as the Structured Clinical Interview for DSM–IV (First, Spitzer, Gibbon, & Williams, 1996). Experienced PTSD practitioners may elect to assess PTSD symptoms with an unstructured clinical interview (supplemented, as needed, with questions from the Structured Clinical Interview for *DSM–IV*). For the purpose of PTSD treatment-outcome research, however, it is preferable to use standardized PTSD measures. Useful measures include the Clinician-Administered PTSD Scale (Blake et al., 1997), the Posttraumatic Stress Diagnostic Scale (Foa, 1995), the Trauma Symptom Inventory (Briere, 1995), and the Accident Fear Questionnaire (for motor-vehicle accident patients: Kuch, Evans, & Schulman, 1994).

In assessing PTSD symptoms, we split the avoidance and numbing scales into separate subscales, one for avoidance and another for numbing. We do this because (a) avoidance and numbing are factor-analytically distinct from one another (Asmundson et al., 2000; King, Leskin, King, & Weathers, 1998), which suggests that they should be assessed separately; (b) pretreatment avoidance and numbing have different predictive properties—numbing predicts poorer outcome for cognitive-behavior therapy (CBT), whereas avoidance does not (Taylor et al., 2001); (c) avoidance and numbing are associated with different patterns of treatment response—behavior therapy, compared to relaxation training and eye movement desensitization and reprocessing, is superior at reducing avoidance, whereas the three treatments do not differ in their effects on numbing (Taylor et al., 2003; and see chapter 2).

With regard to pain assessment, the multidimensional nature of pain means that clinicians ought to assess its various sensory, cognitive, affective, and behavioral aspects. This is particularly important in the pretreatment assessment, which is used to develop a treatment plan. Clinicians experienced in pain assessment might simply opt to use an unstructured interview to assess pain. This can be supplemented with self-report measures. Useful multidimensional measures include the McGill Pain Questionnaire (Melzack, 1975, 1987) and the Multidimensional Pain Inventory (Kerns, Turk, & Rudy, 1985).

To monitor treatment progress, we have found it useful to use brief self-report instruments, administered at the beginning of each session. A short battery could consist of the PTSD Symptom Scale (from Foa, 1995) and a short rating of pain. The type of pain measure would depend on the nature of the patient's pain problems (e.g., a simple rating of one or two key aspects of the patient's pain). For people with relatively constant pain, for example, the scale might consist of a 0 to 10 rating scale (0 = no pain, 10 = severe pain). This could be used to measure the average pain intensity each day. For patients with intermittent pain (e.g., recurrent headaches or back pain), they could be asked to report the number of pain episodes over, say, the past week.

TREATMENT STRATEGIES

Behavioral and Cognitive-Behavioral Approaches

A large body of research shows that behavior therapy and cognitive-behavior therapy are among the most effect treatments for PTSD, and can reduce associated psychopathology such as depression (Taylor et al., 2003; van Etten & Taylor, 1998). Behavioral and cognitive-behavioral methods are also important interventions for chronic pain (Turk & Rudy, 1994). However, there has been relative little research on the treatment of co-morbid PTSD and chronic pain. Available evidence suggests that comorbid pain may interfere with the treatment of PTSD, thereby suggesting that conventional PTSD protocols may need to be modified when pain is present (Taylor et al., 2001). Thus, the treating clinician is faced with several important questions: Which interventions are most useful for patients with PTSD and chronic pain? Which interventions should be modified or avoided? What is the best way to organize the sequence of treatment? For example, should we first treat pain and then PTSD? Should we try to treat pain and PTSD simultaneously? There are no simple answers to these questions. At the present time, treatment decisions must be made on a case-by-case basis. Even so, the treatment-outcome literature offers some guidance for selecting and sequencing interventions.

Research suggests that presence of chronic pain need not rule out empirically supported psychosocial treatments for PTSD, such as CBT. Although PTSD treatment may be less effective when chronic pain is present, these interventions can still be useful. To illustrate, Muse (1986) reported findings supporting the value of CBT for PTSD when chronic pain is present. Patients first completed a multidisciplinary pain management program and then were treated for PTSD. Symptoms of PTSD did not change during the pain program, but did improve when PTSD was treated with imaginal exposure (in the form of systematic desensitization).

Hickling and Blanchard (1997) treated 10 patients with MVA-related PTSD symptoms. The majority of patients also had accident-related pain. Treatment (9 to 12 weekly sessions) consisted of a manualized multicomponent package, which included psychoeducation, relaxation training, exposure therapy, cognitive restructuring, and pleasurable activity scheduling. At posttreatment, there was a substantial decrease in posttraumatic, depressive, and general anxiety symptoms, and these gains were largely maintained at a 3-month follow-up. However, role limitations (e.g., work-related impairments) continued to be an ongoing problem, which the authors attributed to the persistent physical difficulties. Other studies using this treatment package have similarly found that CBT can reduce PTSD even when chronic pain is present (Blanchard et al., 2003; Taylor et al., 2001). And PTSD treatment can lead to some reduction in chronic pain (Fedoroff et al., 2000), although pain may continue to be a problem.

Despite the benefits of CBT for PTSD, there is ample room for improving treatment efficacy. One approach is to identify the way that chronic pain interferes with PTSD treatment, and try to find ways of circumventing the problem. Chronic pain can interfere with PTSD treatment by reducing the patient's participation in imaginal and in vivo exposure to trauma cues (Koch & Taylor, 1995). During exposure, chronic pain patients may experience muscle spasms. This disrupts or even terminates the exposure exercise and makes patients reluctant to engage in further exposure. To offset this problem, the clinician can devote more time to training the patient in relaxation exercises and to implementing relaxation exercises immediately before and after each exposure exercise. The "tense-release" component of relaxation training (i.e., the exercise in which patients tense and then release various muscle groups) should be avoided, in order to limit the likelihood of triggering muscle spasms or other forms of pain.

CBT for PTSD may also be improved by integrating it with a multidisciplinary pain management program. For severe, chronic pain, multidisciplinary pain management is considered to be among the most effective interventions. This type of program typically involves medical, psychological, and physical rehabilitation. The psychological component of pain management programs typically uses cognitive behavioral principles and interventions (Turk & Rudy, 1994). Specific interventions typically include psychoeducation, relaxation training, and cognitive restructuring (Currie, Wilson, Pontefract, & deLaplante, 2000).

Patients with comorbid pain and PTSD could first complete the pain program and then receive PTSD treatment. This approach may limit the problem of exposure-related pain exacerbation. A problem with this approach, however, is that many pain programs involve group therapy, consisting of people with chronic pain and perhaps one or two patients with comorbid chronic pain and PTSD. Pain/PTSD patients are often unsuitable for these groups because the manifestation of PTSD symptoms in group can be very distressing for the other members. For severe cases of PTSD, pain specialists may request that the PTSD be treated first. What sometimes happens is these patients get shuffled between pain and PTSD clinics, with each clinic insisting that the other problem be treat first (e.g., pain clinics requesting that PTSD be treated first, and PTSD clinics wanting the pain treated first). Some type of agreement with the treating professionals on a comprehensive treatment plan would be helpful for these complex cases, so that an integrated treatment can be provided to concurrently treat pain and PTSD. Unfortunately, such integrated programs are the exception rather than the rule. More typically, pain/PTSD patients are triaged on the basis of their most severe problem; those with pain as their most severe problem are first treated in pain clinics, whereas those with PTSD as the major problem are first treated for PTSD.

For pain/PTSD patients who first receive pain treatment, it is important that the skilled learned in the pain management program continue to be utilized during PTSD treatment. Throughout PTSD treatment, patients may need to be periodically reminded to continue to practice their pain management techniques. Another approach that we are currently pilot-testing is to use interoceptive exposure. Here, the goal is to reduce anxiety sensitivity, and thereby indirectly reduce pain and PTSD. Table 11.1 lists some further ways in which CBT for PTSD can be modified when the patient also suffers from chronic pain. These suggestions are drawn from the treatment literature and from our clinical experiences.

PHARMACOTHERAPIES

According to the Expert Consensus Panel Guidelines (Foa, Davidson, & Frances, 1999), a combination of psychological and pharmacological therapies may be needed when PTSD is comorbid with other disorders. Several types of medications, most notably the selective serotonin reuptake inhibitors (SSRIs: e.g., fluoxetine, fluvoxamine, sertraline), are effective in reducing PTSD (van Etten & Taylor, 1998). For coexisting PTSD and chronic pain, the Consensus Panel recommended the use of SSRIs, nefazodone, and venlafaxine. These drugs are also suggested for individuals with comorbid PTSD and depression. These recommendations are based on the available research and clinical experiences of PTSD experts. Unfortunately, randomized controlled trials have not yet been done to compare the efficacy of monotherapies (e.g., CBT alone or medication alone) against combination therapies (drugs plus CBT).

Table 11.1 Cognitive-Behavioral Strategies for PTSD, and Modified Interventions When Pain is Comorbid

PTSD Intervention	Components	Modifications when pain is comorbid
Psychoeducation	• Introduce cognitive-behavioral treatment model and rationale • Discuss the importance of homework	• Add information about the things that perpetuate chronic pain (e.g., inactivity), and about interrelationships between pain and PTSD • Validate pain symptoms
Applied relaxation training	• Education about stress-symptom relationship and benefits of relaxation training • Introduce and practice various relaxation techniques (e.g., diaphragmatic breathing, rapid relaxation, cued relaxation)	• Use passive relaxation techniques; avoid "tense-release" exercises to avoid pain flare-ups
Cognitive interventions	• Review CBT model, discussing interrelationships between thoughts, feelings, and behaviors • Introduce and practice various cognitive techniques (e.g., cognitive restructuring; cognitive rehearsal, goal setting)	• Review links between pain and PTSD • Discuss how catastrophizing about pain increases distress and perceived pain intensity
Imaginal exposure	• Develop a detailed script, describing traumatic event(s) in detail, including descriptions of sights, sounds, smells, tastes, bodily sensations, thoughts, and feelings during trauma • Script is written down and re-read repeatedly, or narrated into a tape recorder and listened to, repeatedly	• Use a more gradual approach to avoid tension-induced pain • Include brief relaxation exercise (e.g., rapid-relaxation) between trials • Reduce exposure length (in session and homework)
In vivo exposure	• Collaboratively develop graduated exposure hierarchy • Patient chooses exposure goals • Exposure is to distressing but safe situations • May be therapist-accompanied or assigned as homework	• Use a more gradual approach to avoid tension-induced pain • Include brief relaxation exercise (e.g., rapid-relaxation) between trials • Reduce exposure length (in session and homework) • Graduated exposure may also be employed for fears of pain and reinjury
Other	• Develop coping strategies to deal with stressors (e.g., job stress) that may exacerbate symptoms • Implement assertiveness training, couples therapy, family therapy, as needed • Relapse prevention: Develop a written plan for dealing with future occurrences of symptoms	• To facilitate occupational rehabilitataion, examine workplace factors (ergonomic and psychosocial) that may exacerbate pain • Gradually increase activity to prevent physical deconditioning (which may worsen pain) • Involvement of a physiotherapist would be useful because of patients' fearful beliefs about pain and injury

Much remains to be learned about the merits of other types of medication, either alone or in combination with CBT. The second-generation anticonvulsants Neurontin and topiramate have both been found to be effective in reducing at least some forms of chronic pain (Finnerup, Gottrup, & Jensen, 2002). Recently, a handful of uncontrolled studies suggest that these medications might also reduce PTSD (e.g., Berlant & van Kammen, 2002; Hamner, Brodrick, & Labbate., 2001; Malek-Ahmadi, 2003). It remains to be seen whether these medications are effective for comorbid pain and PTSD.

The growing body of research on pain sensitization—the gradual increase in pain due to particular kinds of nerve injuries—suggests that early and aggressive treatment may help acute pain from becoming chronic (e.g., Schwartzman, Grothusenm, Kiefer, & Rohr, 2001). Early pain management might also reduce the traumatic nature of the pain experience itself and hence potentially reduce the risk of subsequently developing PTSD (Schreiber & Galai-Gat, 1993). Preliminary evidence similarly suggests that medications that inhibit physiological arousal (e.g., propranolol, clonidine) following a traumatic injury might also decrease the risk of developing PTSD (Morgan, Krystal, & Southwick, 2003). It is possible that early pharmacotherapy with a combination of analgesic and arousal-inhibiting medications might prevent the development of comorbid PTSD and chronic pain.

CASE STUDIES

The following two case studies highlight some of the challenges encountered when treating patients with comorbid pain and PTSD. The patients were referred through family physicians for assessment and treatment of PTSD. Patients met diagnostic criteria for PTSD, which originated from a MVA, and suffered from chronic pain. The patients were female and married, and 23 and 40 years of age. Both were involved in litigation over the accident. Both were treated by a doctoral-level psychologist experienced in CBT for chronic pain and CBT.

Prior to admission, patients gave informed consent and received the Structured Clinical Interview for DSM–IV to determine current and lifetime Axis I disorders. Treatment outcome was assessed by (a) the Clinician Administered PTSD Scale, which assessed PTSD symptoms over the past month, and (b) a battery of self-report measures. The latter included the PTSD Symptom Severity Scale, which is part of the Posttraumatic

Stress Diagnostic Scale (Foa, 1995). The Symptom Severity Scale contains 17 items corresponding to the *DSM–IV* PTSD symptoms. This inventory was also administered at each weekly treatment session to monitor treatment progress. We divided this scale into four subscales in order to assess the severity of symptoms on each of the four PTSD dimensions over the past week: reexperiencing (items 1–5), avoidance (items 6–7), numbing (items 8–12), and hyperarousal (items 13–17). To facilitate comparison across subscales, scores were computed as the mean item score (e.g., for the reexperiencing subscale, a patient's score at a given assessment period is the mean of items 1 to 5). The scores on all subscales ranged from 0 to 3.

Other self-report outcome measures included (a) the Beck Depression Inventory (Beck & Steer, 1987) to measure depression over the past week; (b) the Beck Anxiety Inventory (Beck & Steer, 1993) to measure general anxiety over the past week; (c) the Anxiety Sensitivity Index (Peterson & Reiss, 1992) to measure anxiety sensitivity; (d) the trait from of the State-Trait Anger Expression Inventory (Spielberger, 1988) to measure anger proneness (high trait anger is a common associated feature of PTSD and chronic pain); (e) the Posttraumatic Cognitions Inventory (Foa, Ehlers, Clark, Tolin, & Orsillo, 1999) to measure trauma-related dysfunctional beliefs (negative thoughts about oneself, negative thoughts about the world, and self-blame); and (f) the Accident Fear Questionnaire (Kuch et al., 1994) to measure the severity of avoidance of motor vehicle travel. Pain was assessed by clinical interview (e.g., assessing the frequency of pain flare-ups and pain intensity ratings on a verbal rating scale).

Treatment primarily consisted of behavior therapy for PTSD (imaginal and in vivo exposure), with two modifications. First, pain management techniques were added, as needed (e.g., activity scheduling, extensive use of relaxation training). Second, interoceptive exposure was added, as a means of reducing anxiety sensitivity (see chapter 4). Given the potential role of anxiety sensitivity in pain and PTSD, interoceptive exposure may be a useful intervention. Interoceptive exposure involves inducing feared bodily sensations to teach patients that the sensations are harmless (e.g., voluntary hyperventilation to induce palpitations and dizziness; breathing through a narrow straw to induce dyspnea: see Taylor, 2000, for a detailed description).

Case 1: BC

Case 1 was referred for treatment 1 month after her MVA. During the accident she sustained soft tissue injuries to the left side of her body.

Although these had healed, she continued to experience intermittent episodes of pain. At admission, her primary disorder (most severe) was acute PTSD (moderate severity). She also met criteria for major depressive disorder (moderate severity, single episode). BC suffered from panic attacks triggered by trauma-related stimuli, but did not meet diagnostic criteria for panic disorder. She reported having daily headaches, which fluctuated in severity from 3 to 10 on a 10-point verbal rating scale (0 = no pain; 10 = severe pain). She also described having constant pain along her left side (neck, shoulder, lower back, hip, and leg), which varied in severity from 6 to 9 on the verbal rating scale. For pain control, she was using over-the-counter pain relievers, and she was receiving weekly massage and chiropractic treatments. She reported no preinjury psychiatry history or contact with mental health professionals. BC was not taking any form of anxiolytic or antidepressant medication.

BC's treatment was initially designed to consist of weekly appointments consisting of two sessions of relaxation training (60-minute sessions intended primarily for pain management), four sessions of interoceptive exposure (60-minute sessions), four sessions of imaginal exposure (90-minute sessions), and four sessions of in vivo exposure (90-minute sessions). The treatment was also designed to include weekly homework exercises, to be practiced on a daily basis (e.g., practicing the exercises that had been conducted during the sessions, such as relaxation training or imaginal exposure).

As treatment progressed, the patient and therapist jointly decided to modify the protocol because of exposure-induced pain flare-ups. The modifications included those suggested in Table 11.1. First, we added another session of interoceptive exposure to see if we could further reduce her anxiety sensitivity before moving on to the imaginal exposure. We modified the interoceptive, imaginal, and in vivo exposure sessions by encouraging her to practice rapid relaxation (2–3 minute) before and after each exposure trial. A brief relaxation exercise (10–15 minute) was incorporated at the end of each imaginal and in vivo exposure session. In another session (session 10), which was intended to be an imaginal exposure session, BC felt unable to complete any of the imaginal exercises due to increased pain. We replaced the exposure with relaxation training and reviewed other pain management options. Further details about the treatment sessions are as follows.

- *Session 1*: Psychoeducation about pain and PTSD, and an introduction to applied relaxation training. Release-only relaxation and rapid relaxation techniques were described and practiced in the session and assigned for daily homework.

- *Session 2*: Review of symptoms and homework. Release-only relaxation and rapid relaxation were practiced again and assigned for homework.
- *Session 3*: Introduction to interoceptive exposure therapy. Prior to the exercises, BC completed a checklist of medical conditions that might contraindicate the use of particular exercises. She attempted 9 (out of 10) brief and commonly used interoceptive exposure exercises (Taylor, 2000) designed to induce arousal-related body sensations (e.g., jogging on the spot for 1 minute, spinning around while standing for 1 minute, hyperventilating for 1 minute). She was also instructed to use the rapid relaxation exercise for a minute or so after each exercise.
- Following each exercise, we recorded information about the duration completed, the sensations, and their intensity (0–10: 0 = no sensations present , 10 = very intense sensations), peak anxiety rating during the exercise (0–10: 0 = no anxiety, 10 = extreme anxiety), and similarity to "real-life" anxiety symptoms (0–10: 0 = not similar at all to real life anxiety, 10 = identical to real life anxiety). The presence of catastrophic thoughts (and images) and trauma memories during the exercise were also examined. The therapist and patient then collaboratively established a graded interoceptive exposure hierarchy by ranking the exercises from least to most anxiety provoking. The homework assignment consisted of practicing the exercise ranked least anxiety provoking on the scale and one that she had a high degree of confidence in completing. For homework, she was instructed to practice an exercise 10 to 15 minute a day over two to three practice sessions, and she was asked to record her peak anxiety after each trial.
- *Sessions 4 to 8*: Interoceptive exposure therapy. During each session, the therapist and BC collaborated and planned the interoceptive exposure exercises for the session. Before each exercise, the therapist and patient also examined two predictions. BC was asked to identify a specific catastrophic belief about the potential negative consequences of the feared sensations, as well as an alternative noncatastrophic prediction. BC also rated the strength of these beliefs on a scale from 0 to 100% (0% = do not believe that _____ to 100% = completely believes that _____ is true). For example, one of her catastrophic beliefs was "Tensing my legs will make me lose

control and I will have a heart attack and die." Her alternative prediction was "Tensing will be temporarily uncomfortable but I can manage this and nothing bad will happen." Over repeated trials her peak anxiety decreased, the strength of her catastrophic prediction decreased, and the strength of her non-catastrophic belief increased. Toward the end of the interoceptive exposure component of her treatment, BC reported that she had started to resume a number of activities that were previously avoided after her accident due to her fears of arousal-related sensations (e.g., going for walks with her husband, using aerobic exercise equipment, taking the stairs instead of the elevator).

- *Session 9*: Introduction to imaginal exposure. During the session, BC was asked to recall the trauma vividly, speaking in the present tense. After each exposure trial, she was asked to describe the most distressing aspect of the accident and rate her peak anxiety during the exposure. The weekly homework during the imaginal exposure involved, for 1 hour a day, listening to the retelling of the traumatic event that was audiotaped during the session. She was asked to record the amount of time spent listening to the tape each day and her peak anxiety while completing the homework.

- *Session 10*: Given that BC reported significant pain at the beginning of the session, it was jointly decided to discuss pain management strategies and postpone imaginal exposure until the following session. The session consisted of reviewing her pain management strategies, specifically relaxation techniques and activity pacing (to gradually resume pre-injury activity levels). She was encouraged to discuss the potential benefits of obtaining a physiotherapy referral with her family physician. Pain imagery distraction techniques were introduced and practiced for the remainder of the session.

- *Sessions 11 to 13*: Imaginal exposure.

- *Session 14*: Introduction to in vivo exposure. A graduated in vivo exposure hierarchy was established, which consisted of identifying harmless real-life situations (objects, situations, places, activities) that were related to BC's accident, which she found to be distressing and avoided. She began the exposure with a situation ranked lowest on her hierarchy (e.g., looking at pictures of other car accidents). For in vivo exposure homework, she was asked to practice the exposure exercise from the session each day for 60 minutes.

- *Sessions 15 to 17*: In vivo exposure. Termination issues were addressed in the last session, which included a review of gains made in therapy, areas still in need of improvement, and relapse prevention.

As noted, pain appeared to interfere with PTSD treatment at various times. BC often experienced pain flare-ups between sessions. Although she was diligent in attempting all the exposure homework, she frequently needed to split the homework up to help keep the pain at a manageable level (e.g., listening to the tape 20 minutes, three times a day, instead of one 60 minute period per day). Although the exposure portion of the imaginal and in vivo sessions was scheduled to last 60 minutes a day, she could only tolerate 30 to 45 minutes; longer exposures triggered pain.

Table 11.2 shows the outcome of BC's treatment, as assessed by the CAPS and self-report measures. Here it can be seen that her scores on all measures declined over the course of treatment, to the point that she was only experiencing mild, residual symptoms and no longer met diagnostic criteria for PTSD. Figure 11.1 shows her scores on the self-report measure of PTSD symptoms over the course of treatment. The figure shows that there was some decline in her PTSD scores during the interoceptive exposure. She experienced a temporary increase in PTSD symptoms in the initial sessions of imaginal exposure, which was associated with a flare-up of pain. Pain management techniques, followed by the above-mentioned modification to the exposure protocol (i.e., shorter exposures, interspersed with relaxation) appeared to solve the problem of exposure-related pain exacerbation. From session 10 onward her PTSD symptoms steadily declined and exposure-induced pain flare-ups became infrequent. She also described a significant improvement in her pain during her daily life. For example, in the last session, her average weekly pain severity had decreased to 4 on the 10-point verbal rating scale. These gains were also maintained despite nearly being involved in two car accidents that occurred toward the end of her treatment.

Case 2: DE

DE was several months pregnant at the time of her MVA, which occurred 1 year prior to the initial assessment at our clinic. During the accident she sustained soft tissue injuries to her upper body (back, abdomen, ribcage, and head) and was hospitalized overnight to monitor the baby's condition. She described having severe and unremitting pain in her upper body since the accident, and she regularly experienced breathing difficul-

Table 11.2 Results from the Clinician Administered PTSD Scale (CAPS) and Self-Report Measures

Measure	Case 1: BC		Case 2: DE		
	Pretreatment	Posttreatment	Pretreatment-1	Pretreatment-2	Posttreatment
CAPS total	75	6	77	NA	79
PTSD Symptom Severity Scale	49	2	41	41	38
Anxiety Sensitivity Index	43	4	21	24	29
Beck Depression Inventory	21	1	25	26	31
Beck Anxiety Inventory	43	2	23	27	25
Posttraumatic Cognitions Inventory	169	43	109	131	115
State-Trait Anger Expression Inventory-Trait Form	29	10	23	23	24
Accident Fear Questionnaire	57	6	26	25	35

NA = not administered.

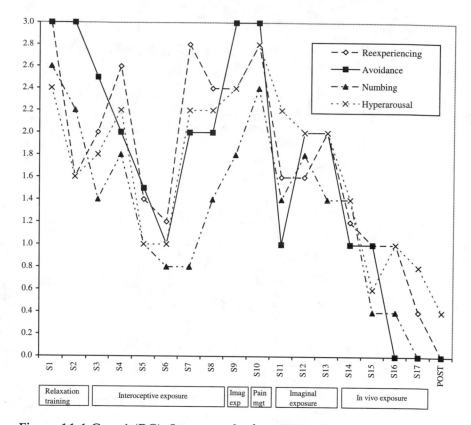

Figure 11.1 Case 1 (BC): Scores on the four PTSD dimensions, as assessed by the PTSD Symptom Severity Scale at the beginning of each weekly treatment session and at posttreatment (S = treatment session).

ties due to the injuries sustained to her ribcage and diaphragm. At the pretreatment assessment, she estimated that her pain in her back and abdominal regions ranged from 5 to 9 on the 10-point verbal rating scale and she did not report any pain-free days. DE was taking sertraline (100 mg/day) and was not using any analgesic medication. For pain management, she was receiving regular physiotherapy and massage therapy.

DE's primary (most severe) problem at the intake assessment was chronic pain, and she also met diagnostic criteria for chronic PTSD (moderate severity) and major depressive disorder (moderate severity, single episode). Given that she was seeking treatment for PTSD but had severe chronic pain, we offered her a modified treatment program and conducted a more comprehensive pain evaluation than the first case. Pretreatment data from the Multi-

Dimensional Pain Inventory (Kerns et al., 1985) showed that DE was experiencing severe pain intensity and interference with daily activities. The Pain Disability Index (Tait, Chiball, & Krauser, 1990) suggested a high level of perceived disability across different activity domains (e.g., family/home responsibilities, social activity). She reported no psychiatric history or contact with mental health professionals prior to her accident.

Treatment was planned to consist of four weekly sessions of pain management (60-minute sessions) followed by eight weekly sessions (90-minute sessions) of trauma-based exposure therapy (four imaginal sessions and four in vivo sessions). The pain management portion of treatment included the following.

- *Session 1*: Psychoeducation about pain and its relationship to PTSD, an introduction to relaxation training, and goal setting. Release-only relaxation and rapid relaxation were described and practiced in the session and assigned for daily homework. She was also asked to generate a list of realistic and specific goals pertaining to her treatment and pain management.
- *Session 2*: Relaxation training. Release-only relaxation and rapid relaxation were practiced again and assigned for homework.
- *Session 3*: In this session DE presented with significant emotional distress and reported being overwhelmed by the multiple effects of the accident and her persistent pain. As a general coping strategy, she was asked to generate a problem list and prioritize the items by their importance. Her treatment goals were reviewed, and activity scheduling and activity pacing were introduced. The cognitive-behavioral framework of pain management was also reviewed. Specifically, the interrelationships between pain-related cognitions, feelings, and behaviors were explored. For example, DE was encouraged to identify links between catastrophic beliefs (e.g., "I will never get better") and negative emotional reactions (e.g., increased anxiety and depression) and increased pain intensity. She was then asked to formulate alternative statements that would be more realistic and helpful. For homework, she was asked to schedule daily activities and implement activity-pacing strategies.
- *Session 4*: Cognitive restructuring and problem solving with regard to her pain. A pain distraction technique using imagery was introduced and practiced. For homework, she was asked to monitor thoughts that co-occur with periods of increased pain and was encouraged to practice cognitive restructuring. Pain management strategies were reviewed and she was also asked to practice pain imagery techniques on a daily basis.

The format and structure of the imaginal and exposure sessions were the same as those of the first case. Similar to BC's treatment, we modified the exposure sessions by encouraging DE to practice rapid relaxation (2–3 minutes) before and after each exposure trial. A brief relaxation exercise (10–15 minutes) was incorporated at the end of each imaginal and in vivo exposure session. DE experienced increased pain symptoms during all the exposure sessions. To make treatment more tolerable we reduced the exposure portion to 30 to 45 minutes. Despite her pain, she completed most of the homework each week.

DE was assessed at two pretreatment periods, separated by a period of one week. Table 11.2 shows that DE's symptoms tended to be stable during this baseline. The table also shows that her symptoms were not reduced by treatment. Neither pain management nor exposure exercises appeared to have any clear benefit on her PTSD, pain, or other symptoms.

Figure 11.2 shows DE's scores on the PTSD Symptom Severity Scale across treatment sessions. The figure shows that numbing and hyperarousal symptoms remained particularly elevated, and there was a slight increase in reexperiencing symptoms during the imaginal exposure portion of treatment. DE's pain symptoms were assessed throughout treatment via clinical interview. In terms of severity and functional interference, her pain remained relatively constant throughout treatment. For example, in the last session, she reported that her average pain severity over the previous week was a 9 on the 10-point verbal rating scale. There was no improvement in her scores on either the Multi-Dimensional Pain Inventory or Pain Disability Index.

COMMENT

Patients BC and DE were similar in their scores on several pretreatment measures (Table 11.2), including PTSD severity, depression, and trait anger. BC had higher scores on measures of anxiety sensitivity, general anxiety, and MVA-related avoidance (as assessed by the Accident Fear Questionnaire), and stronger dysfunctional trauma-related beliefs. Although BC tended to have more severe pretreatment psychopathology, she gradually responded to treatment, whereas DE showed no evidence of treatment response. DE had a longer duration of PTSD than BC, although our previous research has shown that PTSD duration does not predict treatment outcome (Taylor et al., 2001; and see chapter 2).

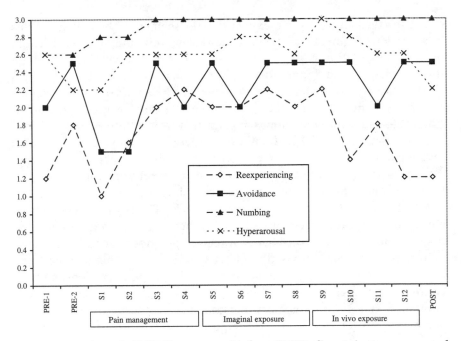

Figure 11.2 Case 2 (DE): Scores on the four PTSD dimensions, as assessed by the PTSD Symptom Severity Scale at two pretreatment assessments (baseline), the beginning of each weekly treatment session, and at post-treatment (S = treatment session).

DE had more severe, more enduring pain than BC. Our clinical impression is that this seemed to be the critical variable that interfered with PTSD treatment. BC had pain flare-ups that interfered with PTSD treatment, although we were able to manage them by implementing pain management methods (especially a greater emphasis on relaxation training), and by breaking the exposure exercises down into shorter units. Through this intervention her pain and PTSD were reduced.

In comparison, DE showed no evidence of treatment response, and failed to benefit from either pain management or PTSD treatment. This finding runs counter to the notion that patients with PTSD and severe chronic pain, compared to patients who only suffer from PTSD, simply require a longer course of treatment that includes PTSD treatment and pain management. DE showed no response to either PTSD or pain management, and the session-by-session results offered no evidence of a trend for symptom reduction.

BC received interoceptive exposure, and seemed to benefit from this intervention (Figure 11.1). DE did not receive this intervention. It could be argued that DE might have benefited from this intervention. Although this is possible, we found that a third patient with PTSD and severe chronic pain (a treatment dropout) did not benefit from interoceptive exposure. Although one should not place too much weight on uncontrolled case studies, our findings suggest that interoceptive exposure may be most useful for PTSD with mild or moderate chronic pain. PTSD with severe chronic pain does not seem to be responsive to interoceptive exposure or to other cognitive-behavioral PTSD interventions for that matter. Controlled studies are needed to test these impressions.

So what should be done to help patients with PTSD and severe chronic pain? Our clinical impression is that psychosocial interventions may be insufficient. It may be necessary to integrate psychosocial and drug treatments, such as medications that target chronic pain. This impression is consistent with the recommendations of the Expert Consensus Panel Guidelines (Foa et al., 1999a), which suggest that a combination of psychological and pharmacological therapies may be needed when PTSD is comorbid with chronic pain. Although DE had been treated before and during our treatment with an SSRI by her primary care physician, this did not relieve her symptoms. Treatment with other medications (e.g., Neurontin or topiramate) may have been more effective. Also, when the patient has severe chronic pain like DE, the optimal approach may be to implement PTSD treatment in the context of a multidisciplinary pain clinic. When PTSD is comorbid with milder pain, such as in the case of BC, a modified PTSD protocol may be sufficient, following the guidelines in Table 11.1.

DISCUSSION

PTSD is frequently comorbid with chronic pain, often arising from a common source such as an MVA or a work-related injury. Little is known about the best way to treat comorbid PTSD and chronic pain. Sometimes, pain abates when PTSD is treated, even though the focus of clinical attention is on PTSD rather than pain. Stress-related tension headaches, for example, may decline in frequency when PTSD hyperarousal symptoms are reduced. In other cases, however, pain warrants direct treatment because of its severity and because it seems to interfere with PTSD treatment. Behavioral and cognitive-behavioral PTSD treatments can be fruitfully modified to incorporate pain management techniques and other methods for avoiding pain exacerbations from exposure exercises (Table 11.1). Modified treatment seems most promising when chronic pain is not severe (in terms of frequency or severity). Our experience is that PTSD and severe chronic pain can be difficult to treat if one relies only on psychosocial methods. Such cases seem to be best treated with a combination of psychosocial and pharmacological therapies, in the context of a multidisciplinary pain program.

REFERENCES

Amir, M., Kaplan, Z., Neumann, L., Sharabani, R., Shani, N., & Buskila, D. (1997). Posttraumatic stress disorder tenderness and fibromyalgia. *Journal of Psychosomatic Research, 42,* 607–613.

Asmundson, G. J. G. (1999). Anxiety sensitivity and chronic pain: Empirical findings, clinical implications, and future directions. In S. Taylor (Ed.), *Anxiety sensitivity: Theory, research, and treatment of the fear of anxiety* (pp. 269–285). Mahwah, NJ: Erlbaum.

Asmundson, G. J. G., Coons, M. J., Taylor, S., & Katz, J. (2002). PTSD and the experience of pain: Research and clinical implications of shared vulnerability and mutual maintenance models. *Canadian Journal of Psychiatry, 47,* 930–937.

Asmundson, G. J. G., Frombach, I., McQuaid, J., Pedrelli, P., Lenox, R., & Stein, M. B. (2000). Dimensionality of posttraumatic stress symptoms: A confirmatory factor analysis of DSM–IV symptom clusters and other symptom models. *Behaviour Research and Therapy, 38,* 203–214.

Asmundson, G. J. G., Norton, G. R., & Allerdings, M. D. (1998). Posttraumatic stress disorder and work-related injury. *Journal of Anxiety Disorders, 12,* 57–69.

Beck, A. T., & Steer, R. A. (1987). *Manual for the revised Beck Depression Inventory.* San Antonio, TX: Psychological Corporation.

Beck, A. T., & Steer, R. A. (1993). *Manual for the Beck Anxiety Inventory.* San Antonio, TX: Psychological Corporation.

Berlant, J., & van Kammen, D. P. (2002). Open-label topiramate as primary or adjunctive therapy in chronic civilian posttraumatic stress disorder: A preliminary report. *Journal of Clinical Psychiatry, 63,* 15–20.

Blake, D.D., Weathers, F.W., Nagy, L.M., Kaloupek, D.G., Charney, D.S., & Keane, T. M. (1997). *Clinician administered PTSD scale (revised).* Boston: Behavioral Science Division, National Center for Post-Traumatic Stress Disorder.

Blanchard, E. B., Hickling, E. J., Devineni, T., Veazey, C. H., Galovski, T. E., Mundy, E., Malta, L. S., & Buckley, T. C. (2003). A controlled evaluation of cognitive behavioral therapy for posttraumatic stress in motor vehicle accident survivors. *Behaviour Research and Therapy, 41,* 79–96.

Blanchard, E. B., Hickling, E. J., Taylor, A. E., Loos, W. R., Forneris, C. A., & Jaccard, J. (1996). Who develops PTSD from motor vehicle accidents? *Behavior Research and Therapy, 34,* 1–10.

Breslau, N., Davis, G.C., Andreski, OP. & Peterson, E. (1991). Traumatic events and posttraumatic stress disorder in an urban population of young adults. *Archives of General Psychiatry, 48,* 216–222.

Briere, J. (1995). *Trauma Symptom Inventory professional manual.* Odessa, FL: PAR.

Bryant, R. A., & Harvey, A. G. (1995). Avoidant coping style and post-traumatic stress following motor vehicle accidents. *Behaviour Research and Therapy, 33,* 631–635.

Bryant, R. A., & Harvey, A. G. (2003). The influence of litigation on the maintenance of posttraumatic stress disorder. *Journal of Nervous and Mental Disease, 191,* 191–193.

Bryant, R. A., Marosszeky, J. E., Crooks, J., Baguley, I. J., & Gurka, J. A. (1999). Interaction of posttraumatic stress disorder and chronic pain following traumatic brain injury. *Journal of Head Trauma Rehabilitation, 14,* 588–594.

Chibnall, J. T., & Duckro, P. N. (1994). Post-traumatic stress disorder in chronic post-traumatic headache patients. *Headache, 134,* 357–361.

Currie, S. R., Wilson, K. G. P., Pontefract, A. J., & deLaplante, L. (2000). Cognitive-behavioral treatment of insomnia secondary to chronic pain. *Journal of Consulting and Clinical Psychology, 68,* 407–416.

Dersh, J., Polatin, P. B., & Gatchel, R. J. (2002). Chronic pain and psychopathology: Research findings and theoretical considerations. *Psychosomatic Medicine, 64,* 773–786.

Ehlers, A., Mayou, R. A., & Bryant, B. (1998). Psychological predictors of chronic posttraumatic stress disorder after motor vehicle accidents. *Journal of Abnormal Psychology, 107,* 508–519.

Eimer, B. N., & Freeman, A. M. (1998). *Pain management psychotherapy: A practical guide.* New York: Wiley.

Fedoroff, I. C., Taylor, S., Asmundson, G. J. G., & Koch, W. J. (2000). Cognitive factors in traumatic stress reactions: Predicting PTSD symptoms from anxiety sensitivity and beliefs about harmful events. *Behavioural and Cognitive Psychotherapy, 28,* 5–15.

Fernandez, E., & Turk, D. C. (1995). The scope and significance of anger in the experience of chronic pain. *Pain, 61,* 165–175.

Finnerup, N. B., Gottrup, H., & Jensen, T. S. (2002). Anticonvulsants in central pain. *Expert Opinion on Pharmacotherapy, 3,* 1411–1420.

First, M. B., Spitzer, R. L., Gibbon, M., & Williams, J. B. W. (1996). *Structured Clinical Interview for DSM–IV Axis I—Patient edition.* New York: Biometrics Research Department, New York State Psychiatric Institute.

Foa, E. B. (1995). *The Posttraumatic Diagnostic Scale (PDS) manual.* Minneapolis, MN: National Computer Systems.

Foa, E. B., Davidson, J. R. T., & Frances, A. (1999a). Treatment of PTSD: The NIH expert consensus guideline series. *Journal of Clinical Psychiatry, 60* (Suppl. 16), 4–76.

Foa, E. B., Ehlers, A., Clark, D. M., Tolin, D. F., & Orsillo, S. M. (1999). The

Posttraumatic Cognitions Inventory (PTCI): Development and validation. *Psychological Assessment, 11,* 303–314.

Foa, E. B., & Rothbaum, B. O. (1998). *Treating the trauma of rape: Cognitive-behavioral therapy for PTSD.* New York: Guilford.

Gasma, A. (1994). The role of psychological factors in chronic pain. II. A critical appraisal. *Pain, 57,* 17–29.

Geisser, M. E., Roth, R. S., Bachman, J. E., & Eckert, T. A. (1996). The relationship between symptoms of post-traumatic stress disorder and pain, affective disturbance and disability among patient with accident and non-accident pain. *Pain, 66,* 207–214.

Hamner, M. B., Brodrick, P. S., & Labbate, L. A. (2001). Gabapentin in PTSD: A retrospective, clinical series of adjunctive therapy. *Annals of Clinical Psychiatry, 13,* 141–146.

Hickling, E. J., & Blanchard, E. B. (1992). Posttraumatic stress disorder and motor vehicle accidents. *Journal of Anxiety Disorders, 6,* 285–291.

Hickling, E. J., & Blanchard, E. B. (1997). The private practice psychologist and manual-based treatments: Post-traumatic stress disorder secondary to motor vehicle accidents. *Behaviour Research and Therapy, 35,* 191–203.

Hickling, E. J., Blanchard, E. B., Schwartz, S. P., & Silverman, D. J. (1992). Headaches and motor vehicle accidents: Results of psychological treatment of post-traumatic headaches. *Headache Quarterly, 3,* 285–289.

Holzman, A. D., & Turk, D. C. (1986). *Pain management.* New York: Pergamon.

Kerns, R. D., Turk, D.C., & Rudy, T. E. (1985). The West-Haven-Yale Multidimensional Pain Inventory (WHYMPI). *Pain, 23,* 345–356.

King, D. W., Leskin, G. A., King, L. A., & Weathers, F. W. (1998). Confirmatory factor analysis of the clinician-administered PTSD Scale: Evidence for the dimensionality of posttraumatic stress disorder. *Psychological Assessment, 10,* 90–96.

Koch, W. J., & Taylor, S. (1995). Assessment and treatment of motor vehicle accident victims. *Cognitive and Behavioural Practice, 2,* 327–342.

Kuch, K., Evans, R. J., & Shulman, I. (1994). Phobias, panic, and pain in 55 survivors of road accidents. *Journal of Anxiety Disorders, 8,* 181–187.

Lebovitz, A. H., Yarmush, J., & Lefkowitz, M. (1990). Reflex sympathetic dystrophy and posttraumatic stress disorder. Multi-disciplinary evaluation and treatment. *Clinical Journal of Pain, 6,* 153–157.

Malek-Ahmadi, P. (2003). Gabapentin and posttraumatic stress disorder. *Annals of Pharmacotherapy, 37,* 664–666.

Mayou, R., Tyndel, S., & Bryant, B. (1997). Long-term outcome of motor vehicle accident injury. *Psychosomatic Medicine, 59,* 578–584.

Melzack, R. (1975). The McGill Pain Questionnaire: Major properties and scoring methods. *Pain, 1,* 277–299.

Melzack, R. (1987). The short-form McGill Pain Questionnaire. *Pain, 30,* 191–197.

Merskey, H., & Bogduk, N. (1994). *Classification of chronic pain* (2nd ed.). Seattle, WA: IASP.

Morgan, C. A., Krystal, J. H., & Southwick, S. M. (2003). Toward early pharmacological posttraumatic stress intervention. *Biological Psychiatry, 53,* 834–843.

Muse, M. (1986). Stress-related post-traumatic chronic pain syndrome: Behavioral approaches to treatment. *Pain, 25,* 389–394.

Peterson, R. A., & Reiss, S. (1992). *Anxiety Sensitivity Index manual* (2nd ed.). Worthington, OH: International Diagnostic Systems.

Riggs, D. S., Dancu, C. V., & Gershuny, B. S. (1992). Anger and post-traumatic stress disorder in female crime victims. *Journal of Traumatic Stress, 5,* 613–625.

Salomons, T. V., Osterman, J. E., Gagliese, L., & Katz. J. (in press). Pain flashbacks in posttraumatic stress disorder. *Clinical Journal of Pain.*

Schreiber, S., & Galai-Gat, T. (1993). Uncontrolled pain following physical injury as the core-trauma in post-traumatic stress disorder. *Pain, 54,* 107–110.

Schwartzman, R. J., Grothusen, J., Kiefer, T. R., & Rohr, P. (2001). Neuropathic central pain: Epidemiology, etiology, and treatment options. *Archives of Neurology, 58,* 1547–1550.

Sharp, T. J., & Harvey, A. G. (2001). Chronic pain and posttraumatic stress disorder: Mutual maintenance? *Clinical Psychology Review, 21,* 857–877.

Spielberger, C. D. (1988). *State-Trait Anger Expression Inventory: Professional manual.* Odessa, FL: PAR.

Tait, R. C., Chibnall, J. T., & Krause, S. (1990). The Pain Disability Index: Psychometric properties. *Pain, 40,* 171–182.

Taylor S. (2000). *Understanding and treating panic disorder.* New York: Wiley.

Taylor, S., Fedoroff, I. C., Koch, W.J., Thordarson, D.S., Fecteau, G., & Nicki, R. M. (2001). Posttraumatic stress disorder arising after road traffic collisions: Patterns of response to cognitive-behavior therapy. *Journal of Consulting and Clinical Psychology, 69,* 541–551.

Taylor, S., & Koch, W. J. (1995). Anxiety disorders due to motor vehicle accidents: Nature and treatment. *Clinical Psychology Review, 15,* 721–738.

Taylor, S., Thordarson, D. S., Maxfield, L., Fedoroff, I. C., Lovell, K., & Ogrodniczuk, J. (2003). Comparative efficacy, speed, and adverse effects of three treatments for PTSD: Exposure therapy, EMDR, and relaxation training. *Journal of Consulting and Clinical Psychology, 71,* 330–338.

Turk, D. C., & Rudy, T. E. (1994). A cognitive-behavioral perspective on chronic pain: Beyond the scalpel and syringe. In C. D. Tollison, J. R. Satterthwaite, & J. W. Tollison (Eds.), *Handbook of pain management* (2nd ed., pp. 136–151). Baltimore: Williams and Wilkins.

van Etten, M., & Taylor, S. (1998). Comparative efficacy of treatments for posttraumatic stress disorder: A meta-analysis. *Clinical Psychology and Psychotherapy, 5,* 126–145.

Vlaeyen, J. W. S., & Linton, S. J. (2000). Fear-avoidance and its consequences in musculoskeletal pain: A state of the art. *Pain, 85,* 317–332.

Chapter 12

PTSD, DISSOCIATION, AND TREATMENT

Norah C. Feeny and Carla Kmett Danielson

INTRODUCTION

Dissociative symptoms, such as subjective sense of numbing or detachment, reduced awareness of one's surroundings, derealization, depersonalization, and dissociative amnesia, are often considered cardinal features of posttraumatic stress disorder (PTSD). As early as 1889, Pierre Janet wrote about dissociative symptoms and their relation to long-term psychological difficulties following traumatic experiences (Janet, 1889). Still today, many trauma theorists conceptualize PTSD as a biphasic disorder, alternating between intrusive reexperiencing of the trauma and the shutting down of emotional responsiveness associated with dissociation (e.g., Horowitz, 1986). Indeed, the DSM–IV [American Psychiatric Association (APA), 1994] definition of PTSD reflects this conceptualization by including the avoidance symptoms of "psychic numbing" or "emotional anesthesia," reflecting diminished emotional responsiveness to the external world.

While dissociation and PTSD have been linked conceptually, the empirical investigation of their relationship often has led to mixed results. In some studies, the presence of dissociative symptoms either during or immediately after a trauma has predicted later PTSD (e.g., Classen, Koopman, Hales, & Spiegel, 1998; Koopman, Classen, & Spiegel, 1994; Marmar et al., 1994; McFarlane, 1986) and in others it has not (e.g., Barton, Blanchard, & Hickling, 1996; Dancu, Riggs, Hearst-Ikeda, Shoyer, & Foa,

This chapter was supported in part by a grant awarded by the Anxiety Disorders Association of America (ADAA) to the first author.

1996). Dissociation is most likely a multifaceted construct (Briere, Weathers, & Runtz, in press); thus, some of our current empirical difficulties may lie in definitional inconsistency across studies. Nevertheless, dissociation is a key clinical construct that consistently distinguishes between trauma-exposed individuals with PTSD and those without (e.g., Bernstein & Putnam, 1986; Whalen & Nash, 1996). This chapter further discusses background information on PTSD, definitional issues of dissociation, and the relationship between dissociation and chronic PTSD. In addition, it discusses the potential impact of dissociative symptoms on treatment for PTSD and discuss how to manage these symptoms in the course of exposure treatment.

PTSD DIAGNOSTIC CRITERIA AND PREVALENCE

Although the *DSM–III–R* (APA, 1987) defined trauma as an event outside the realm of typical human experience, epidemiological studies have since revealed that traumatic events are instead quite common (e.g., Breslau, Davis, Andreski, & Peterson, 1991; Kessler, Sonnega, Bromet, Hughes, & Nelson, 1995; Norris, 1992; Resnick, Kilpatrick, Dansky, Saunders, & Best, 1993). Accordingly, the DSM–IV (APA, 1994) defines trauma as an event that involves a perceived or actual threat and elicits an extreme emotional response (i.e., helplessness, horror, or terror). PTSD is an anxiety disorder that may develop in response to a traumatic event. Three clusters of symptoms characterize PTSD: reexperiencing (e.g., intrusive, upsetting trauma-related thoughts or images, nightmares), avoidance of trauma-related memories or stimuli, and hyperarousal (e.g., sleep, irritability, and concentration problems).

Whereas many individuals experience symptoms of PTSD in the immediate aftermath of a traumatic event, most do not develop long-term psychopathology (e.g., Riggs, Rothbaum, & Foa, 1995; Rothbaum, Foa, Riggs, Murdock, & Walsh, 1992). Lifetime rates of PTSD have been estimated to be about 8% in the general population (Kessler et al., 1995) and 24% in samples of trauma survivors (Breslau et al., 1991). Among those who have experienced traumatic events, rates of current PTSD vary, ranging from 15% of Vietnam combat veterans (Kulka et al., 1990), up to 40% of those in serious motor vehicle accidents (Taylor & Koch, 1995), and between 12% and 47% of female assault survivors (Resnick et al., 1993; Rothbaum et al., 1992). Once established, its course is commonly chronic and unremitting (e.g., Kessler et al., 1995).

In the past 10 to 15 years, we have learned much about how to effectively treat PTSD. Among psychosocial interventions, cognitive behavioral therapies (CBT) have been tested the most frequently and rigorously; randomized controlled trials have demonstrated that most patients who complete CBT improve substantially and maintain their gains over the course of up to a year (e.g., Foa et al., 1999; Foa, Rothbaum, Riggs, & Murdock, 1991; Marks, Lovell, Noshirvani, Livanou, & Thrasher, 1998; Resick, Nishith, Weaver, Astin, & Feuer, 2002). However, not all clients benefit equally from these treatments; outcome depends on both client characteristics and treatment characteristics (e.g., Feeny, Zoellner, & Foa, 2000a,b; Taylor et al., 2001). Indeed, dissociation may be one client characteristic that dramatically impacts PTSD treatment.

Definition and Prevalence of Dissociation

Although emotional detachment was discussed in the late nineteenth century as a defense against overwhelming emotions (Breuer & Freud, 1895), Janet was the first to label the lack of connection between aspects of memory or conscious awareness observed during and after extreme stress as *dissociation* (Janet, 1907). Several characteristics of dissociation have been proposed over the past thirty years. These characteristics include (a) an alteration in sense of one's identity (Nemiah, 1981), (b) a disturbance in memory of the specific experience during a dissociative period (Nemiah, 1981), and (c) an association with a traumatic experience (Coons, & Milstein, 1986; Putnam, 1989; Spiegel, 1986). Thus, early and more recent conceptualizations of dissociation have emphasized disruptions in memory, self, and consciousness as cardinal features.

Along these lines, according to the *DSM–IV*, dissociation involves a "disruption in the usually integrated functions of consciousness, memory, identity, or perception of the environment" (APA, 1994, p. 477). That is, normal cognitive processes that are typically integrated become separated from awareness or consciousness. This structured separation is often conceptualized as consisting of three factors: absorption-imaginative involvement (i.e., becoming so involved in tasks that one loses the sense of time and surroundings), amnesia (i.e., forgetting part or all of past or current experiences), and depersonalization-derealization (i.e., feeling detached from oneself and/or as if surroundings are unreal; Ross, 1996).

Considerable debate exists as to whether dissociation should be viewed on a continuum or whether it has categorical or taxonic properties (e.g.,

Waller, Putnam, & Carlson, 1996). Viewing dissociation on a continuum, dissociative symptoms have been reported in the context of nonpathological experiences, such as during some forms of meditation and hypnosis (e.g., Amodeo, 1981) and in common everyday experiences such as driving the car (e.g., Cubelli, 2003). Further, transient dissociative symptoms such as depersonalization symptoms are often prevalent among some psychiatric conditions and in the context of traumatic events (Cardena & Spiegel, 1996). Yet, evidence is emerging suggesting that extreme dissociation may not be best viewed on a continuum and may actually be qualitatively different from other types of dissociation. For example, using the self-report Dissociative Experiences Scale (DES; Bernstein & Putnam, 1986), Waller, Putnam & Carlson (1996) detected a pathological dissociation taxon in a mixed sample of 228 patients with dissociative identity disorder and 228 normal controls. In a second study, Waller and Ross (1997) investigated dissociative symptoms in a very large community sample and again found evidence of a pathological dissociative taxon or category. Consistent with this taxometric view, specific dissociative syndromes have been identified based on alterations in memory (e.g., dissociative amnesia), identity (e.g., dissociative fugue, dissociative identity disorder), and consciousness (e.g., depersonalization disorder). However, results from a recent study examining the test-retest stability of the previously identified taxon (Waller et al., 1996; Waller & Ross, 1997) in a large sample of undergraduates challenge the existence of a pathological dissociation taxon (Watson, 2003). Specifically, taxon scores were only modestly stable over time, and taxon membership was not consistent (Watson, 2003). Additional research is need to determine more decisively whether a continuum or taxonic (i.e., categorical) conceptualization of dissociative symptoms is most representative and clinically useful.

In addition to the debate regarding dissociation as a qualitatively distinct phenomenon, another issue of considerable debate is whether dissociation is largely a unitary or multifaceted construct. Recently, Briere et al. (in press) examined the factor structure of dissociation in a combined sample of clinical and normal participants using the Multidimensional Dissociation Inventory (MDI; Briere, 2002). Interestingly, trauma exposure accounted for only 3% to 7% of the variance in MDI factors. Five moderately intercorrelated factors were identified: disengagement, identity dissociation, emotional constriction, memory disturbance, and depersonalization-derealization. Thus, the notion of dissociation as a general trait was not supported; and instead, the authors suggested that dissociation may represent a variety of phenomenologically distinct and only moderately related symptom clusters whose ultimate commonality is more theoretical than empirical. Clearly, replication of this factor structure is needed, but these results argue against the notion of dissociation as a unitary construct.

In terms of prevalence, at this point we do not have good data for the dissociative disorders, but what we do know suggests that these disorders are quite rare. On the other hand, dissociative symptoms are substantially more common. Among clinical and inpatient populations, rates of dissociation are consistently higher than in the general population (e.g., Ross, Anderson, Fleisher, & Norton 1991; Ross, Joshi, & Currie, 1990). Studies examining inpatient populations have found that approximately 15 to 20% report extreme levels of dissociative symptoms (e.g., Chu & Dill, 1990). Similarly, among those who have experienced traumatic events, rates of dissociation also are elevated. We will discuss this in more detail below.

The Relationship Between PTSD and Dissociation

As mentioned above, stress has long been identified as playing a role in dissociation and the dissociative disorders. In fact, the construct of dissociation is largely defined by a set of symptoms that have been observed in those who have experienced trauma, including amnesia, emotional detachment, feelings of depersonalization, out-of-body experiences, dreamlike recall of events, feelings of estrangement, flashbacks, and abreaction (Foa, Steketee, & Rothbaum, 1989). In the earlier part of the twentieth century, the link between dissociation and traumatic events was highlighted when clinicians and researchers noted dissociative symptoms in individuals who had served in war. For example, Kardiner (1941) noted the central role of dissociation in his traumatized war veterans when he observed that a patient would speak and behave in such a way suggestive that he was trying to defend himself (as during a military assault) in response to a cue in the environment (e.g., flashbacks while riding the subways into the tunnels of New York). Since that time, this association with dissociative symptoms has been well established in other areas of civilian trauma. In fact, Whalen and Nash (1996) recently reviewed studies examining trauma and dissociation and found that all studies indicated higher levels of dissociation among individuals who had been traumatized (Briere & Runtz, 1988, 1989; Chu & Dill, 1990; DiTomasso & Routh, 1993; Goff, Brotman, Kindlon, & Waites, 1991; Pribor &

Dinwiddle, 1992; Sandberg & Lynn, 1992; Sanders & Giolas, 1991; Strick & Wilcoxon, 1991).

The relationship between dissociation and PTSD has been conceptualized and researched in several different ways. van der Kolk, van der Hart, and Marmar (1996) have discussed dissociation as a way of *organizing* information obtained during a traumatic event. Specifically, victims of a traumatic event may compartmentalize the experience, so that elements of the trauma are not integrated into a unitary whole. van der Hart and colleagues (1996) have proposed three types of dissociation based on the manner in which information about the traumatic event is organized. *Primary dissociation* is a reaction to the traumatic event or threat wherein the individual is completely overwhelmed by the event and is unable to integrate the full experience of what is occurring into consciousness. This involves situations where dissociated traumatic memories are demonstrated as the most severe PTSD symptoms (i.e., intensely intrusive memories, nightmares, and flashbacks. *Secondary dissociation* is a distancing strategy that allows individuals to observe their traumatic event as a spectator, so as to limit their pain and distress and protect them from awareness of the full impact of the event. In other words, secondary dissociation, also referred to as "peritraumatic dissociation," puts people out of touch with their emotions related to the trauma they have experienced (e.g., emotional numbing). *Tertiary dissociation* is a complex reaction wherein the individual sometimes experiences strong emotions (e.g., fear, anger) in response to memories of the trauma, whereas other times the individual appears unaware of the trauma and its effects. These conceptualizations have assumed a causal relationship between dissociation and traumatic events. Recent empirical investigations have attempted to examine this assumption and its relevance to PTSD.

Some researchers have attempted to identify the *chronology* of the relationship among dissociation, trauma, and PTSD. One hypothesis is that early or previous trauma exposure makes individuals more dissociative. Indeed, data suggest that early childhood trauma (e.g., childhood sexual abuse; Putnam, 1985; Terr, 1991), as well as trauma experienced later in life (e.g., Burgess & Holmstrom, 1976) plays an important role in the etiology of dissociation. However, the notion that the relationship between traumatic experiences and dissociation is a straightforward, causal relationship has been challenged (for a discussion see Merckelbach & Muris, 2001). A second corollary hypothesis is that the presence of dissociation makes individuals more vulnerable to the development of chronic PTSD. Some research has demonstrated that dissociative processes and increased use of dissociative strategies may play a role in the development of PTSD (e.g., Briere & Conte, 1993; Marmar et al., 1994; Shalev, Peri, Caneti, & Schreiber, 1996). Specifically, the presence of dissociative symptoms such as emotional numbing, either during or immediately after the trauma, has been shown to predict later psychological disturbance (Classen et al., 1998; Koopman et al., 1994; Marmar et al., 1994; McFarlane, 1986).

Given that peritraumatic dissociation, or dissociation during or immediately after a traumatic event, may be a response to elevated arousal and panic, an alternative hypothesis is that the presence of panic serves as a mediator between dissociation and the development of chronic PTSD. Bryant and Panasetis (in press) have recently studied a sample of 51 traumatized individuals with or without acute stress disorder. Acute stress and posttraumatic symptoms, anxiety symptoms, peritraumatic dissociative symptoms, and panic reactions were assessed within 1 month of their trauma. The researchers found that panic symptoms that occurred during the trauma accounted for most of the variance of subsequent dissociation (i.e., 45% of the variance of peritraumatic dissociation), more so than reexperiencing, avoidance, anxiety, and depressive reactions to trauma. The findings are consistent with proposals that acute dissociation is associated with panic that occurs during the traumatic experience, and specifically, the role of acute dissociation in posttraumatic stress may be mediated by panic during the trauma.

It is important to note though, that research has not been consistent in supporting dissociation as a predictor of PTSD. As we described in the introduction, some studies have found that the presence of dissociative symptoms either during or immediately after a trauma predicts later PTSD (e.g., Classen et al., 1998; Koopman et al., 1994; Marmar et al., 1994; MacFarlane, 1986) and others have not (e.g., Barton et al., 1996; Dancu et al., 1996). Feeny, Zoellner, and Foa (2000) explored the relationship between anger and dissociation and their relationship to symptoms of posttrauma pathology in female assault victims and found that 4 weeks post-assault, anger expression, *but not dissociation* (as measured by the Dissociative Experiences Scale; Bernstein & Putnam, 1986), was predictive of later PTSD severity. However, dissociation was predictive of poorer later functioning, indicating that these symptoms may serve a mediating role with regard to trauma and pathological reactions (although perhaps not PTSD).

As mentioned above, it may be that different aspects or characteristics of dissociation better predict the development of chronic PTSD than others.

To explore this hypothesis, Feeny, Zoellner, Fitzgibbons, and Foa (2000) separated emotional numbing from other dissociative symptoms and explored their ability to predict the development of chronic PTSD. Indeed, among female assault survivors, high initial levels of emotional numbing were predictive of PTSD severity 3 months later, whereas dissociative symptoms soon after the trauma were *not* predictive of PTSD. Initial emotional numbing, two weeks after the assault, was related to initial levels of depression, dissociation, and PTSD. After accounting for depression and dissociation, initial emotional numbing remained associated with PTSD severity, which indicates that emotional numbing may be its own construct. Thus, emotional numbing may be clinically distinct from other dissociative symptoms,— and distinct in their likelihood to hinder recovery. One hypothesis that has been suggested to explain this distinction is that emotional numbing, more so than dissociative symptoms, reflects the survivor's inability to engage emotionally with the traumatic memory and thus impair the processes that promote recovery (Foa, Riggs, Massie, & Yarczower, 1995). Feeny, Zoellner, Fitzgibbons, and Foa, (2000) proposed that the lack of predictive ability of dissociation for later PTSD in these studies may reflect that the relationship between these domains is more complex than those of the other variables. In fact, these results may be consistent with Briere et al. (in press) suggesting that dissociation is better conceptualized as a multifaceted construct, representing phenomenologically distinct and only moderately related symptom clusters.

DISSOCIATION AND TREATMENT FOR PTSD

As indicated earlier in the chapter, several cognitive-behavioral therapies (CBT) have received empirical support in prospective, randomized studies for PTSD (for reviews see Foa & Meadows, 1997; Foa & Rothbaum, 1998). Among them are prolonged exposure (e.g., Foa et al., 1999) stress inoculation training (e.g., Foa et al., 1999), cognitive restructuring (e.g., Marks et al., 1998), cognitive processing therapy (e.g., Resick et al., 2002), and eye movement desensitization and reprocessing (e.g., Taylor et al., 2003). The recent treatment guidelines published by the International Society for Traumatic Stress Studies (ISTSS) concluded that exposure therapy was the most empirically supported intervention for PTSD. Moreover, at least two recent studies have shown that exposure therapy (alone or in combination with affect regulation training) for PTSD reduces dissociative symptoms, as well as PTSD and other psychopathology (Cloitre,

Koenen, Cohen, & Han, 2002; Taylor et al., 2003). As such, we will focus our discussion of dissociation and treatment for PTSD on exposure therapy. To provide a framework for understanding how dissociation might impact exposure treatment for PTSD, we will first describe the theoretical underpinnings of this treatment.

Exposure Therapy

Foa and colleagues (Foa & Riggs, 1993; Foa et al., 1989; Foa & Rothbaum, 1998) have proposed that impaired emotional processing of the traumatic event underlies PTSD. Further, they suggest that in those who develop PTSD, memories of the trauma have pathological elements as a result of this impaired processing. According to Foa and Kozak's (1986) emotional processing theory, pathological fear is differentiated from typical fear by (a) disruptive intensity, (b) associations that do not accurately represent reality; and (c) incorrect interpretations such as, "my anxiety means I'm incompetent." Building on this theory, they propose that two conditions are necessary for corrective emotional processing to occur: (a) activation of the fear structure, and (b) the incorporation of new information that is incompatible with the pathological elements of the structure (e.g., overgeneralization of fear). Thus, from the perspective of emotional processing theory, treatment for PTSD should facilitate emotional engagement with traumatic memories in order to promote trauma-related fear reduction, reduce avoidance, and modify the distorted interpretations that contribute to the maintenance of PTSD.

To provide opportunity for such emotional engagement, exposure treatments typically include two main types of confrontation with feared memories and situations: imaginal exposure, which consists of repeatedly recounting the traumatic event and describing feelings and thoughts that occurred at the time, and in vivo exposure, which requires confrontation with situations, places, or activities that are avoided due to trauma-related fear.

PTSD AND DISSOCIATIVE SYMPTOMS: FACTORS TO CONSIDER WHEN UTILIZING EXPOSURE THERAPY

As illustrated by the discussion above, the emotional processing facilitated by exposure is thought to be central to successful treatment of PTSD.

Dissociation, on the other hand, often is thought to impede such emotional processing (e.g., Whalen & Nash, 1996). Dissociation and emotional numbing are used as strategies to avoid trauma-related emotional distress (Davidson & Foa, 1991). Such strategies may impede treatment progress by thwarting effective emotional engagement.

While exposure therapy is a clearly efficacious intervention for PTSD, treatment can be stressful for patients as it involves addressing the very memories the patient is working to avoid. Therapists should be aware that the stress of treatment may *temporarily* exacerbate dissociative and other trauma-related symptoms (Foa, Zoellner, Feeny, Hembree, & Alvarez-Conrad, 2002). Similarly, during exposure therapy, patients who have dissociated in the past to avoid emotional distress may become overwhelmed during imaginal exposure and may begin to dissociate in session. If this occurs, the therapist should utilize therapeutic modifications designed to titrate emotional engagement, which will be discussed below in more detail.

In addition, given the observed connection between panic and dissociation, as discussed by Bryant and Panasetis (in press), clinicians also should be aware of the potential relationship between panic experienced during a trauma and subsequent dissociation. It is important to note that panic in response to trauma reminders is quite common and does not warrant an additional diagnosis of panic disorder, nor does it require modification of validated treatment for PTSD. In contrast, in cases where both "classic," out of the blue panic and dissociative symptoms are present in a trauma survivor, treatment of the panic symptoms (such as through interoceptive exposure exercises) may reduce related dissociative symptoms.

Clinicians also should be cognizant that individuals with PTSD and high levels of dissociative symptoms may tend to have worse outcomes than those without dissociative symptoms, although empirical investigations of this relationship are limited. For example, dissociation has been identified as a predictor of both self-mutilation and suicide attempts (van der Kolk, Perry, & Herman, 1991). Thus, if dissociative symptoms are recognized in a patient, the therapist should be careful to assess risk for self-harm. In addition, as reported earlier, dissociation among women with PTSD has been found to predict poorer long-term functioning (Feeny, Zoellner, Fitzgibbons, & Foa, 2000). These factors highlight the importance of thorough assessment of clients with PTSD to measure history of dissociation.

MANAGING DISSOCIATIVE SYMPTOMS DURING PTSD TREATMENT: FACILITATING EFFECTIVE EMOTIONAL ENGAGEMENT

While at least two studies show that exposure therapy for PTSD significantly reduces dissociative symptoms, we have presented theoretical reasons to predict that high levels of dissociation may impede treatment progress. Thus, in this section, we will focus on how to effectively manage dissociative symptoms during the delivery of exposure therapy for PTSD. Exposure therapy typically consists of a variety of therapeutic components, including education about PTSD and common reactions to traumatic events, breathing retraining, repeated recounting of the traumatic event (i.e., imaginal exposure), and encouragement to confront, rather than avoid, trauma cues and reminders (i.e., in vivo exposure). For a detailed description of the treatment program see Foa and Rothbaum (1998).

Emotional processing theory suggests that in order to modify fear structures that perpetuate extreme anxiety, treatment for PTSD should include engaging emotionally with traumatic memories. Flashbacks, emotional numbing, and extreme anxiety may be problematic to effective engagement (e.g., Hembree, Marshall, Fitzgibbons, & Foa, 2001; Jaycox & Foa, 1996). We will discuss each of these impediments and how to deal with them in the context of exposure treatment for PTSD below.

Flashbacks. Some clients who present with PTSD and dissociative symptoms struggle with intense flashbacks of the traumatic event. Unless the client has an identified primary dissociative disorder, flashbacks that occur during exposure therapy should not typically be reason to discontinue therapy. In the context of exposure therapy, there are several ways to handle these flashbacks. First, the therapist can attempt to ground the client and titrate the exposure to decrease the likelihood that she will dissociate. This can be done by attempting to start the imaginal exposure at a manageable level and by increasing supportive comments that remind the client that she is safe and that the trauma is not recurring (e.g., "you're safe here.... remember this is a memory; it is not happening again.... you are with me"). It can be helpful to discuss and implement "grounding" techniques prior to starting the imaginal exposure. For example, for some clients holding on to their chair arms or to an object (e.g., clay, a clump of tissues, etc.) are ways to remind them that they are safe in their therapist's office and that the traumatic event is not reoccurring. In addition, simple modifications to standard exposure procedures such as having the client recount the trauma memory with her eyes open, instead of closed, can facilitate staying grounded in the present and can prevent flashbacks.

However, for those clients who routinely have severe flashbacks, preventing them during exposure may not be realistic. In the event of flashbacks during exposure, the therapist can sympathetically encourage clients to deal with their flashbacks in a calm and soothing voice. It is important that therapists not respond to flashbacks with fear, but instead label the experience as a flashback and teach the client how to manage the experience. For example, this can be done by encouraging the use of breathing techniques taught at the start of treatment and by reminding the client that she is safe and experiencing a very intense *memory*. Similarly, when flashbacks are over, the therapist can praise the client for her ability to calm herself down, to tolerate the experience, and to regain her sense of reality. Optimally, the client should begin to regard her flashbacks as not dangerous and not as a reason to avoid the memory, and in turn, the flashbacks should decrease.

Emotional numbing. At the other end of the spectrum, clients who are experiencing dissociative symptoms also may experience emotional numbing during imaginal exposure. As described above, emotional numbing and dissociation appear to be related, but distinct constructs (Feeny et al., 2000). While most therapists worry about clients having flashbacks or panic attacks during exposure, clinical experience indicates that emotional disengagement is substantially more common. Indicators that your client is numb or disengaged include low ratings of distress during imaginal exposure, rushing through particular sections of the trauma narrative, or recounting the event in "police report" style, with "just the facts" and little or no emotional connection. When emotional numbing or disengagement is prominent, it is important to repeat the rationale for processing traumatic events through imaginal exposure to ensure that the client understands why it is necessary to engage with trauma-related memories. In addition, explore with your client what is preventing her from connecting with the memory. Some clients may worry about losing control of their emotions if they really let themselves connect with the memory. In this event, the therapist can be empathetic and validating of these feelings, but reiterate that with time, the distress will decrease. In contrast to the procedural adaptations designed to decrease engagement or to deal with flashbacks, to facilitate engagement, encourage clients to keep their eyes closed and to use the present tense consistently. Similarly, avoid conversations with the client during imaginal exposure as they typically reduce emotional engagement with the memory. Once engaged in imaginal exposure, another way to facilitate engagement is to prompt clients for additional details. This prompting can include questions about details of what happened, and what the client was thinking, feeling, seeing or hearing at the time of the traumatic event.

Extreme anxiety or panic. Clients with dissociative symptoms can become extremely anxious or "overengaged" during imaginal exposure. A minority will become so anxious that they fear they will lose control of themselves and their emotions. As we have described already, it is important that clients with PTSD engage with the memory in order to process it and become less fearful. However, as suggested by Jaycox and Foa (1996), extreme levels of anxiety during exposure can impede treatment progress. Clients need to maintain the sense that they are safe and in the present while recounting the trauma memory with their therapist. This can be particularly challenging when working with clients who have very severe PTSD or who have severe dissociative symptoms. In these cases, exposure procedures often need to be slightly modified to modulate clients' distress to tolerable levels. As identified above, under strategies to use with patients experiencing flashbacks, such procedural modifications include instructing the patient to keep her eyes open, using the past tense, making eye contact with and conversing with the patient about the story she is relating, and providing frequent, "grounding" comments (e.g., "the memory can not hurt you.... I'm here to help you").

CONCLUSION

Dissociation and PTSD have long been linked conceptually as reactions to traumatic experiences. Indeed, dissociative symptoms such as amnesia and emotional numbing have been considered by some to be cardinal symptoms of PTSD. However, empirical investigation of the relationship between PTSD and dissociation has led to conflicting results. In this chapter, we reviewed theoretical conceptualizations and empirical data relevant to the construct of dissociation and its relationship to PTSD. We also discussed the potential impact of dissociation on treatment for PTSD. Emotional processing theory suggests that in order to modify fear structures that perpetuate extreme anxiety, treatment for PTSD should include en-gaging emotionally with traumatic memories. In contrast, dissociation is thought to be a strategy to avoid trauma-related emotional distress (e.g., Davidson & Foa, 1991). Thus, dissociation may impede treatment progress by thwarting effective emotional engagement. In light of this, we high-lighted factors to consider when treating PTSD in the presence of comor-bid dissociative symptoms and guidelines for enhancing effective emotional engagement. Ultimately, being aware of the likely multidimensional na-ture of dissociation and its impact on PTSD may help clinicians and researchers better understand how to most effectively implement treat-ment for trauma survivors.

REFERENCES

American Psychiatric Association. (1980). *Diagnostic and statistical manual of mental Disorders,* 3rd ed. Washington, DC: Author.

American Psychiatric Association. (1987). *Diagnostic and statistical manual of mental disorders* (3rd ed., revised). Washington, D.C.: American Psychiatric Press.

American Psychiatric Association. (1994). *Diagnostic and statistical manual of mental disorders,* (4th edition). Washington, D.C.: American Psychiatric Press.

Amodeo, J. (1981). Focusing applied to a case of disorientation in meditation. *Journal of Transpersonal Psychology, 13,* 149–154.

Barton, A., Blanchard, E., & Hickling, E. J. (1996). Antecedents and consequenc-es of acute stress disorder among motor vehicle accident victims. *Behaviour Research and Therapy, 34,* 805–813.

Bernstein, E. M., & Putnam, F. W. (1986). Development, reliability, and validity of a dissociation scale. *Journal of Nervous & Mental Disease, 174,* 727–734.

Breslau, N., Davis, G.C., Andreski, P., Peterson, E. (1991). Traumatic events and posttraumatic stress disorder in an urban population of young adults. *Archives General Psychiatry, 48,* 218–228.

Breuer, J., & Freud, S. (1895). *Studies on hysteria.* New York: Basic Books.

Briere, J. (2002). *Multiscale Dissociation Inventory (MDI).* Odessa, FL: Psycholog-ical Assessment Resources.

Briere, J., & Conte, J. (1993). Self-reported amnesia for abuse in adults molested as children. *Journal of Traumatic Stress, 6,* 21–32.

Briere, J., & Runtz, M. (1988). Post sexual abuse trauma. *Journal of International Violence, 2,* 367–379.

Briere, J., & Runtz, M. (1989). The trauma symptom checklist (TSC-33): Early data on a new scale. *Journal of Interpersonal Violence, 4,* 151–163.

Briere, J., Weathers, F. W., & Runtz, M. (in press). Is dissociation a multidimen-sional construct? Data from the Multiscale Dissociative Inventory. *Journal of Traumatic Stress.*

Bryant, R. A., & Panasetis, P. (in press). The role of panic in peritraumatic dissociation. *British Journal of Clinical Psychology.*

Burgess, A. W., & Holmstrom, L. L. (1976). Coping behavior of the rape victim. *American Journal of Psychiatry, 133,* 413–418.

Cardena, E., & Spiegel, D. 1996. Diagnostic issues, criteria, and comorbidity of dissociative disorders. In L. K. Michelson & W. J. Ray, Eds., *Handbook of dissociation: Theoretical, empirical, and clinical perspectives.* New York: Plenum Press.

Chu, J. A., & Dill, D. L. (1990). Dissociative symptoms in relation to childhood physical and sexual abuse. *American Journal of Psychiatry, 147,* 887–892.

Classen, C., Koopman, C., Hales, R., & Spiegel, D. (1998). Acute Stress Disorder as a predictor of posttraumatic stress symptoms. *American Journal of Psychiatry, 155,* 620–624.

Cloitre, M., Koenen, K. Cohen, L.R. & Han, H. (2002). Skills training in affective and interpersonal regulation followed by exposure: A phase-based treatment for PTSD related to childhood abuse. *Journal of Consulting and Clinical Psychology, 70,* 1067–1074.

Coons, P., & Milstein, V. (1986). Rape and post-traumatic stress in multiple personality. *Psychological Reports, 55,* 839–845.

Cubelli, R. (2003). Defining dissociations. *Cortex, 39,* 211–214.

Dancen, C.V., Riggs, D.S., Hearst, Ikeda, D., & Shoyer, B.G., (1996). Dissociative experiences and posttraumatic stress disorder among female victims of criminal assault and rape. *Journal of Traumatic Stress, 9.* 253–267.

Davidson, J., & Foa, E. B. (1991). Diagnostic issues in post-traumatic stress disorder: Consideration for the DSM–IV. *Journal of Abnormal Psychology, 100,* 346–355.

DiTomasso, M. J., & Routh, D. K. (1993). Recall of abuse in childhood and three measures of dissociation. *Child Abuse & Neglect, 17,* 477–485.

Feeny, N. C., Zoellner, L. A., Fitzgibbons, L. A., & Foa, E. B. (2000). Exploring the roles of emotional numbing, depression, and dissociation in PTSD. *Journal of Traumatic Stress, 13,* 489–498.

Feeny, N. C., Zoellner, L. A., & Foa, E. B. (2000a). Anger, dissociation, and posttraumatic Stress Disorder among female assault victims. *Journal of Traumatic Stress, 13,* 89–100.

Feeny, N. C., Zoellner, L. A., & Foa, E. B. (2000b). *Patterns of recovery women with chronic PTSD.* Symposium paper presented at annual AABT conference, New Orleans, LA.

Foa, E. B., Dancu, C. V., Hembree, E. A., Jaycox, L. H., Meadows, E. A., & Street, G. P. (1999). A comparison of exposure therapy, stress inoculation training, and their combination for reducing posttraumatic stress disorder in female assault victims. *Journal of Consulting and Clinical Psychology, 67,* 194–200.

Foa, E. B., & Hearst-Ikeda, D. (1996). Emotional dissociation in response to trauma. In L. K. Michelson & W. J. Ray, Eds., *Handbook of dissociation: Theoretical, empirical, and clinical perspectives.* New York: Plenum Press.

Foa, E. B., & Kozak, M. J. (1986). Emotional processing: Theory, research and clinical implications for anxiety disorder. In J. Safran & L. S. Greenberg, Eds., *Emotion psychotherapy and change.* New York: Guilford Press.

Foa, E. B., & Meadows, E. A. (1997). Psychosocial treatments for post-traumatic stress disorder: A critical review. In J. Spence, J. M. Darley, & D. J. Foss (Eds.), *Annual Review of Psychology* (Vol. 48., pp. 449–480), Palo Alto, CA: Annual Reviews Inc.

Foa, E.B., & Riggs, D. S. (1993). Post-traumatic stress disorder in rape victims. In J. Oldham, M. B. Riba, & A. Tasman (Eds.) *American psychiatric press review of psychiatry,* Volume 12. Washington, D. C.: American Psychiatric Press, pp. 273–303.

Foa, E. B., Riggs, D. S., Massie, E. D., & Yarczower, M. (1995). The impact of fear activation and anger on the efficacy of exposure treatment for posttraumatic stress disorder. *Behavior Therapy, 26,* 487–499.

Foa, E. B. & Rothbaum, B. O. (1998). *Treating the trauma of rape.* New York: Guilford Press.

Foa, E. B., Rothbaum, B. O., Riggs, D. S., & Murdock, T. (1991). Treatment of post-traumatic stress disorder in rape victims: A comparison between cognitive-behavioral procedures and counseling. *Journal of Consulting and Clinical Psychology, 59,* 715–723.

Foa, E. B., Steketee, G., & Rothbaum, B. O. (1989). Behavioral/cognitive conceptualizations of posttraumatic stress disorder. *Behavior Therapy, 20,* 155–176.

Foa, E. B., Zoellner, L. A., Feeny, N. C., Hembree, E. A., & Alvarez-Conrad, J. (2002). Is imaginal exposure related to an exacerbation of symptoms? *Journal of Consulting and Clinical Psychology, 70,* 1022–1028.

Goff, D. C., Brotman, A. W., Kindlon, D., & Waites, M. (1991). The delusion of possession in chronically psychotic patients. *Journal of Nervous & Mental Disorders, 179,* 567–571.

Harvey, A. G., & Bryant, R. A. (1998). The relationship between acute stress disorder and posttraumatic stress disorder: A prospective evaluation of motor accident survivors. *Journal of Consulting & Clinical Psychology, 66,* 507–512.

Helzer, J. E., Robins, L. N., & McEvoy, L. (1987). Post-traumatic stress disorder in the general population: Findings of the Epidemiologic Catchment Area Survey. *The New England Journal of Medicine, 317,* 1630–1634.

Hembree, E. A., Marshall, R., Fitzgibbons, L., & Foa, E. B. (2001). The difficult to treat PTSD patient. In M. Dewan & R. Pies (Eds.), *The difficult to treat psychiatric patient (pp 149–178).* Washington, DC: American Psychiatric Press.

Horowitz, M. J. (1986). *Stress response syndromes* (2nd ed.). Northvale, NJ: Jason Aronson.

Janet, P. (1889). *Psychological automatisms.* Paris: Alcan.

Janet, P. (1907). *The major symptoms of hysteria.* New York: Macmillan.

Jaycox, L. H., & Foa, E. B. (1996). Obstacles in implementing exposure therapy for PTSD: Case discussions and practical solutions. *Clinical Psychology and Psychotherapy, 3,* 176–184.

Kardiner, A. (1941). *The traumatic neuroses of war.* New York: Basic Books.

Kessler, R. C., Sonnega, A., Bromet, E., Hughes, M., & Nelson, C. B. (1995). Posttraumatic stress disorder in the National Comorbidity Survey. *Archives of General Psychiatry, 52,* 1048–1060.

Kolodner, G., & Frances, R. (1993). Recognizing dissociative disorders in patients with chemical dependency. *Hospital and Community Psychiatry, 44,* 1041–1043.

Koopman, C., Classen, C., & Spiegel, D. (1994). Predictors of posttraumatic stress symptoms among Oakland/Berkeley firestorm survivors. *American Journal of Psychiatry, 151,* 888–894.

Kulka, R.A., Schlenger, W.E., Fairbank, J.A., Hough, R.L., Jordon, B.K., Marmar, C.R., et al. (1990). *Trauma and the Vietnam war generation.* New York: Brunner/ Mazel.

Maldonado, J. R., & Spiegel, D. (1994). The treatment of post-traumatic stress disorder. In S. J. Lynn & J. W. Rhue (Eds.). *Dissociation: Clinical & theoretical perspectives* (pp. 215–241). New York: The Guilford Press.

Marks, I., Lovell, K., Noshirvani, H., Livanou, M., & Thrasher, S. (1998). Treatment of posttraumatic stress disorder by exposure and/or cognitive restructuring. *Archives of General Psychiatry, 55,* 317–325.

Marmar, C. R., Weiss, D. S., Schlenger, D. S., Fairbank, J. A., Jordan, B. K., Kulka, R. A., et al., (1994). Peritraumatic dissociation and posttraumatic stress in male Vietnam theater veterans. *American Journal of Psychiatry, 151,* 902–907.

McFarlane, A. C. (1986). Posttrauma morbidity in a disaster. *Journal of Nervous & Mental Disorders, 174,* 4–14.

Merckelbach, H. & Muris, P. (2001). The causal link between self reported trauma and dissociation: A critical review. *Behaviour Research and Therapy, 39,* 245–254.

Nash, M. R., & Lynn, S. J. (1986). Child abuse and hypnotic ability. *Imagination, Cognition, and Personality, 5,* 211–218.

Nemiah, J. 1981. Dissociation disorders. In A. M. Freeman & H. I. Kaplan, Eds., *Comprehensive textbook of psychiatry,* 3rd ed. Baltimore: Williams & Wilkins.

Norris, F. H. (1992). Epidemiology of trauma: Frequency and impact of different potentially traumatic events on different demographic groups. *Journal of Consulting and Clinical Psychology, 60,* 409–418.

Pribor, E. F., & Dinwiddle, S. H. (1992). Psychiatric correlates of incest of incest in childhood. *American Journal of Psychiatry, 149,* 52–56.

Putnam, F. W. (1985). Dissociation as a response to extreme stress. In R. K. Kluft, Ed., *Childhood antecedents of multiple personality.* Washington, DC: American Psychiatric Press.

Putnam, F. W. (1989). *Diagnosis and treatment of multiple personality disorder.* New York: Guilford Press.

Quimby, L. G., & Putnam, F. W. (1991). Dissociative symptoms and aggression in a state mental hospital. *Dissociation, 4,* 21–24.

Resick, P. A., Nishith, P., Weaver, T., Astin, M. C., & Feuer, C. A. (2002). A comparison of cognitive processing therapy, prolonged exposure, and a waiting condition for the treatment of posttraumatic stress disorder in female rape victims. *Journal of Consulting and Clinical Psychology, 70,* 867–879.

Resnick, H. S., Kilpatrick, D. G., Dansky, B. S., Saunders, B. E. & Best, C. L. (1993). Prevalence of civilian trauma and posttraumatic stress disorder in a representative national sample of women. *Journal of Consulting and Clinical Psychology, 61,* 984–991.

Riggs, D. S., Rothbaum, B. O., & Foa, E. B. (1995). A prospective examination of symptoms of posttraumatic stress disorder in victims of non-assault. *Journal of Interpersonal Violence, 2,* 201–214.

Ross, C. A. (1996). History, phenomenology, and epidemiology of dissociation. In L. K. Michelson & W. J. Ray, Eds., *Handbook of dissociation: Theoretical, empirical, and clinical perspectives (pp.3–24).* New York: Plenum Press.

Ross, C. A., Anderson, G., Fleisher, W. P., & Norton, G. R. (1991). The frequency of multiple personality disorder among psychiatric inpatients. *American Journal of Psychiatry, 148,* 1717–1720.

Ross, C. A., Joshi, S., & Currie, R. (1990). Dissociative experiences in the general population. *American Journal of Psychiatry, 147,* 1547–1552.

Rothbaum, B. O., Foa, E. B., Riggs, D. S., Murdock, T., & Walsh, W. (1992). A prospective examination of post-traumatic stress disorder in rape victims. *Journal of Traumatic Stress, 5,* 455–475.

Sandberg, P. A., &Lynn, S. L. (1992). Dissociative experiences, psychopathology and adjustment, and child and adolescent maltreatment in female college students. *Journal of Abnormal Psychology, 101,* 717–723.

Sanders, B., & Giolas, M. H. (1991). Dissociation and childhood trauma in psychologically disturbed adolescents. *American Journal of Psychiatry, 148,* 50–54.

Saxe, G. N., van der Kolk, B. A., Berkowitz, R., Chinman, G., Hall, K. L., Lieberg, G., & Schwartz, J. (1993). Dissociative disorders in psychiatric inpatients. *American Journal of Psychiatry, 150,* 1037–1042.

Shalev, A. P., Peri, T., Caneti, L., & Schreiber, S. (1996). Predictors of PTSD in injured trauma survivors: A prospective study. *American Journal of Psychiatry, 153,* 219–225.

Spiegel, D. (1986). Dissociating damage. *American Journal of Clinical Hypnosis, 29,* 123–131.

Spiegel, D. (1997). Trauma, dissociation, and memory. In R. Yehuda & A. C. McFarlane (Eds.), *Psychobiology of PTSD.* New York: New York Academy of Sciences.

Spiegel, D., & Cardena, E. (1991). Disintegrated experience: The dissociative disorders revisited. *Journal of Abnormal Psychology, 100,* 366–378.

Strick, F. C., & Wilcoxon, S. A. (1991). A comparison of dissociative experiences in adult female outpatients with and without histories of early incestuous abuse. *Dissociation: Progress in the Dissociative Disorders, 4,* 193—199.

Taylor, S., & Koch, W. J. (1995). Anxiety disorders due to motor vehicle accidents: Nature and treatment. *Clinical Psychology Review, 15,* 721–738.

Taylor, S., Koch, W. J., Fecteau, G., Fedoroff, I. C., Thordarson, D. S., & Nicki, R. M. (2001). Posttraumatic stress disorder arising after road traffic collisions: Patterns of response to cognitive-behavioral therapy. *Journal of Consulting and Clinical Psychology, 63,* 541–551.

Taylor, S., Thordarson, D. S., Maxfield, L., Fedoroff, I. C., Lovell, K., & Ogrodniczuk, J.
(2003). Comparative efficacy, speed, and adverse effects of three PTSD treatments: Exposure therapy, EMDR, and relaxation training. Journal of Consulting & Clinical Psychology, 71, 330–338.

Terr, L. C. (1991). Childhood traumas: An outline and overview. American Journal of Psychiatry, 148, 10–20.

van der Hart, O., van der Kolk, B. A., & Boon, S. (1996). The treatment of dissociative disorders. In J. D. Bremner & C. R. Marmar, (Eds.), Trauma, memory, and dissociation. Washington, DC: American Psychiatric Press.

van der Kolk, B. A., Pelcovitz, D., Roth, S., Mandel, F. S., McFarlane, A. C., & Herman, J. L. (1996). Dissociation, somatization, and affect dysregulation: The complexity of adaptation to trauma. American Journal of Psychiatry, 153, 83–93.

van der Kolk, B. A., Perry, C., & Herman, J. L. (1991). Childhood origins of self-destructive behavior. American Journal of Psychiatry, 148, 1665–1671.

van der Kolk, B. A., van der Hart, O., & Marmar, C. R. (1996). Dissociation and information processing in posttraumatic stress disorder. In B. A. van der Kolk, A. C. McFarlane, & L. Weisaeth (Eds.), Traumatic Stress: The effects of overwhelming experience on mind, body, and society. New York: The Guilford Press.

Watson, D. (2003). Investigating the construct validity of the dissociative taxon: Stability analyses of normal and pathological dissociation. Journal of Abnormal Psychology, 112, 298–305.

Waller, N. G., Putnam, F. W., & Carlson, E. B. (1996). Types of dissociation and dissociative types: A taxometric analysis analysis of dissociative experiences. Psychological Methods, 1, 300–321.

Waller, N. G., & Ross, C. A. (1997). The prevalence and biometric structure of pathological dissociation in the general population: Taxometric and behavior genetic findings. Journal of Abnormal Psychology, 106, 499–510.

Whalen, J. E., & Nash, M. R. 1996. Hypnosis and dissociation: Theoretical, empirical, and clinical perspectives. In L. K. Michelson & W. J. Ray, Eds., Handbook of dissociation: Theoretical, empirical, and clinical perspectives. New York: Plenum Press.

Chapter 13

COGNITIVE-BEHAVIORAL INTERVENTIONS FOR CHILDREN AND ADOLESCENTS WITH PTSD

Philip A. Saigh, Marla R. Brassard, and
Stephen T. Peverely

HISTORICAL BACKGROUND

Historically, different forms of exposure-based anxiety-reduction procedures have been used for hundreds of years (Saigh, 2002; Saigh, Yasik, Oberfield, & Inamder, 1999). Goethe's autobiography presents a graphic account of his self-induced treatment of acrophobia (Boudewyns & Shipley, 1983). More recently, Malleson (1959) described a course of imaginal or in vitro exposure that was used to reduce distress of a test-phobic graduate student. The student was described as "classically panic stricken... sobbing and fearful, bewailing his fate, and terrified of the impending examination" (p. 225). In lieu of prescribing the standard treatment of that era (i.e., psychoanalysis), Malleson asked the student to "tell of the awful consequences that he felt would follow his failure—derision from his colleagues . . . disappointment from his family and financial loss" (p. 225). The student was also instructed that when he "felt a little wave of spontaneous alarm, he was not to push it aside, but was to augment it, to try to experience it more profoundly and more vividly" (p. 225). Although the regimen was associated with a degree of distress, the patient adhered to Malleson's instructions and reported that he was almost unable to experience test-related anxiety as the date of the examination approached. As it were, he passed the exam with ease.

In 1961 Stampfl coined the term *"implosive therapy"* to describe a treatment that "may be regarded as a synthesis between Freudian oriented and Mowerian approaches to psychotherapy" (p. 1). This treatment involved imaginal exposure to fear stimuli. Stampfl and Levis (1967) developed an elaborate description of the procedure and generated a theoretical rationale to account for its efficacy. They reported that the initial objective of implosive therapy involves the identification of discrete exteroceptive- and interoceptive-conditioned stimuli or cues that phobic patients avoid. Stampfl and Levis reasoned that fear-inducing stimuli are apparent in a variety of forms (e.g., auditory, olfactory, tactile, and cognitive). They also proposed that these cues are interdependent and arranged in serial hierarchies that correspond to the degree of fear and avoidance. Cues were said to be the product of personal experiences wherein "objects or situations are known to have high-anxiety eliciting value, as in specific traumatic situations, material produced by dreams or symbolism of a psychoanalytic nature" (p. 502). Given this rationale, the Stampfl and Levis treatment modality initially called for the identification of traumatic cues. In-depth clinical interviews were used to identify these cues. Patients were subsequently asked to imagine and verbalize symptom contingent cues until extinction occurred.

Rachman (1966) subsequently introduced the term *flooding* to the clinical literature. Rachman attributed the term to Pollin (1959) who employed it to describe the aversive component of an infrahuman laboratory experiment involving extinction. Although Rachman's (1966) paper concluded that systematic desensitization was more effective than flooding (i.e., prolonged imaginal exposure) in reducing the fears of phobic adults, he cautioned that the "disparate results can be accounted for by differences in method" (p. 5). Rachman also acknowledged that the participants had received less than 2 minutes of anxiety-inducing imaginal exposure at a time and that it was "possible therefore that the crucial element omitted in the present technique is prolonged exposure" (p. 6).

Following Rachman's (1966) initial paper, a number of reports involving longer periods of imaginal exposure (i.e., 40 to 60 minutes of stimulation) were carried out (e.g., Hogan & Kirchner, 1967; Levis & Carrera, 1967; Yule, Sacks, & Hersov, 1974). By 1972, flooding studies had been carried out by different investigators across a wide range of participants and settings. Following a review of the flooding literature, Marks (1972) formulated an important definition of the flooding process. According to this definition, flooding and systematic desensitization are seen as constituting two ends of a continuum of therapeutic approaches to distressing situations. Marks also maintained that "the difference between the two is largely one of degree. The more sudden the confrontation, the more it is prolonged, and the greater the emotion that accompanies it, the more apt is the label *flooding* for that procedure" (Marks, 1972, p.154). Although it is beyond the scope of this chapter to present a thorough review of this literature base, it may be said that flooding has been successfully used to treat a wide range of simple and social phobia cases (Marks, 1981; Spiegler & Guevermont, 1998).

PROLONGED THERAPEUTIC EXPOSURE TRIALS WITH TRAUMATIZED ADULTS

Given the efficacy of flooding procedures with simple and social phobics, Fairbank, DeGood, and Jenkins (1981) tested the efficacy of a multifaceted flooding program in the treatment of a 32-year-old female motor vehicle accident victim. Although the patient had physically recovered from her injuries and was able to drive, she experienced panic attacks when she attempted to drive. Employing directed relaxation, self-monitoring, and imaginal exposure, the investigators eliminated her startle reaction and appreciably reduced her self-reported anxiety estimates after five treatment sessions. Treatment gains continued to be evident at 1, 4, and 6-month follow-up evaluations.

Keane and Kaloupek (1982) went on to publish a paper on "imaginal flooding in the treatment of posttraumatic stress disorder" (p. 138). The article was based on the treatment of a 36-year-old male Vietnam veteran with war-related posttraumatic stress disorder [PTSD; American Psychiatric Association (APA), 1980]. Through a series of clinical interviews, Keane and Kaloupek identified a number of highly disturbing thoughts and nightmares. The patient was instructed to imagine the traumatic cues during nineteen 40-minute treatment sessions. Keane and Kaloupek reported significant reductions in self-reported anxiety. They also reported a significant increase in the amount of sleep and work-related productivity. Follow-up assessments denoted continued efficacy at 3- and 12-month follow-ups.

Following the reports by Fairbank et al. (1981) and Keane and Kaloupek (1982), investigators have repeatedly documented the efficacy of prolonged exposure therapy with adult PTSD patients in a series of single-case (e.g., Black & Keane, 1982; Fairbank, Gross, & Keane, 1983; Fairbank & Keane, 1982) and experimental investigations (e.g., Boudewyns & Hyer, 1990; Cooper & Clum, 1989; Keane, Fairbank, Caddel, & Zimmering, 1989; Richards, Lovell, & Marks, 1994; Thompson, Charlton,

Kerry, Lee, & Turner, 1995). More recently, treatments incorporating prolonged exposure and stress inoculation training (Foa, Rothbaum, Riggs, & Murdock, 1991; Marks, Lovell, Noshirvani, & Thrasher, 1998; Resick & Schnicke, 1992) have reflected efficacy across a variety of adult PTSD patients.

CHILD-ADOLESCENT SINGLE-CASE RESEARCH STUDIES

Given the absence of information involving the effects of flooding with traumatized youth and the clinical need to provide services for traumatized youth during the Lebanese war, Saigh carried out a number of single-case flooding trials at the American University of Beirut Hospital. Saigh (1987a) initially described the treatment of a 14-year-old Lebanese boy who had been abducted and tortured. Six months after the abduction, the youth met criteria for PTSD as measured by the Children's PTSD Inventory (CPTSDI; Saigh, 1989a*). A 12-item Behavioral Avoidance Test (BAT) was developed to quantify aspects of the boy's trauma-related avoidance behaviors. The BAT called for a 10-minute behavioral walk wherein the boy left his home and followed the route that he had previously taken to the location where the abduction occurred. As PTSD at that time was indicated in part by deficits in short-term memory and concentration (*DSM–III*, APA, 1980), the WISC-R Digit Span and Coding subtests were administered. The boy also completed the State Trait Anxiety Inventory (STAI; Spielberger, Gorsuch, & Lushane, 1968), Beck Depression Inventory (BDI; Beck, Ward, Mandelson, Mock, & Erbaugh, 1961) and the Rathus Assertiveness Schedule (RAS; Rathus, 1973).

The parents and child were informed about the nature and course of posttraumatic stress syndrome (PTSD), the flooding process, short-term reactivity, and the importance of securing reliable and valid indices before, during, and following treatment. Given their informed consent, four anxiety-evoking scenes were identified through a series of clinical interviews with the boy. These scenes reflected the sequence of traumatic events that the youth had experienced (e.g., being stopped, forced into a car at gun point, blindfolded, driven away, interrogated, tortured, experi-

---

*The Children's PTSD Inventory was developed in 1982 and its psycometric properties were published in 1989. This instrument reflected the diagnostic criteria for PTSD as indicated in the third edition of the APA's (1980) Diagnostic and Statistical Manual of Mental Disorders (*DSM–III*). The instrument has been revised to reflect the *DSM–IV* PTSD criteria (Saigh, 2004).

encing mock executions, and listening to the abductors discuss the merits of requesting a ransom vs. execution).

The flooding regimen was initiated by 10 minutes of therapist-directed deep muscle relaxation exercises. The exercises were followed by 60 minutes of prolonged exposure. In this context, the youth was asked to imagine the contents of the anxiety-evoking scenes. These scenes were presented sequentially according to a multiple baseline across traumatic scenes design. Emotional distress relative to the traumatic scenes or cues was measured by subjective units of disturbance (SUDs) ratings. The youth rated each scene according to a 0- to 10-point scale with 10 denoting "maximum discomfort" and 0 denoting "no discomfort." SUDs ratings were recorded at 2-minute intervals during each scene presentation. Extensive debriefing was provided following treatment sessions.

Figure 13.1 shows SUDs levels appreciably decreased following seven exposure sessions. A 4-month follow-up determined that the boy reported almost no distress relative to the trauma-related scenes that he was asked to imagine. Appreciable posttreatment gains relative to the baseline levels were apparent on his WISC-R Coding and Digit Span performance. Posttreatment and 4-month follow-up assessments also reflected clinically significant reductions on self-reported estimates of anxiety, depression, and aggression as measured by the STAI, BDI, and RAS. Whereas the youth was able to complete one-third of the BAT activities before the treatment, he performed 100% of the BAT activities after the last treatment session. These gains were maintained at a 4-month follow-up evaluation.

Given the observed efficacy of the initial trial, Saigh (1987b, 1987c, 1987d, 1989b) conducted four single-case systematic replications wherein prolonged imaginal exposure was used to treat children or adolescents with war-related PTSD. Traumatic scenes were identified and presented according to a multiple-baseline across traumatic scenes design. Stimulus and response imagery cues were employed during the exposure process. Stimulus cues involved visual, auditory, tactile, and olfactory components of each scene. Response cues involved the behavioral and cognitive aspects of the scene. Table 13.1 presents the transcript of a session with a 9-year-old girl who developed PTSD after she was exposed to an artillery barrage (Saigh, 1987b).

The number of intrusive trauma-related thoughts (excluding those that were induced in therapy) was self-monitored on pocket frequency counters by three of the child PTSD patients (Saigh, 1987c). Although imaginal exposure was associated with an initial increase in the number of

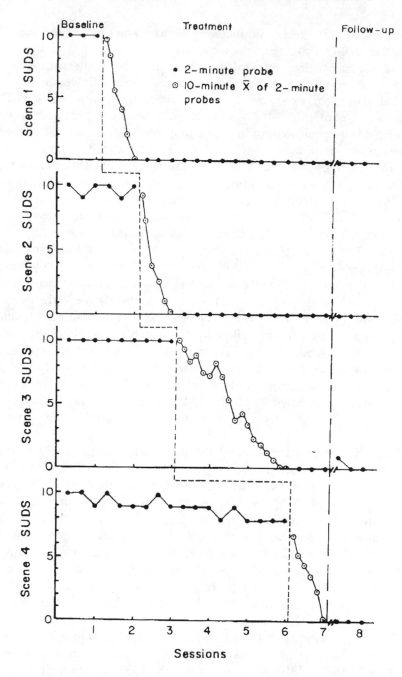

Figure 13.1 SUDs ratings across assessment situations.

Table 13.1 Case Example of the Imaginal Flooding Process with a 10-Year-Old Girl

Therapist:	Imagine that you are playing in a neighborhood garden in the afternoon. Imagine the color of the grass and the plants. Imagine the people slowly walking by. Can you picture this?
Mariam:	Yes.
Therapist:	Imagine running after the ball that your mother threw. Now, imagine that you are looking at the shrubs. Imagine how you are separating the shrubs in search of the ball. Can you imagine yourself doing this?
Mariam:	Yes.
Therapist:	Now I want you to keep on imagining that you are leafing through the shrubs. Imagine the texture of the shrubs against your hands. Imagine the color of the underside of the leaves. Can you imagine this?
Mariam:	Yes.
Therapist:	According to the scale that we discussed, how much does this bother you?
Mariam:	Seven.
Therapist:	Very good. Keep on picturing this. (Ten second pause). Now imagine that you can hear loud noises that sound like thunder in the distance as you are looking for the ball. Can you imagine these noises?
Mariam:	Yes.
Therapist:	Good. Now I want you to imagine that you are still looking for the ball in the shrubs. (Ten second pause). Suddenly, you hear a very loud explosion nearby. Imagine that you are looking up. People are running away. Imagine how everyone is running. Can you do this?
Mariam:	Yes.
Therapist:	How much does it bother you?
Mariam:	Ten.
Therapist:	Keep on imagining how people are running away. Imagine that you are turning away from the shrub. You want to find your mother. Imagine looking at the place where your mother had been. She is not there. Imagine that you suddenly hear a very loud explosion. Imagine that you are starting to run to the place where your mother had been. Can you picture this?
Mariam:	Yes. It's very bad.
Therapist :	How disturbing is it?
Mariam:	Ten.

This table represents the transcript of a flooding session involving a 10-year-old Lebanese girl who developed PTSD after being exposed to an artillery barrage (Saigh, 1987b). Stimulus and response imagery cues (Levis, 1980) were used during the imaginal flooding process. Stimulus cues involved the visual, auditory, olfactory, and tactile components of each scene. Response cues involved the behavioral and cognitive aspects of the scene.

spontaneous trauma-related thoughts, the frequency of these thoughts appreciably decreased during the course of the treatment and at follow-up.

Pre- to posttreatment improvements were observed on the WISC-R Digit Span and Coding subtests in all of the Saigh single-case treatment studies. Major reductions in the levels of self-reported reactivity to the traumatic scenes were evident on the SUDs ratings as monitored before therapy, during therapy, at posttreatment, and follow-up assessments. Appreciable reductions in distress were also observed on the Revised Children's Manifest Anxiety Scale (RCMAS, Reynolds & Richmond, 1978), Children's Depression Inventory (CDI; Kovacs, 1992), and the Conners Teacher Rating Scale (CTRS; Conners, 1995). Four of the Lebanese child-adolescent reports (Saigh, 1987a, 1987b, 1987c, 1989b) included performance measures. Appreciably less avoidance was evident as measured by BATs at posttreatment and 6-month follow-up assessments. Finally, anecdotal observations strongly supported the social validity (Wolf, 1978) of the intervention as the participants reported that the outcomes justified the temporary discomfort that they experienced.

Cocco and Sharpe (1993) employed an auditory variation of eye movement desensitization and reprocessing (EMDR; Shapiro, 1989) in the treatment of a 4-year-old Australian male assault victim. Generally, EMDR therapists ask patients to imagine trauma-related stimuli while visually tracking their finger movements and articulating negative and positive statements (Shapiro, 1989, 1995). As based on parent and child reports, the youth met criteria for PTSD. Cocco and Sharpe reported that the boy had been experiencing nightmares, sleeping in his parents' bed, wetting the bed, asking for reassurance, and carrying a toy gun since the assault. They also reported that these problems had been occurring for 1 year.

Cocco and Sharpe (1993) reported that the boy was not able to imagine the traumatic event and track the therapist's finger movements at the same time. In lieu of the conventional EMDR regimen that involves the visual tracking of an object during exposure (Shapiro, 1995; Wilson, Becker, & Tinker, 1995), they asked the child to draw a picture of the assailants and a picture of a super hero. The youth was instructed to look at the picture of the assailants and think about the traumatic event as the therapist clicked his fingers at a rate of 4 clicks per second for 12 seconds. The boy was subsequently instructed to look at the picture of the super hero and verbalize what the hero was going to do to the assailants. The boy was also asked to look at both pictures and imagine how the hero was attacking the assailant as a therapist clicked his fingers. The therapist employed the auditory clicking procedure as the youth was engaged in this process. Cocco and Sharpe reported that after 14 clicks, the boy independently began to stab the picture of the assailants with a pen and spontaneously declared "They're dead . . . they're dead" (p. 375). Cocco and Sharpe also reported that 48 clicks were presented as the youth stabbed the picture and verbalized.

The authors reported that the boy did not experience nightmares, seek reassurance, wet his bed, sleep with his parents, or carry the toy gun after treatment. Treatment gains relative to nightmares, reassurance, and the carrying of the toy gun were reported at 3- and 6-month follow-ups. 3- and 6-month follow-up data also indicated that the frequency of bed wetting and sleeping in the parents' bed reverted to premorbid levels.

Comment

Examined in toto, the Lebanese multiple-baseline trials evidenced rapid improvements across a host of standardized and nonstandardized measures after 8 to 15 treatment sessions. In all instances, multiple SUDs ratings were recorded before, during, and after treatment. Data regarding level, trend, and variability clearly revealed that the SUDs ratings were stable before and after treatment. The data were also marked by very apparent decelerating trends during the intervention phases. These findings should also be viewed with the realization that the prevalence of PTSD frequently independently remits within a year after traumatization (Saigh, 1988; Saigh, Green, & Korol, 1996; Saigh, Yasik, Sack, & Koplewicz, 1999) and that the Lebanese youth had been symptomatic for a year or more. As such, the rapid and sustained improvements suggest that historical factors did not influence the results. While the Lebanese studies clearly denoted efficacy across a number of participants and measures, information pertaining to treatment integrity (i.e., evidence that treatment was implemented as specified in the reports) was not reported. As such, the possibility that procedural variance may have contributed to the results should be considered. The aggregate Lebanese trials must also be viewed with the understanding that single-case multiple-baseline elements have less predictive power relative to true experimental designs. Given the limited number of participants in the Lebanese trials, one should not assume that similar results would be observed among treated youth with divergent personal characteristics (IQ, language comprehension skills, and the ability to sustain in vitro traumatic images).

The modified EMDR Australian study also reported treatment gains over time. Although PTSD had been evident for more than a year, rapid gains were reported following a single treatment session. Given the relative chronicity of the case, the rapid improvements suggest that historical factors did not contribute to the observed effects. Despite these impressive findings, information regarding treatment integrity was not reported. Moreover, the Cocco and Sharpe report did not include information about level, trend, or degree of symptom variability before, during, and after treatment. In view of this, and the absence of standardized test scores, the internal validity of the findings is limited.

CHILD-ADOLESCENT TIME SERIES GROUP STUDIES

Deblinger, McLeer, and Henry (1990) used clinical interviews and the Schedule for Affective Disorders and Schizophrenia for School Age Children Epidemiological Version (K-SADS-E; Puig-Antich, Orvaschel, Tabrinzi, & Chambers, 1980) to identify 19 female child abuse victims with PTSD. The sample ranged in age from 3 to 16 years. A multifaceted child intervention program was implemented. More specifically, the program involved the modeling of coping behaviors, gradual exposure to abuse-related information, and sexual abuse education. Participants were asked to select the type of exposure procedure therapy that they wanted to receive (e.g., confronting abuse-related issues through a choice of imagery, doll play, drawing, reading, or singing). Child participants received 10 treatment sessions (duration was not specified). Non-offending parents received information regarding child abuse education, training in child-parent communication, and the use of behavior management. Deblinger et al. reported that the participants evidenced significantly fewer trauma-related reexperiencing, avoidance, and arousal symptoms after they completed the treatment. Significant reductions over baseline assessments were reported on the CDI, the STAI, and the Internalizing and Externalizing indices of the *Child Behavior Checklist* (CBCL; Achenbach, 1991).

March, Amaya-Jackson, Murray, and Schulte (1998) administered the Clinician Administered PTSD Scale-Child and Adolescent Version (CAPS-CA; Nader, Blake, Kriegler, & Pynoos, 1994) to 1,800 children at two elementary schools and two junior high schools. Seventeen students (age range 10 to 15 years) were identified as potential candidates for treatment. Ten of the 17 experienced two or more traumatic incidents and none had a positive history for abuse. Examples of the stressors that were reported included motor vehicle accidents, accidental injury, gunshot wounds, and fire-related injuries. Inclusion criteria consisted of a PTSD diagnosis as denoted by the CAPS-CA and "motivation to work on PTSD as an identified problem, general cognitive abilities, and social problem-solving skills" (p. 586). Participants received 18 multifaceted treatment sessions. Sessions were approximately 50 minutes. The treatment consisted of: goal setting, an explanation of how the treatment was going to be applied in group settings, anxiety management training, guided muscle relaxation, generation of distress ratings through the use of a fear thermometer, anger management training, positive self-talk, construction of trauma-specific fear hierarchies, corrective information regarding trauma-specific attributions, and imaginal exposure to traumatic material.

March et al. (1998) reported that 14 of the 17 participants completed the program. Eight (57%) cases no longer criteria for PTSD as measured by the CAPS-CA immediately after the treatment was completed and 12 (86%) did not evidence PTSD at a 6-month follow-up. Significant reductions relative to the number of reported PTSD symptoms were evident on the Child and Adolescent Trauma Survey (CATS; March & Amaya-Jackson, 1998) after treatment and at a 6-month follow-up. Significantly lower posttreatment and follow-up scores were also reported on the Clinical Global Improvement Scale (CGIS; Guy, 1976), Multidimensional Anxiety Scale for Children (March, Parker, Sullivan, Stallings, & Conners, 1997), State Trait Anger Expression Inventory (STAEI; Spielberger, 1988), CDI, and CTRS.

Comment

Clearly, the reported outcomes of the group time series results are encouraging as efficacy was evident across a number of standardized tests with well-documented psychometric qualities. Nevertheless, several concerns are apparent. The Deblinger et al. (1990) and March et al. (1998) investigations did not provide information regarding the interval between traumatization and clinical evaluation. As control groups were not used and as the prevalence of PTSD decreases over time, the contribution of spontaneous remission cannot be excluded. Moreover, the Deblinger and March studies did not control for treatment integrity. In view of this and as the interventions were multifaceted, the possibility that the independent variable may not have been presented as described in the article has to be considered. Additional concern is noted as the Deblinger et al.

(1990) participants did not receive the same intervention within treatment groups (participants selected the modality of exposure therapy that they received). This form of unsystematic variance greatly limits conclusions regarding treatment efficacy. Finally, group time series elements do not provide the same degree of external validity as true experimental designs (Hayes, Barlow, & Nelson, 1999). Despite these reservations, the two group time series elements clearly denoted efficacy across a number of standardized measures and participants.

CHILD-ADOLESCENT EXPERIMENTAL STUDIES

Two studies have employed experimental designs to examine the effects of cognitive-behavioral packages with abused youth. Deblinger, Lippmann, and Steer (1996) randomly assigned 100 sexually abused children between the ages of 7 to 13 years to one of four treatment groups: (a) standard community care, (b) child intervention, (c) non-offending parent intervention, and (d) a combined child and parent intervention. The authors reported that 71% of the sample met *DSM–III–R* criteria for PTSD (APA, 1987) as measured by the K-SADS-E, and 29% evidenced a minimum of three PTSD symptoms. It was further reported that 66% of the participants were sexually abused 6 months prior to the initiation of the study.

Parents who were assigned to the standard community care group were informed about the expression of PTSD and encouraged to put their children in treatment. Children in the child intervention group received training involving (a) relaxation procedures, (b) emotional expression skills, (c) cognitive coping skills, and (d) abuse education. In addition, participants in the child intervention condition received their choice abuse-related exposure exercises (a) doll play, discussion, (b) reading, or singing. In the parent regimen, therapists "accepted and validated mothers' experiences and corrected common misconceptions that might have given rise to their heightened negative emotional reactions" (Deblinger et al., 1996, p. 315). Parents also received training involving how to discuss issues related to sexual abuse and sex-related issues with their children. In addition, parents were trained in the use of behavior management skills. Participants in the combined child-parent intervention group received the child and parent interventions as described above.

Following treatment, Deblinger et al. (1996) reported that the *combined* child only and parent and child groups exhibited significantly fewer

PTSD symptoms relative to the *combined* community and parent only groups. The authors also reported that mothers in the parent training group and the mothers in the combined child-parent group reported a significantly greater use of parenting skills as measured by the Parent Practices Questionnaire (PPQ; Strayhorn & Weidman, 1988) relative to the combined child only and standard community care groups. The authors further represented that mothers in the child-parent and parent groups rated their offspring as having significantly lower CBCL externalizing ratings relative to the ratings of the combined child and community groups. Likewise, participants in the combined child-parent and the parent only groups reported significantly lower depression scores on the CDI as compared with the combined child only and standard community care groups. It was also reported that the groups did not significantly differ between the CBCL internalizing ratings and STAI scores.

More recently, King et al. (2000) identified 36 sexually abused youth with PTSD or "subclinical PTSD" (i.e., at least three PTSD symptoms) as measured by Silverman and Albano's (1986) Anxiety Interview Schedule for the *DSM–IV* (ADIS). The selected sample consisted of 25 males and 11 females. Their mean age was 11.4 years with a range of 5.2 to 17.4 years. King et al. randomly assigned participants to one of three groups. One group received 20 weekly 50-minute sessions of individual child cognitive-behavior therapy (child CBT). Participants received training involving goal setting, child abuse, PTSD, and the cognitive behavior therapy process. Child CBT participants also received training in cue-directed relaxation, recognition of stress-inducing cognitions, assertion training, graded exposure via in vitro exercises, self-created drawings, and role play exercises. A second group received 20 sessions of family cognitive-behavioral therapy (Family CBT). In this context, separate sessions were conducted with children and non-offending mothers. In addition to receiving the same training that the child CBT group received over 20 weeks, the mothers of the participants received 20 weekly sessions of training in child behavior management and communication skills. A third group was assigned to a 24-week waitlist control condition.

Three youths dropped out of treatment from the child CBT group and three dropped out of the family CBT group. Two children dropped out of the WLC group. As such, the final sample consisted of 9 child CBT completers, 9 family CBT completers, and 10 WLC completers. All of the participants made ratings on author-devised abuse-related fear thermometers and coping questionnaires. They also completed the more standardized RCMAS and CDI. The mothers independently marked the CBCL.

The treating therapists evaluated the participants according to the Global Assessment of Functioning scale (GAF; APA, 1987). Assessments were conducted at pretreatment, posttreatment, and at a 12-week follow-up.

King and his colleagues (2000) reported that the child and family CBT groups did not significantly differ on any of the self-report measures (including ADIS PTSD symptom number), parental CBCL Internalizing and Externalizing scores and CBCL items that correspond to PTSD symptoms, and therapist GAF ratings at posttreatment and follow-up. The authors reported that the combined treatment groups (i.e., child CBT and family CBT) evidenced significantly fewer PTSD symptoms as indicated by the ADIS relative to the WLC group at posttreatment and follow-up. The fear thermometer ratings of the combined treatment groups were significantly lower than the ratings of the WLC group at posttreatment and at follow-up. Likewise, treated youth had lower scores on CBCL items that are suggestive of PTSD at posttreatment and follow-up. King at al. also reported that the therapist-completed GAF ratings of the combined treatment groups were significantly greater (i.e., improved) than the ratings of the WTC group at posttreatment and follow-up.

Although nonsignificant differences were evident when the RCMAS scores of the treatment completers and the WLC group were compared at posttreatment, the treatment groups had lower scores at the 12-month follow-up. Nonsignificant differences were reported when the parental CBCL Internalizing and Externalizing ratings were compared at posttreatment and follow-up. Between-group comparisons involving an author-devised coping questionnaire and the CDI were not reported.

Comment

The Deblinger and King studies clearly reflected efficacy across a number of outcome variables. To their credit, the authors employed structured clinical interviews, randomly assigned participants to groups, and used a wide-range of norm-referenced child and parent scales to assess efficacy. The authors also deserve recognition for having advanced the field beyond *in vitro* exposure. Certainly, the inclusion of coping strategies and the involvement of parents are theoretically appropriate treatment components given the symptoms and scope of the disorder. Despite these efforts, methodological concerns are apparent. Although Deblinger et al. (1996) used a treatment manual, quantifiable estimates of treatment integrity were not reported. Given that a number of treatment components were presented, the omission of information on treatment integrity presents a serious threat to the internal validity of the study. Moreover, data from different treatment groups were combined and information regarding the efficacy of specific treatments (e.g., child only vs. combined child-parent) was not reported. Pooling data from groups that received different treatments raises a number of unanswerable questions. Did the child CBT package account for the reported differences or was the child and parent package responsible for the observed variations? The interpretation of the Deblinger et al. findings is further confounded by the unsystematic way that the treatments were applied within groups (i.e., participants received their choice of different interventions). It is also of concern to note that follow-up assessments were not performed and that the long-term efficacy of the Deblinger investigation is unknown. Certainly, the possibility of spontaneous remission cannot be ruled out because 66% of the participants were abused 6 months or less before the study was initiated and as it is not known if the time between traumatization and intervention was comparable across treatment groups. Finally, the external validity of the study is limited because 29% of the participants did not have PTSD before the treatment was applied.

While the King et al. (2000) child group received the 20 weekly sessions of child CBT, the family CBT received the child component and an extra 20 sessions of parent training. Despite this difference, the efficacy of the *independent treatment conditions* relative to the control group was not addressed. As in the case of the Deblinger report, one may ask: Was the child CBT package responsible for the differences or did the combined child and family CBT package account for the variations? It is also of concern to note that the King investigation did provide information regarding the interval between traumatization and intervention. If there were significant variations between groups in this regard, spontaneous remission may have affected the outcome. Concern is also noted with respect to the size of the sample that was treated. The external validity of the study relative to youth with PTSD should also be viewed with the realization that 31.4% of the treated cases did not meet full criteria for PTSD at pre-treatment.

SUMMARY AND FUTURE DIRECTIONS

The child-adolescent single-case, group time series and experimental trials suggest that the cognitive-behavioral regimens effectively reduced PTSD symptoms and a number of the associated features of the disorder. On the other hand, additional research must be conducted before a more definitive conclusion can be reached.

Research designed to identify child-adolescent PTSD patient, therapist, treatment, and family factors that are associated with successful outcomes is clearly in order. At this time there is a pressing need to look beyond treatment efficacy and consider process-related dependent variables. There is a need to determine what treatments work and why they work. Accordingly, researchers may wish to develop and administer measures that are sensitive to the expression of trauma-specific cognitive processing before, during, and after intervention. Information involving child-adolescent factors that may be associated with treatment efficacy (e.g., age, the quality of visual imagery, ability to follow instruction, threshold for fatigue, and verbal comprehension) is necessary. The influence of moderator variables such as the quality of therapeutic relations and the qualitative aspects of parental support also warrant examination.

Given that all of the child-adolescent PTSD interventions employed multifaceted treatment packages, there is a clear need to conduct dismantling studies. Such studies may serve to identify salient or inert treatment components. Given the complexity of the child-adolescent PTSD treatment studies, researchers need to implement mechanisms to document treatment integrity. Investigators also need to realize that recently diagnosed PTSD frequently remits. Accordingly, the efficacy of nonexperimental studies that treat recently diagnosed children and adolescents with PTSD will be open to question. In a similar vein, experimental investigations need to incorporate methods to control for historical factors such as including the interval between traumatization and intervention as a covariate. Certainly, it is important to conduct studies with samples that are large enough to denote significant changes.

Finally, the inclusion of traumatized youth who do not have PTSD in treatment samples is not recommended, as research suggests that the traumatized children without PTSD did not significantly differ from nonclinical controls on a variety of anxiety, depression, cognitive, and misconduct measures (Saigh, 2002; Saigh, Yasik, Oberfield, & Halamandaris, 2002).

Although a few of the single-case studies employed selected subtests of the WISC-R as treatment outcome measures (Saigh, 1987a, 1987b, 1987c, 1989b), cognitive indices of treatment efficacy were not employed by subsequent investigators. Recently, Saigh, Yasik, and Oberfield (2003) determined that the WISC-III scores of youth with PTSD were significantly lower than the scores of traumatized non-PTSD youth and non-traumatized controls. Saigh et al. (2003) also reported that the significant group differences were limited to discrete indices of verbal intelligence.

In view of this information, investigators may wish to consider the use of cognitive indices that measure verbal resources. We recommend the Working Memory Index of the Wechsler Memory Scale III (Wechsler, 1996) because this measure is associated with reading performance and a number of academically important outcomes (Daneman, 2003). Given the association between long-term memory and academic achievement (Peverly, Brobst, Graham, & Shaw, 2003), researchers may also wish to consider The Wide Range Assessment of Memory and Learning Delayed Recall test (Sheslow & Adams, 1990) as an index of treatment efficacy over time.

REFERENCES

Achenbach, T. M. (1991). *Manual for the child behavior checklist and revised child behavior profile.* Burlington, VT: University of Vermont, Department of Psychiatry.

American Psychiatric Association. (1980). *Diagnostic and statistical manual of mental disorders* (3rd ed.). Washington, DC: Author.

American Psychiatric Association. (1987). *Diagnostic and statistical manual of mental disorders* (3rd ed. revised). Washington, DC: Author.

Beck, A. T., Ward, C. H., Mandelson, M., Mock, J., & Erbaugh, J. (1961). An inventory for measuring depression. *Archives of General Psychiatry, 4,* 561–571.

Black, J.L., & Keane, T.M. (1982). Implosive therapy in the treatment of combat related fears in a World War II veteran. *Journal of Behavior Therapy and Experimental Psychiatry, 13,* 163–165.

Boudewyns, P. A., & Hyer, L. A. (1990). Physiological responses to combat memories and preliminary treatment outcome in Vietnam veteran PTSD patients with direct therapeutic exposure. *Behavior Therapy, 21,* 63–87.

Boudewyns, P. A., & Shipley, R. H. (1983). *Flooding and implosive therapy.* New York: Plenum Press.

Cocco, N., & Sharpe, L. (1993). An auditory variant of eye–movement desensitization in a case of childhood posttraumatic stress disorder. *Journal of Behaviour Therapy and Experimental Psychiatry, 24,* 373–377.

Conners, C. (1995). *Conners Rating Scales.* Toronto, Ontario: Multi–Health.

Cooper, N. A., & Clum, G. A. (1989). Imaginal flooding as a supplementary treatment for PTSD in combat veterans: A controlled evaluation. *Behavior Therapy, 20,* 381–391.

Daneman, M. (2003). Learning disabled individuals show deficits on working memory tasks. The question is why? *Issues in Education: Contributions from Educational Psychology, 7,* 79–85.

Deblinger, E., Lippmann, J., & Steer, R. (1996). Sexually abused children suffering posttraumatic stress symptoms: Initial treatment outcome findings. *Child Maltreatment, 1,* 310–321.

Deblinger, E., McLeer, S. V., & Henry, D. (1990). Cognitive behavioral treatment for sexually abused children suffering from posttraumatic stress: Preliminary findings. *Journal of the American Academy of Child and Adolescent Psychiatry, 29,* 747–752.

Fairbank, J. A., DeGood, D. D., & Jenkins, C. W. (1981). Behavioral treatment of a persistent posttraumatic startle response. *Journal of Behavior Therapy and Experimental Psychiatry, 12,* 321–324.

Fairbank, J. A., Gross, R. T., & Keane, T. M. (1983). Treatment of posttraumatic stress disorder: Evaluating outcome with a behavioral code. *Behavior Modification, 7,* 557–568.

Fairbank, J. A., & Keane, T. M. (1982). Flooding for combat–related stress disorders: Assessment of anxiety reduction across traumatic memories. *Behavior Therapy, 13,* 499–510.

Foa, E. B., Rothbaum, B. O., Riggs, M. J., & Murdock, T. (1991). Treatment of posttraumatic stress disorder in rape victims: A comparison between cognitive–behavioral procedures and counseling. *Journal of Consulting and Clinical Psychology, 59,* 715–723.

Guy, W. (1976). *ECDEU Assessment manual for psychopharmacology.* (DHEW Publication ABM 76–388). Washington, DC: U.S. Government Printing Office.

Hayes, S. C., Barlow, D. H., & Nelson, R. O. (1999). *The scientist practitioner: Research and accountability in the age of managed care.* (2nd ed). Boston: Allyn & Bacon.

Hogan, R. A., & Kirchner, J. H. (1967). Preliminary report on the extinction of learned fears via short term therapy. *Journal of Abnormal Psychology, 72,* 106–109.

Keane, T. M., Fairbank, J. Cadell, J. M., & Zimering, R. T. (1989). Implosive (flooding) therapy reduces symptoms of PTSD in Vietnam combat veterans. *Behavior Therapy, 20,* 245–260.

Keane, T. M., & Kaloupek, D. G. (1982). Imaginal flooding in the treatment of posttraumatic stress disorder. *Journal of Consulting and Clinical Psychology, 50,* 138–140.

King, N. J., Tonge, B. J., Mullen,P., Myerson, N., Heyne, D., Rollings, S., et al. (2000). Treating sexually abused children with posttraumatic stress symptoms: A randomized clinical trial. *Journal of the Academy of Child and Adolescent Psychiatry, 39,* 1347–1355.

Kovacs, M. (1992). *The Children's Depression Inventory.* North Tonowanda, NY: Multi–Health Systems.

Levis, D. J. (1980). Implementing the technique of implosive therapy. In A. Goldstein & E. Foa (Eds.). *Handbook of behavioral interventions: A clinical guide* (pp. 51–92). New York: Wiley.

Levis, D. J., & Carrera, R. N. (1967). Effects of ten hours of implosive therapy in the treatment of outpatients: A preliminary report. *Journal of Abnormal Psychology, 72*, 504–508.

Malleson, N. (1959). Panic and phobia: A possible method of treatment. *Lancet, 1*, 225–227.

March, J. S., & Amaya–Jackson, L. (1998). *Child and Adolescent Trauma Survey.* Duke University Medical Center, Department of Psychiatry.

March, J. S., Amaya–Jackson, L., Murray, M. A., & Schulte, A. (1998). Cognitive–behavioral psychotherapy for children and adolescents with posttraumatic stress disorder after a single incident stressor. *Journal of the American Academy of Child and Adolescent Psychiatry, 37*, 585–593.

March, J. S., Parker, J., Sullivan, K., Stallings, P., & Conners, C. (1997). The Multidimensional Anxiety Scale for Children (MASC): Factor structure, reliability, and validity. *Journal of the American Academy of Child and Adolescent Psychiatry, 36*, 554–565.

Marks, I. (1972). Flooding (implosion) and allied treatments. In S. Agras (Ed.), *Behavior modification: Principles and clinical applications* (pp.151–211). Boston: Little, Brown, & Co.

Marks, I. (1981). *Care and cure of neuroses.* New York: Wiley.

Marks, I., Lovell, K., Noshirvani, L. M., & Thrasher, S. (1998).Treatment of posttraumatic stress disorder by exposure and/or cognitive restructuring: A controlled study. *Archives of General Psychiatry, 55*, 317–325.

Nader, K, Blake, D., Kriegler, J., & Pynoos, R. (1994). *Clinician Administered PTSD Scale for Children (CAPS–C), current and lifetime diagnosis version and instructional manual.* UCLA Neuropsychiatric Institute, Los Angeles, CA and National Center for PTSD, Boston.

Peverely, S. T., Brobst, K., Graham, M., & Shaw, R. (2003). College adults are not good at self–regulation: A study on the relationship of self–regulation, note–taking, and test–taking. *Journal of Educational Psychology, 95*, 335–346.

Pollin, A.T. (1959). The effects of flooding and physical suppression as extinction techniques on an anxiety motivated avoidance locomotor response. *Journal of Psychology, 47*, 235–245.

Puig–Antich, J., Orvaschel, H., Tabrinzi, M.H., & Chambers, W. (1980). *The Schedule for Affective Disorders and Schizophrenia for School Age Children epidemiological version (Kiddie SADS–E).* New York Psychiatric Institute, New York and Yale University School of Medicine, New Haven, CT.

Rachman, S. J. (1966). Studies in desensitization–II: Flooding. *Behaviour Research and Therapy, 4*, 1–6.

Rathus, S. A. (1973). A 30–item schedule for assessing assertive behavior. *Behavior Therapy, 4*, 398–406.

Resick, P.A., & Schnicke, M.K. (1992). Cognitive processing therapy for sexual assault victims. *Journal of Consulting & Clinical Psychology, 60*, 748–756.

Reynolds, C., & Richmond, B. (1978). What I think and feel: A revised measure of children's manifest anxiety. *Journal of Abnormal Child Psychology, 6*, 271–280.

Richards, D. A., Lovell, K., & Marks, I. M. (1994). Posttraumatic stress disorder: Evaluation of a behavioral treatment program. *Journal of Traumatic Stress, 7*, 669–680.

Saigh, P. A. (1987a). In vitro flooding of an adolescent's posttraumatic stress disorder. *Journal of Clinical Child Psychology, 16*, 147–150.

Saigh, P. A. (1987b). In vitro flooding of a childhood posttraumatic stress disorder. *School Psychology Review, 16*, 203–211.

Saigh, P. A. (1987c). In vitro flooding of childhood posttraumatic stress disorder: A systematic replication. *Professional School Psychology, 2*, 133–145.

Saigh, P. A. (1987d). In vitro flooding of a 6–year–old boy's posttraumatic stress disorder. *Behaviour Research and Therapy, 24*, 685–689.

Saigh, P. A. (1988). Anxiety, depression, and assertion across alternating intervals of stress. *Journal of Abnormal Psychology, 97*, 338–342.

Saigh, P. A. (1989a). The development and validation of the Children's Posttraumatic Stress Disorder Inventory. *International Journal of Special Education, 4*, 75–84.

Saigh, P. A. (1989b). The use of *in vitro* flooding in the treatment of traumatized adolescents. *Journal of Behavioral and Developmental Pediatrics, 10*, 17–21.

Saigh, P.A. (2002, January). *Cognitive and psychological correlates of PTSD in children and adolescents.* Invited paper presented at the NIMH Early Trauma Responses and Psychopathology Conference, Bethesda, MD.

Saigh, P. A. (2004). *The Children's PTSD Inventory.* San Antonio, TX: Psychological Corporation.

Saigh, P. A., Green, B., & Korol, M. (1996). The history and prevalence of posttraumatic stress disorder in children and adolescents. *Journal of School Psychology, 34*, 107–132.

Saigh, P. A., Yasik, A. E., & Oberfield, R. (2003). *The WISC–III performance of traumatized youth with or without PTSD.* Manuscript submitted for publication.

Saigh, P. A., Yasik, A. E., Oberfield, R. O., & Halamandaris, P. (2002). A comparative analysis of the internalizing and externalizing behaviors o traumatized urban youth with and without PTSD. *Journal of Abnormal Psychology, 111*, 462–470.

Saigh, P. A., Yasik, A. E., Oberfield, R., & Inamder, S. (1999). Behavioral treatment of traumatized youth. In P. A. Saigh & J. D. Bremner (Eds.), *Posttraumatic stress disorder: A comprehensive text.* (pp. 354–375). Needham Heights, MA: Allyn & Bacon.

Saigh, P. A., Yasik, A., Sack, W., & Koplewicz, H. (1999). Child–adolescent posttraumatic stress disorder: Prevalence, comorbidity, and risk factors. In P.A. Saigh & J. D. Bremner (Eds.) *Posttraumatic stress disorder: A comprehensive text* (pp. 19–43). Needham Heights, MA: Allyn & Bacon.

Shapiro, F. (1989). Efficacy of the eye movement desensitization procedure in the treatment of traumatic memories. *Journal of Traumatic Stress, 2*, 199–223.

Shapiro, F. (1995). *Eye movement desensitization and reprocessing: Basic principles, protocols, and procedures.* New York: Guilford Press.

Sheslow, W., & Adams, D. (1990). *wide range assessment of memory and learning.* Wilmington, DE: Jastak Associates, Inc.

Silverman, W. K., & Albano, A. M. (1997). *The Anxiety Disorders Interview for Children (DSM–IV).* San Antonio, TX: Psychological Corporation.

Spiegler, D. S., & Guevermont, D. C. (1998). *Contemporary behavior therapy.* Pacific Grove, CA: Brooks/ Cole.

Spielberger, C. D. (1988). *State–Trait Anger Expression Inventory professional manual.* Odessa, FL: Psychological Assessment Resources.

Spielberger, C. D., Gorsuch, R. L., & Lushane, R. E. (1968). *Manual for the State Trait Anxiety Inventory.* Palo Alto, CA: Consulting Psychologist Press.

Stampfl, T. G. (1961). *Implosive therapy: A learning theory derived psychodynamic technique.* Unpublished manuscript, John Carroll University, Cleveland, OH.

Stampfl, T. G., & Levis, D. J. (1967). Essentials of implosive therapy: A learning–based psychodynamic behavioral therapy. *Journal of Abnormal Psychology, 72,* 496–503.

Strayhorn, J. M., & Weidman, C. S. (1988). A parent practices scale and its relation to parent and child mental health. *Journal of the American Academy of Child and Adolescent Psychiatry, 27,* 613–618.

Thompson, J. A., Charlton, P. F., Kerry, R., Lee, D., & Turner, S. W. (1995). An open trial of exposure therapy based on deconditioning for posttraumatic-stress disorder. *British Journal of Clinical Psychology, 34,* 407–416.

Wechsler, D. (1996). *The Wechsler Memory Scale—Third edition.* San Antonio, TX: Psychological Corporation.

Wilson, S. A., Becker, L. A., & Tinker, R. H. (1995). Eye movement desensitization and reprocessing (EMDR) treatment for psychologically traumatized individuals. *Journal of Consulting and Clinical Psychology, 63,* 928–937.

Wolf, M. M. (1978). Social validity: The case of subjective measurement or how applied behavior analysis is finding its heart. *Journal of Applied Behavior Analysis, 11,* 315–329.

Yule, W., Sacks, B., & Hersov, L. (1974). Successful treatment of a noise phobia in an 11 year old. *Journal of Behavior Therapy and Experimental Psychiatry, 5,* 209–211.

PART **IV**

PERSPECTIVES ON FUTURE DIRECTIONS

Chapter 14

A GLASS HALF EMPTY OR HALF FULL? WHERE WE ARE AND DIRECTIONS FOR FUTURE RESEARCH IN THE TREATMENT OF PTSD

Shawn P. Cahill and Edna B. Foa

INTRODUCTION

In 1992, Solomon, Gerrity, and Muff conducted a comprehensive survey of the published treatment outcome literature on posttraumatic stress disorder (PTSD) and found 11 randomized controlled studies investigating the efficacy of medication (5 studies) or psychotherapy (6 studies). They concluded there was "a modest but clinically meaningful effect" for medication (p. 633) and that "[s]tronger effects were found for behavioral techniques involving direct therapeutic exposure," (p. 633) although they expressed concern about safety of exposure therapy, citing a case series by Pitman et al. (1991). Moreover, they called for more research before pronouncing any treatment as an effective, lasting treatment for PTSD. To that end, Solomon et al. made the following suggestions for future directions in research. (a) Comparisons between individual and combined treatments in order to "understand which components, in which combinations, result in treatment gains", (p. 637) and to specifically test the hypothesis that "flooding may prove to be most effective when combined with cognitive forms of therapy, designed to address irrational cognitions and provide the patient with coping skills" (p. 637). (b) Determination of the optimal conditions for each treatment approach, including such variables as duration and timing of treatment (e.g., whether to intervene during the acute period or delay treatment until it is clear the person is not likely to experience natural recovery). (c) Determination of whether comorbid diagnoses moderate the outcome of treatment for PTSD. (d) Comparison of response to treatment for PTSD across a range of traumatic events. More recent reviews (e.g., Foa & Meadows, 1997; Foa, Rothbaum, & Furr, 2003; Frueh et al., 1995; Harvey, Turner, & Beidel. 2003; Paunovic, Bryant, & Tarrier, 1997) have documented the significant progress and growth in our knowledge about the nature, treatment, and prevention of PTSD that has been made since the Solomon et al. review.

While acknowledging the progress that has occurred in the past 11 years, the primary goal of this chapter is to provide a self-critical review of the literature to identify the limits in our current knowledge and offer updated recommendations for future research. To this end, we first provide a summary of what is currently known about treatments for chronic PTSD and for the treatment of acute stress reactions/prevention of chronic PTSD. Second, and the main focus of this chapter, we discuss three limitations to our ability to provide effective treatments (a) lack of access to empirically supported treatments, (b) treatment dropouts, and (c) nonresponders and partial responders to current treatments. For each of these limitations, we have reviewed the available research and then offered suggestions for future research. We close the chapter with a general summary and discussion of the issues presented therein.

THE GLASS HALF FULL

Treatment of Chronic PTSD

Cognitive-behavior therapy. We have learned a lot over the past 11 years about the treatment of chronic PTSD, filling in many of the gaps identified in the Solomon et al. (1992) review. For example, several forms of cognitive-behavior therapy (CBT) are now known to be effective in reducing the symptoms of chronic PTSD and associated anxiety and depression compared with waitlist or minimal treatment control conditions (e.g., supportive counseling, relaxation). Cognitive-behavioral treatments that have been found effective include exposure therapy (e.g., Foa, Dancu, et al., 1999; Foa, Hembree, Feeny, & Zoellner, 2002; Bryant, Moulds, Guthrie, Dang, & Nixon, 2003; Foa, Rothbaum, Riggs, & Murdock., 1991; Marks, Lovella, Nashrivani, Livanou, & Thrasher, 1998; Resick,

Nishith, Weaver, Astin, & Feurer, 2002; Taylor et al., 2003), stress inoculation training (Foa, Dancu, et al., 1999; Foa et al.,1991), variations of
cognitive therapy (Ehlers et al., in press; Foa, Hembree, et al., 2002;
Marks et al., 1998; Resick et al., 2002; Tarrier, Pilgrim, et al., 1999), and
EMDR (e.g., Rothbaum, 2002; Power et al., 2002; Taylor et al., 2003). In
addition, a number of researchers have developed and found efficacious
treatments that combine exposure therapy with elements of other treatments, such as cognitive therapy, anxiety management training, and dialectical behavior therapy (e.g., Blanchard et al., 2003; Bryant, Moulds,
Guthrie, Dang, et al., 2003; Cloitre, Koenen, Cohen, & Han, 2002; Echeburua, Corral, Zubizaretta, & Sarasua, 1997; Foa, Dancu, et al., 1999;
Foa, Hembree, et al., 2002; Kubany et al., 2003; Marks et al., 1998; Power
et al., 2002). The efficacy of several of these treatment programs is illustrated in Table 14.1, which presents the prevalence of PTSD after treatment (all participants were required to meet full criteria for PTSD prior to

Table 14.1 Responders to CBT in the Treatment of PTSD

Study	Treatment	% Without PTSD	% Achieved good end-state functioning	Definition of good end-state functioning
Bryant et al. (2003)	IE	67%	20%	CAPS < 19 and BDI < 10
	IE/CR	87%	60%	
	SC	40%	0%	
Cloitre et al. (2002)	STAIR/IE	77%	46%	MPSS-SR < 20, STAI-S
	MA	25%	4%	< 40, and BDI score < 10
Foa, Dancu, et al. (1999)	PE	65%	57%	PSS-I < 20, STAI-S < 40,
	SIT	58%	42%	and BDI score < 10
	PE/SIT	54%	36%	
	WL	0%	0%	
Marks et al. (1998)	PE	75%	53%	Minimum 50% reduction
	CR	65%	32%	on PSS-SR, STAI-S < 35,
	PE/CR	63%	32%	and BDI < 7
	RLX	55%	15%	
Resick et al. (2002)	PE	82%	58%	PSS-SR < 20 and BDI < 10
	CPT	80%	76%	
	MA	2%	0%	

Note. IE = imaginal exposure, PE = prolonged exposure, SIT = stress inoculation
training, CR = cognitive restructuring, CPT = cognitive processing therapy, STAIR =
skills training in affect and interpersonal regulation, RLX = relaxation, MA = minimal attention, WL = waitlist. MPSS-SR = Modified PTSD Symptom Scale—Self-report; STAI-S = State-Trait Anxiety Inventory—State portion; BDI = Beck Depression
Inventory; PSS-I = PTSD Symptom Scale—Interview; PSS-SR = PTSD Symptom Scale—
Self-report.

beginning treatment) and the proportion of participants achieving good end-state functioning status at the end of treatment. As can be seen, treatment with CBT was associated with a reduction of PTSD incidence by 54 to 82%, compared with 0 to 25% for those receiving minimal or no treatment (i.e., waitlist), and 40 to 55% for those receiving treatment with supportive counseling or relaxation. Similarly, good end-state functioning status was achieved by 20 to 76% of participants receiving CBT, compared with 0 to 4% of participants receiving minimal or no treatment and 0 to 15% for those receiving supportive counseling or relaxation. Several studies have included follow-up assessments, ranging between 3 months to 2 years, showing that treatment gains are generally retained (e.g., Blanchard et al., 2003; Blanchard et al., in press; Cloitre et al., 2002; Ehlers et al., in press; Foa et al., 1991; Foa, Dancu, et al., 1999; Resick et al., 2002; Taylor et al., 2003; Tarrier, Sommerfield, Pilgrim & Humphreys, 1999).

CBT for PTSD has been found effective in randomized controlled trials across a variety of trauma populations. Samples studied include female victims of rape (Echeburua, et al., 1997; Foa et al., 1991; Foa, Hembree, et al., 2002; Foa, Dancu, et al., 1999; Resick et al., 2002; Rothbaum, 2002), physical assault (Foa, Dancu, et al., 1999; Foa, Hembree, et al., 2002), domestic violence (Kubany et al., 2003), and physical (Cloitre et al., 2002) and sexual abuse in childhood (Cloitre et al., 2002; Echeburua et al., 1997; Foa Hembree, et al., 2002); male combat veterans (Cooper & Clum, 1989; Glynn et al., 1999; Keane, Fairbank, Caddell, & Zimmering, 1989); male and female survivors of motor vehicle accidents (Blanchard et al., 2003; Fecteau & Nicki, 1999), refugees (Otto et al., in press; Paunovik & Ost, 2001), and mixed trauma samples (Bryant, Moulds, Guthrie, Dang, & Nixon, 2003; Marks et al., 1998; Power et al., 2002; Tarrier, Pilgrim, et al., 1999; Taylor et al., 2003) comprised primarily of physical and sexual assault victims and survivors of motor vehicle accidents.

Three additional samples of interest have been studied in open trials of CBT with promising results. These samples are men and women seeking treatment for comorbid PTSD and cocaine-dependence (Back, Dansk, Carrol, Foa, & Brady, 2001; Brady, Dansk, Back, Foa, & Carrol, 2001), an act of mass terrorism (Gillespie, Duffy, Hackman, & Clark, 2002) and "traumatic grief" (Shear et al., 2001). In the study of comorbid PTSD and cocaine dependence, the treatment (Back et al., 2001) consisted of sequentially combining cognitive-behavioral coping skills for substance abuse (adopted from the CBT protocol for alcohol dependence in Project Match,

1997) and the Foa, Dancu, et al. (1999) PE protocol for PTSD. Preliminary results from this study (Brady et al., 2001) indicated there was a
high dropout rate (24 of 39 entrants dropped after less than 10 sessions
of a 16-session protocol), although the majority of dropouts (75%) occurred prior to the initiation of PE. Among those who completed at least
10 sessions (at least 3 of which included imaginal exposure), there were
significant reductions in PTSD severity, depression, and cocaine use at
posttreatment that were maintained at the 6-month follow-up. Shear et al.
(2001) tested a 16-session treatment that combined elements of interpersonal therapy for depression (Klerman, Weissman, Rounaville, & Chevron, 1984) with the Foa et al. PE protocol for the treatment of traumatic
grief. Participants reported significant reductions on measures of grief,
depression, and general anxiety. Gillespie et al. (2002) administered a
multicomponent intervention-based on the Ehlers and Clark (2000) model
of PTSD to survivors of the 1998 car bombing in Omagh, Northern Ireland, and achieved posttreatment outcomes similar to those obtained in a
randomized controlled trial of the same treatment completed by Ehlers,
Clark and colleagues (in press).

Thus, the efficacy of CBT has been demonstrated across a wide range
of trauma populations. However, few studies have directly compared treatment response across trauma types within the same study. In one of the
two exceptions to the preceding generalization, Echeburua et al. (1997)
randomly assigned 20 women to treatment with either the combination
of exposure plus cognitive therapy or relaxation. Nine of the women
identified childhood sexual abuse as the index trauma and 11 identified
rape in adulthood as the index trauma. Collapsing across trauma type,
Echeburua et al. found exposure plus cognitive therapy to be superior to
relaxation. Collapsing across type of treatment, Echeburua et al. found
similar response to treatment for both trauma groups.

CBT for PTSD has been shown to not only reduce the severity of
PTSD, but also been other negative emotional states associated with PTSD.
Quite consistently, treatments that reduce PTSD symptoms also result in
reductions in both general anxiety and depression. Beyond anxiety and
depression, studies have found treatment for PTSD to decrease measures
of anger (e.g., Cahill, Rauch, Hembree, & Foa, 2003), trauma-related
guilt (Kubany et al., 2003; Resick et al., 2002), and shame (Kubany et al.,
2003), increase self-esteem (Kubany et al., 2003), and alter trauma-related cognitions (Foa & Rauch, in press; Paunovic & Ost, 2001). Cloitre et
al. (2003) implemented a treatment that sequentially combined skills
training in affective and interpersonal regulation with imaginal exposure

in the treatment of PTSD resulting from assaults occurring in childhood. Within group effect sizes for the exposure therapy phase of treatment were as large or larger than the corresponding effect sizes for the skills training phase on measures of dissociation, alexithymia, and depression, measures which showed no improvement in a waitlist control group (Cahill, Zoellner, Feeny, & Riggs, in press).

A few studies have evaluated the relationship between comorbidity and treatment outcome of CBT for PTSD. In a series of analyses investigating predictors associated with outcome of cognitive therapy and imaginal exposure therapy, Tarrier, Pilgrim, et al. (1999) found that comorbid generalized anxiety disorder (GAD) was one of three variables that predicted poorer outcome at the 6-month follow-up assessment. Taken together, the number of missed sessions, living alone, and presence of GAD accounted for 37% of the variability in treatment outcome, with the first two factors together accounting for 32% of the variance. Interestingly, Blanchard et al. (2003) found that CBT directed at PTSD resulted in a significant reduction in the prevalence of co-morbid GAD and major depression compared with either supportive counseling or waitlist, which did not differ from one another. Feeny, Zoellner, and Foa (2002) reanalyzed data from the Foa, Dancu, et al. (1999) study of prolonged exposure (PE), stress inoculation training (SIT), and PE/SIT to investigate whether treatment for PTSD would be affected by the presence of borderline personality disorder characteristics. Results revealed no significant differences among treatment completers for those with and without these characteristics in their response to treatment measures of PTSD severity, depression, state- and trait-anxiety. Falsetti, Resnick, Davis, & Gallagher, (2001) evaluated the efficacy of a treatment, called multi-channel exposure therapy (M-CET) that combined Resick and Schnicke's (1993) cognitive processing therapy with aspects of Barlow and Craske's (1994) panic control treatment for the treatment of women with PTSD and comorbid panic attacks. Compared with a waitlist control condition, treatment with M-CET resulted in a significant decrease in both PTSD severity and panic frequency.

Although the results of individual studies may vary a bit, the general pattern for direct head-to-head comparisons between different forms of CBT is that these different treatments yield similar results (Foa, Dancu, et al., 1999; Foa, Hembree, et al., 2002; Foa et al., 1991; Marks et al., 1998; Power et al., 2002; Resick et al., 2002; Rothbaum, 2002; Tarrier, Pilgrim, et al., 1999). Moreover, studies explicitly testing the effects of combining treatments, such as adding cognitive therapy or stress inoculation training to the combination of imaginal plus in vivo exposure therapy have failed to find evidence for enhanced outcome for the combined treatments (Foa, Dancu, et al., 1999; Foa, Hembree, et al., 2002; Marks et al., 1998; Paunovik & Ost, 2001). Bryant, Moulds, Guthrie, and Nixon (2002) compared the combination of imaginal exposure, in vivo exposure, and cognitive restructuring with imaginal exposure alone, in vivo exposure alone, and supportive counseling and found the combination was superior to the other treatments. Bryant, Moulds, Guthrie, Dang, and Nixon (2003) also found the combination of imaginal exposure plus cognitive restructuring was superior to either imaginal exposure alone or supportive counseling. Because of the lack of a treatment condition that combined both imaginal and in vivo exposure without cognitive therapy in the two studies by Bryant and colleagues, the overall pattern of results across studies suggests that the addition of cognitive therapy can enhance outcome when exposure therapy is limited to imaginal exposure (the two Bryant et al. studies), but does not add to outcome when exposure therapy consists of both imaginal and in vivo exposure (Foa, Hembree, et al., 2002; Marks et al., 1998; Paunovic & Ost, 2001).

Medication. Since 1994, three SSRI medications have been shown to be more effective than placebo in the treatment of PTSD: fluoxetine (Connor, Sutherland, Tupler, Malik, & Davidson, 1999; Martenyi, Brown, Zhang, Prakash, & Koke, 2002; van der Kolk et al., 1994), sertraline (Brady et al., 2000; Davidson, Rothbaum, van der Kolk, Sikes, & Farfel, 2001), and paroxetine (Marshall, Beebe, Oldham, & Zaninell, 2001; Tucker et al., 2001). The latter two medications have received the FDA indication for treatment of PTSD. Table 14.2 presents the percentage of participants in each of these studies judged to be treatment responders for both medication and placebo conditions. As can be seen, treatment with medication was consistently associated with the majority of participants (53–85%) being classified as treatment responders, and significantly more participants receiving medication were judged to be responders than participants who received placebo (32–62%). The samples in all of the above studies included both men and women, although the majority of participants were women, and they recruited participants across a range of traumas, although physical or sexual assault and motor vehicle accidents were the most common types of trauma.

Two studies have investigated the effect of medication discontinuation on relapse by re-randomizing treatment responders to continue on

Table 14.2 Responders to Medication and Placebo in the Treatment of PTSD

Study	Treatment	% Responders	Definition of responder
Brady et al. (2000)	SERT	53%	Minimum 30% reduction in PTSD severity (CAPS total score) and a CGI-I score ≤ 2
	PBO	32%	
Connor et al. (1999)	FLU	85%	CGI-I score ≤ 2
	PBO	62%	
Davidson et al. (2001)	SERT	60%	Minimum 30% reduction in PTSD severity (CAPS total score) and a CGI-I score ≤ 2
	PBO	38%	
Marshall et al. (2001)	PAR-20	62%	CGI-I score ≤ 2
	PAR-40	54%	
	PBO	37%	
Martenyi et al. (2002)	FLU	60%	Minimum 50% reduction in PTSD severity (TOP-8) and a CGI-I score ≤ 2
	PBO	44%	
Tucker et al. (2001)	PAR	59%	CGI-I score ≤ 2
	PBO	38%	

Note. SERT = sertraline, FLU = fluoxetine, PAR = paroxetine and PBO = placebo. CAPS = Clinician Administered PTSD Scale; TOP-8 = Treatment Outcome PTSD Scale; CGI-I = Clinical Global Impression Improvement.

medication or shift to placebo. Davidson, Pearlstein, et al. (2001) investigated the effects of discontinuing sertraline and found that, depending on the criterion used to define a relapse, between 26–52% of participants relapsed when shifted to placebo, compared with between 5 to 16% of participants maintained on medication. Martenyi, Brown, Zhang, Koke, and Prakash (2002) found that only 17% of participants maintained on fluoxetine relapsed compared with 34% of participants shifted to placebo. As with medication treatment for other anxiety disorders and depression, relapse on discontinuation is a frequent occurrence. Although there are no studies directly comparing medication with CBT, comparisons across long-term follow-up studies of CBT and discontinuation studies of medication seem to indicate that relapse on discontinuation of medication is more common than relapse following completion of CBT.

Treatment of Acute Stress Reactions/Prevention of Chronic PTSD

Although not studied as extensively, we have also learned about the nature and efficacy (or lack thereof) of brief psychological treatments administered in the acute aftermath of a traumatic event designed to foster recovery and prevent the development of chronic PTSD. The two psychosocial approaches to preventing posttrauma psychopathology that have received the most research are psychological debriefing and brief CBT packages that contain many of the same elements utilized in the treatment of chronic PTSD. Following the recently published Practice Guidelines from the International Society for Traumatic Stress Studies (Bisson, McFarlane, & Rose, 2000), we use the term psychological debriefing in a general way to refer to very brief (one or a few sessions) interventions that are typically applied shortly after a traumatic event (frequently within 48 to 72 hours, but not necessarily) and which share a number of features. Such common features include discussion of the facts of the traumatic event as well as the trauma survivors' beliefs about what happened; an opportunity to express thoughts, impressions, and emotional reactions; normalization of the trauma survivors' reactions; and planning for coping with the trauma and its sequelae. For a detailed description of Critical Incident Stress Management, one form of psychological debriefing, see Everly, Flannery, Eyler, and Mitchell, (2001).

In the research literature, psychological debriefing has been administered in both group and individual therapy settings. Although the results of randomized controlled trials are somewhat mixed, an important pattern is emerging. In general, participants in studies of psychological debriefing subjectively find the intervention to be helpful (i.e., high consumer satisfaction) and that posttreatment levels of symptoms are lower than they were at pretreatment. However, in comparison to untreated control conditions, there is little evidence that treatment facilitated recovery (e.g., Conlon, Fahy, & Conroy, 1999; Rose, Brewin, Andrews, & Kirk, 1999). Thus, the symptom reduction following psychological debriefing is better attributed to natural recovery, rather than active treatment. In addition, some studies have found a possible iatrogenic effect of psychological debriefing such that treatment may actually interfere with natural recovery, particularly among those with the most severe initial posttrauma reactions (e.g., Mayou et al., 2000).

Brief (4–5 sessions) of CBT utilizing the same anxiety management and exposure therapy techniques developed for the treatment of chronic PTSD implemented starting 2 to 4 weeks posttrauma has been substantially

more effective in reducing acute stress reactions and preventing the development of chronic PTSD. Foa, Hearst-Ikeda, and Perry, (1995) initially
developed and tested a four-session intervention that combined psychoeducation and stress inoculation training with imaginal and in vivo exposure therapy. Participants in this study were female victims of sexual and
nonsexual assault. Bryant and colleagues (1998, 1999; Bryant, Moulds,
Guthrie, & Nixon, 2003) subsequently tested a five-session version of
this same treatment among men and women meeting symptom criteria
for acute stress disorder following motor vehicle accidents, industrial
accidents, and nonsexual assaults. Previously, Harvey and Bryant, Harvey,
Sackville, Dang, and Basten (1998) and Bryant, Sackville, Dangh, Moulds,
and Guthrie (1999) demonstrated that meeting criteria for acute stress
disorder following motor vehicle accidents was predictive of later development of PTSD. The results of all four studies, in terms of the percent
of participants not meeting criteria for PTSD posttreatment and at 6-
month follow-up are summarized in Table 14.3. As can be seen, the vast
majority of participants receiving brief CBT or PE across the four studies
(80–92%) did not meet criteria for PTSD after treatment or at 6-month
follow-up (77–85%). By comparison, only a minority of participants did
not have PTSD in the assessment control and supportive counseling conditions at posttreatment (17–42%) and at follow-up (33–42%). Bryant,
Moulds, and Nixon (in press) provide four-year follow-up data on participants receiving CBT and supportive counseling from the studies by Bry-

Table 14.3 Responders to CBT for Treatment of Acute Stress Disorder/ Prevention of Chronic PTSD

Study	Treatment	% Without PTSD at Posttreatment	% without PTSD at 6-month follow-up
Foa et al. (1995)	CBT	90%	—
	AC	30%	—
Bryant et al. (1998)	CBT	92%	83%
	SC	17%	33%
Bryant et al. (1999)	CBT	80%	77%
	PE	86%	85%
	SC	44%	33%
Bryant et al. (2003)	CBT	92%	83%
	SC	42%	42%

Note: CBT = brief cognitive-behavior therapy PE plus SIT; PE = prolonged exposure
consisting of imaginal plus in vivo exposure; AC = assessment control; SC = supportive counseling.

ant et al. (1998) and Bryant et al. (1999). In an analysis of participants who completed the 4-year follow-up assessment (approximately 50% of participants were lost to long-term follow-up in each condition) 2 of 25 participants receiving CBT (8%) met criteria for PTSD compared with 4 of 16 participants (25%) in the supportive counseling condition. In an intent-to-treat analysis utilizing the last available observation, rates of PTSD were 30% and 33% for CBT and supportive counseling, respectively. Thus, brief CBT similar to treatments used for chronic PTSD can speed recovery from severe acute stress reactions. Given the similarity in rates of PTSD at long-term follow-up for the intent-to-treat sample and the lack of a no-treatment control group, it is not clear whether CBT actually prevented the development of chronic PTSD.

Summary

As the above review illustrates, substantial research has been conducted since 1994 and has addressed many of the points Solomon et al. (1992) identified as directions for future research. Specifically, there is solid evidence now for the basic efficacy of serotonin reuptake inhibitor medications and for various forms of CBT including exposure therapy, stress inoculation training, cognitive therapy, various combinations of the preceding treatments, and eye movement desensitization (EMDR). Studies that have looked at long-term outcome indicate that discontinuation of medication results in a significant increase in the likelihood of relapse. By contrast, response to psychotherapy appears to be maintained.

The benefits of treatment for PTSD with CBT have been demonstrated over a wide range of trauma populations and outcome measures. Direct comparisons between different forms of CBT have not yielded any particular pattern of superiority for one treatment over another, while direct comparisons between medication and psychotherapy have not been conducted. Contrary to the expectations of many, studies that added elements of either stress inoculation training or cognitive therapy to exposure therapy have as yet failed to find superior outcome for the combined treatments. While one study found that the presence of comorbid GAD was associated with poorer outcome on measures of PTSD, another study found that CBT for PTSD resulted in reductions in the incidence of comorbid GAD.

Recent studies of CBT for treating acute stress disorder or preventing chronic PTSD have yielded a remarkably similar pattern. Brief CBT that combines elements of exposure with stress inoculation training has been shown to speed recovery from acute trauma reactions and, in some studies, reduce the incidence of chronic PTSD. The one available dismantling study found no difference between the full CBT package and just the exposure therapy components.

THE GLASS HALF EMPTY

Despite the progress to date, there is still much work to do. In the section below, we discuss three specific areas we recommend should be priorities for future research. Given the demonstrated efficacy of certain treatments for PTSD, we view successful dissemination of these treatments as being the highest priority. In addition, further research is warranted into reducing dropouts from effective treatments for PTSD and improving outcome for the minority of participants who show partial or no response to current treatments.

Lack of Access to Empirically Supported Treatments

The existence of empirically supported treatments for PTSD is of limited value if mental health professionals do not provide these treatments. Indeed, one significant barrier for patients is the lack of access to CBT for PTSD. Although many therapists treat patients with PTSD, very few of them are actually trained in the use of CBT for PTSD and even many of those trained in CBT do not provide it to their patients. A recent survey by Becker, Zayfert, and Anderson (in press) serves to illustrate these points with regard to exposure therapy for the treatment of PTSD. Similar surveys for other CBT treatments (e.g., stress inoculation training, cognitive therapy, EMDR) have not been conducted, although some of their findings may be relevant to other forms of CBT.

Becker et al. (in press) report results from a main sample of 207 psychologists and an additional specialist sample of 29 members of the Association for Advancement of Behavior Therapy's Disaster and Trauma Special Interest Group. Results for the main sample indicated that although 63% of therapists had treated 11 or more patients with PTSD, only 29% of the therapists had received training in exposure therapy for PTSD (even fewer had received training in the use of exposure therapy for other anxiety disorders). Moreover, 46% of therapists who had been trained in exposure therapy reported that they had never used it to treat PTSD. Unfortunately, the survey does not tell us what techniques were used to treat PTSD instead of exposure. It seems unlikely, however, that other forms of CBT (e.g., stress inoculation training, cognitive therapy) were being used instead, given the fact that only 29% of the sample identified their theoretical orientation as being cognitive or cognitive-behavioral whereas the majority of the sample identified themselves as either eclectic (37%) or psychodynamic (28%). The three most commonly endorsed reasons for not employing exposure therapy were lack of training (60%), a preference for "individualized" treatment over manualized treatment (25%), and the fear that patients would decompensate (22%).

Among members of the Disaster and Trauma SIG, 76% of the respondents identified their theoretical orientation as CBT and 93% had received training in exposure therapy for PTSD (76% also had training in exposure therapy for other anxiety disorders). In addition, more than 90% of these specialist therapists reported feeling somewhat or very familiar with and comfortable in using exposure therapy for the treatment of PTSD. Despite this, 34% of these experts had never used exposure therapy to treat PTSD and only 55% of the expert sample utilized exposure therapy in 50% or more of their PTSD cases. Interestingly, this group endorsed the same reasons for not utilizing exposure therapy more frequently: inadequate training (40%), concerns about patients decompensating (35%), and a preference for individualized treatment over manualized treatment (20%).

The barrier for using CBT is not unique to exposure therapy for PTSD. As noted above, the greatest barrier to use of this treatment was lack of training. While only 28.5% of clinicians in the Becker et al's (in press) study said they had training in exposure therapy for PTSD, even fewer (12.5%) reported training in exposure therapy for other anxiety disorders. It follows that the likelihood of these same clinicians to use exposure therapy for other anxiety disorder is even smaller than for PTSD. Indeed, Issakidis and Andrews (2002) found that only 11% of patients with anxiety disorders ever receive evidence based treatments.

In contrast to the limited access to CBT, access to SSRI medication is widely available. However, a recent study of treatment preference has shown an overwhelming preference for exposure therapy over medication. Zoellner, Feeny, Cochran, and Pruitt, (in press) provided a large group of women (nontreatment seeking) with descriptions of exposure therapy and the medication sertraline as effective treatments for PTSD and asked them to rate each treatment for credibility and to make a forced choice among treatment with exposure therapy, sertraline, or no treatment. Exposure therapy was rated as more credible than sertraline and 88% of the women expressed a preference for exposure therapy compared with 7% for sertraline and 6% selecting no treatment. A subgroup of women in the study met criteria for PTSD. Among this subgroup, 74% of the women preferred exposure therapy compared with 22% selecting sertraline and 3% selecting no treatment.

The results of the Zoellner et al. (in press) study could reflect a preference for psychotherapy over medication, rather than a preference for exposure therapy per se. Thus, given a choice between sertraline and supportive counseling, it could be that patients would prefer counseling, even though there is more evidence supporting the efficacy of SSRI medication in the treatment of PTSD than there is for supportive counseling. It therefore is of concern that the limited availability of CBT for PTSD combined with a strong preference for psychotherapy could potentially lead patients to select less effective therapy for their PTSD. Accordingly, significant efforts are needed toward the dissemination of empirically supported psychological treatments for PTSD to practicing clinicians and patient education about effective treatment option, both medication and psychotherapy. In addition, further research is warranted into the factors that influence people's (both therapists and patients) choices among available treatments and to determine the extent to which matching specific patients with specific treatments will enhance outcome.

Safety of Exposure Therapy for PTSD

Concern has been expressed about the safety of exposure therapy in the treatment of at least some populations presenting with PTSD (e.g., Cloitre et al., 2002; Kilpatrick & Best, 1984; Pitman et al., 1991), which is reflected in one of the reasons for not providing exposure therapy in the Becker et al. (in press) survey of therapists discussed above. Despite this concern, there has been little empirical investigation of the safety of any form of CBT for PTSD. Until recently, the primary published source of evidence for these concerns was a series of six case studies described by Pitman et al. (1991) drawn from a larger study of exposure therapy for PTSD among veterans (Pitman et al., 1996). The paper reported casual observations of a variety of complications that arose during and after the veterans' participation in exposure therapy, such as an increase in PTSD symptoms; feelings of guilt and shame at how the veteran behaved during the traumatic event; and relapse of other psychiatric conditions such as panic attacks, depression, and substance abuse. However, in the entire sample (Pitman et al., 1996), guilt, anger, and shame were found to be unrelated to outcome of exposure therapy and mobilization of self-reported anger or guilt during the imaginal exposure was not found to predict a worse therapeutic outcome. Moreover, anger, shame, and guilt showed the same pattern of decrease form pre- to posttreatment as did fear and physiological arousal.

More recently, Tarrier, Pilgrim, et al. (1999) conducted a study comparing imaginal exposure and cognitive therapy in the treatment of chronic PTSD in a general sample of civilian trauma survivors, excluding victims of childhood abuse. Participants who continued to meet criteria for PTSD after 4-week self-monitoring run-in phase were randomly assigned to either 15 one-hour sessions of either imaginal exposure to the trauma memory or Beck-style cognitive therapy. No differences were found between treatments on standard measures of PTSD symptom severity, depression, and anxiety. To assess symptom worsening after treatment, they defined symptom worsening as a posttreatment score on the CAPS that was greater than the corresponding pretreatment score by one or more points. Results revealed that significantly more participants receiving imaginal exposure (9 of 29, or 31%) showed a worsening of symptoms at posttreatment than in the cognitive therapy condition (3 of 33, or 9%), although the difference was no longer significant at the 6-month follow-up assessment (5 of 27 vs. 3 of 29, respectively).

Several considerations limit the conclusion that can be drawn from the Tarrier, Pilgrim, et al. (1999) results. First, on several measures such as the CAPS global improvement and retention of PTSD diagnosis, the group that received imaginal exposure achieved better outcome than the cognitive therapy group, although the differences did not reach significance. Thus, there was no general pattern of inferior outcome in the imaginal exposure group. Second, Tarrier et al. defined worsening as increase by one or more points on a single measure. Given that all instruments have measurement error associated with them, an increase by one point can easily fall within the margin of error (Devilly & Foa, 2001). Third, as discussed in greater detail below, the high rates of symptom worsening in the Tarrier, Pilgrim, et al. study (19% overall at posttreatment and 14% at 6-month follow-up) have not been replicated across other samples.

In addition, an interpretative difficulty in both the Pitman et al. (1991) case series and in the Tarrier, Pilgrim, et al. (1999) study stems from the lack of a comparison group to determine how many patients would have shown deterioration in the absence of treatment. Given the lack of a no-treatment control group, we cannot determine whether the rates of symptom worsening following treatment reflect an increase or a decrease in the likelihood of getting worse in the absence of treatment.

Symptom Worsening

In discussing the issue of symptom worsening associated with treatment, it is important to distinguish between symptom worsening that is present following a full course of treatment and a temporary symptom exacerbation occurring early in therapy that may be resolved prior to termination. In the case of symptom worsening at the end of treatment, the important issues are whether similar symptom worsening would have occurred in the absence of treatment and whether poor outcome is more likely to occur with one type of treatment or another. In the case of symptom exacerbation early in treatment, the important issues are whether such increases are associated with either premature termination of treatment or predictive of poor treatment outcome.

Symptom worsening at outcome. Three published studies have reported information relevant to the first two of the above questions. Gillespie et al. (2002) administered a treatment for PTSD based on Ehlers and Clark's (2000) cognitive theory of PTSD to survivors of the 1998 Omagh car bombing in Northern Ireland. This treatment included many components of cognitive and behavioral interventions, including exposure and cognitive restructuring. Their results indicated that all participants obtained at least 20% reduction in PTSD severity and no participants displayed symptom worsening. Cloitre et al. (2002) compared a treatment using the sequentially combined skills training in affect and interpersonal regulation (STAIR) with imaginal exposure (IE) with a waitlist control condition. One person (4.5%) showed symptom worsening in the STAIR/IE condition compared with (25%) in the waitlist condition. Given the lack of an exposure therapy–only condition in these two studies, it cannot be determined whether or not the low rates of symptoms worsening in the treatment conditions were due to the additional treatment components. However, the Cloitre et al. study illustrates the potential danger in withholding treatment. Taylor et al. (2003) compared PE to EMDR and relaxation training and found no cases of symptom worsening for exposure therapy and one case in each of EMDR (7%) and relaxation (7%).

In addition to the three published studies, we (Cahill, Riggs, Rauch, & Foa, 2003) have recently presented data from two of our studies (Foa, Dancu, et al., 1999; Foa, Hembree, et al., 2002) addressing all three questions. We first looked at symptom worsening defined as at least a one-point increase on the PSS-I, our interview measure of PTSD severity. Across the two studies we did not have any instances of symptom worsening in either PE only condition, compared with three cases (7.7%) across the two waitlist conditions. In addition, there were no cases of symptom worsening for a treatment that combined PE with cognitive restructuring (PE/CR), no cases in the SIT condition of the Foa, Dancu, et al. (1999) study, and one case (4.5%) in the PE/SIT condition from the Foa, Dancu, et al. (1999) study. We further extended the analysis by investigating symptom worsening on the Beck Depression Inventory (both studies), the state-anxiety portion of the State-Trait Anxiety Inventory (Foa, Dancu, et al., 1999), and the Beck Anxiety Inventory (Foa , Hembree, et al., 2002). Rates of symptom worsening in the two waitlist conditions on these measures of depression and anxiety ranged between 33 and 40%, compared with less than 5% in the two PE alone and the PE/CR conditions, 0 and 10.5% in the SIT condition, and 4.5 and 22.7% in the PE/SIT condition.

Finally, following the recommendations of Devilly and Foa (2001), we utilized the same procedures as in a study by Foa, Zoellner, Feeny, Hembree, and Alvaraz-Conrad (2002) to investigate reliable symptom worsening—increases on measures of PTSD, depression, and anxiety that are greater than the standard error of the difference between two measurements. Reliable PTSD symptom worsening by this criterion did not occur in any of the groups in either study and occurred on depression in less than 2% of cases receiving treatment, compared with 5.67% of cases in waitlist. On measures of anxiety, reliable worsening occurred in four cases (2.5%) receiving active treatment compared with seven cases (20.6%) in waitlist.

Symptom exacerbation during treatment. Foa, Zoellner, et al. (2002) took advantage of a unique design feature of our recently completed study comparing PE alone vs. PE combined with cognitive restructuring (PE/CR; Foa, Hembree, et al., 2002) to investigate reliable symptom worsening during treatment, its relationship with the initiation of imaginal exposure, and its associations with dropouts and treatment outcome. All participants completed self-report measures of PTSD, anxiety, and depression at the beginning of Sessions 2, 4, and 6. The treatment protocol called for the initiation of in-session imaginal exposure in Session 3 for participants randomly assigned to the PE only condition. In contrast, Session 3 in the PE/CR condition was focused on introducing cognitive restructuring and imaginal exposure did not begin until Session 4. Following the recommendations of Devilly and Foa (2001), Foa, Zoellner, et al. (2002) investigated the incidence of reliable worsening of PTSD, anxiety, and depression occurring between Sessions 2 and 4. Moreover, because participants had been randomly assigned to begin imaginal exposure in either Session 3 or Session 4, they were able to determine if there was an association between initiating imaginal exposure and the percentage of participants showing reliable symptom worsening. The majority of participants did not show any symptom worsening across measures of PTSD (85% and 97% for PE and PE/CR conditions, respectively), anxiety (72% and 91%), and depression (87% and 97%). Among participants who showed reliable worsening on anxiety, significantly more participants were in the PE-only condition and the same pattern was observed for PTSD and depression but the results were not significant. Thus, there was evidence that reliable worsening did occur in a minority of participants, and such worsening was associated with the initiation of imaginal exposure therapy. However, participants who showed symptom worsening early in therapy were no more likely to drop out from treatment (15%) than participants who did not experience symptom worsening (17%). Moreover, treatment outcome was not different for participants who showed symptom worsening compared with those who did not.

Evaluating Efforts to Disseminate CBT for PTSD

Data from the previously mentioned Becker et al. (in press) survey on the use of exposure therapy for PTSD indicate the most common source of training was through a workshop for continuing education credits. Although there are no systematic data to indicate whether attendees of such brief (typically between 3 hours and 2 days) workshops master the skills being taught or alter their clinical practices as a result of the training, one of the authors (EBF), along with other members of the Center for the Treatment and Study of Anxiety (CTSA), have extensive experience in providing such workshops. It has been our collective experience that, although such workshops often generate enthusiasm for the use of PE in the treatment of PTSD, few of the attendees feel confident enough in their ability to implement PE independently and therefore do not use it in their regular practice. In many cases, we agree with their view that short workshops do not sufficiently prepare for the proper use of PE and therefore we have been involved in the development and assessment of two more intensive training models that appear to have great promise for success. The first model focuses on intensive training and supervision of the therapists who will be administering the treatment. The second model also includes intensive initial training of the therapists but focuses more on use of local supervisors to provide ongoing supervision of the therapists and initial training of new therapists as needed. The two models are described below, along with a summary of relevant outcome data. For a more detailed discussion of our efforts to disseminate PE, see Cahill, Hembree, and Foa (in press).

Model I: Intensive initial training of therapists followed by ongoing expert supervision. We recently completed a study that utilized this model to disseminate PE with and without cognitive restructuring to Philadelphia's community-based rape treatment program, Women Organized Against Rape (WOAR). Prior to our involvement with WOAR, their primary treatments consisted of individual and group supportive counseling. In our research with WOAR, female sexual assault victims seeking services through WOAR's referral network were invited to participate in a study that involved random assignment to treatment with 9 to 12 sessions of PE alone, PE/CR or waitlist. Members of the CTSA provided WOAR therapists with a 1-week workshop that provided background into the theory and efficacy data supporting the use of PE in the treatment of PTSD and training, through role plays and videotapes, in how to conduct the treatment components (e.g., calming breathing, psychoeducation, imaginal and in vivo exposure). A second week-long workshop on cognitive restructuring provided by David M. Clark and assisted by members of the CTSA, again provided background into the theory of cognitive restructuring and training, through role plays and videotapes, in how to conduct cognitive restructuring. The therapists at WOAR were all women with master's degrees in counseling or social work who had worked with survivors of sexual assault for several years. None of the WOAR therapists had previous training in cognitive-behavioral interventions and none had previously participated in research or delivered manualized treatment protocols. Each therapist then completed at least two training cases under careful weekly supervision by a CTSA supervisor. Supervision included not only discussing each case on a weekly basis, but actually reviewing videotapes of the therapy sessions. No therapist began seeing actual randomized study cases until they were deemed competent with the treatment protocols. Six months after the initial training, a 2-day booster workshop was conducted in which therapists presented cases, and videotapes of therapy sessions were reviewed. Throughout the course of the study, a CTSA supervisor continued to provide weekly supervision to the WOAR therapists that included reviewing videotapes of select portions of therapy sessions.

In parallel fashion, participants were also recruited through the CTSA and randomly assigned to PE, PE/CR or WL and were treated by CTSA therapists with expertise in CBT for PTSD. The CTSA therapists also participated in weekly supervision that included review of videotapes of therapy sessions. Indeed, the supervision established at WOAR was modeled after the standard supervision practices at the CTSA. The results from this study revealed that, compared with WL, both treatments were very effective in reducing symptoms of PTSD, anxiety, and depression, and contrary to expectations, PE/CR was not superior to PE alone. Importantly, there were no differences in treatment outcome between the two sites: participants treated by community therapists under CTSA supervision showed the same treatment response as participants treated by CTSA expert therapists.

We are currently conducting two additional dissemination studies in Philadelphia. The first of these studies is a continuation of work with WOAR therapists in which we have reduced the level of supervision to determine whether WAOR as an agency can maintain their level of fidelity to the treatment protocol without our intensive involvement and to compare outcomes from this maintenance stage of our dissemination research with that obtained during the initial study. Our second study is a replication of our basic training and supervision procedures with a second local agency to determine if we can repeat the success realized with WOAR with another community clinic. If the initial dissemination to this other clinic is successful, we will replicate the titration of supervision to again determine whether community agencies can maintain their level of treatment fidelity and outcome with minimal expert involvement.

Gillespie et al. (2002) utilized a similar model to train therapists to provide cognitive therapy based on Ehlers and Clark's (2000) model of PTSD to survivors of the 1998 car bombing of Omagh in Northern Ireland. Shortly after the bombing, community therapists were given intensive training in this form of cognitive therapy. The five study therapists came from varying backgrounds (psychiatry, nursing, and social work) and none had previously specialized in psychological trauma. Initial training consisted of three steps. First, there were several phone consultations with David M. Clark to identify key therapeutic procedures and discuss how to apply them in the current circumstances. Second, there was a lecture on PTSD and cognitive models of PTSD. Third, Clark and his colleagues conducted a 2-day workshop. In addition, ongoing supervision was provided locally by a CBT expert (Gillespie) and, once every 4 to 6 weeks, by Clark and colleagues via teleconferencing technology. Although the treatment permitted flexibility in the total number of sessions, the median number of sessions was 8 and 76% of participants completed treatment within 15 sessions. On average, participants displayed a 64% reduction in PTSD severity, ranging between 20 to 100% reduction. These results are comparable with those obtained in a randomized controlled trial completed by Ehlers, Clark, and others (in press).

The existing evidence therefore suggests that CBT can be successfully disseminated using the model described above. However, our experience is that this model is labor intensive and requires the involvement of the expert site for an extended period of time, which may not be practical in many community service situations. Moreover, dissemination following this model is limited to places with local CBT experts. The second emerging dissemination model is an attempt to address these limitations.

Model II: Intensive initial training of therapists and a local supervisor. The goal of the second dissemination model is to reduce reliance on currently established expert sites for training of new therapists and ongoing supervision by developing local experts who assist in the training of the first generation of therapists. Furthermore, the goal is to take on the long-term responsibility of providing ongoing supervision and training of new therapists.

This model developed out of the experiences of one of us (EBF) in conducting brief workshops (between 3 hours and two days) in Israel. Increased interest in effective treatments for PTSD developed after the onset of the Al Aktza Intifada toward the end of September 2000, due to the increase in the number of victims exposed to terrorist attacks. As a result, clinicians working in settings that served victims of recent terrorist attacks and patients with combat-related PTSD came to the CTSA for extended (2–5 weeks) training in PE. In addition, public and private organizations sponsored 3 to 5 day workshops for clinicians that worked with traumatized populations. The most systematic of these efforts is one initiated by the American Jewish Joint Distribution Committee, an American Jewish charitable organization, through its Israel operation, JDC Israel, under the direction of Ruth Regulant-Levi.

The first step in this endeavor was a 5-day workshop given in July 2002. In attendance were 35 Israeli therapists who worked in various civilian and military clinical centers that provided services to trauma victims. The team of trainers consisted of two faculty from our center and three Israeli therapists who we previously trained in PE at the CTSA. The content and form of the training was based on the materials and procedures developed previously in the training of therapists at WOAR. The next step was the development of three supervision groups in different locations in Israel. Six months later, a 2-day booster training was then held in which video and audiotapes from PE sessions were presented and discussed by one of us (EBF). These supervision groups continue to meet regularly and, although we remain available for consultation, our current involvement as consultants has been quite limited. Importantly, outcome data for the first 10 patients, all male combat veterans with chronic PTSD, were presented at the 2003 meeting of the Israeli Psychiatric Association (Nacasch et al., 2003). After 10 to 12 sessions of PE, the mean reduction of symptoms was 58%, a reduction that is comparable with that of our clinic and at WOAR with female victims of physical and sexual assault. The third and most recent step has been a replication of the training procedure with a psychologist and a psychiatrist from the Israel Defense Forces being trained to serve as local supervisors for a group of 35 additional therapists at Ha'emek hospital in Afula who underwent our 5-day workshop in July of 2003 conducted by Foa and local colleagues.

Summary and Recommendations

Available evidence indicates that lack of training represents the single greatest barrier to the widespread use of exposure therapy, and probably other effective forms of CBT as well. Moreover, many therapists who have received some training in exposure therapy do not use it, calling into question the efficacy of current training practices. Training models that go beyond a brief workshop for continuing education credits need to be developed and evaluated. The training not only should impart information about how to implement these treatments and for whom they are appropriate, but also should to address such issues as (a) the relative efficacy, safety, and tolerability of various treatments, (b) the therapists' negative attitudes toward manualized treatments, and (c) the provision of adequate training consisting not only of learning the treatments but also providing supervision support to encourage the use of these treatments in their clinical practice.

The urgent need for disseminating evidence-based treatments has been recognized by the U.S. Department of Health and Human Services' Substance Abuse and Mental Health Services Administration (SAMHSA). Each year this agency selects model treatments and assists in disseminating them to mental health professionals. In 2001 PE bestowed the Exemplary Substance Abuse Prevention Program Award. In addition, SAMHSA designated PE as one of 42 model programs for mental health services that have been targeted for national dissemination.

In our ongoing experience with the dissemination of PE for PTSD, we have formalized two different training models. The first model, which we have more experience with and formal data regarding treatment adherence and treatment outcome, involves intensive training of community therapists followed by regular ongoing supervision by experts from our center over an extended period of time. This approach has yielded excellent outcomes thus far, and we are currently exploring the extent to which we can replicate our success at WOAR with another agency, and the extent to which WOAR can maintain their level of competence and perpetuate the use of PE when staff members change over. The second model is an attempt to create local expertise so that dissemination is not as expensive or limited to cities in which current experts reside. We have less experience with this model, but the results to date are promising. Research efforts are needed to determine which treatment protocols should be targeted for widespread dissemination and the most effective and efficient methods to accomplish this. Considerations for deciding which treatment among the various empirically supported methods is best suited for dissemination include efficacy and efficiency of the treatment method, the breadth of trauma populations for which the treatment has been shown effective, and the ease with which therapists can learn the treatment.

Treatment Dropouts

As with the dissemination issue described above, the availability of an effective treatment for PTSD is limited if patients are not willing to undergo the treatment or prematurely terminate the treatment. Indeed, there is a strong belief that exposure therapy in particular is prone to causing dropout or that certain trauma populations (e.g., adult survivors of childhood abuse) are especially likely to drop out from exposure therapy (Cloitre et al., 2002). In a recent metaanalysis of dropout rates from various CBT treatments for PTSD, Hembree et al. (in press) found similar dropout rates across active treatments such as exposure therapy (20.5%), SIT or cognitive therapy alone (22.1%), exposure therapy combined with SIT or cognitive therapy (26.9%), and EMDR (18.9%), while active treatment yielded greater dropout rates than control conditions (11.4%). Thus, dropout rates from PE are no different from other CBT treatments. Moreover, dropout rates from CBT studies compare favorably with those from SSRI medication studies for PTSD. Across six recent medication studies (Brady et al., 2000; Connor et al., 1999; Davidson, Rothbaum, et al., 2001; Marshall et al., 2001; Tucker et al., 2001; van der Kolk et al., 1994) dropout rates ranged between 22 and 38% for active medication and between 12 and 41% for placebo. Thus, approximately one out of four or five participants randomly assigned to an active CBT for PTSD terminates treatment prior to completion of the treatment protocol along with nearly one out of three participants randomly assigned to SSRI medication.

Do the dropout rates found by Hembree et al. (2003) reflect a limitation that is specific to CBT in controlled studies? This does not seem to be the case. In fact, the frequency of premature treatment termination appears to be higher in clinical settings than in controlled studies. Major reviews of the treatment dropout literature (e.g., Baekland & Lundwall, 1978; Garfield, 1986; Wierzbicki & Pakarik, 1993) estimate dropouts from clinical services to range from 30 to 60%. The most recent of these reviews (Wierzbicki & Pakarik, 1993) was a metaanalysis of 125 studies of psychotherapy dropout that obtained an average dropout rate of 47%. Only 4 of 32 variables were found to be significantly related to dropout rates. The first of these variables was the definition of dropout. Dropout rates were significantly lower (36%) when defined as a patient failing to attend a scheduled session than when defined in terms of the therapists' judgment (48%) or completion of a set number of sessions (48%). The remaining variables were patient-related variables: race, education, and socioeconomic status. Demographic variables may help us identify which patients may be at greater or less risk for dropping out, but it is not clear why such variables as race or education are associated with greater dropout, nor do they provide any obvious suggestions as to the kinds of interventions that may be useful to promoting staying in treatment. The role of socioeconomic status may be related to both the direct (i.e., fees) and indirect financial costs (e.g., transportation and child care) of being in therapy. In such cases, dropouts could potentially be reduced by making treatment available at low costs, providing on-site childcare, and being accessible by public transportation.

More recently, Zayfert and Becker (2000) have investigated the use of exposure therapy for PTSD and dropouts from treatment in a medical school–based outpatient clinic. Of 91 patients evaluated, 74% returned for treatment, and of those, 39% received one or more exposure therapy sessions. Thus, even in settings where clinicians are trained in the use of exposure therapy for PTSD and disposed toward using it, many patients still may not receive it. Interestingly, more patients who received exposure therapy completed treatment compared with those who received other, nonspecified treatments. Specifically, of the 67 patients who entered treatment, 9 patients completed treatment at the time of the report, all of whom had received exposure therapy. Thirty-seven of the 67 entrants had dropped out of treatment, only 6 of whom had received exposure therapy. The remaining patients were still in active treatment, with approximately half of them (12 of 22) receiving exposure therapy. One factor complicating the interpretation of these findings is that some of the patients who received exposure therapy also received interventions based on principles of dialectical behavior therapy (DBT), which the authors hypothesize to improve patients' ability to tolerate subsequent exposure therapy. In the absence of an appropriate comparison group, it is impossible to determine why patients receiving exposure were more likely to complete treatment and less likely to drop out. However, in the Cloitre et al's (2002) study in which emotional regulation program preceded imaginal exposure, the dropout rate was 30%, suggesting that a the addition of a DBT-like treatment did not yield a lower rate of dropout from that found for PE alone in the Hembree et al. (2003) metaanalysis. In summary, Zayfert and Becker's (2000) results illustrate that, similar to the randomized controlled trial (RCT) data summarized in the Hembree et al. (2003) metaanalysis, the use of exposure therapy in outpatient clinics is not associated with greater dropout than alternative treatment.

Zayfert and Becker (2000) also investigated reasons for not receiving treatment among a sample of 65 patients who did not receive exposure therapy. A small percentage of patients (6%) reported that they improved enough with the assessment that they felt they did not require additional treatment. Another 11% did not receive exposure therapy because of active suicidal or dissociative behavior and 12% were already in another active treatment. Twenty-seven percent of patients cited logistical and life problems as the reason they did not enter treatment and 26% did not provide a reason. Only 17% of the sample cited refusal to engage in imaginal exposure as the reason for not entering treatment. These data indicate that, although there may be a subset of patients who will refuse exposure therapy because of its requirement to confront the feared memory, the majority of patients did not receive exposure therapy for reason that were equally applicable to any treatment for

PTSD and other disorders (i.e., logistical and life problems, already in treatment elsewhere, suicidal, "unknown").

Summary and Recommendations

Even under circumstances in which empirically supported treatments for PTSD are available, some individuals may fail to receive adequate treatment because they choose not to begin treatment or they terminate treatment early. This is neither unique to treatment for PTSD nor is it unique to treatment with prolonged exposure for PTSD. In the context of randomized controlled trials, the average rate of dropout from CBT for PTSD is approximately 22% and does not systematically vary across different types of CBT (Hembree et al., in press), a figure that compares favorably to the approximately 30% of participants who drop out from randomized controlled trials of medication for PTSD and quite favorably to the approximately 47% of people who drop out of psychotherapy generally when it is not part of a randomized controlled trial (Wierzbicki & Pekarik, 1993). Moreover, Zayfert and Becker (2000) found that in a clinic where exposure therapy is provided, the number of patients who refused exposure therapy was relatively low and the dropout rate from exposure therapy was not higher than that from other treatment. That said, even in randomized controlled trials where investigators are particularly motivated to have as many participants as possible complete the treatment, approximately one in five people will drop out of treatment. Thus, one way to increase the number of people who receive effective treatment for PTSD is to decrease the number of people who drop out from treatment. The available evidence on factors associated with dropout suggest that interventions that will be most effective in reducing dropout need to address the logistical barriers to treatment. Research is particularly needed to identify methods to reduce dropout from treatment in community settings where dropout rates appear to be substantially higher than in the kind of academic settings where randomized controlled trials are typically conducted.

Nonresponders and Partial Responders to Treatment

Although the best validated CBT and pharmacological treatments for PTSD yield statistically significant improvements compared with appropriate control conditions, and a large number of patients in these studies experience clinically significant improvement, the facts remain that a significant minority of patients do not respond to treatment and a substantial number of patients classified as treatment responders continue to experience residual symptoms and functional impairment. To illustrate this point, reconsider the information summarized in Tables 14.1 to 14.3. As noted previously, between 54 and 82% of participants receiving CBT no longer met criteria for PTSD after treatment and between 20 and 76% met criteria for good end-state functioning (Table 14.1). This means that between 18–66% of participants continued to have PTSD after treatment and an even greater percent (24–80%) did not achieve good end-state functioning status. Medication studies reveal similar findings. The fact that 53 to 85% of participants are judged to be medication "responders" also means that between 15 and 47% of participants were "nonresponders" (Table 14.2). Moreover, given that responder status is determined by improvement alone, without reference to absolute score, it is possible for a person to be a responder but still experience significant levels of symptoms and impairment. With respect to brief CBT to treat ASD or to prevent the development of chronic PTSD (Table 14.3), the currently available data would indicate that 8 to 20% of participants developed PTSD despite the receipt of treatment, and both the 6-month (15–23% PTSD) and 4-year (8–30% PTSD) follow-up data suggest these numbers remain relatively constant over time.

Thus, we can conclude that there has been great progress in the past 15 years in treating chronic PTSD with medication and with psychotherapy, and in preventing chronic PTSD with therapy. However, there also remains room for improvement in treatment outcome. Currently, there is little research devoted to identifying ways to improve treatment outcome. What research has been done can be divided into two general categories: extending current treatment and combining treatments.

Extending Current Treatment

Perhaps the simplest strategy for helping non- or partial responders to an initial course of a treatment is to continue with more of the same treatment. The most common way to accomplish this is to administer the same treatment at the same intensity for a longer period of time. Indeed, the norm in clinical practice is to extend the treatment if the patient does not respond well, at least within reasonable limits. It is therefore surprising there isn't much research on the utility of this commonplace practice.

Londborg et al. (2001) investigated the effects of continuation treatment with sertraline for PTSD. Participants in the Londborge et al. study were a group of 126 participants who had previously received 12 weeks of treatment with sertraline in either of the Brady et al. (2000) or Davidson, Rothbaum, et al. (2001) randomized, placebo-controlled studies. These participants received open-label continuation treatment with sertraline for an additional 24 weeks. Using a the criteria of a minimum 30% reduction in CAPS scores plus a CGI-Improvement score < 2 (Much or Very Much Improved), 74 participants were classified as responders after the initial 12-week phase of blind treatment with sertraline, 92% of whom maintained their responder status at last observation during the 24-week open-label continuation phase.

Fifty-two participants were classified as nonresponders after the initial 12-week phase of blinded treatment with sertraline, 54% of whom subsequently became responders at their last observation during the 24-week open label continuation phase. These data suggest that response rates to medication may be as high as 81%, given a long enough trial (up to 36 weeks in this case). However, this estimate does not take into consideration the effects of dropouts (more than 30%) from the initial 12-week treatment phase, potential self-selection biases as to which participants from the original RCTs agreed to enter the continuation phase, and the effect of shifting treatment from double-blind conditions to open-label conditions, all factors which may have inflated the apparent efficacy of a 36-week trial of medication relative to a 12-week trial.

We have observed a similar phenomenon in our recently completed study of CBT for PTSD. Female assault victims were randomly assigned to prolonged exposure, prolonged exposure plus cognitive restructuring, or waitlist. Participants in the two treatment conditions were evaluated at session 8 and a determination was made whether to terminate treatment at session 9 or to continue treatment to session 12. Participants who demonstrated a minimum 70% reduction in their self-reported PTSD symptom severity completed treatment at session 8, while the remaining participants received the extension sessions. A preliminary analysis (Foa, Hembree, Rauch, & Cahill, 2003) comparing these two groups of treatment participants revealed at session 8, participants scheduled to terminate at session 9 had an average 81% reduction in self-reported PTSD symptom severity compared with 26% for those scheduled for additional sessions. However, the group that received additional treatment showed further improvement such that after session 12, this group now showed an average 63% reduction in PTSD symptom severity. Notably, the two groups did not differ in their pretreatment levels of PTSD severity. Therefore, the difference between groups at session 8 is not an artifact of the partial responders having started with greater symptom severity. Rather, the difference at session 8 reflects a difference in the rate of improvement.

While the above results are promising, a few limitations should be noted. First, as with the Londborg et al. (2001) study discussed above, our results do not take into consideration the effects of dropouts prior to session 8 when the decision was made to either terminate at session 9 or continue through session 12. Second, even with the additional sessions the group of partial responders still did not achieve the same degree of improvement as the full responder group achieved during their first nine sessions. Although it is possible that the group of partial responders would catch up to the group of full responders if given more treatment sessions, additional research is needed to determine if this is the case.

Third, the lack of a comparison group that did not meet termination criteria by session 8 and did not receive additional treatment prevents us from knowing for sure that it was the additional treatment that was responsible for the additional improvement. Specifically, we cannot rule out the possibility that additional improvement would have occurred even in the absence of additional treatment. Foa et al. (1991), for example, reported additional improvement after treatment with PE, but not SIT or supportive counseling, during their 3-month treatment-free follow-up period. However, given the magnitude of improvement over a relatively short time, it is unlikely the additional improvement can be attributed solely to a "sleeper effect" of prior treatment. As a pragmatic matter, then, we are recommending that therapists utilizing PE be flexible in the number of sessions offered and that, provided that at least some improvement is observed within the first 8 weeks of treatment, therapy continue until patients have achieved a good outcome or at least completed 15 sessions. Researchers should develop treatment protocols that provide for adequate treatment duration or that specifically manipulates treatment duration to investigate its impact on treatment outcome.

Combining Treatments

The strategy for enhancing outcome that has been the subject of most research to date involves combining treatments. However, the nature of the treatment combinations (i.e., which treatments are combined) and the manner by which they are combined (e.g., simultaneously vs. sequentially) has varied considerably.

Additional treatment administered concurrently. Studies have consistently shown that the concurrent addition of CBT procedures do not enhance the efficacy of PE alone (for a review see Foa, Rothbaum, & Furr, 2003). As mentioned briefly in the first section of this chapter, several studies have investigated whether adding elements of stress inoculation training or cognitive therapy to exposure therapy enhances outcome. Foa, Dancu, et al. (1999) compared PE, SIT, and their combination with a waitlist control group in the treatment of chronic PTSD. Results found all three treatments were more effective than WL and no clear superiority for either PE or SIT. Importantly, the combined treatment was not superior to either of the individual treatments. Indeed, when there were differences, the combined treatment was slightly less effective. Bryant et al. (1999) compared PE/SIT with PE and a supportive counseling control group in the treatment of ASD with similar results: both PE and PE/SIT were more effective than SC, but combined treatment was not superior to PE alone.

Marks et al. (1998) compared PE, cognitive restructuring (CR), and their combination with a relaxation training control group in the treatment of chronic PTSD. Results found all three active treatments were superior to relaxation and no clear superiority for either PE or CR. Once again, the combined treatment was not superior to the individual treatments. In our recently completed study, we compared the combination of PE/CR with PE alone and waitlist control, obtaining similar results. Although both treatments were superior to WL, the addition of CR to PE did not enhance outcome across a wide range of dependent variables for PTSD symptoms severity, depression, anxiety, and drop out from treatment. Paunovic and Ost (2001) similarly compared PE/CR with PE alone, but did not include a control group. While both treatments were associated with significant improvement from the pre- to posttreatment assessments, PE/CR was not superior to PE alone.

Bryant and his colleagues have conducted a series of studies investigating procedures to improve outcome by adding procedures to imaginal exposure therapy (in contrast to PE, which incorporates both imaginal and in vivo exposure). Bryant et al. (2002) compared imaginal exposure alone, in vivo exposure alone, and the combination of imaginal and in vivo exposure plus cognitive restructuring with a supportive counseling control group in the treatment of chronic PTSD. Imaginal exposure alone and the combined treatment were both superior to supportive counseling and to in vivo exposure alone, while in vivo exposure alone did not differ from supportive counseling. The combined treatment was superior to imaginal exposure alone. However, because Bryant et al. did not include a PE condition (which includes both imaginal and in vivo exposure) , it is not clear whether the superiority of the combined treatment to imaginal exposure was due to the addition of in vivo exposure, cognitive restructuring, or both.

In a second study with chronic PTSD, Bryant, Moulds, Woody Guthrie, Dang, and Nixon (2003) compared imaginal exposure alone, imaginal exposure plus CR, and supportive counseling control. While both treatment conditions were superior to control, combined treatment was superior to imaginal exposure alone. In a third study described in a review by Harvey, et al. (2003), imaginal exposure alone was compared with imaginal exposure plus hypnosis and with supportive counseling in the treatment of ASD. Hypnosis in the combined treatment group was administered immediately before conducing imaginal exposure with the goal of enhancing emotional engagement during imagery. Results indicated that both exposure treatments were more effective than supportive counseling in reducing ASD and prevention of chronic PTSD. There were no differences between treatments in the percentage of patients who subsequently met criteria for PTSD at the 6-month follow-up (21% for imaginal exposure alone, 22% for combined treatment). Combined treatment was found to be superior to imaginal exposure on the intrusive symptom subscale of the Impact of Event Scale, but not the avoidance subscale.

The pattern of results that is emerging suggests that it is difficult to enhance the effects of exposure therapy by the concurrent addition of other treatment techniques when exposure therapy consists of both imaginal and in vivo exposure (i.e., PE). However, when exposure therapy is restricted to imaginal exposure alone or in vivo exposure alone, then it is possible to enhance the effects of therapy by adding the missing exposure modality (i.e., adding in vivo exposure to imaginal exposure or vice versa) and/or adding cognitive restructuring. By comparison, the effect of adding hypnosis to enhance imaginal exposure seems less promising. It is unknown whether adding stress inoculation training will enhance the outcome when exposure therapy is limited to a single modality. Additional research is needed to identify which combination of treatment techniques yield the best outcome, paying particular attention to the effects of imaginal and in vivo exposure modalities when used separately or when combined. In addition, it may be useful to investigate why so many attempts to improve outcome by combining different treatments have not been successful. The three interventions that have been found effective in treating PTSD (exposure therapy, cognitive restructuring, and stress inoculation training) have traditionally been thought to involve different mechanisms of action. Therefore it is surprising that combined treatments have not been more successful than the individual components. One possible explanation is that these treatments operate through the same mechanisms and that each one provides a full dose of the effective component and therefore combining them does not result in further benefit. For example, it is possible that exposure therapy, stress inoculation training, and cognitive therapy all produce modification of perceptions that are thought to underlie PTSD: perception of self as extremely incompetent, and the world as extremely dangerous (e.g., Foa & Cahill, 2001; Foa & Rothbaum, 1998). Several studies supported the relationship between these cognitions and PTSD (Ehlers, Mayou, & Bryant, 1998; Foa, Ehlers, Clark, Tolin, & Orsillo, 1999). Moreover, several studies support the view that both exposure therapy and cognitive therapy modify negative cognitions associated with the particular anxiety disorder that is being treated (panic disorder; Williams & Falbo, 1996; social phobia; Hope, Heimberg, & Bruch, 1995). If true, it is not surprising that combining treatments that operate through the same mechanisms do not result in greater improvement than using one treatment only. Indeed Foa and Rauch (in press) found that PE alone reduced negative perception about self and the world as much as did PE combined with cognitive restructuring. Moreover, Foa and Rauch (in press) found significant correlations between reductions in these cognitions and reduction in PTSD symptoms. If the various treatments address the same mechanisms, the question remains which treatment is the most effective and efficient in producing the cognitive changes. In a recent meta-analyses, Foa, Cahill, and Moser (2003) concluded that the addition of cognitive therapy to exposure therapy that includes both imaginal and in vivo exposure did not enhance treatment effects. In contrast, the addition of some form of exposure therapy to cognitive therapy does enhance treatment efficacy.

A second possibility is that these treatments operate through different mechanisms that are partially antagonistic to one another. For example, the goal in exposure therapy is sometimes construed as enhancing habituation of fear by confronting trauma-related memories and reminders in and activating the underlying fear structure. By contrast, the goal in stress inoculation training is to teach patients techniques such as relaxation to be used in anxiety- evoking situations to counter the anxiety. Perhaps attempts to reduce anxiety via relaxation interfere with anxiety reduction via habituation.

Foa, Dancu, et al. (1999) proposed yet a third possibility. They noted that the study protocol was designed to keep the number and duration of sessions the same across treatments. Thus, the PE/SIT condition required that all of the SIT and all of the PE procedures be covered in the same time frame that would be used to cover just PE or SIT in the individual treatment conditions. Participants in the combined condition, therefore, may have experienced an information overload and if so, were not able to learn and utilize the techniques as well as participants in the individual treatment conditions. This same design feature is relevant to the studies by Marks et al. (1998), Paunovic and Ost (2001) and, to a lesser extent, our recently completed study comparing PE alone and PE with CR (Foa, Hembree, et al., 2002). Indeed, one impetuous reason for comparing PE and PE/CR was to reduce the information load in the previous PE/SIT condition by selecting what we thought to be the most effective component of SIT.

Additional treatment administered sequentially. One potential way to address the problem of information overload with multicomponent treatments is to present the treatments sequentially, rather than simultaneously. Moreover, the sequential arrangement of treatments allows a greater opportunity for the effect of one treatment to influence the other, such as in cases where skills acquired in the first of the two treatments are hypothesized to be prerequisites to benefiting from the second of the two treatments. In addition, the sequential presentation of treatments may help to address the potential for a floor effect when combining two separately effective treatments. If both treatments are, on average, moderately effective with most participants, then it becomes difficult to see the benefit of combined treatments because the benefit would be limited only to those people who did not fully benefit from one of the individual treatments. When combined treatments are administered simultaneously, it is impossible to identify which of the participants who responded to the combined treatment actually required both treatments. However, when treatments are administered sequentially, it is possible to identify those individuals who were either none or partial responders to the first treatment in order to test whether adding the second treatment yields further benefit.

Cloitre et al. (2002) developed and tested the efficacy of a treatment that sequentially combined skills training in affective and interpersonal regulation (STAIR) with imaginal exposure for the treatment of PTSD resulting from abuse in childhood. Descriptive information on victims of child abuse indicates that in addition to PTSD they experience difficulties with affect regulation and with interpersonal relationships. Based on this,

Cloitre et al. hypothesized that these additional difficulties would interfere with childhood abuse survivors participating in and benefiting from exposure therapy. Accordingly, treatment with STAIR first was designed to ameliorate the affect regulation and interpersonal skills deficits so that participants would be in a position to benefit from imaginal exposure therapy for their PTSD. Compared with a minimum attention control group, women receiving STAIR/IE showed significant improvements in affect regulation skills and reductions in PTSD symptom severity and associated anxiety and depression. However, the absence of a comparison group that received treatment with imaginal exposure without prior treatment with STAIR precludes drawing conclusions about whether STAIR enhanced the efficacy of exposure therapy. Moreover, the magnitude of within-group effect sizes on three of the four measures of affect regulation, which ostensibly were targeted during STAIR, were as large or larger following the imaginal exposure component of treatment than following STAIR (see Cahill et al., in press). This pattern of results questions the rationale for providing treatment with STAIR prior to conducting imaginal exposure. Thus, further research is needed to determine if preparatory training in affect regulation and interpersonal skills enhances subsequent treatment with exposure therapy.

In a review of exposure therapy in the treatment of combat-related PTSD, Frueh, et al. (1995) concluded that, while exposure therapy appeared effective in reducing symptoms of reexperiencing and hyperarousal, "the data do not indicate that exposure therapy has a significant effect upon the 'negative' symptoms of PTSD (e.g., avoidance, social withdrawal, and emotional numbing), nor on certain aspects of emotion management (e.g., anger control)" (p. 813). Accordingly, Frueh, Turner, Beidel, Mirabella, and Jones (1996) tested a treatment that sequentially combined 14 sessions of PE followed by 14 sessions of training in social and anger management skills. Results revealed that treatment with PE was associated with a reduction in anxiety, improvement in sleep, and less physiological reactivity in response to script-driven imagery of the veterans' index trauma memory. Subsequent skills training was associated with further reductions in anxiety and an increase in the veterans' social activities. Although strong conclusions cannot be made given the absence of any control conditions, the findings are consistent with the hypothesis that veterans were able to further their treatment benefits by adding skills training after completing exposure therapy.

Glynn et al. (1999) also investigated a multicomponent treatment that was administered sequentially among veterans. Participants were assigned to receive 18 sessions of imaginal exposure plus cognitive restructuring, 18 sessions of imaginal exposure plus cognitive restructuring followed by 16 sessions of behavioral family therapy, or waitlist control. Behavioral family therapy included training in communication, anger management, and problem solving. It was hypothesized that imaginal exposure therapy plus cognitive restructuring would reduce the "positive" symptoms of PTSD (i.e., reexperiencing, hyperarousal) but have no effect on the negative symptoms (e.g., social withdrawal, numbing), while behavioral family therapy would reduce the negative symptoms. Results revealed that, compared with no treatment, both treatment groups showed significant improvement on a composite measure of positive PTSD symptoms. However, neither group showed significant improvement on the negative symptoms of PTSD. Moreover, there were no differences among the three groups on overall social adjustment. These results, therefore, are not consistent with the findings of Frueh et al. (1995) regarding the benefits of skills training following exposure therapy among veterans.*

Stein, Kline, and Matloff (2002) recruited a group of veterans with PTSD who were judged to be minimally responsive to 12 weeks of treatment with one of three selective serotonin reuptake inhibitors (SSRIs: fluoxetine, paroxetine, or sertraline), with at least a minimum of 4 weeks at the maximally tolerable dose. These veterans were maintained on their original medication and then randomly assigned to 8 weeks of augmentation with either placebo or the atypical neuroleptic olanzapine under double-blind conditions. Compared with placebo, the addition of olanzapine resulted in a significant reduction in PTSD symptom severity and depression, accompanied by an increase in sleep quality. However, olanzapine was also associated with an average 13-pound weight increase, which is likely to be viewed as an unwanted secondary effect of the medication and may have compromised the study blind. In addition, the study design does not permit determination of whether it is necessary to continue the SSRI and add olanzapine, or replace the SSRI with olanzapine.

---

*The explicit distinction between "positive" and "negative" symptoms of PTSD seems to appear only in a few studies of veterans. However, several outcome studies with civilian populations have reported results for the different PTSD symptom clusters. For example, Lovell, Marks, Noshrivani, Thrasher, and Livanou (2001) re-analyzed data from the Marks et al. (1998) trial to test the hypothesis that PE would have its strongest effects on fear and avoidance, cognitive therapy would have its strongest effects on numbing symptoms and associated features of PTSD (e.g., guilt, depression), and that combined treatment would yield best outcome. Results showed that PE, CR, and PE/CR were superior to relaxation control on all clusters, and there were no differences among active treatments.

We have recently completed a multicenter study with Davidson (Duke University) and Rothbaum (Emory University) that investigated the effects of sequentially adding PE to treatment with sertraline in a general civilian trauma population. In the first phase of the study, all participants received 10 weeks of open-label treatment with sertraline. All participants who experienced at least 20% reduction in their PTSD symptom severity entered the second phase in which they were randomly assigned to 5 weeks of continuation on sertraline alone or continuation of sertraline augmented with 10 twice-weekly sessions of PE. A preliminary analysis (Foa, Franklin, & Moser, 2002) revealed that continuation of sertraline alone resulted in no further improvement while the addition of PE produced further treatment gains. This augmentation effect was particularly noticeable for participants who were partial responders to medication during the first phase. A subsequent analysis (Cahill, et al. 2003) found the addition of CBT also reduced the likelihood of relapse 6 months after the completion of treatment.

Otto et al. (in press) conducted a study that combined elements of concurrent and sequential treatment additions. Participants in this study were 10 Cambodian refugees with PTSD despite ongoing treatment with the combination of clonazepam and an adequate dose of an SSRI medication other than sertraline. All participants were maintained on the clonazepam for the course of the study and the existing SSRI was gradually replaced with sertraline. In addition to the change in SSRI, five randomly selected participants were provided with 10 sessions of CBT that consisted of education, exposure to trauma memories, interoceptive exposure exercises to physical sensations associated with anxiety, stress management training, cognitive restructuring, and scheduling pleasant activities. Results revealed the combination of medication plus CBT was more effective than medication alone on measures of PTSD, anxiety, somatization, and anxiety sensitivity, but not on depression. This study has several design difficulties that limit the conclusions that can be drawn. First, the lack of a control group that was maintained on their original SSRI precludes drawing any conclusions about the efficacy of switching to sertraline when treatment with a prior SSRI has not been successful. Second, the study provides no information about the utility of combining an SSRI with a benzodiazepine. Third, the fact that all participants were maintained on their clonzepam and shifted to sertraline precludes knowing whether it was the combination of medication and CBT that was responsible for improvement or CBT alone.

SUMMARY AND RECOMMENDATIONS

Although currently available treatments are effective with most study participants who complete the intended treatment, there is variability in the degree to which treatment is effective and a significant number of patients are left with substantial residual symptoms. Improving treatment outcome for these partial- and nonresponders should be set as one of the priorities for further research. Two general approaches have been studied: continuing an existing treatment and combining treatments. With regard to the former approach, existing research, although limited, is suggestive that extending treatment for partial responders, either medication or PE, can result in further gains, although appropriate control groups are needed to make strong conclusions about this issue.

More research has addressed the usefulness of combining treatments for PTSD. Although psychosocial treatments that combine elements of exposure therapy, stress inoculation, and cognitive therapy are effective, there is little evidence to indicate that combined treatments are more effective than the individual treatments. The two exceptions to this rule appear to be when exposure therapy is limited to just one modality, either imaginal or in vivo, and when cognitive therapy does not include some exposure procedure. The combination of imaginal and in vivo exposure is superior to either of the individual components, and combining imaginal exposure with cognitive therapy is superior to imaginal exposure alone. However, there is no evidence of further benefit to adding cognitive therapy to the combination of imaginal and in vivo exposure. To date, these studies have investigated treatments in which all components are administered more or less concurrently, and therefore cannot determine whether nonresponders to one treatment become responders with the addition of the second treatment.

Other studies of combined treatments have looked at the impact of the combining treatment for PTSD with treatment for some other target, such as social (Frueh et al., 1995) and marital functioning (Glynn et al., 1999); affect regulation (Cloitre et al., 2002); and comorbid panic attacks (Falsetti et al., 2001) and substance dependence and PTSD (Back et al., 2001; Brady et al., 2001). The results of these studies have been mixed. Glynn et al. found no evidence that adding behavioral marital therapy to the combination exposure therapy plus cognitive restructuring improved outcome on measures of PTSD or marital functioning. Frueh et al. (1995) found evidence of improved social functioning when anger management and social skills training were implemented after completion of exposure therapy, but the lack of control group cannot rule out the possibility that social functioning would have improved without the additional treatment. Similarly, participants who completed treatment for cocaine dependence and subsequently received PE showed additional improvements on measures of PTSD but again the lack of a control group cannot rule out the possibility that PTSD would have improved without target treatment once the substance abuse was addressed. Combined treatment for PTSD and comorbid panic resulted in improvements for targets (Falsetti, 2001), but the lack of a control group that received just one of the two treatments cannot rule out the possibility that treatment of one condition resulted in improvements in the other.

Three studies have looked at the effects of adding a second treatment following an initial treatment. One small study found that the addition of an atypical neuroleptic medication resulted in greater improvement than the addition of a placebo among a group of nonresponders to SSRI medication. A second study found a similar augmentation effect for the addition of PE to an initial course of treatment with sertraline. The third study found that the combination of shifting from one SSRI (other than sertraline) to sertraline plus CBT resulted in far greater improvement than just shifting to sertraline among a group of participants who had previously failed to respond to an adequate treatment of a previous SSRI other than sertraline.

Taken as a whole, these studies seem to suggest that combined treatments administered concurrently do not result in significant improvement compared with the individual treatments. By contrast, studies that provide medication and CBT sequentially, and particularly those that target nonresponders to the initial treatment, appear to be more effective in detecting positive effects of combined treatments. However, the number of studies inversitigating this strategy is quite small and has utilized small sample sizes. Moreover, the use of sequentially combined treatments requires facing a number of methodological challenges. For example, given an effective initial treatment, it would require the recruitment of a large number of participants in order to have an adequate number of partial- and nonresponders available for randomization to second treatment or appropriate control condition. In addition, care needs to be taken in the selection of an appropriate control group in order to determine that it was the specific addition of the new treatment that was responsible for additional improvement and not just a result of the prior treatment (i.e., a "sleeper effect" as hypothesized by Foa et al., 1991) or the result of simple continuation (as in the study by Londborg et al., 2001, and the analyses reported by Foa, Hembree, et al., 2003). Continued research into various methods to improve treatment outcome for non- and partial responders to existing treatments is warranted.

CONCLUSION

This chapter has highlighted the significant progress made in the treatment of chronic PTSD and interventions of ASD/prevention of chronic PTSD while also specifying the areas still in need of additional research. The most important challenge at the present time is to effectively disseminate information about effective treatment programs to therapists, patients, and the general public. It is important to note that the obstacles to widespread dissemination of evidence- based treatment are not specific to PTSD nor are they specific to a particular form of treatment, such as exposure therapy. The majority of therapists have not received training in the use of empirically supported treatments for any disorder. Indeed, many therapists eschew the use of "manualized" treatments, preferring instead to offer "individually tailored" treatments. One possible cause for this position is the widely held belief that the kind of patients seen in randomized controlled trials are very different from what community clinicians see in their everyday practice. In addition, most consumers of mental health services are not aware that different types of therapy exist and that some treatments have greater evidence for their efficacy than others. Again, these issues are not specific to PTSD, as empirically supported treatments for other anxiety disorders and depression are also not well disseminated and are underutilized. One exception is the use of exposure and response prevention for the treatment of obsessive-compulsive disorders (OCD). Compared with other disorders, it is now widely known by patients with OCD and the professionals that treat them that the treatments of choice for this condition are SSRI medications and exposure and response prevention. The two other challenges that we face are improving outcome for partial responders and reducing the proportion of patients who refuse treatment or drop out of treatment. Again, neither of these challenges is specific to PTSD or to a specific type of treatment such as exposure therapy.

One additional challenge that is unique to PTSD is that, compared with other anxiety disorders such as phobias, obsessive-compulsive disorder, and panic disorder, there are at least four treatment approaches that have empirical support: exposure therapy, stress inoculation training, cognitive therapy, and EMDR. Thus, our field faces the additional challenge of deciding which protocol or protocols to target for widespread dissemination. At the present, we believe the evidence favors PE, the combination of imaginal and in vivo exposure therapy, because of four primary reasons. First, the efficacy of exposure therapy has been repeatedly shown in randomized controlled trials across a wide range of trauma populations by researchers in the United States, Canada, Europe, and Australia. Second, PE is the only treatment that has been directly compared with each of the remaining treatments. The results of these studies have generally found PE produces as good as or somewhat better outcome than the comparison treatments. By contrast, stress inoculation training, cognitive therapy, and EMDR have not been compared with one another. Third, attempts to improve treatment by adding elements of stress inoculation training or cognitive therapy to PE have not resulted in demonstrably better outcome. Thus, the additional difficulty of learning cognitive restructuring or stress inoculation in addition to PE is not warranted. And fourth, the results of our initial work evaluating the efficacy of PE in hands of community therapists, such as our collaboration with WOAR and our efforts with JDC Israel, has to date been quite successful. No other treatment program has yet established as complete and successful a track record as PE.

Research on treatments for PTSD has come a long way since the Solomon et al. (1992) review, and there is good reason to feel optimistic about our ability to help many people suffering from acute and chronic posttrauma reactions. At the same time, there is much work remaining to reduce treatment dropouts, improve outcome for those who do not fully benefit from existing treatments, and make sure that therapists who treat PTSD are trained in and will utilize one of the currently available empirically supported treatments for PTSD.

REFERENCES

Back, S. E., Dansky, B. S., Carroll, K. M., Foa, E. B., & Brady, K. T. (2001). Exposure therapy in the treatment of PTSD among cocaine-dependent individuals: Description of procedures. *Journal of Substance Abuse Treatment, 21,* 35–45.

Baekland, F., & Lundwall, L. (1975). Dropping out of treatment: A critical review. *Psychological Bulletin, 82,* 738–783.

Barlow, D. H., & Craske, M. G. (1994). *Mastery of your anxiety and panic II: Client workbook.* San Antonio, TX: Psychological Corporation.

Becker, C. B., Zayfert, C., & Anderson, E. (in press). A survey of psychologists' attitudes toward and utilization of exposure therapy for PTSD. *Behaviour Research and Therapy.*

Bisson, J. I., McFarlane, A. C., & Rose, S. (2000). Psychological debriefing. In E. B. Foa, T. M. Keane, & M. J. Friedman (Eds.), *Effective treatments for PTSD* (pp. 39–59). New York: Guilford Press.

Blanchard, E. B., Hickling, E. J., Devineni, T., Veazey, C. H., Galovski, T. E., Mundy, E., et al. & Buckly, T. C. (2003). A controlled evaluation of cognitive-behavioral therapy for posttraumatic stress in motor vehicle accident survivors. *Behaviour Research and Therapy, 41,* 79–96.

Blanchard, E. B., Hickling, E. J., Malta, L. S., Freidenberg, B. M., Canna, M. A., Kuhn, E., Sykes, et al.. (in press). One—and two–year prospective follow–up of cognitive-behavior therapy or supportive psychotherapy. *Behaviour Research and Therapy.*

Brady, K. T., Dansky, B. S., Back, S. E., Foa, E. B., & Carroll, K. M. (2001). Exposure therapy in the treatment of PTSD among cocaine–dependent individuals: Preliminary findings. *Journal of Substance Abuse Treatment, 21,* 47–54.

Brady, K., Pearlstein, T., Asnis, G. M., Baker, D., Rothbaum, B., Sikes,et al. (2000). Efficacy and safety of sertraline treatment of posttraumatic stress disorder. *JAMA, 283,* 1837–1844.

Bryant, R. A., Harvey, A. G., Sackville, T., Dang, S. T., & Basten, C. (1998). Treatment of acute stress disorder: A comparison between cognitive–behavioral therapy and supportive counseling. *Journal of Consulting and Clinical Psychology, 66,* 862–866.

Bryant, R. A., Moulds, M. L., Guthrie, R. M., Dang, S. T., Nixon, R. D. V., & Felmingham, K. (2002, November). Imaginal exposure, in vivo exposure, and their combination in treating PTSD. In R. A. Bryant (Chair), *Treating PTSD.* Symposium conducted at the annual convention of the Association for Advancement of Behavior Therapy, Reno, NV.

Bryant, R. A., Moulds, M. L., Guthrie, R. M., Dang, S. T., & Nixon, R. D. V. (2003). Imaginal exposure alone and imaginal exposure with cognitive restructuring in treatment of posttraumatic stress disorder. *Journal of Consulting and Clinical Psychology. 71,* 706–712.

Bryant, R. A., Moulds, M., Guthrie, R., & Nixon, R. D. V. (2003). Treating acute stress disorder following mild traumatic brain injury. *American Journal of Psychiatry, 160,* 585–587.

Bryant, R. A., Moulds, M., & Nixon, R. D. V. (in press). Cognitive behaviour therapy of acute stress disorder: A four–year follow–up. *Behaviour Research and Therapy.*

Bryant, R. A., Sackville, T., Dangh, S. T., Moulds, M., & Guthrie, R. (1999). Treating acute stress disorder: An evaluation of cognitive-behavior therapy and supportive counseling techniques. *American Journal of Psychiatry, 156,* 1780–1786.

Cahill, S. P., Foa, E. B., Rothbaum, B. O., Connor, K., Smith, R., & Davidson, J. R. T. (2003, March). *Augmentation of sertraline with prolonged exposure (PE) in the treatment of PTSD: Does PE protect against relapse?* Poster presented at the annual convention of the Anxiety Disorders Association of America, Toronto, Ontario, Canada.

Cahill, S. P., Hembree, E. A., & Foa, E. B. (in press). Dissemination of prolonged exposure therapy for posttraumatic stress disorder: Successes and challenges. In Y. Neria, R. Gross, R. Marshall, & E. Susser (Eds.), 9/11: Public health in the wake of terrorist attacks. Cambridge, UK: Cambridge University Press.

Cahill, S. P., Riggs, D. S., Rauch, S. A. M., & Foa, E. B. (2003, March). Does prolonged exposure therapy for PTSD make people worse? Poster presented at the annual convention of the Anxiety Disorders Association of America, Toronto, Ontario, Canada.

Cahill, S. P., Rauch, S. A. M., Hembree, E. A., & Foa, E. B. (2003). Effect of cognitive–behavioral treatments for PTSD on anger. *Journal of Cognitive Psychotherapy, 17,* 113–131.

Cahill, S. P., Zoellner, L. A., Feeny, N. C., & Riggs, D. S. (in press). Sequential treatment for child abuse–related PTSD: Methodological comment on Cloitre et al. (2002). *Journal of Consulting and Clinical Psychology.*

Cloitre, M., Koenen, K., Cohen, L. R., & Han, H. (2002). Skills training in affective and interpersonal regulation followed by exposure: A phase–based treatment for PTSD related to childhood abuse. *Journal of Consulting and Clinical Psychology, 70,* 1067–1074.

Conlon, L., Fahy, T. J., & Conroy, R. (1999). PTSD in ambulant RTA victims: A randomized controlled trial of debriefing. *Journal of Psychosomatic Research, 46,* 1, 37–44.

Connor, K. M., Sutherland, S. M., Tupler, L. A., Malik, M. L., & Davidson, J. R. T. (1999). Fluoxetine in post–traumatic stress disorder: Randomised, double–blind study. *British Journal of Psychiatry, 175,* 17–22.

Cooper, N. A., & Clum, G. A. (1989). Imaginal flooding as a supplementary treatment for PTSD in combat veterans: A controlled study. *Behavior Therapy, 20,* 381–391.

Davidson, J., Pearlstein, T., Londborg, P., Brady, K. T., Rothbaum, B., Bell, J., et al. (2001). Efficacy of sertraline in preventing relapse of posttraumatic stress disorder: Results of a 28–week double–blind, placebo–controlled study. *American Journal of Psychiatry, 158,* 1974–1981.

Davidson, J. R. T., Rothbaum, B. O., van der Kolk, B. A., Sikes, C. R., & Farfel, G. M. (2001). Multicenter, double–blind comparison of sertraline and placebo in the treatment of posttraumatic stress disorder. *Archives of General Psychiatry, 58,* 485–492.

Devilly, G. J., & Foa, E. B. (2001). Comments on Tarrier et al.'s study and the investigation of exposure and cognitive therapy. *Journal of Consulting and Clinical Psychology, 69,* 114–116.

Echeburua, E., Corral, P. D., Zubizarreta, I., & Sarasua, B. (1997). Psychological treatment of chronic posttraumatic stress disorder in victims of sexual aggression. *Behavior Modification, 21,* 433–456.

Ehlers, A., & Clark, D. M. (2000). A cognitive model of posttraumatic stress disorder. *Behaviour Research and Therapy, 38,* 319–345.

Ehlers, A., Clark, D.M., Hackmann, A., McManus F., Fennell, M., Herbert, C., et al. (in press). A randomized controlled trial of cognitive therapy, self–help booklet, and repeated assessment as early interventions for PTSD. *Archives of General Psychiatry.*

Ehlers, A., Mayou, R.S., & Bryant, B. (1998). Psychological predictors of chronic posttraumatic stress disorder after motor vehicle accidents. *Journal of Abnormal Psychology, 107,* 508–519.

Everly, G. S., Flannery, R. B., Eyler, V., & Mitchell, J. T. (2001). Sufficiency analysis of an integrated multicomponent approach to crisis intervention: Critical incident stress management. *Advances in Mind Body Medicine, 17,* 174–183.

Falsetti, S. A., Resnick, H. S., Davis, J., & Gallagher, N. G. (2001). Treatment of posttraumatic stress disorder with comorbid panic attacks: Combining cognitive processing therapy with panic control treatment techniques. *Group Dynamics: Theory, Research, and Practice, 5,* 252–260.

Fecteau, G., & Nicki, R. (1999). Cognitive behavioural treatment of post traumatic stress disorder after motor vehicle accident. *Behavioural and Cognitive Psychotherapy, 27,* 201–214.

Feeny, N. C., Zoellner, L. A., & Foa, E. B. (2002). Treatment outcome for chronic PTSD among female assault victims with borderline personality characteristics: A preliminary examination. *Journal of Personality Disorders, 16,* 30–40.

Foa, E. B., & Cahill, S. P. (2001). Psychological therapies: Emotional processing. In N.J. Smelser & P. B. Bates (Eds.), *International encyclopedia of the social and behavioral sciences* (pp. 12,363–12,369). Oxford: Elsevier.

Foa, E. B., Cahill, S. P., & Moser, J. S. (2003). *Psychosocial treatments for posttraumatic stress disorder: A bird's eye view.* Manuscript in preparation.

Foa, E. B., Dancu, C. V., Hembree, E. A., Jaycox, L. H., Meadows, E. A., & Street, G. P. (1999). A comparison of exposure therapy, stress inoculation training, and their combination for reducing posttraumatic stress disorder in female assault victims. *Journal of Consulting and Clinical Psychology, 67,* 194–200.

Foa, E.B., Ehlers, A., Clark, D.M., Tolin, D.F., & Orsillo, S.M. (1999). The posttraumatic cognitions inventory (PTCI): Development and validation. *Psychological Assessment, 11,* 303–314.

Foa, E. B., Franklin, M. E., & Moser, J. (2002). Context in the clinic: How well do cognitive–behavioral therapies and medications work in combination? *Biological Psychiatry, 52,* 987–997.

Foa, E. B., Hearst–Ikeda, D., & Perry, K. J. (1995). Evaluation of a brief cognitive–behavior program for the prevention of chronic PTSD in recent assault victims. *Journal of Consulting and Clinical Psychology, 63,* 948–955.

Foa, E. B., Hembree, E. A., Feeny, N. C., & Zoellner, L. A. (2002, March). Posttraumatic stress disorder treatment for female assault victims. In L. A. Zoellner (Chair), *Recent innovations in posttraumatic stress disorder treatment.* Symposium presented at the annual convention of the Anxiety Disorders Association of America, Austin, TX.

Foa, E. B., Hembree, E. A., Rauch, S. A. M., & Cahill, S. P. (2003, November). CBT for PTSD for partial treatment responders. In R. Bryant (Chair), *Improving treatment for posttraumatic stress disorder.* Symposium presented at the annual convention of the International Society for Traumatic Stress Studies, Chicago.

Foa, E. B., & Meadows, E. A. (1997). Psychosocial treatments for posttraumatic stress disorder: A critical review. In J. Spence, J. M. Darley, & D. J. Foss (Eds.), *Annual review of psychology* (Vol. 48, pp. 449–480). Palo Alto, CA: Annual Reviews.

Foa, E. B., & Rauch, S. A. M. (in press). Cognitive changes during prolonged exposure alone versus prolonged exposure and cognitive restructuring in female assault survivors with PTSD. *Journal of Consulting and Clinical Psychology.*

Foa, E. B. & Rothbaum, B. O. (1998). *Treating the trauma of rape.* New York: Guilford.

Foa, E. B., Rothbaum, B.O., & Furr, J. M. (2003). Augmenting exposure therapy with other cognitive-behavior therapy procedures. *Psychiatric Annals, 33,* 47–53.

Foa, E. B., Rothbaum, R. O., Riggs, D. S., & Murdock, T. B. (1991). Treatment of posttraumatic stress disorder in rape victims: A comparison between cognitive–behavioral procedures and counseling. *Journal of Consulting and Clinical Psychology, 59,* 715–723.

Foa, E. B., Zoellner, L. A., Feeny, N. C., Hembree, E. A., & Alvarez–Conrad, J. (2002). Does imaginal exposure exacerbate PTSD symptoms? *Journal of Consulting and Clinical Psychology, 70,* 1022–1028.

Frueh, B. C., Turner, S. M., Beidel, D. C. (1995). Exposure therapy for combat-related PTSD: A critical review. *Clinical Psychology Review, 15,* 799–817.

Frueh, B. C., Turner, S. M., & Beidel, D. C., Mirabella, R. F., & Jones, W. J. (1996). Trauma management therapy: A preliminary evaluation of a multicomponent behavioral treatment for chronic combat–related PTSD. *Behaviour Research and Therapy, 34,* 533–543.

Garfield, S. L. (1986). Research on client variables in psychotherapy. In S. L. Garfield & A. E. Bergin (Eds.), *Handbook of psychotherapy and behavior change* (3rd ed., pp. 213–256). New York: Wiley.

Gillespie, K., Duffy, M., Hackmann, A., & Clark, D. M. (2002). Community based cognitive therapy in the treatment of posttraumatic stress disorder following the Omagh bomb. *Behaviour Research and Therapy, 40,* 345–357.

Glynn, S. M., Eth, S., Randolph, E. T., Foy, D. W., Urbaitis, M., Boxer, L., et al. (1999). A test of behavioral family therapy to augment exposure for combat-related posttraumatic stress disorder. *Journal of Consulting and Clinical Psychology, 67,* 243–251.

Harvey, A. G., & Bryant, R. A. (1998). The relationship between acute stress disorder and posttraumatic stress disorder: A prospective evaluation of motor vehicle accident survivors. *Journal of Consulting and Clinical Psychology, 66,* 507–512.

Harvery, A. G., Bryant, R. A., & Tarrier, N. (2003). Cognitive behaviour therapy for posttraumatic stress disorder. *Clinical Psychology Review, 23,* 501–522.

Hembree, E. A., Foa, E. B., Dorfan, N. M., Street, G. P., Tu, X., & Kowalski, J. (in press). Do patients drop out prematurely from exposure therapy for PTSD? *Journal of Traumatic Stress.*

Hope, D.A., Heimberg, R.G., & Bruch, M.A. (1995). Dismantling cognitive–behavioral group therapy for social phobia. *Behaviour Research and Therapy, 33,* 637–650.

Issakidis, C., & Andrews, G. (2002). Service utilisation for anxiety in an Australian community sample. *Social Psychiatry and Psychiatric Epidemiology, 37,* 153–63.

Keane, T. M., Fairbank, J. A., Caddell, J. M., & Zimmering, R. T. (1989). Implosive (flooding) therapy reduces symptoms of PTSD in Vietnam combat veterans. *Behavior Therapy, 20,* 245–260.

Kilpatrick, D. G., & Best, C. L. (1984). Some cautionary remarks on treating sexual assault victims with implosion. *Behavior Therapy, 15,* 421–423.

Klerman, G. L., Weissman, M. M., Rounsaville, B. J., & Chevron, E. S. (1984). *Interpersonal psychotherapy for depression.* New York: Basic Books.

Kubany, E. S., Hill, E. E., & Owens, J. A. (2003). Cognitive trauma therapy for battered women with PTSD: Preliminary findings. *Journal of Traumatic Stress, 16,* 81–91.

Londborg, P. D., Hegel, M. T., Goldstein, S., Goldstein, D., Himmelhoch, J. M., Maddock, R., et al. (2001). Sertraline treatment of posttraumatic stress disorder: Results of 24 weeks of open–label continuation treatment. *Journal of Clinical Psychiatry, 62,* 325–331.

Lovell, K., Marks, I. M., Noshirvani, H., Thrasher, S., & Livanou, M. (2001). Do cognitive and exposure treatments improve various PTSD symptoms differentially? A randomized controlled trial. *Behavioural and Cognitive Psychotherapy, 29,* 107–112.

Marks, I., Lovell, K., Noshirvani, H., Livanou, M., & Thrasher, S. (1998). Treatment of posttraumatic stress disorder by exposure and/or cognitive restructuring. *Archives of General Psychiatry, 55,* 317–325.

Marshall, R. D., Beebe, K. L., Oldham, M., & Zaninelli, R. (2001). Efficacy and safety of paroxetine treatment of chronic PTSD: A fixed–dose, placebo–controlled study. *American Journal of Psychiatry, 158,* 1982–1988.

Martenyi, F., Brown, E. B., Zhang, H., Koke, S. C., & Prakash, A. (2002). Fluoxetine v. placebo in prevention of relapse in post–traumatic stress disorder. *British Journal of Psychiatry, 181,* 315–320.

Martenyi, F., Brown, E. B., Zhang, H., Prakash, A., & Koke, S. C. (2002). Fluoxetine versus placebo in posttraumatic stress disorder. *Journal of Clinical Psychiatry, 63,* 199–206.

Mayou, R. A., Ehlers, A., & Hobbs, M. (2000). Psychological debriefing for road traffic accident victims. *British Journal of Psychiatry, 176,* 589–593.

Nacasch, N., Cohen–Rapperot, G., Polliack, M., Knobler, H.Y., Zohar J., & Foa, E., B. (2003). *Prolonged exposure therapy for PTSD: The dissemination and the preliminary results of the implementation of the treatment protocol in Israel.* Abstract in the Proceedings of the 11th Conference of the Israel Psychiatric Association. April, 2003, Haifa, Israel.

Otto, M. W., Hinton, D., Korbly, N. B., Chea, A., Ba, P., Gershuny, B. S., et al. (in press). Treatment of pharacotherapy–refractory posttraumatic stress disorder among Cambodian refugees: A pilot study of combination treatment with cognitive–behavior therapy vs. sertraline alone. *Behaviour Research and Therapy.*

Paunovic, N. (1997). Exposure therapy for post–traumatic stress disorder: Its relative efficacy, limitations, and optimal application. *Scandinavian Journal of Behaviour Therapy, 26,* 54–69.

Paunovic, N., & Ost, L. G. (2001). Cognitive–behavior therapy vs exposure therapy in the treatment of PTSD in refugees. *Behaviour Research and Therapy, 39,* 1183–1197.

Pitman, R. K., Altman, B., Greenwald, E., Longpre, R. E., Macklin, M. L., Poire, R. E., et al. (1991). Psychiatric complications during flooding therapy for post–traumatic stress disorder. *Journal of Clinical Psychiatry, 52,* 17–20.

Pitman, R. K., Orr, S. P., Altman, B., Longpre, R. E., Poire, R. E., Macklin, M. L., et al. (1996). Emotional processing and outcome of imaginal flooding therapy in Vietnam veterans with chronic posttraumatic stress disorder. *Comprehensive Psychiatry, 37,* 409–418.

Power, K. G., McGoldrick, T., Brown, K., Buchanan, R., Sharp, D., Swanson, V., et al. (2002). A controlled comparison of eye movement desensitization and reprocessing versus exposure plus cognitive restructuring, versus waiting list in the treatment of posttraumatic stress disorder. *Journal of Clinical Psychology and Psychotherapy, 9,* 299–318.

Project MATCH Research Group. (1997). Matching alcoholism treatment to client heterogeneity: Project MATCH posttreatment drinking outcomes. *Journal of Studies on Alcohol, 58,* 7–29.

Resick, P. A., Nishith, P., Weaver, T. L., Astin, M. C., & Feurer, C. A. (2002). A comparison of cognitive–processing therapy with prolonged exposure and a waiting condition for the treatment of chronic posttraumatic stress disorder in female rape victims. *Journal of Consulting and Clinical Psychology, 70,* 867–879.

Resick, P.A., & Schnicke, M.K. (1993). *Cognitive processing therapy for rape victims.* Newbury Park, CA: Sage.

Rothbaum, B. O. (2002, March). A controlled study of PE versus EMDR for PTSD rape victims. In L. A. Zoelnner (Chair), *Recent innovations in posttraumatic stress disorder treatment*. Symposium presented at the annual convention of the Anxiety Disorders Association of America, Austin, TX.

Rose, S., Brewin, C. R., Andrews, B., & Kirk, M. (1999). A randomized controlled trial of individual psychological debriefing for victims of violent crime. *Psychological Medicine, 29*, 793–799.

Shear, M. K., Frank, E., Foa, E., Cherry, C., Reynolds III, C. F., Vander Bilt, J., et al. (2001). Traumatic grief treatment: A pilot study. *American Journal of Psychiatry, 158*, 1506–1508.

Solomon, S. D., Gerrity, E. T., & Muff, M. (1992). Efficacy of treatments for posttraumatic stress disorder: An empirical review. *JAMA, 268*, 633–638.

Stein, M. B., Kline, N. A., & Matloff, J. L. (2002). Adjunctive olanzapine for SSRI-resistant combat–related PTSD: A double–blind, placebo–controlled study. *American Journal of Psychiatry, 159*, 1777–1779.

Tarrier, N., Pilgrim, H., Sommerfield, C., Faragher, B., Reynolds, M., Graham, E., et al. (1999). A randomized trial of cognitive therapy and imaginal exposure in the treatment of chronic posttraumatic stress disorder. *Journal of Consulting and Clinical Psychology, 67*, 13–18.

Tarrier, N., Sommerfield, C., Pilgrim, H., & Humphreys, L. (1999). Cognitive therapy or imaginal exposure in the treatment of post–traumatic stress disorder: Twelve–month follow–up. *British Journal of Psychiatry, 175*, 571–575.

Taylor, S., Thordarson, D. S., Maxfield, L., Federoff, I. C., Lovell, K., & Ogrodniczuk, J. (2003). Efficacy, speed, and adverse effects of three PTSD treatments: Exposure therapy, relaxation training, and EMDR. *Journal of Consulting and Clinical Psychology, 71*, 330–338.

Tucker, P., Zaninelli, R., Yehuda, R., Ruggiero, L., Dillingham, K., & Pitts, C. D. (2001). Paroxetine in the treatment of chronic posttraumatic stress disorder: Results of a placebo–controlled, flexible–dosage trial. *Journal of Clinical Psychiatry, 62*, 860–868.

van der Kolk, B. A., Dreyfuss, D., Michaels, M., Shera, D., Berkowitz, R., Fisler, R. E., et al. (1994). Fluoxetine in posttraumatic stress disorder. *Journal of Clinical Psychiatry, 55*, 517–522.

Wierzbicki, M., & Pakarik, G. (1993). A meta–analysis of psychotherapy dropout. *Professional Psychology: Research and Practice, 24*, 190–195.

Williams, S. L., & Falbo, J. (1996). Cognitive and performance–based treatments for panic attacks in people with varying degrees of agoraphobic disability. *Behaviour Research and Therapy, 34*, 253–264.

Zayfert, C., & Becker, C. B. (2000). Implementation of empirically supported treatment for PTSD: Obstacles and innovations. *The Behavior Therapist, 23*, 161–162, 164–168.

Zoellner, L. A., Feeny, N. C., Cochran, B., & Pruitt, L. (in press). Treatment choice for PTSD. *Behaviour Research and Therapy*.

INDEX

Springer Publishing Company

Stress Management

A Comprehensive Handbook of Techniques and Strategies

Jonathan C. Smith, PhD

"...a state-of-the-art book...practical methods of treatment for those who need help managing stress in their lives...ideal as a graduate level text or resource..."

—**Martin Weinstein,** PhD, Associate Professor
   Roosevelt University, School of Psychology

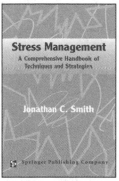

"...an invaluable tool in educating both undergraduate and graduate students, in psychology and across disciplines...clinicians and their clients would be hard-pressed to find a more useful text..."

—**Dena Traylor,** PsyD, Roosevelt University

This clinical manual contains detailed descriptions of tactics for training the user in the methods of relaxation, positive thinking, time management, and more. Features validated self-tests (normed on over 1000 individuals), and first-time-ever stress management motivations and irrational beliefs inventories.

Partial Contents:

Part I. Stress Basics • Stress Competency and the Smith Stress Management Skills Inventory • Stress Concepts, Exercises

Part II. The Four Pillars of Stress Management • Progressive Muscle Relaxation and Autogenic Training • Breathing and Stretching Exercises • Sense Imagery and Meditation • Relaxation, Centering, and Stress Management Exercises • Identifying Clear and Concrete Problem Cues • Stress Inoculation and Relapse Prevention

Part III. Interpersonal Skills: Relationships and Stress Management • Assertiveness, Exercises • Empathy and Assertive Coping • Goals and Priorities • Relaxation Beliefs, Active Coping Beliefs, and Philosophy of Life

2002   280pp   0-8261-4947-2   hardcover

11 West 42nd Street, New York, NY 10036-8002 • **Fax: 212-941-7842**
Order Toll-Free: 877-687-7476 • **Order On-line: www.springerpub.com**

Springer Publishing Company

Comparative Treatments for Anxiety Disorders

Robert A. DiTomasso, PhD, ABPP
Elizabeth A. Gosch, PhD, Editors

Anxiety disorders are costly, common, and debilitating. They often present challenging problems in the caseloads of practicing clinicians today. This volume compares and contrasts various models of and treatment approaches to anxiety disorders. Each contributor, a master clinician, analyzes the same case and presents a thorough description of the model. Detailed descriptions of therapists' skills and attributes, assessment plans, treatment goals, intervention strategies, common pitfalls and mechanisms of change are included.

Among the 11 therapies presented are Cognitive-Behavioral, Problem-Solving, Acceptance and Commitment, Contextual Family Therapy, Supportive-Expressive, Psychodynamic, and Psychopharmacological. The volume concludes with a useful table that succinctly summarizes the tenets of all these major approaches. For practitioners, graduate students, and professionals preparing for licensure.

Partial Contents:
- Anxiety Disorders: An Overview, *R.A. DiTomasso and E.A. Gosch*
- Cognitive-Behavioral Treatment, *E.A. Meadows and K.A. Phipps*
- Acceptance and Commitment Therapy, *S.C. Hayes, et al.*
- Context-Centered Therapy, *J.S. Efran and L.C. Sitrin*
- Contextual Family Therapy, *B. Lackie and M. Olson*
- Adlerian Therapy, *R.R. Kopp*
- Interpersonal Therapy, *R.D. Goldstein and A.M. Gruenberg*
- Person-Centered Therapy, *S.A. Williams*
- Supportive-Expressive Therapy, *A.L. Schwartz and K. Crits-Cristoph*
- Psychodynamic Therapy, *P.M. Lerner*

Sprinter Series on Comparative Treatments for Psychological Disorders
2002   368pp   0-8261-4832-8   hard

11 West 42nd Street, New York, NY 10036-8002 • Fax: 212-941-7842
Order Toll-Free: 877-687-7476 • Order On-line: www.springerpub.com